Who Made the West

Other Histories from New London Librarium

Quilombo dos Palmares:
Brazil's Lost Nation of Fugitive Slaves

Vertiginous Life

Thanksgiving:
The Pilgrims' First Year in America

How a Nation Grieves:
Press Accounts of the Death of Lincoln, the Hunt for Booth,
and America in Mourning

Good Days! Chronicles by Machado de Assis 1888-1889

Religions in Rio

Stories from Yantic Cemetery

To the Ends of the Earth:
Memoir of a Missionary Sister of the Sacred Heart of Jesus

Who Made the West

A Ranking of the 30 Most Influential Figures in Western History

Ian Alan Cheney

NEW LONDON LIBRARIUM

Who Made the West

A Ranking of the 30 Most Influential Figures in Western History

by Ian Alan Cheney

Copyright © 2021 Ian Alan Cheney

Published by
New London Librarium
Hanover, CT 06350
NLLibrarium.com

No part of this book may be reproduced in any medium without the express permission of the author or publisher.

ISBNs
Paperback: 978-1-947074-47-7
Hardcover: 978-1-947074-48-4
eBook: 978-1-947074-49-1

For Mom and Dad,

my most influential figures

Contents

Foreword	ix
Introduction to the Top 30	1
They Didn't Make It	9
#30: Plato & Aristotle (tie)	19
#29: Philip "the Fair" of France	36
#28: Nicolaus Copernicus	48
#27: Joan of Arc	59
#26: Peter the Great	72
#25: Gregory Pincus	85
#24: Thomas Jefferson	95
#23: Constantine the Great	110
#22: Voltaire	126
#21: Charlemagne	136
#20: Henry Ford	149
#19: Queen Elizabeth	158
#18: Thomas Edison	173
#17: Adolf Hitler	183
#16: Napoleon Bonaparte	204
#15: Charles Darwin	221

#14: George Washington	232
#13: Charles Martel	248
#12: Galileo	260
#11: Albert Einstein	272
#10: William Shakespeare	281
#9: Karl Marx	291
#8: Louis Pasteur	307
#7: Jesus	316
#6: Martin Luther	329
#5: James Watt	346
#4: John Locke	360
#3: Isaac Newton	377
#2: Johannes Gutenberg	391
#1: Christopher Columbus	405
About the Author	435
New London Librarium	436
Index	437

Foreword

In December of 2012, I had a terrible idea. Over the next eight years, that terrible idea spun out of control, ultimately landing in your hands at this moment. Who are we to blame for this future paperweight?

Many, many people.

Let's back up to that fateful December. I was six years into what is now a fifteen-year career as a history teacher at Waterford High School in Waterford, CT. I had just finished covering the 2012 election for *Construction Literary Magazine*, an online publication started by founders Nathan Schiller and Masha Udensiva-Brenner. I had been writing about the election for my own website, *Presidential Politics for America*, when one of my oldest friends and the most talented writer I know outside of my family, Stephen Kurczy, recommended to Nathan and Masha that I could be useful to their website. Irresponsibly, they agreed.

With the election's conclusion in November, my journey with *Construction* arrived at a crossroads. The plummeting demand for political content forced me to consider how else I could contribute to the site. There was an obvious choice. My educational background and career was actually not in politics. It was in history. Such a broad area, however, needed focus.

I determined that I would be able to submit monthly columns, and I'd want to submit them across two-and-a-half years. That approach would get me halfway through 2015, which is when we could expect the 2016 presidential primaries to heat up, at which point I'd switch back to politics. Two-and-a-half years equal 30 months, so that gave me the idea to write a 30-part series. A ranking naturally flowed from that idea. Since my educational and vocational backgrounds covered just about every era of Western history, I proposed ranking its most influential figures. Each entry would be a consumable, bite-sized snack[1] on an influential historical figure so that a reader would have a better feel for the person and their era.

Nathan and Masha not only agreed, they did a great job pretending it was a good idea.[2] I generated the list, and by January of 2013 I had tapped out a piece on Plato and Aristotle.

The entry was—and I can't emphasize this enough—atrocious. I wasn't anywhere near finding my history voice, and trying to articulate Plato and Aristotle's philosophies and contributions with digestible lan-

---

[1] Appetites may vary.

[2] So, if you're keeping track of who to blame for this book, we're already up to three people. Nathan and Masha deserve a great deal of blame. Before them, it all started with Steve, who didn't even read most of my entries because they were, in his words, "just so long."

Foreword

guage and length wasn't in my skill set.³ But I kept going. Month after month, I somehow submitted a three (or four) thousand word entry on a historical figure, and I think they generally got better. I'm still indebted to my two editors for the opportunity and their patience. I'm also grateful to readers who complimented the early entries, although for some reason their voice was about an octave higher than normal.

Though the entries improved, I did find it difficult to keep up with the monthly pace while also needing so much time to be an effective teacher. To complicate matters, the unthinkable happened: ably assisted by my wife, I procreated. We had a son. I was a father.

I knew I couldn't possibly juggle the three roles of history teacher, family man, and fake writer, and so one had to go. My wife refused my offer to divorce and my principal declined my offer to quit,⁴ so I sullenly reported to my editors that the Top 30 series would be placed on hold, perhaps indefinitely. At that point, I was 15 months in—exactly halfway through. Once Napoleon clocked in at #16, I clocked out at *Construction*. It was halftime.

My son Arden is as much a miracle now as he was then. An easy baby with a stellar mother, he quickly allowed me to find my footing. By the end of 2015, I resurrected my old website and began covering the 2016 presi-

---

³ I still think it's the worst entry of the series. Even after two rewrites, I've been unable to shed its initial flaws. I even considered re-ranking the Top 30 to knock Plato and Aristotle out in favor of someone who missed the cut. I thought better of it, however, as a ranking of the West's most influential figures that doesn't include two of its founders is no ranking at all. Anyway, if you find yourself bored at #30, hang in there. I'd say 29 and 28 are better.

⁴ Both of which I thought would be to their benefit.

dential election.[5] Once it was over, I faced the same dilemma I'd had four years earlier—I wanted to write, but I needed something to write about.

The Top 30 beckoned from my brain's attic. At that point, it had been halftime for two years. In the spring of 2017, I finally returned to it. Having secured permission and support from my old editors to take the ranking to my own website, I did precisely that. I first edited and re-ran the initial 15 entries—from Plato to Napoleon—which bought me time to write the rest.

And this time, I followed through. Thirty months later, the Top 30 was complete.

I'm not sure I would have made it without endless encouragement from many sources. Every time I thought I was running out of gas, someone's compliment or anticipation of the next entry fueled me to go further. Even after the ranking was complete, further praise came in some version of, "You *have* to make this into a book!"

Did people mean it or were they just trying to make me feel good? I didn't know. But if it was the latter, it was working! I began believing maybe I should indeed publish the series.

I would need an editor, however. That brings me to other acknowledgements. Although I couldn't possibly name all my appreciated readers who took the time to click, share, retweet, or send me a heartening line saying they valued my political or historical columns, I can list the 30 who sacrificed some time to edit this book. Early in 2021, I sent out an email to just over 30 friends, colleagues, and former students, most of them among my most loyal readers, asking for each to volunteer to read a single Top 30 entry and offer their thoughts. I wasn't sure I could actual-

---

[5] You won't BELIEVE who won.

Foreword

ly get 30 readers, and I expected to instead beg some people to read a second or third entry.

To my surprise and appreciation, the response was overwhelming. Within two days, I had 29 volunteers. The 30th came two days later.[6] Those valued readers are colleagues Brian Ash, Matt Cadorette, Jay Criscuolo, Courtney Hesch, Ann Marie Keating, Alison Moger, Kathy Morgan, Suzanne Sturm, Elizabeth Sutman, and Mike Uscilla; former students Sean Corman, Jessica Creevy, Nataly Estrin, Joshua Kelly, Anthony Steady, Mike Stroneski, and Baird Welch-Collins; and dear friends Gabriella Aisenberg, Bob Batten, Rich Carmona[7], Lianne Coble, Scott Dispensa, David Frye, Elizabeth Foley, Frank Foley, Patrick Foley, Greg Gwudz, Brett Levanto, Karl Sauvant, and Nathan Schiller.[8]

They are just the beginning of a longer list. Topping my personal Most Influential figures ranking is my mother, Solange Aurora Cavalcante Cheney. Her lack of inclusion in the Top 30 is an omission for which I've profusely apologized. Notably, over the course of the Top 30's online unveiling, Mom set the record for most Facebook shares for the purposes of something other than advancing a political position.

I deeply appreciate the analytical eyes of editors Ralph Hunter Cheney and Denise Dembinski. I owe special thanks to two of my most loyal readers, Derek and D'Anne Dibble. Month after month, they raised encouragement from a seemingly bottomless well of it. Their daughter Marinne, also known as, impossibly, my wife, perhaps played the most

---

[6] Apparently no one wants to read about James Watt. Thankfully, a childhood friend came to the rescue.

[7] He of James Watt savior status.

[8] So they all share blame too—and that's double jeopardy now for Nathan.

important role of all: that of patient co-parent and recipient to innumerable versions of, "I just have to finish this paragraph!"

Among my earliest sources of encouragement was my late grandfather, Theodore Rees Cheney, who started a now three-generation run of published authors. His insights into writing proved invaluable, and they still ring in my ears 13 years after his passing. His son and my father, Glenn Alan Cheney, inherited all of Ted's talents, not least of which was as an endless source of inspiration for what the written word can do. I'm relieved to have now contributed just one book to continue the half-century legacy of the two role models who came before me.[9]

Finally, here's the thing about rankings, including this one. They are absurd. Although I love them, I don't pretend that we can know or calculate with any certainty history's most influential figure, nor America's greatest president, nor football's greatest quarterback, nor science's greatest invention.[10]

However, a ranking is at its most absurd if we see it as the end of the conversation. That should not be a ranking's aim. It is certainly not the aim of this one.

No, rankings should be where the conversation begins. No one should agree with the order. If two people debate this list, or think that I, the ranker, am wrong, that is a welcome sign they're thinking deeply about what has been written. I hope this book can therefore start some

---

[9] Here's the baton, Arden. No pressure.

[10] Although obviously the answer to the last three are Abraham Lincoln, Tom Brady, and the Scrub Daddy.

Foreword

conversations, and perhaps even an argument or two. If it does, it was well worth the eight years.

Thanks for reading.

IAN A. CHENEY
GALES FERRY, CONN.

Introduction to the Top 30

Over the next 30 chapters, I will count down the 30 most influential people in Western history.[1] You have my deepest apologies.

My qualifications are not overwhelming, but what I lack in prestige I make up with pluck.[2] My bachelor's degree was in history and my master's in American studies. I've also taught various courses of Western history for the last 15 years. Perhaps my most important qualification is that I obsess over lists and rankings, creating them for just about every part of my existence, including historical figures, athletes, movies, *Star Trek* episodes, the founding fathers, project Apollo missions,[3] breakfast cereals, you name it. I live for rankings. I even rank my rankings![4]

---

[1] I'll admit now that there are actually 31 people on the list, as there's a tie for #30. There are no ties afterward, though, so the list's integrity is maintained. For example, there won't be a tie for #18, which would mean I skip over #19.

[2] That sounded awesome in my head and looks pathetic on the page, likely foreshadowing what's to come.

[3] My Apollo ranking is buried deep in this book somewhere. Happy hunting.

[4] This one's #4.

To whet your appetite for this ranking, below I serve up a dozen caveats, parameters, and other criteria.

Here are the Top 30's considerations:

1) This ranking is a list of *influential* figures. I considered making a "Greatest Figures" list, but I didn't want the wording to be confusing, misleading, or controversial. People of questionable character can make this list. Adolf Hitler *did* make this list. I'm looking for influence—it doesn't have to be positive.

2) This ranking is a list of *Western* figures. Unfortunately, the Western world is not a specific term. For the purposes of this series, the West consists of civilization from the Greco-Roman world, its cultural descendants in Europe, and the colonies that most seamlessly adopted the culture of those founders. A figure must hail from one of history's "Western" territories. Figures who are not of these origins but still heavily impacted Western history—think Zoroaster, Attila the Hun, Mohammed, Genghis Khan, and Mao, among many others—do not qualify for the list. The reason for their exclusion is because I only feel comfortable ranking Westerners, as the West has been my area of study and teaching for two decades. I wouldn't presume to understand the importance of Confucius, the Buddha, Emperor Qin, Emperor Meiji, or Mohandas Gandhi.

3) I was not kind to monarchs. Of the 30 figures, I have only 6 autocrats, which aren't a lot considering 80 percent of the list did not have their kind of political power. Moreover, no autocrat made the top half of the list. Colossally famous and reasonably important kings like William the Conqueror, Henry VIII, and Louis XIV did not make the cut at all. Still, I'll mention scores of monarchs along the way.

Introduction

4) Similarly, I disqualified any leaders who coincidently presided over enormous sociopolitical change. For example, is King John influential because he was forced to sign the Magna Carta? Is Louis XVI influential for being the king forced to call the Estates General after a century of financial and political mismanagement before his reign? In both cases, and in many more where an embattled leader is powerless to stop events much larger than their own crown, I say nay.

5) I had difficulty weighing the importance of artists, musicians, and authors. Ultimately, no artists or musicians made the list. Aside from one exception, no authors made the cut unless that vocation was not their primary one. (Thomas Jefferson and Isaac Newton are published authors, for example, but they're much better classified as something else.) While I have enormous appreciation for the arts and adore classical music, I simply could not make the case that any one artist or musician changed the West's development more than those who made this ranking. Perhaps the best way to look at it is that these cultural icons were superb reflections of an era; when studying a period, it's good to study the titans of music and art, much like an archaeologist unearths artifacts to draw conclusions about a past culture. Yet, they do not shape their era or future ones as much as others on this list.

6) Instead of artists, I hedged toward leaders and those with big, paradigm-shifting ideas. I believe these are the people that influence, rather than merely reflect, the West's development. For that reason, this list of 31 figures (remember, #30 is a tie) has:

- 11 political and military leaders
- 10 that were either scientists, inventors, or both

- 7 who are best described as philosophers or thinkers.

For the arithmetically challenged, that leaves only three people who do not place into one of those categories.

7) This list in some ways is American-heavy, but in other ways it's not. Five Americans and a German-American make the list. No other country received more entries. Some might resent the heavy American presence, considering the United States has existed for less than one-tenth of Western history, but I'll try to make the best defense I can with each figure. For now, I'll say that only the German-American made the top dozen, so while they might win the quantity contest, other countries have more quality. France and England have five each in the top 30, but whereas France doesn't sniff the top 10, their old rivals across the English Channel own 30 percent of it (40 percent if you throw in the rest of Great Britain).

Other represented countries are Germany with four; ancient Greece, ancient Rome, early modern Italy, and the medieval Frankish kingdom with two each; and we have one Scot, one Pole, and one Russian.[5] Spain didn't place anyone, but what can you expect from a country that takes a daily siesta?

8) Keep in mind that beyond the Top 30, I will mention many more names that missed the cut. I will frequently dedicate some space to others of the same field or era who one could argue should have made the list. In the next chapter, I'll summarize the "Next 30"—or the people I'd rank down to about 60.

---

[5] So many clues!

Introduction

9) Only two women made the list,[6] and I might not have any minorities, depending on how one wants to classify Jesus. Instead, the ranking is almost totally comprised of white men.

Since this list measured influence, many amazing and talented people in history, including such notable white men as Mozart and da Vinci, didn't make the cut. The reason is because I wasn't evaluating greatness and talent unless it contributed to the impact one left on the development of Western history.

It's irrefutable that for nearly all of Western history, power and influence has been concentrated in the hands of white men. I'll leave analysis and criticism of this sad fact to more insightful writers and their more sobering works, but it'll remain a sad fact. Although plenty of women and minorities across Western history have been some combination of inspirational, underappreciated, accomplished, and flat out great, only in the last century or so have they been in a position to effect change on the macro level. In fact, we still see systemic racism and sexism evidenced by the comparatively few female and minority leaders in politics, science, and industry.

This ranking is, admittedly, just the latest example of discrimination against women and minorities, but I think it more a reflection of that discrimination than a continuation of it. A list of underappreciated figures, one that reveals the many important women and minorities often forgotten by history, would be appropriate, but that's not what this book is.

10) Regarding that twentieth century number, one might think that having five relatively recent people is too many, considering the grand

---

[6] Sorry, Mom.

scope of history. One might argue that someone from early history created more ripples over the centuries than someone alive in the 1900s.

Perhaps. However, I wanted to avoid assuming that earlier is necessarily more consequential, as that kind of logic could ensnare us in quite the trap. For example, Isaac Newton is an extraordinarily influential figure—perhaps the most important scientist of all time and surely in anyone's top 10 historical figures list. But without his mother, there's no Isaac Newton. And since his mother created Newton and surely had at least one other effect on something else, does she now supersede Newton in influence? And, by the same logic, what about *her* mother? Thus, the trap.

I hope you'll agree that identifying the laws of gravity and motion is more important than expelling Isaac Newton out of a birth canal. Earlier is not necessarily more influential just because of the added ripples across time. Instead, I'll try to identify whose actions are most responsible for the modern West. As such, yes, five twentieth century figures do make the list. Moreover, another five saw the nineteenth century, four the eighteenth, four the seventeenth, and three the sixteenth. In other words, the most recent 21 figures on this list are almost evenly spaced out across the last five centuries. Only the remaining 10 had their hallmark achievements in the two millennia before the year 1500.[7]

11) One reason why so few are so early is because we know less and less as we examine earlier and earlier history. Which Phoenician deserves

---

[7] Many, like the Thomases Edison and Jefferson, were influential across centuries. In almost all cases, I "rounded up" their centuries in that paragraph. (If I had more Thomases in the Top 30, I would have listed them there. Hobbes and Aquinas just missed. Better luck next time to Becket, More, Cromwell, Wolsey, and Paine.)

Introduction

credit for the alphabet? Which proto-civilization the wheel? History scrutinizes and calls into question the stories and even existence of Abraham and Moses, so to which Biblical patriarch do we credit the beginning of the unbroken chain of Judeo-Christian ethical monotheism? Because these developments happened so early, it's impossible to feel as confident discussing the people behind them. Even a trusted grade-school fact like "Hammurabi was the first one to write down a law code" has been obliterated by further study.

The further back we go, the less we know. Thus, the ancients, though perhaps the most impressive people to ever walk the West, are underrepresented in my ranking.[8]

12) It goes without saying how difficult it is to measure influence. In fact, it's *im*measurable. There are many pitfalls to avoid. While someone can be colossally important to their own country or their own century, I tried to consider what impact they had on the West's development and how we live today. As stated, I tried to be careful about earlier figures necessarily having more influence, and I tried to think about how the West would be different without each figure.

I also acknowledge that none of these figures could do what they did without contributions from earlier men and women. What could Washington have accomplished without the musket, Einstein without harnessed electricity, and Shakespeare without paper, the pen, an education, a literate and cultured West, and the welcoming political climate of Elizabethan England? Probably not a lot. Moreover, almost all these fig-

---

[8] My deepest apologies to the estates of Pythagoras, Thales, Euclid, Hippocrates, and Archimedes.

ures had contemporary help, too—unsung heroes working with them every day. These friends, co-workers, employees, subordinates, and acquaintances were imperative in the operation, but mostly forgotten by history.

Therefore, each of the 31 figures on this list is ultimately just a mosaic; look closely enough and the *tesserae* emerge, each a smaller piece of the larger picture. The famous figure is merely the face on the poster; his or her collaborators are listed at the bottom in small print.

Ultimately, throughout this series, I will try to keep in mind one of my favorite quotes about history. Author-historian David McCullough described history as "who we are and why we are the way we are." Who shaped the West to make it look like it does today? Who gave us our society, our culture, our ideas, our borders, our thirst for knowledge, our soul, and everything else that makes the West what it is? Which historical figures are most responsible for *who* we are and *why* we are the *way* we are?

With this series, I'll attempt to answer those questions and more. I hope you learn something.

They Didn't Make It

Before we get into the Top 30, you might want to know some famous historical figures who *didn't* make the ranking.[1]

I'll start with some big names who were as quickly dismissed as they were conjured. They didn't even make the "next" 30. All, of course, are extremely important. These figures would be on a list of the hundred or thousand most influential Westerners of all time, which is really high up there.[2] Nonetheless, on this competitive list, at least 60 names are more influential than them.

I'll split them up into mini-categories so you can know why They Didn't Make It.

The comparatively overrated political leaders: Louis XIV, Catherine the Great, Vladimir Lenin, Josef Stalin, Benito Mussolini, Franklin Roosevelt

---

[1] Prepare to be furious.

[2] I mean, there've been billions of us.

Who Made the West

The talented artists/composers/authors who aren't influential enough: Michelangelo, Raphael, Bach, Mozart, Beethoven, The Beatles, Dante, Chaucer, Tolstoy, Dickens

The hugely influential Westerners whose impacts were felt more in non-Western areas: Alexander the Great, Norman Borlaug

Are you sure they existed and did what you think they did? Abraham, Moses, Homer

Others were on the verge of doing what they did: Ferdinand Magellan, Adam Smith, Alexander Graham Bell, Louis Daguerre, Wright Brothers, Sigmund Freud

Vital inventors/scientists with relatively less influence compared to higher ranked inventors/scientists: William Harvey, Andreas Vesalius, Francis Bacon, Johannes Kepler, Antoine Lavoisier, Antonie van Leeuwenhoek, Gugliemo Marconi, Benjamin Franklin, Charles Babbage, James Clerk Maxwell, Jonas Salk, Nikola Tesla

The brilliant but perhaps too early Greeks: Archimedes, Aristarchus, Eratosthenes, Hippocrates, Pythagoras, Thales

Supremely talented people whose influence was relatively limited compared to those ranked ahead of them: Leonardo da Vinci, Carl Friedrich Gauss

Still alive, so the jury is out: Bill Gates, James Watson of Watson & Crick, Mark Zuckerberg, my mother

They Didn't Make It

The Next 30

Next is a group I call the "Next 30." Before we get to 41 through 30, you'll first get a tier that I would rank 41 through 60 in some order (alphabetical here):

Thomas Aquinas (1225-1274, Italian theologian): His introduction of scholasticism allowed classicism, Aristotelianism in particular, back into the good graces of the Catholic Church—and therefore back into western Europe as well. This "recovery of Aristotle" helped bring about the Renaissance. (More on that in the Aristotle entry.)

St. Augustine (354-430, Roman African theologian): His Christian theology was accepted by the Roman Catholic Church as it began its ascent to become the West's central authority. He was probably Christianity's most important thinker between St. Paul (first century) and Aquinas (thirteenth).

Otto von Bismarck (1815-1898, German statesman): He was the mastermind behind assembling the nation of Germany, one of the most important countries in modern history.

Winston Churchill (1874-1965, British prime minister): His leadership of the U.K. in World War II's darkest days kept Britain alive until the Allies could wrest back momentum from the Axis. The pressure was on him to come to terms with Hitler. He refused.

Marie Curie (1867-1934, Polish-French scientist): She was the first woman to win a Nobel Prize. Our earliest breakthroughs in understanding radioactivity are due to her. (Her death, unfortunately, was from radioactivity.)

René Descartes (1596-1650, French polymath): Leonardo da Vinci was the prototypical "Renaissance man," but Descartes embodied the post-Renaissance man, helping to set up the Enlightenment. Unlike da Vinci, he left a direct impact on philosophy (classical rationalism) and mathematics (most notably the Cartesian plane).

Michael Faraday (1791-1867, British scientist): He invented the dynamo, the first machine to generate electricity. He also advanced the field of magnetism.

Thomas Hobbes (1588-1679, English political philosopher): I have a lot to say about Hobbes in a Top 5 entry.

Queen Isabella (1451-1504, Spanish queen): She'll also be discussed at length in a Top 5 entry.

Steve Jobs (1955-2011, American entrepreneur): You won't see Bill Gates on this list because he's still alive and not done yet. The late Steve Jobs, however, was strongly considered. I predict he'll make a new Top 30 when I revise the ranking in a couple centuries after my consciousness is downloaded into an Apple product.

They Didn't Make It

John Maynard Keynes (1883-1946, British economist): He spearheaded a macroeconomic revolution in the West. Gone are the days of true laissez-faire economics. Western governments now regularly use a Keynesian approach, injecting themselves into economies, particularly when contractions threaten recession. His advocacy for using fiscal policy to regulate the business cycle is now the norm.

Abraham Lincoln (1809-1865, American statesman): He saved the United States. A key argument to George Washington will be the importance of the U.S. to the modern world. Though Washington helped birth the nation, it was Lincoln who guided it through adolescence. Still, unlike Washington, Lincoln did not humble the world's foremost empire, and he was not as contributory to the fundamentals of American government.

Niccolo Machiavelli (1469-1527, Italian political scientist): Author of *The Prince,* the ideology he proposed to his powerful benefactors became a justification and guide for power-hungry politicians who believe the ends justify the means.

Gregor Mendel (1822-1884, Austrian scientist): The founder of modern genetics. (Or, rather, the "father" of genetics.[3])

Marco Polo (1254-1324, Italian explorer): Before Christopher Columbus sailed west to Fake Asia, Marco Polo traveled east to the real one. In time, his writings about his experiences in China inspired others to

---

[3] Your groans make me stronger.

search for a route there, which led to the accidental discovery of the Americas.

Wilhelm Röntgen (1845-1923, German scientist): This Nobel Prize winner was the inventor of the X-ray machine, perhaps the world's most important modern invention.

Jean-Jacques Rousseau (1712-1778, Swiss-French philosopher): His ideas drove the worldviews of many American and French revolutionaries in their struggles against the old regimes. I considered Voltaire more influential, however.

Margaret Sanger (1879-1966, American sex educator): Read my Gregory Pincus chapter to know how important I think birth control is. Of the many people crucial to the development of realistic and safe birth control, Pincus is the most important, but Sanger is second.

Urban II (1035-1099, French-Italian pope): Surprisingly, only three popes were even strongly considered for the list, and only this one came close.[4] Urban gave us the first of the Crusades, a series of wars in the Middle East that introduced Arab ideas and luxuries, and reintroduced preserved Roman culture, to the Western world. The Renaissance followed shortly thereafter. The Crusades also soured relations between

---

[4] Innocent III, probably history's most powerful pope, was one of these three, but his influence doesn't match up to Urban's. Gregory XIII gave us our calendar, but Caesar had already set up the basic parts of it, and Gregory's major influence was limited to the calendar alone.

They Didn't Make It

Western Christians and the Arab world, a souring which had many effects, including some to this day.

William the Conqueror (1028-1087, English king): Before 1066, the Anglo-Saxons of England were German and the French of France were Latin. William's Norman Invasion of England merged them. The result was a hybrid culture that was later exported throughout the world through the language of English. These French rulers eventually bothered their German subjects so much that many of them rose up and demanded liberties which became a key part of English, and later American, government.

The Next 10

And finally, here is the "Next 10." In some order (alphabetical below), they are the next ten most influential figures in Western history, ranked after only the 30 written about in this book.

Augustus (63 BCE-14 CE, Roman emperor): I've seen his name high on some lists. Though he was the first Roman Emperor and one of the 40 most influential figures in Western history, it's Julius Caesar who deserves more credit for making the empire possible and influential. Augustus gets knocked off my list as a result.

Julius Caesar (100 BCE – 44 BCE): See Augustus. Caesar was one of my last cuts from the Top 30 and may in fact have been the first person ranked directly behind Plato and Aristotle. Consider all the culture (language, calendar, science, art, roads, and more) we've inherited from ancient Roman civilization, which greatly expanded under Caesar's leadership. I see him as more important than Augustus, who more solidified many of the reforms and conquests started by Caesar. Still, the responsibility of Rome's rise is split among so many people that they were all kept off the list.

Cicero (106 BCE – 43 BCE, Roman statesman and orator): Thanks to his prolific writings and the many cultural influencers that studied him, perhaps no one had a greater impact on Latin and the modern Western languages that come from it. Centuries later, Petrarch's discovery of Cicero's writings helped catalyze the early Renaissance period. Enlightenment leaders also looked to him for inspiration.

Euclid (mid-300s BCE-mid-200s BCE, Greek mathematician): As the father of geometry, I hate Euclid's Greek guts,[5] but I recognize his importance. His book, "Elements," was the leading mathematical textbook from the age of Aristotle to the age of Newton.

Alexander Fleming (1881-1955, Scottish scientist): The inventor of antibiotics, he was a tough omission.

Henry VIII (1491-1547, English king): He fathered three English monarchs (including the 19th most influential figure in Western history) and created the Anglican Church, which smoothed England's later decision to ignore the Church's decree that only Spain and Portugal could colo-

---

[5] Apologies to my wondrously wise and patient ninth-grade geometry teacher, Mr. Lamothe.

They Didn't Make It

nize abroad. If you're a white Anglo-Saxon Protestant living in America (and there's a lot of you), Henry's creation of the Church of England is a primary reason why you are what you are.

Edward Jenner (1749-1823, English scientist): I have more to say about him in a Top 10 entry. It's been said that his work with immunology and vaccines saved more lives than anyone else in history.[6]

St. Paul (c. 5 – c. 64, Roman religious co-founder): I have much more to say about him in the chapter on Jesus.

Petrarch (1304-1374, Italian poet and humanist): When Petrarch uncovered some of Cicero's old letters, he was inspired to break away from traditional medieval philosophy and start a new "humanistic" movement, a decision credited by many as the catalyst behind the Renaissance. He vocally dissented from the old way of thinking—which he was the first to dub the "Dark Ages"—and helped us pivot into the modern age.

Socrates (470 BCE-399 BCE, Greek philosopher): The first great Western philosopher, he was nonetheless outdone by his pupil and his pupil's pupil.[7] Speaking of them...

---

[6] I often wish I made more than 30 spots.

[7] I expect the same will be said of me.

Who Made the West

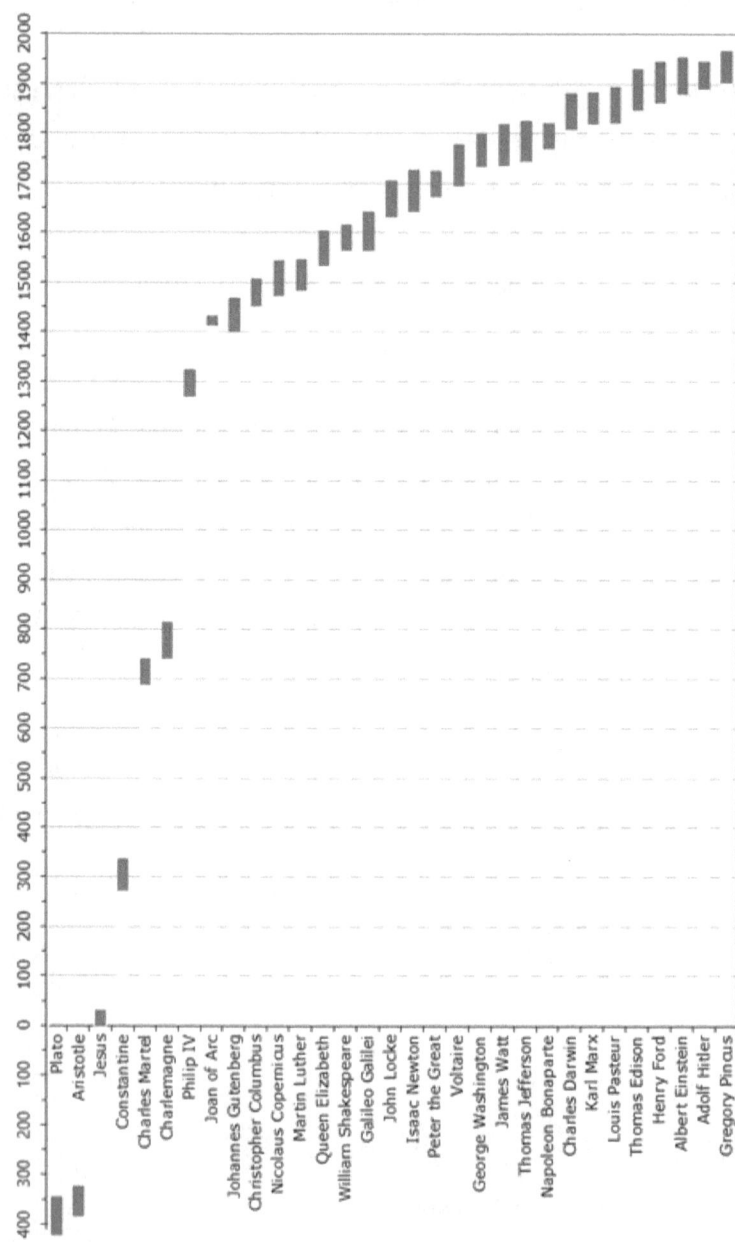

#30: Plato & Aristotle (tie)

"Do we say that justice itself is something? Of course. And the fair and the good? Surely. Then have you ever seen any of these sorts of things with your eyes? In no way. But then have you grasped them with any other sense through the body. . . . Is it through the body then that what is most true of these things is contemplated? Or does it hold thus?"

–Plato ("Phaedo")

"No one is able to attain the truth adequately, while, on the other hand, no one fails entirely, but everyone says something true about the nature of things, and while individually they contribute little or nothing to the truth, by the union of all a considerable amount is amassed."

–Aristotle ("Metaphysics")

"You will always be a child of two worlds. . . . The question you face is: which path will you choose?"

–Sarek to his half-human, half-Vulcan son, Spock (*Star Trek*)

Part I: Plato

For the last 2,500 years, the Western world has hosted a battlefield—a philosophical tug of war, if you will. Repeatedly stretched and torn, the West has developed under two almost diametrically opposed and competing worldviews. It's remarkable that it mends, but it does. The two teams in this struggle are the philosophical descendants of Plato (c. 428 – c. 348 BCE) and his student Aristotle (384 – 322 BCE).

You might not know it, but you probably adhere, with some minor deviations, to one of their schools of thought. You're either a Platonist, who believes in absolute morals, the supremacy of the ultimate good, perceived truths unveiled by a series of deductions, and the potential release of the immortal spirit from our material world into an idealized higher plane of existence; or you're an Aristotelian, one who looks to this material world for answers in a never-ending, empirical quest to learn about the universe, studying and categorizing all findings, using not just deduction but also inductive reasoning to incrementally accrue knowledge.

These competing schools have competed for the West's soul. As a result, Plato and Aristotle, ancient Greece's most important titans of thought, share my designation as the 30th most influential figure in Western history.

Despite their philosophical differences, even the most ardent Aristotelian must have a great deal of respect for Plato. The English philosopher Alfred North Whitehead once argued that "The safest general characterization of the European philosophical tradition is that it consists of a series of footnotes to Plato."[1]

Plato learned under the legendary Socrates and his eponymous method. Consequently, Plato's prime years were filled with wondering, questioning, re-questioning, and challenging preconceived notions. Through this critical analysis, Plato developed into a renowned philosopher in his own right, and it's his own writings that make Socrates a legend at all.[2]

Plato's inclusion in my Top 30 stems mainly from his contributions to government, metaphysics, and epistemology, much of which was grafted onto future Western institutions. Centuries after his 348 BCE death, his worldviews were largely appropriated by Christianity, particularly the Roman Catholic Church. Later still, constitutional framers saw wisdom in Plato's writings as well.

"The Republic," perhaps his most famous work, outlines Plato's ideal form of government. Disillusioned with the democratic process that killed his mentor in 399—a vote from 501 Athenians ruled Socrates guilty of impiety and corruption of the youth, charges that carried the penalty of death—Plato instead argues for a meritocracy. This

---

[1] Like so.

[2] Socrates won't make our list of 30, although I do rank him in the "Next 10." His teachings, method, and philosophy were never recorded by him. Rather, it was his students, Plato especially, who preserved and circulated Socrates's ideas. The idolization of their master, especially after his heroism in the face of a flawed trial and execution, surely infected the students' accounts of their great teacher. The inability to precisely know what Socrates thought, said, and did has become known as the "Socratic Problem." Thus, his dependency on Plato for posterity and his problematic historicity bump Socrates from our list in favor of his pupil and pupil's pupil.

form of government is comprised of the most capable citizens, and this group perpetuates itself by selecting its qualified successors. Neither democratic nor despotic, such a state would avoid the volatile whims of an impulsive mob as well as the menacing moods of an arrogant autocrat. These enlightened leaders, or "philosopher-kings," would be educated in the affairs of the state, own little land, make little money, have no familial distraction, and would place the health of the state above all personal concerns. While no actual state has fully adopted this mode of governing, many of these ideas have nevertheless been attempted in Western governments.

For example, under ancient Rome's "Five Good Emperors" (96 – 180), the last four of these emperors were adopted by their predecessor based on merit, which was similar to Plato's proposal. It's under their leadership that Rome reached its zenith.[3] More recently, the American founding fathers did their best to set up a meritocracy, creating a constitution that ensured their own office, erected barriers between voters and most federal offices, and placed numerous checks on the power of democracy over the new government.[4] In fact, the founding fathers sometimes pejoratively used the term "democracy," often comparing it more to mob rule than a wise and fair governing system. I assure you they had read their Plato.

---

[3] The termination of the adoption line—marked by the ascension of Emperor Commodus, the true son of the last of the Five Good Emperors, Marcus Aurelius—is hailed by many as the beginning of Rome's lengthy downfall. Point Plato.

[4] Only one-sixth of the original federal government—the House of Representatives—was directly elected by voters. The other half of the legislative branch—the Senate—was initially chosen by state legislatures. The president was picked by the Electoral College, which was originally not tied to

Plato & Aristotle

Though these governments were "Republic"-adjacent, another powerful organization came even closer to Plato's ideals: the Roman Catholic Church. Like Plato advised, the Church's officials—from popes down to priests—are chosen from within the organization after years of ecclesiastical education, and most of its clergy have lived humbly, with little land and no wife or children.[5]

Plato's impact on Western religion goes well beyond "The Republic." Not limited to just the Church's clerical hierarchy, Christianity's roots drink deeply from the wellspring of Platonism. Plato proposed that the material world perceived by our basic senses is filled with imperfect manifestations of idealized "Forms," which exist on a conceptual plane of reality that most of us cannot yet perceive. The things we perceive around us are imperfect copies of those Forms. Examples include shapes, like circles and squares. No perfect circle or square exists materially; inspect either closely enough and flaws will emerge. The circle isn't perfectly round. The square's sides aren't identically long. Yet, we know circles and squares conceptually, and we agree on these forms' properties even if we can't reproduce them materially.

---

states' popular votes. Finally, the judicial branch was picked by the unelected president on advice and consent from the unelected Senate. Underscoring all these barriers between the people and the national government was that the original electorate was a tiny slice of the population—mostly just land-owning white men. This was hardly a democracy—and thank goodness, too, says Plato.

[5] Admittedly, the historical exceptions to this lifestyle number too many to count. Catholic clergy own an abhorrent record in matters of greed, lust, and the other five sins, too.

When expanding the analogy beyond shapes, it's understandable why early Christians appropriated many facets of Platonism to strengthen their doctrine. Instead of shapes like circles, think about concepts such as beauty and goodness. Like shapes, they are universal concepts; yet, in practice—in the material world—they are rarely perfect. Take "Goodness," for example. For millennia, ethics and philosophy classes have debated the idea of a "universal good." Are there moral absolutes? Is anything universally right and good or wrong and bad?[6] For many, it's a messy debate with no easy answers.

But for Platonists and Christians, there are, in fact, moral absolutes. There *is* an absolute Good. Plato analogized the Good to the sunlight outside his famous allegory's cave. The sun emits a warm beam of knowledge and grace withheld from those stuck in a dark dungeon. Christians, similarly, propose God as the originator of morals prescribed to the world through the Bible. In Plato, all goodness emanates from the sun; the more one allows the light to be a guide, the closer to Good and Knowledge one gets. Christians, too, spend lifetimes studying their religion, trying to move closer to God and His knowledge. In either case, just as we can't create perfect shapes, we can't reproduce perfect Beauty and Good; to err is still human. Yet, according to Platonism and its Christian offspring, the forms of Beauty and Good exist conceptually thanks to the Sun/God, and we're encouraged to move toward them. The

---

[6] Most commonly, murder is brought up as an example of an absolute wrong. However, when it comes to defending one's homeland, family, or self, all of a sudden killing seems appropriate. Modern terrorists are excoriated for killing innocents, but President Truman and the Enola Gay bombers get praise for incinerating 70,000 Japanese civilians. Even killing can be acceptable under the right parameters.

kicker: Plato, in "Phaedo," suggests that at death, our immortal soul is released from the material world into that higher plane. The Christian connection is clear.

Centuries after his death mid-fourth century BCE death, a revival of Platonism coincided with the second century rise of Christianity. This new strain, called Neoplatonism, was soon appropriated by the new faith. Early Christian thinkers merged Neoplatonic philosophy into their religion, solidifying Plato's ongoing influence on the West's dominant religion.[7] Even when the Greco-Roman classical world crumbled in the fourth and fifth centuries, the Platonized Roman Catholic Church during the subsequent Middle Ages became the dominant political and social institution in the Western world. Thus, even in the greatest socioeconomic collapse in civilized history, Christianity survived and propagated. The result was that Plato, "the Athenian Moses," continued to deliver the truth to the Christian people.

As the Middle Ages progressed under the premise of a singular, ultimate Good, the Church used its authority to control western Europe. After all, if there is only one truth and one perfect Good, anyone who disagreed with it must be less good—and maybe even bad.

No longer was one allowed a personal, local relationship to God or the gods. The Church did its best to homogenize Christianity. The swords of armies commanded by Constantine, Clovis, Charlemagne, and

---

[7] Interestingly, after "Neoplatonism" was introduced into third century Christianity, mostly thanks to St. Augustine (who just missed the Top 30) and Pseudo-Dionysius (not to be confused with the real Dionysius), many historians and some small Christian denominations argue that this meddling changed Christ's original message, doctrine, and practice.

others ingrained this "Catholic," or "universal," interpretation into the region. Only with Martin Luther and the Protestant Reformation of the sixteenth century did the Church lose its grasp on the West, and only since then has the right of the people to personally interpret the Word returned.[8] Still, from the rise of Christianity to its reformative schism—essentially the timeframe of the entire Middle Ages—the West was decidedly Platonic.

These Middle Ages are bookended by the ancient and modern worlds. The transition from ancient to medieval occurred in a tumultuous fifth century that included three raids on the city of Rome and the dismemberment of the Western Roman Empire by Germanic tribes.[9] When this power vacuum was replaced by an increasingly dominant papacy, Neoplatonism, via Christianity, became the reigning Greek philosophy for the next thousand years.

After that, however—as medievalism gave way to modernity—the Church's power slipped, and Plato's philosophy lost control of the West. It has since been gradually replaced by the philosophy of his star student.

---

[8] For this reason, Martin Luther gets his own chapter on this ranking.

[9] The Roman Empire had officially split in 395 CE. The Eastern Roman Empire, the stronger half, remained for another millennium after the Western Empire's fall, and its strong emperors ruling from the fortified capital of Constantinople were able to maintain the upper hand over the Eastern Church, which later evolved into the Greek-speaking Orthodox Church. The Eastern Roman Empire is often called the Byzantine Empire by historians who don't want us to confuse the continuing Roman Empire with the classical version of it. "Byzantine" stems from "Byzantium," the Greek word for the city that was re-named Constantinople for reasons I'll get into in a later chapter. The empire, however, just kept calling itself "Roman."

Part II: Aristotle

In 1511, the Renaissance artist Raphael completed his masterpiece, *The School of Athens*. It imagines all the great ancient Greeks living at the same time in one room. Among others, we see Socrates, Archimedes, Epicurus, Pythagoras, Parmenides, Euclid, and Ptolemy.

Two, however, take center stage: Plato and his pupil Aristotle. Raphael considered them the most important Greeks of all. So does this ranking.

Historian E.H. Gombrich writes that Aristotle was "the teacher of mankind for 2,000 years. . . . Whenever people failed to agree on one thing or another, they turned to his writings. He was their referee."

One might doubt Gombrich's characterization considering Platonism's supremacy during the Middle Ages. His generalization works, however, when one considers that for the bulk of the medieval era, to disagree with prevailing Catholic wisdom was dangerous. In other words, it was unusual for people to "fail to agree."

The collapse of the Western Roman Empire in the fifth century destabilized western Europe. No strong, organized states remained. This vacuum, however, had a peculiar side-effect: the rise of the Roman Catholic Church, the strongest institution remaining in the region. A few centuries later, it reigned over the continent and influenced powerful state leaders, an empire in all but name.

During the heart of the Middle Ages, few dared stand up to the nearly omnipotent papacy. Heretics were burned at the stake. Princes were brought to their knees. Emperors served at the will of His Holiness, the pope. Philosophers, from Augustine to Aquinas, operated under the assumption of an all-powerful Christian God who sent His Word through the Bible and His son. The world and universe worked according to His will and whim. To doubt any of these presumptions was heretical and punishable by excommunication and even death.

But in select medieval instances of open debate and reference to ancient knowledge, and in the many intellectual breakthroughs since, the guiding philosopher of the West has been Aristotle.

Son of the physician to the Macedonian king, Aristotle was born into science. He was sent to study at the Academy, where Plato cultivated the curious Aristotle's intellectual gifts.

The student, however, ultimately broke with the teacher. For example, whereas Plato's rationalism stated that knowledge is *a priori* (already within us before we peel off the layers hiding it), Aristotle was an empiricist who believed knowledge is *a posteriori* (built after experience). Thus, Platonists rely on deductive logic—a rational series of deductions can turn premises into conclusions, like a syllogism—but Aristotelians favor inductive logic, preferring observation to accrue knowledge, which consequently produces firmer conclusions.[10]

By doing so, Aristotle ultimately eclipsed his teacher just as Plato eclipsed his own. The most prominent "Renaissance man" of the ancient world, Aristotle didn't merely study education, ethics, history, logic, metaphysics, philosophy, physiology, poetry, politics, rhetoric, society, and the sciences (including anatomy, astronomy, biology, geology, meteorology, physics, and zoology); he was considered a foremost expert in

---

[10] You might notice that many arguments today between theists and atheists come down to theists favoring the deductive approach while atheists prefer inductive. You'll also notice that these two sides are always respectful of each other's beliefs.

Plato & Aristotle

those areas. While he didn't invent any of those fields, one could argue that he was the first to standardize them. His body of written works (*corpus Aristotelicum*) is quite the list to behold. The rudimentary titles—"Mechanics," "Metaphysics," "Meteorology," "History of Animals," "On Plants," "On the Universe," "Physics," "Poetics," "Politics," "Rhetoric," and 37 more—are a reminder that he is among the earliest to standardize our most basic fields. He literally wrote the book on those topics. Only 47 of these works survived; he's believed to have written over 120 more. British philosopher Bryan Magee put it best when he said, "it is doubtful whether any human being has ever known as much as he did."[11]

Aristotle's guiding philosophical principle was that the universe was not governed by magic or divine intervention. Rather, it's natural law that governs our world and the cosmos. The trick was to understand them, and the path to understanding was using what we now call the scientific method—observe, measure, experiment, formulate hypotheses, test them, and then test them again. Only then do you truly know something.[12] Aristotle wasn't the first to try this empirical approach, but he

---

[11] I would empty my bank account and take out a second mortgage to pay a newspaper to put that into the first paragraph of my obituary.

[12] Maybe.

may have been the first to formalize it.[13] Scientists and philosophers of the ancient world openly referenced Aristotle for centuries after his 322 BCE death.

Later, however, many in the medieval Catholic Church suppressed his legendary status. Although they would cite him when they endorsed his conclusions—Aristotle was a geocentrist, for example—they demurred when it came to his philosophy.

Take his celebrated work, the "Categories." In it, Aristotle posits that each thing in the universe, in order to be understood, must stand up to ten examinations—that of its substance, quantity, quality, relation, place, time, posture, state, action, and affection. Before the Middle Ages, Aristotle's "Categories" were commonly referenced in all things scientific and dialectic.

With the medieval loss of Aristotelianism, "Categories" faced castigation. After all, God could not be measured by those examinations, yet He very much existed. Anastasius of Sinai, a prominent seventh century abbot, eviscerated the work, saying the ten horns of the dragon from Revelation 12:3 represented Aristotle's ten categories, which Anastasius deemed as ten heresies. As late as 1210, with the Church's "Condemna-

---

[13] It should be noted that his championing of inductive reasoning did not mean he dismissed the deductive reasoning of his teacher. Quite the contrary, as stated in his Posterior Analytics, he felt that deductive logic was helpful in discerning universal truths, to whatever extent those could be known. Many of the ancient Greeks embraced this approach, the most famous manifestations of which are their beloved syllogisms. An example of a syllogism would be "If A = B" and "B = C," then "A = C." Or, to put it into practice: "If Socrates is a mortal" and "All mortals love the Top 30 list," then it stands to reason that "Socrates loves the Top 30 list." See? Universal truths.

tions" of that year, Aristotle's works were anathema to most Western Christians.[14]

In contrast to western Europe, throughout the West's "Dark Ages" —the term sometimes given to the dreariest period of the Middle Ages, up through about 1000 CE—the Eastern Roman (Byzantine) Empire and Muslim world cherished Aristotle. Byzantine and Arab scholars preserved Aristotle's works, which is due in no small part to the regions'

---

[14] I've spared the main body from the following footnoted evidence that you can definitely skip unless you want to wade ankle deep into the schism between early Christians and the Greek tradition.

In First Corinthians, Paul, referring to the curious, scientific, Aristotelian minds of the Greco-Roman tradition, boasts of his new brand of philosophy "destroying the wisdom of the wise" and "frustrating the intelligent."

Three hundred years later, St. Augustine's "City of God" (*De Civitate Dei*) blamed pagan amorality and unchristian philosophers—save Plato—as a reason for the devastating Visigothic sack of Rome in 410 CE.

Fourth century Church father John Chrysostom argued that man should "restrain our own reasoning, and empty our mind of secular learning." Contemporary Basil of Caesarea, a Greek bishop, agreed, writing, "Let Us Christians prefer the simplicity of our faith to the demonstrations of human reason."

Even after the turn of the millennium, Christian leaders such as St. Bernard of Clairvaux criticized using one's "intellect" for any pursuit other than a holy one. Plato is one of the only ancients that survived this Catholic onslaught, mostly because Christians owed him for much of their worldview.

For a summarization on the suppression of Aristotelianism and the Greek tradition of inquiry, I recommend Charles Freeman's "The Closing of the Western Mind."

earlier conquests by Aristotle's warrior-student, Alexander the Great.[15] When Alexander conquered from Greece to Egypt to the Himalayas, the residual Hellenistic culture left in his wake led to the spread of Aristotle's works across north Africa and southwest Asia. In those non-Western places, Aristotle's works never had to withstand the Church's scrutiny.

The eventual return of Aristotle to the Western world can be partially attributed to one of the Church's most ignominious moments—the Crusades. Starting in the late eleventh century, the powerful papacy called on Western Catholics to launch a series of raids into the Muslim-occupied Holy Land. After a triumphant, if bloody, initial showing, each successive Crusade (one doesn't have enough fingers to count them) was one embarrassment after another. The Westerners that traveled to the Middle East, which included journeys through Eastern Roman land, returned with goods, ideas, and manuscripts not seen since the ancient world. The Fourth Crusade of the early 1200s hastened the downfall of Byzantium itself, which allowed Italian merchants to usurp the role of principal European traders in the eastern Mediterranean. What naturally followed was a steady stream of cultural diffusion, mostly from east to west.

The ensuing "Recovery of Aristotle" revolutionized Western thought. The Late Middle Ages re-embraced the lost philosopher. Even Christian theologians—most prominently Thomas Aquinas—used Aristotelianism to further their Christian teachings, a merging known as

---

[15] Alexander ends our famous teacher-student run. Socrates taught Plato who taught Aristotle who taught Alexander the Great. Or, as my students acronymize, "Spaa." Though the meat of this four-Greek sandwich made the Top 30, the two pieces of bread did not.

scholasticism. Aquinas thought that Aristotle should be accepted by Christians. After all, Aristotle was by no means an atheist. He had insisted that there must be an "Unmoved First Mover" whose catalyzing presence allowed all other things in the universe to exist and change.[16] Aquinas felt that the path to strengthening Christianity lay not with fearing and debunking Aristotle, but welcoming him and using his logic to promote and reinforce Christianity. In his hallmark "Summa Theologica," Aquinas sets out to prove the existence of God through Aristotelianism. In his *quinque viae*—five ways—he claims to have done so. The Church approved.

With the approval of Aristotle from Aquinas and, consequently, the rest of the Catholic Church, Aristotelianism thundered back into the Western world. Moreover, thanks to the Crusades and rise of Italian trade, so, too, did Classical writings and Greco-Roman ideas of all kinds. Many in the inspired West soon craved knowledge. New universities across Europe—Salamanca, Paris, Oxford, and many more—developed as places of higher learning. Soon, a new wave of Classically-inspired thinkers promoted humanism and individualism.

Predictably, the evolution of the Middle Ages into the Renaissance and modern world was met with stiff resistance from traditionalists, but they were overwhelmed. The Middle Ages crumbled around an outmatched Church. In the course of about a century, the papacy had to deal with the rise of secular leaders (who siphoned power from the Church),

---

[16] His theory is similar to the deistic values of the Enlightenment in that such a Mover—or, as deists have analogized, a "clockmaker"—must have set the universe in motion, but dissimilar in that Aristotle, like his teacher Plato, cites the Mover as the indivisible source of all things Good. Enlightenment philosophers did not ascribe any morality to their clockmaker.

nationalism (which usurped the allegiance of people from their religion), and Protestantism (which had the audacity to proclaim there were other interpretations of Christianity besides Rome's). Perhaps worst of all, science roared back into the Western world and a weakened Church couldn't stop it. By the mid-sixteenth century, the Scientific Revolution had begun; prominent Western scientists (including a few who will make their way onto this ranking) pursued knowledge having nothing to do with Christianity. Instead, guiding them was the scientific method.

Aristotelianism was back, and it's been here ever since.

It should be noted that Aristotle ultimately turned out to be wrong about many things.[17] Whereas Socrates's questions can always be asked and Plato's unearthly philosophy never proven inaccurate, Aristotle wrote about everything around him and made the best guesses he could with the limited evidence and instruments he had. Inevitably, with the improvement of instrumentation and the accumulation of experience, many of his best guesses have fallen short.

But that doesn't mean he's unimportant. Quite the contrary, his contributions to dozens of fields of study furthered the West's knowledge of them. More importantly, his approach to science stood the test of time. Even his "guesses" became the foundation of Western science. Cracks emerge in foundations over time, but it's with his approach to learning that we could later fill those cracks with new knowledge.

---

[17] Aristotle's inaccuracies arguably slowed the West's scientific advancement as much as the Church did. After his death, to doubt the great Aristotle was akin to a cleric doubting the papacy. Aristotle would have bristled at being such a hindrance.

Plato & Aristotle

As #30 draws to a close, it must feel like Aristotle has separated himself from Plato as ancient Greece's superior ambassador to our modern world—and therefore to have them tied in this ranking makes little sense. But we are so much more than science, aren't we? We cannot separate our Platonic roots from Western history, even if it's Aristotelianism that has blossomed over the last few centuries.

As a people, we look for answers in all sorts of places. In Raphael's *The School of Athens*, the hands of the centered Plato and Aristotle's reveal their identities. Plato points to the heavens, a higher plane of existence that is the source of all knowledge. Aristotle's hand hovers over the material world, which must be studied and categorized in our quest for understanding. We do a little of both, don't we? The West still looks to this linked pair.

And so the tug of war continues. Plato and Aristotle, incompatible yet inseparable, are tied as Western history's 30th most influential person.

#29: Philip "the Fair" of France

"Your venerable stupidity may know, that we are nobody's vassal in temporal matters."

–Philip IV "The Fair," King of France, in a letter to the Pope

Imagine a man more powerful than kings, prime ministers, and presidents. Imagine that this man is above the law, beyond reproach. He and his office have controlled millions of people for centuries. Princes and priests obey his every command. Emperors, desperate for approval and legitimacy, kneel before him. Imagine a man that is not only the temporal judge and jury of everyone on his land, but he also determines the fate of their very soul.

Now imagine the man who kidnaps him.

At the turn of the fourteenth century, the strongest days of the Roman Catholic Church and its papacy were behind them—they just didn't know it yet. The fall of western Europe's strongest political power since the Roman Empire was near. Much like Rome's fall, it didn't happen overnight; it took many years and a cascade of bad decisions.

But what started that chain reaction? Who pushed the Church off medieval Europe's perch and sent it plummeting into the modern world?

Philip "the Fair" of France

His name was Philip IV, the King of France and Navarre, the founder of the Estates General, the kidnapper of his Holy Father, and the 29th most influential person in Western history.[1]

In #30, when discussing the prevalence of Platonism during the Middle Ages, I described the Catholic Church's strength in medieval Europe.

"During the heart of the Middle Ages, few dared stand up to the nearly omnipotent papacy. Heretics were burned at the stake. Princes were brought to their knees. Emperors served at the will of His Holiness, the pope. Philosophers, from Augustine to Aquinas, operated under the assumption of an all-powerful Christian God who sent His Word through the Bible and His son. The world and universe worked according to His will and whim. To doubt any of these presumptions was heretical and punishable by excommunication and even death."

It goes without saying that our current pontiff, Pope Francis, does not wield that kind of power, and that has nothing to do with his revolutionary ideas.[2] The Western world was once almost fully Catholic; now, however, most of the West considers itself something else. What's more, even modern Catholics largely march to their own drum. Chances are you know many Catholics who don't support modern Church doctrine

---

[1] I'd say this Top 30 series has three people to whom even a relatively educated person would respond, "Who?!" Philip IV is one of them. Another will be revealed four chapters from now, while the last one found his way onto the top half of this list.

[2] To say that the papacy is a shell of its former self would be an insult to shells everywhere.

on issues like homosexuality, birth control, and abortion. Francis and his recent predecessors, much like the English monarchy, have been relegated to mostly symbolism, known more for pomp and ritual than power and resolutions.

During the Middle Ages, however, it was unthinkable to cross His Holiness. He was considered to be the Vicar of Christ, God's representative on Earth. A century before King Philip, Pope Innocent III, probably the most powerful pope in history, ruled over western Europe like a continental autocrat. He ordered around kings like they were his children.[3] He collected tithes from all corners of western Europe and ordered the devious Fourth Crusade, which conquered the rival Orthodox Christians of the Byzantine Empire.

Within a few hundred years, however, Catholic control was severely weakened. A few centuries after that, the Pope was used in farcical ad campaigns supporting gay marriage in New Zealand.[4] To what do we owe the decline of the once mighty Church? Many, many things. However, we can trace the beginning of the downfall to the early 1300s, with Philip IV as the catalyst.

Philip Capet was born in 1268 and ascended to the French throne 17 years later. His reign spanned 30 years and laid the foundation for enormous change across western Europe. Known as "the Fair" for his handsome face, he was driven by one guiding principle: power.

---

[3] John of England (he of Magna Carta and Robin Hood fame) and Philip II "Augustus" of France, for examples, feared the back of the Holy Father's holy hand.

[4] He's also purportedly walking into thousands of bars with rabbis and Gandhi.

Philip "the Fair" of France

For much of the Middle Ages, France was not governed by a strong, central government. Nor, for that matter, were other kingdoms across western Europe. Instead, the era was dominated by feudalism. Feudal lords—wealthy nobles scattered throughout a kingdom—governed local lands with considerable autonomy. They also appointed "vassals" to manage smaller sections of these lands. While there were certainly kings during the era, they relied on their lords to manage their kingdom. The lords would owe some sort of fealty to the king, but they often had more power on their own lands than the distant monarch did. In time, however, as the Low Middle Ages (c. 400 – c. 1000) gave way to the High (c. 1000 – c. 1300), feudal lords increasingly saw the pressures and benefits of coalescing around a unifying monarch's strong central authority.

Though feudalism's slow decline gradually subordinated nobles to the monarch, King Philip knew he was still not the most commanding presence in his country. Indeed, Pope Boniface VIII exerted more influence in France from Rome than Philip did from Paris.

Philip wouldn't stand for it. In a drive for wealth, he targeted the richest group in his country—the clergy. [5] The Church was the largest landholder in France, making them a prime source for Philip's greed. The problem was that Church officials, scattered throughout France and the rest of western Europe as wealthy archbishops, rich bishops, and poor priests, were traditionally tax exempt.

Philip taxed them anyway.

Pope Boniface was incensed. He was a man known for his arrogance, intensity, and cruelty. His predecessor, Celestine V, was a humble me-

---

[5] This was after targeting French Jews, a surprising decision considering the smooth history of the Jewish people.

dieval pope, and he in fact abdicated a papacy he might have never wanted.⁶ Rumors suggest that Boniface, in his drive to be pontiff, drove Celestine to insanity. History records that once he did succeed Celestine, he dragged his holy predecessor from retirement, arrested him, and threw him in a cell. Celestine died the following year with a hole in his skull, a likely symptom of a Bonifacian murder. The new pope, free of potential papal rivals, reigned supreme.⁷

Like Innocent III a century earlier, Boniface affirmed papal absolutism over Catholic lands. Like a feudal lord, he considered the kings of Europe as his own vassals.⁸ In other words, Christendom was his empire.

---

⁶ Upon his abdication, he cited a long list of reasons, including "desire for humility, for a purer life, for a stainless conscience, the deficiencies of his own physical strength, his ignorance, the perverseness of the people, [and] his longing for the tranquility of his former life." In his defense, people are pretty perverse.

⁷ Dante later placed Celestine in one of his famous Circles of Hell—not because of any evil action on Celestine's part, but because his abdication allowed the rise of the cruel Boniface: *"I saw and recognized the shade of him/Who by his cowardice made the great refusal."* –Inferno III, 59–60.

⁸ The idea of kings being subservient to the pope dated back to at least Charlemagne, the most powerful of all medieval leaders (and a future chapter in this ranking). In the year 800, after three decades of sewing back together much of what was the Western Roman Empire, Charlemagne was invited to Rome by Pope Leo III for Christmas mass. Leo wanted to thank the Frankish king for defending the papacy against some rebellious nobles. As the story goes, when Charlemagne knelt to pray, Leo crowned Charlemagne "Emperor of the Romans." The Frankish king, not wanting to be rude to the prestigious Bishop of Rome, graciously accepted the crown. He probably also liked the only promotion remaining above king: emperor. However, Charlemagne inadvertently set the precedent of papal investiture. If one wanted to rule, one needed the approval of the pope. After all, even Charlemagne knelt at the Pope's holy feet.

Philip "the Fair" of France

In 1300, he commissioned a papal jubilee. As part of a grand parade, he dressed in imperial garb while touring Rome. In front of him were two swords representing his supremacy over both the here and hereafter. Flanking heralds cheered, "I am Caesar! I am the emperor!" The jubilee went according to plan; paying Europeans, who rarely got the chance to see His Holiness, flocked to the streets and filled the Church's coffers.

Predictably, when Philip the Fair decided to tax French clergy, Boniface resisted. His 1296 papal bull *Clericis laicos* (clergy, laymen) reiterated that "temporal," "lay" rulers could not tax members of the clergy.[9] Moreover, the bull expressly forbade his clerics to cooperate should the seditious royal ignore the papal command.

Philip responded by forbidding all French money and goods from going to Rome. That particularly bothered Boniface who, as seen with his jubilee, needed funds to support his preening papacy. To lose out on significant income from the largest state in Christendom was unacceptable. Boniface steadily realized this defiant French king must be dealt with more directly, and he summoned Philip to the Vatican.

Not only did Philip refuse this directive, he countered with an invitation for the Pontiff to visit him in Paris. These competing summonses

---

[9] "Temporal" and "lay" both convey the essence of *not spiritual*. Temporal—think "temporary"—describes secular leaders and people who are on Earth for a limited time, which contrasts the eternal spirit. "Lay" is similar, and we still see the word used today when asking for something to be explained in "layman's terms." That's because for centuries the clergy was the most educated group in Europe, so if someone said something too complex, one would ask for it to instead be explained so a "lay man," or an uneducated person, could understand it. I feel like you need to know these things.

overtly attempted to display which of these leaders sat preeminently over the other.[10]

In 1302, Boniface took to writing a letter to this insubordinate royal. It was titled *Ausculta Fili*, which, in a tone we can assume was pretty patronizing, translates to "*Listen, son.*" The letter warns that Philip's actions not only contravened Catholic law, but these actions also endangered his fate in heaven. If Philip didn't back down, the letter warned, he was destined for Hell. After all, *ecclesiam nulla salus*—outside the Church there is no salvation. Over every word loomed the threat of excommunication.

Boniface then made it clear that the Vicar of Christ was also the king of kings. In one of the papacy's most infamous bulls, *Unam Sanctum*, Boniface asserted that refusing the pope is akin to refusing God. He emphasized that "God has set popes over kings and kingdoms" and closed with, "We declare, we proclaim, we define that it is absolutely necessary for salvation that every human creature be subject to the Roman Pontiff." In other words, like lords were vassals to kings, kings were vassals to popes, and they served at the pleasure of His Holiness.

Philip's retort set the tone for the subsequent downfall of the papacy and the eventual rise of the modern Western state above the Church. "Your venerable stupidity may know," Philip wrote to Boniface, "that we are nobody's vassal in temporal matters."[11]

His hand forced, Boniface excommunicated the mutinous monarch.

---

[10] "Me come there? No, you come here."

[11] Shots fired!

Philip "the Fair" of France

Philip's response was to set a diabolical scheme into motion. This scheme led not only to the fall of Boniface, but also, in an astonishing development, the papacy's credibility as well.

The first step of Philip's plan, in order to protect himself against retaliation, was to create an inhospitable sociopolitical climate for Boniface. This wasn't difficult. On the heels of the more spiritual Celestine, Boniface came across as a haughty, greedy, unkind pope—accurate descriptors all. Boniface showed little regard for his followers and regularly placed his own needs above Christendom's. To show his power, he destroyed castles. To intimidate Europeans, he burned suspected heretics. He confiscated land at will, including from the prominent Italian Colonna family, just to dole it out to friends. King Philip realized that if he highlighted these actions while securing his own popularity at home, he could act against the Pope with little fear of reprisal from his own people.

To secure his own position, Philip created a political institution that, nearly 500 years later, would actually bring down the French Crown. In a rather progressive move, Philip created the "Estates General," a congress in the vein of the new English Parliament, though it remained mostly advisory. The assembly had representatives from three distinct social classes, or estates: clergy, nobility, and a growing upper-middle class called the bourgeoisie that represented commoners.[12] Philip used the fledgling body to rally support against Boniface, and he asked to try

---

[12] I won't fully address the Estates General in this series, but it, too, can lend credence to Philip the Fair's influence on Western history. The creation of the body may have been progressive for the era, but its rules and organization grew outdated. Each of the estates had one vote when advising the king despite the Third Estate representing about 99 percent of the population. The first two estates, with the similar interest of keeping their extraordinary wealth, routinely outvoted the Third Estate. For example, the

the pontiff for his impudence, among other charges. The French people, never before having representation in government, supported their sovereign over the already unpopular pope.

And so, in 1303, the king sent soldiers to unleash his plan: to kidnap the most powerful man in Europe.[13]

The kidnapping was successful. Held in Anagni, Italy for several embarrassing days, the health of the nearly 70-year-old Boniface quickly deteriorated. His captors gave him no food or drink, all the while shaming and mistreating him. An uprising from the locals freed Boniface, but the victimized and malnourished pope died weeks later from fever and, I can only assume, humiliation.

As procedure dictated, the College of Cardinals met to fill the vacant papacy. It elected Benedict XI, who then suspiciously withdrew Philip's excommunication. However, he then excommunicated an ally of Philip,

---

first two estates remained tax exempt for centuries, and it was the Estates General that helped sustain such a tradition. Anger toward this inequity exploded in the late 1780s when Louis XVI, during a famine and financial crisis, allowed his wife to buy far too many clothes (a circumstance from which many of us suffer). The kingdom ran out of money and sought approval from the Estates General to raise the starving Third Estate's taxes some more. Cue the French Revolution.

[13] The implementation of this plan would make quite the Hollywood movie. Philip put together a sort of commando team to accomplish the mission. The man in charge of the commandos was Guillaume de Nogaret, a militant lawyer whose father was burned alive by the Church as a heretic. Once in Italy, guess who helped de Nogaret find and secure Boniface? The Colonna family! The same family from whom Boniface, years earlier, had gleefully taken land. I mean, you would CARE about these characters, right? I'm just a phone call away, Spielberg.

and Pope Benedict soon found himself poisoned. Eyes turned to Philip as the mastermind behind this event as well.

Philip used his intimidating reputation to control subsequent events. He influenced the next College of Cardinals, arranging the election of a French archbishop who became Pope Clement V—only the sixth French pope of the nearly 200 pontiffs to have held the office to that point. Clement, likely a pawn, did not go to Italy for his coronation. Instead, he ascended in Lyon, France, with an ornate ceremony attended by His Majesty Philip IV. Soon, the newly minted pope moved papal quarters from its ancient home in Rome to Avignon, France. Philip had won.

It should be acknowledged that Philip was not the first ruler to stand up to the Church. Others, like Holy Roman emperors Henry IV (r. 1056-1105) and Frederick Barbarossa (r. 1152-1190), had raised armies against it. Some even had success in deposing a pope. In each of those cases, however, the papacy eventually returned to supremacy. Innocent III was the most powerful pope in history, and his papacy came *after* those rebellious emperors. Even a hundred years later, Boniface, though not with Innocent's competence, claimed absolute authority over Christendom.No earlier king, therefore, marks a true transition into the modern dynamic. That responsibility falls to King Philip IV.[14] Though he died in 1314, he had already set off a chain reaction that transformed the West.

---

[14] Interestingly, historiography might further support Philip's influence on the development of the Western world. The use of the term "Middle Ages" —surely subjective when one considers that the medieval population did not consider themselves in the "middle" of anything, and someday we will be in the middle of history as well—was eventually broken into three mini-eras within the larger one. The "Low" or "Early" Middle Ages began in the fifth century with the fall of Rome, and they ended at the turn of the mil-

Clement V and the next six popes—all French—reigned from France, a period known as the Babylonian Captivity (1309-1377). During this period, respect for the papacy diminished. Was it the Vicar of Christ making decisions, or was it the King of France?[15]

The Avignon Papacy finally ended thanks to pious Pope Gregory XI, who moved the office back to Rome in 1377, but the respectability of the papacy continued to spiral. Upon Gregory's death the following year, a Roman mob, demanding an Italian pope after seven consecutive Frenchmen had sullied the position, rioted outside the papal palace. The cardinals hastily elected Pope Urban VI, but he turned out to be a narrow-minded, intransigent, and possibly insane pontiff. With the backing of the French, many cardinals ran away to elect a different pope, Clement VII. Urban, however, did not abdicate. Thus, with two competing

---

lennium. (The Low Middle Ages is more known for its controversial nickname, the "Dark Ages.") Next, beginning in about 1000 CE, came the High Middle Ages. The reason for the demarcation is because right around then Europe experienced improved climate; an increase in population, trade, and cultural achievements; modern nation-states followed in the wake of feudalism; legal codes and assemblies evolved like the Magna Carta and Parliament; and standard of living increased.

More relevant to today's topic, the High Middle Ages end at the year 1300—precisely the year of Boniface's jubilee. Then, the Late Middle Ages —which lasted from 1300 into the 1400s—laid the foundation for the demise of the Catholic Church. Philip IV set that process in motion, meaning that perhaps no one was more important in ushering in the new historical era.

[15] It was the King of France. Most infamously, Clement issued the papal bull, Pastoralis Praeeminentiae, in order to arrest and execute members of the historic Knights Templar, a group to which Philip owed large sums of money.

claimants, the Great Schism began.[16] Western Europe floundered in this confusion for the next four decades as the two men and their successors claimed primacy over Christendom.[17]

By the time the Council of Constance resolved the dispute in 1417, the damage was done. Many Europeans doubted the pope's legitimacy. With the door open for criticism, scholars of the next century pointed to the Schism as an example of the Pope's dubious claim as clear Vicar of Christ. Erasmus openly satirized the Church, Martin Luther famously split with it, and Catholicism cracked.

By the close of the sixteenth century, the state had triumphed over the Church, and it has since secured our obedience far more than Pope Francis or any other cleric in the Western world. That modern dynamic was made possible by King Philip. As a result, Philip IV of France earns his spot as the 29th most influential Westerner in history.

---

[16] This is not to be confused with the "East-West Schism" of 1054, when the Western, Latin-speaking Catholic Christians and Eastern, Greek-speaking Orthodox Christians officially separated.

[17] At times, there was even a third pope. This era truly broke the scale of the absurdometer.

#28: Nicolaus Copernicus

"Of all discoveries and opinions, none may have exerted a greater effect on the human spirit than the doctrine of Copernicus. The world had scarcely become known as round and complete in itself when it was asked to waive the tremendous privilege of being the center of the universe. Never, perhaps, was a greater demand made on mankind."

–Goethe

It was, quite literally, a revolutionary idea. In 1514, Polish astronomer Mikolaj Kopernik, in his *"Commentariolus,"* posited that the earth is not at the center of everything. With his sun-centered alterntive, he turned the Western world—and, indeed, the entire universe—on its head.

As Goethe suggests, this theory's impact on science was surpassed by its philosophical implications. *Mankind, you are not that important.*

With that assertion, Mikolaj Kopernik—Latinized to Nicolaus Copernicus—ushered a revolution into the West, one that allowed modern science to develop. These contributions rank him as Western history's 28th most influential figure.

Copernicus was born in 1473 Poland to two merchants who afforded him an education that culminated in attending the University of Krakow. Fluent in Latin, German, and his native Polish, with a working knowledge of Greek and Italian, Copernicus matured in an era of renewed intellectualism. The medieval world gasped for air as the Renaissance slowly suffocated it.

Copernicus's lifetime (1473-1543) spanned what was perhaps the most momentous 70-year period in Western history. During the year of his birth, the recently invented printing press was spreading to all corners of Europe. When Copernicus was 19, a Genoese explorer named Christopher Columbus sailed the Atlantic. Ten years after Columbus's return, Leonardo da Vinci began painting the *Mona Lisa*. Within a decade, the Florentine artist Michelangelo completed the Sistine Chapel's ceiling while fellow Italian Niccolo Machiavelli finished an early draft of "The Prince." Soon after, Martin Luther of Saxony posted his *Ninety-Five Theses* and started the Protestant Reformation. Four years later, as Luther refused recantation at Worms, the Portuguese explorer Ferdinand Magellan led the first voyage to circumnavigate the planet, finally showing the world that it was, as Goethe put it, "round and complete in itself."

Throughout this period, the once omnipotent Roman Catholic Church fell under siege by powerful monarchs, satirical writers, humanist philosophers, and Protestant reformers. As Copernicus witnessed this era of immense change, he could scarcely have envisioned how he would one day contribute to it. His crowning achievement ultimately hammered another nail into the coffin of the once mighty medieval papacy.

That crowning achievement was his book "*De revolutionibus orbium coelestium*"–"On the Revolutions of the Heavenly Spheres"–which explains his heliocentric theory. Fearing retribution from resistant traditionalists across Europe, he had sat on the manuscript for years. He finally allowed friends to publish the work in 1543, the year he took his final breath on the tiny planet he rightly displaced. Lore suggests he saw the first copy on his deathbed.

The traditionalists he feared clung to the accepted second century Ptolemaic model of the universe. Ptolemy's universe was geocentric, or Earth-centered, meaning the sun, planets, and stars revolved around Earth. Ptolemy and others noted the misshapen, direction-changing orbits of the visible planets—caused, as we now know, by them and us actually orbiting something else—and explained them by adding inelegant retrograde "epicycles," or mini-loops that briefly move the planets off their orbits around us. In the ancient world, these seemingly indecisive drifters earned the Greek name for wanderers—*planetes*—giving us the term "planets" today.

The Christianized late Roman Empire and subsequent medieval Catholic Church happily adopted geocentrism as its universe of choice. What better place to put God's creation than at the center of everything? Scripture even supported it.[1] Consequently, geocentrism, like the Church, dominated Western science for centuries.

And why not? For millennia, anyone not well-versed in astronomy could be forgiven for their assumption that the earth stands still at the universe's center. After all, we cannot feel Earth spin or travel through

---

[1] Joshua 10:12 writes about God holding still the sun (rather than the earth) in order to postpone nightfall. Psalms 93:1 talks about our immovable world. In Genesis, the creation of heaven, Earth, and man can be interpreted as God's main focus, which implies philosophical, if not literal, geocentrism.

space at thousands of miles per hour. We observe the stars revolve around us as if they're painted on a rotating planetarium ceiling. Indeed, we still say that the sun "rises" in the east and "sets" in the west.[2] Frankly, from a basic observational point of view, it does feel like we stand at a fixed, immobile center of the cosmos.

Nicolaus Copernicus, however, observed something quite different, and he didn't even need a telescope (which was invented over 60 years after his death) to do it. *De revolutionibus*'s proposal was based on naked-eye observation and mathematical calculation. This Aristotelian empiricism (see #30) helped Copernicus realize that the peculiar Ptolemaic model was aesthetically inferior to a heliocentric—or sun-centered—model.[3] A middle-aged Copernicus shared his ideas with friends in his *Commentariolus*, written a few decades before his more complete book.

The "Little Commentary" proposed big changes. It posited that Earth rotates on its axis once every 24 hours, that only the moon revolves around the earth, and, most radically, that the *planetes*, Earth included, actually revolve around the sun.

Commentariolus made its way around elite European circles and even found its way to Rome, where it was given a mixed reception by the Church. Luckily for Copernicus, the pope, Leo X, was relatively humanistic compared to many of his predecessors. He allowed Copernicus to

---

[2] Which I'm totally cool with. I'd rather avoid saying, "Earth's rotation gave our meridian the requisite angle to observe the sun at 6:17 this morning." Trust me, I talk like that if necessary.

[3] The prevalent geocentric theory of the time was so accepted that Copernicus, after realizing a heliocentric model of the universe seemed to make more mathematical sense, repeatedly checked and rechecked his figures. The notion that the earth was moving seemed absurd on the face of it, even to him. In this case, truth was indeed stranger than fiction.

continue.[4] Copernicus trod carefully for three decades while quietly constructing the larger *De revolutionibus*.

Predictably, the more thorough work faced rebuke from religious contemporaries. Few things united the rival Protestants and Catholics of the sixteenth century, but this heretical idea was one of them. Martin Luther was among the first to rip apart blasphemous heliocentrism:

"People give ear to an upstart astrologer who strove to show that the earth revolves, not the heavens or the firmament, the sun and the moon. . . . This fool wishes to reverse the entire scheme of astrology; but sacred Scripture tells us that Joshua commanded the sun to stand still, not the earth."

Another major Protestant reformer, John Calvin, echoed those sentiments, citing the 93rd Psalm: *"'The world also is stabilized, that it cannot be moved.' . . . Who will venture to place authority of Copernicus above that of the Holy Spirit?"*

The Catholic Church certainly didn't venture it. *De revolutionibus* made its way onto the Church's *Index Librorum Prohibitorum*—the "List of Prohibited Books."

The resistance from multiple wings of Christianity was understandable. Copernicus's proposition wasn't just physical. It was metaphysical as well.

---

[4] The fact that Martin Luther was about to give Leo all he could handle probably helped Copernicus off the hook. Later, heliocentrists like Giordano Bruno, who was burned at the stake (for many heterodox positions), and Galileo Galilei, who was tried by the Church, forced to recant, and imprisoned for life, were not so lucky.

Geocentrism is inextricably paired with egomania.[5] Think of what's implied when one accuses another of thinking they're "at the center of the universe" or that the "world revolves around them." The West suffered from that arrogant affliction for nearly its entire history. *God created us at the center of everything. We are important. He made the universe for us. We are His most precious creation.* From this geocentric premise, Westerners naturally felt like the surrounding universe evidenced our own significance.

Contrarily, evicting Earth from the universe's epicenter triggers many aftershocks. If we're not at the center, where are we? Why are we so far from the center? How did we get here? *Is* there a center of the universe? While we're at it, what *is* the universe? How big is it? Are there other planets with life out there, just as unimportant as we are? Did God create them in six days, too?

Post-Copernican science confirmed not only that we are not at the universe's center, but we're actually just one of eight planets[6] orbiting around the sun, which itself is just one star of a few hundred billion that are part of this galaxy, which itself is just one galaxy of perhaps trillions. The numbers boggle the mind, and with the thousands of exoplanets found in the last decade alone, we start to realize that the probability for other life out there is all but certain. We are merely a speck of dust in a vast cosmic ocean.[7] Luther, Calvin, and the Church did their best to re-

---

[5] Indeed, the words geocentrism and egocentrism are almost identical. (Admit it. Your mind is blown.)

[6] Orbit In Peace, Pluto, you adorable dwarf.

[7] Perhaps no piece of art or literature better puts that realization in perspective than Carl Sagan's "Pale Blue Dot." Look it up.

sist Copernicus's idea, but they were on the wrong side of the facts and on the wrong side of history.[8]

Copernicus forced us not only to rethink our position in the universe, but he gave us a badly needed kick in our prime meridian. *No, mankind. You are not that important, and you aren't nearly as smart as you think you are. So pick up the pace.* Copernicus never said such a thing, but his proposal screamed it.

Copernicus's accomplishments catalyzed a new era of scientific wonder, starting with his beloved field of astronomy. Few historical figures have a "revolution" attached to their name, but with the Copernican Revolution, the Polish astronomer earned it. Future astronomers, if they wanted to be taken seriously, needed to adopt his model.[9] In 1605, Johannes Kepler proposed a more accurate solar system which included elliptical orbits and changing planetary speeds instead of the perfectly round orbits and steadily paced planets proposed by his Polish predecessor. Giordano Bruno and Galileo Galilei also improved upon the Coper-

---

[8] Later that century, in a correspondence between scholar Jerome Wolf and astronomer Tycho Brahe, Wolf wrote, "No attack on Christianity is more dangerous than the infinite size and depth of the universe."

[9] The afore-footnoted Brahe was probably the last legitimate astronomer to entertain geocentrism, and his Tychonic system offered to merge Ptolemy and Copernicus's models into a sort of compromise universe. In essence, Earth would still be at the center, but the other planets would still revolve around the sun, which in turn revolved around the earth. It was a good try, but far too conservative given Copernicus's breakthrough. For his efforts, Brahe earned an eponymous lunar crater.

nican model, Isaac Newton explained how it worked, and then Albert Einstein explained why.[10]

Importantly, these astronomers' improvements on Copernicus's universe start to explain why Copernicus isn't higher on this Top 30 list. Indeed, other similar[11] lists of influential historical figures often have him near or in their top 10. If he proposed an accurate universe and was the first to do so, he would have ranked a bit better for me as well. However, for my list (which, of course, is the definitive word), he's relegated to "only" #28 for several reasons.

First, as just stated, his system, though an enormously important step forward, was seriously flawed. For example, he not only placed the sun at the center of the solar system, he placed it at the center of the universe, a big mistake that's merely less wrong than putting the earth there. Furthermore, because he didn't abandon perfectly circular orbits and the single-speed motion of the planets, he needed to build in his own, less inelegant epicycles to make the timing of his system work. He also supported the mystical explanation of celestial spheres keeping the heavenly bodies in space, a notion that quickly grew archaic. Frankly, it was not until Kepler that we had an accurate map of the visible planets' orbits. In fact, no astronomer ever fully accepted Copernicus's model; his reactionary contemporaries tried to re-center Earth, while by the early seventeenth century, Kepler, Galileo, and their successors obliterated each of Copernicus's proposals, save the solar system's heliocentrism.

---

[10] Galileo, Newton, and Einstein will be getting their own entries later in the book. The fun is just beginning, folks.

[11] Inferior

What's more, Copernicus wasn't even the first person to propose heliocentrism. A fourth century BCE Greek, Heraclides Ponticus, proposed that a rotating Earth, not a circling sun, caused day and night. Followers of famed mathematician Pythagoras joined him.[12] The following century, the first outright heliocentrist in Western history, Aristarchus of Samoa, truly made the breakthrough. Seleucus of Seleucia later used trigonometry to prove Aristarchus correct.[13]

Another mark against Copernicus might be his field of study. Some people could well argue that, "It's just astronomy. Who cares?" What applications were there to heliocentrism? When comparing the relevance of astronomy to the more practical sciences—physics, biology, anatomy, physiology, chemistry—one sees how relatively unimportant astronomy is in our daily lives. It is, in fact, just astronomy. Who cares?[14]

---

[12] Today, people fawn over athletes, pop stars, and reality TV celebrities. But the Greeks? They followed around mathematicians. The lesson, as always: the Greeks were awesome.

[13] Plus, if we leave the West behind and venture into terra incognita for yours truly, we'll find Indian and maybe even Egyptian scholars who also beat Copernicus to the punch. But I would no sooner leave the West behind than I would wander into a foreign forest at nightfall. I'll stick to familiar, well-lit surroundings, thank you very much.

[14] I don't want to be overly critical of astronomy as a science. I think few sciences engage young people as much as astronomy does—I speak from experience as a former child and now a father—which is probably critical in developing the future scientists of the world. Moreover, there actually have been practical applications to more modern astronomy. Many crucial advances in navigation, communications, and physics were impossible without studying the universe.

Nicolaus Copernicus

In this particular case, *everyone* should care. After four paragraphs arguing against Copernicus's importance, it's time to do what he did. Let's put things in perspective.

I'll admit it right now: I left off many scientists and inventors who had more "practical" inventions and ideas than Copernicus did.[15] However, I'd argue that the innumerable technological and scientific advancements of the last five centuries were made in a universe where their originator's brilliant minds knew that the earth was not at the universe's center, that Church doctrine was not infallible, that its reach did not extend to the stars, and that individuals, properly equipped with facts, figures, and observation, could advance our body of knowledge.

In essence, Copernicus created a universe that encouraged science, individualism, and the advancement of man. It is no accident of periodization that the West's "Scientific Revolution" began in 1543, the year of Copernicus's big publication.[16] Following Copernicus was an explosion of scientific curiosity and accomplishment. Copernicus not

---

[15] Very tough cuts: inventors and scientists like William Harvey, Antoine Lavoisier, Alexander Fleming, Joseph Lister, Nikola Tesla, William Gilbert, Eli Whitney, the Curies, Jonas Salk, Michael Faraday, William Shockley, Alexander Graham Bell, Max Plank, Charles Babbage, Antonie van Leeuwenhoek, Robert Oppenheimer, Enrico Fermi, Dmitri Mendeleev, Neils Bohr, Gregor Mendel, Watson and Crick, Werner Heisenberg, Samuel Morse, Robert Fulton, the Wright Brothers, Thomas Newcomen, and Benjamin Franklin. If you think I'm crazy for leaving them off, consider that I just listed 30 names right there. These difficult eliminations kept me up at night. Many, many important people have changed the Western world. In other words, this list wasn't easy... so back off.

[16] Not to be overlooked is Andreas Vesalius's landmark De humani corporis fabrica ("On the Fabric of the Human Body"), which was also published in 1543 and set the foundation for modern anatomy.

only gave us modern astronomy—his paradigm shifting model was far more important than Kepler's refinement of it—but he also showed that science must be a servant to facts, not dogma. Aristarchus's heliocentrism was lost to the West for nearly two millennia, but when Copernicus brought it back and showed the irrefutable arithmetic that disproved the prevailing wisdom of the intimidating Catholic Church, the door opened for so many others in so many fields to do the same. I'm not too sure that a world where more practical advancements is possible without a post-Copernican West to allow and embrace their contributions. The Scientific Revolution was first necessary, and Copernicus was its catalyst. The man changed the universe.

Given the wealth of scientific achievements since Copernicus, like venturing away from Earth and into (and out of!) his restructured solar system, perhaps we can now say that mankind turned out to be pretty important after all. This species' significance, however, does not stem from God placing us at the universe's center. If we are important creatures, we've proven it not through unfounded faith in the importance itself, but through our curiosity and our accomplishments. Copernicus ushered in the era where those characteristics could shine like the sun around which they orbit.

For these reasons, Nicolaus Copernicus deserves his spot as the 28th most influential figure in Western history

#27: Joan of Arc

"Then occurred a miracle, or the nearest thing to an attested miracle in recorded history."

–Historian Morris Bishop on Joan of Arc

She is the smallest person on this list, and she died the youngest. She had no noble or royal blood. She won no election. She had no formal education or military experience.

Yet, despite these characteristics, this teenage peasant turned the tide of a war that began over 70 years before she was born. As a result of her heroics, she altered the course of French history and, by consequence, English history, and, by consequence of that, world history as well. Her unique legacy and iconic image have served as inspirations ever since.

If there are such things as miracles, then Joan of Arc, the 27th most influential person in Western history, was surely one.

Joan of Arc was born to Jacques Darc and Isabelle Romée in 1412. She was raised in Domrémy, a village in northeast France.[1]

Like most medieval Europeans, the Darcs were a peasant family. They worked 50 acres of land and hoped for little more than to outlast famines, wars, malnutrition, and plagues before getting into heaven after merciful death ended their short, brutal lives.[2]

Young Joan—a description that could be used for her entire life— helped in the fields, minding crops and herding animals. She spun and wove like a good girl. A formal education was impossible for a vast majority of medieval Europeans, particularly a female peasant. She stayed illiterate except for memorizing the alien shapes that were the letters of her name.

Yet, somehow, this uneducated peasant girl would redirect the momentum of the interminable Hundred Years' War. Before we get to the voices in Joan's head or her miraculous leadership of the dwindled and demoralized French army, we must first establish just how poorly things were going for the Kingdom of France in the 1420s.[3]

---

[1] Joan of Arc was not from a place called Arc. Arc, in fact, was not a place at all. The family name was probably Darc. Apostrophes in French surnames did not yet exist, but they did in England, so the English later determined the name was "d'Arc," which gave us the "of Arc" part. Instead of imaginary Arc, the Darcs lived in Domrémy, which has since been renamed to Domremy-la-Pucelle in honor of Joan and her nickname, la Pucelle d'Orléans— "the Maid of Orléans." And as long as we're talking about shaky names, Joan's name was Jehanne, but the English Anglicized the name to their closest female approximation of John.

[2] Good times.

[3] Historian Kelly DeVries said of Joan's story, "If anything could have discouraged her, the state of France in 1429 should have."

Joan of Arc

The term "Hundred Years' War" is misleading in a couple of ways, though it does lend an accurate portrayal of a miserable century. First, the beginning and end dates are actually 116 years apart—the war started in 1337 and ended for good in 1453. Moreover, it wasn't one continuous war; its three main stages were the Edwardian War (1337-1360), the Caroline War (1369-1389), and the decisive Lancastrian War (1415-1453).[4]

The conflict began over competing inheritance claims for the French throne. The King of England claimed it, and the people of France resisted.[5] Ninety years later, long after the original competing claimants and their children were dead and buried, the battle for France's crown raged on.

Though the length of the war shows it was not totally one-sided, the overall trend for France, until Joan of Arc's time, was negative. In 1415, by Joan's third birthday, all of northern France was in enemy hands. Fought exclusively on French land, the war had taken over a million French lives. Among the many fallen French cities were the capital of

---

[4] See? There were only 81 years of war. That's barely a skirmish!

[5] This is why I have footnotes, as this information has nothing to do with Joan but everything to do with the war she joined. The initial controversy was the result of direct Capetian line ending after the three sons of Philip IV (#29) died without heirs. England's King Edward III claimed the throne on account of being Philip IV's grandson. True enough, Philip's daughter, Isabella, had married the English king Edward II in 1308. Their child, Edward III, was therefore half Capetian through his mother. Once no full Capetians remained, he claimed the throne. The French nobility predictably opposed being ruled by an Englishman and hurriedly appointed Philip IV's nephew, Philip of Valois, as the next king, inaugurating the new Valois Dynasty and the old tradition of every king annoyingly having the same name.

Paris and the city of Reims, whose cathedral was the coronation site of French kings dating back to the late fifth century.[6]

War wasn't the only scourge to visit the kingdom. The virulent Black Death made itself right at home. Across the continent, it killed about one-in-three Europeans. Paris lost as much as two-thirds of its population of roughly one hundred thousand. Between plague and war, the population of France is thought to have fallen from 17 million before the war to half that by its end.

If war and plague weren't enough, the French government was in utter shambles. Joan's first ten years of life came under the reign of King Charles VI (r. 1380-1422). Bouts of madness and delusion mired Charles's reign. He thought he was made of glass, he denied the existence of his wife and children, he randomly attacked servants, and once he ran and ran without stop until he collapsed in a heap of not-so-regal exhaustion. Toward the end of his rule, he earned the moniker "Charles the Mad." In an effort to right the sinking ship, Charles's younger brother, Louis of Orléans, wrested some power away to manage the kingdom. In 1407, however, he was assassinated on the orders of cousin John the Fearless, who himself had dreams of the throne. John, too, became em-

---

[6] Why Reims? I'm glad you asked. In 496, Clovis, King of the Franks, became the first of all the medieval European kings to convert to Catholicism, and he did so at Reims through a baptism by its archbishop. His kingdom converted with him, which would have been a blip on the historical radar if it weren't for a later Frank by the name of Charlemagne spreading Catholicism throughout western Europe, ingraining the denomination into the region's culture. The Frankish Kingdom later evolved into France, and the French retconned Clovis into the first of eighteen "Louis"es. To say that Catholicism would not be the world's largest denomination without Clovis's conversion is not an unreasonable argument. (And yet, he doesn't make my Top 30. I've said it before and I'll say it again: this list was not easy.)

broiled in French government, scandal, and the Hundred Years' War before also falling victim to assassination.[7] It seemed as if the only thing that truly reigned was chaos.

The war thundered on. In 1415, the Battle of Agincourt seemed to mark the beginning of the end for the Kingdom of France. King Henry V of England (and Shakespeare fame) spurred his army to overcome France's superior numbers to win the field. An estimated 40 percent of France's nobility rallied to Agincourt's cause and were among the thousands killed. Henry, whose outnumbered army captured thousands more, felt the prisoners were too numerous to control and ordered their deaths.

The situation grew bleaker still. By 1419, Henry brokered an alliance with the Duchy of Burgundy. Its presence east of France, paired with England having nearly conquered France's northern half, further encircled the suffocating French Kingdom.

Then, adding insult to injury, King Henry married King Charles's daughter.[8] He forced Charles to sign the Treaty of Troyes, which acknowledged that a future son of Henry and his French bride was heir to the French throne. However, when Charles and Henry coincidentally both died in 1422, many French ignored the treaty. Henry's son, Henry VI, was but an infant, and it was established that France didn't want to be ruled by any Englishman, to say nothing of an English baby. Thus, many believed that Charles's teenage son, also named Charles, was the true heir.

---

[7] I'm telling you, the country was a mess.

[8] That's what historians call, "not cool."

Unfortunately—and importantly in the story of Joan—young Charles was not yet officially King of France, as he was not able to be crowned at Reims while the enemy controlled it. He was known, then, merely as Charles "the Dauphin," or heir apparent to the throne. Thus, for the bulk of the 1420s, the French were not only losing ground, they were without a king.

Eventually, the English came across the city of Orléans, a sizeable town in central France on the banks of the strategic Loire River. The longest river in the kingdom, it started in the Cévennes Mountains in southeast France, cut through the heart of the country where Orléans sat, then emptied into the Atlantic. Orléans was the most important position on France's most important river.

The English could not get inside Orléans's fortified defenses, so for six months they lay siege to the city. They waited for starvation, knowing that with the city's fall, the rest of France would quickly fall with it. Orléans became the last bastion and hope of the French people. Historian Régine Pernoud encapsulates the moment perfectly: "On the fate of Orléans hung that of the entire kingdom."

Naturally, saving Orléans and the rest of France from their imminent demise was an illiterate peasant girl from Domrémy.

We now arrive at the entrance of our miraculous main character. During the English domination of the 1420s, she began to hear, and see visions of, the saints Michael, Margaret, and Catherine.[9] They had a mission for her: they instructed that she break the siege of Orléans, take

---

[9] So beautiful were these visions, she recounted, that she cried when they left her.

France's land back from its English occupiers, and get Charles the Dauphin to Reims to be crowned king.

So that's what she did.

In 1428, a 16-year-old Joan visited a fortress captain near her town. She told him everything. He sent her home. She returned in early 1429 and demanded an audience with the Dauphin. She was said to be so insistent and convincing that the captain acquiesced and sent her and two guards to see Charles.

The Dauphin, warned of her arrival, attempted to avoid her, but Joan was nothing if not persistent. She found him and told him her tale. Suspecting witchcraft or insanity, Charles had her examined. A doctor and two noble women confirmed not only her sanity, but, importantly, her virginity as well. Joan's story was aided by a medieval prophecy which predicted that France, in its worst of times, would be saved by a virgin girl. Joan fit the bill, and Charles was won over. He gave her a suit of armor, a lance, and a horse. A delighted teenage Joan rode out to a nearby field to play, slaying imaginary Englishmen with her new toys. Morris Bishop writes that this was probably the only fun she had in her short life.

With little to lose, Charles allowed her to travel to Orléans to try and lift the six-month siege.[10] Joan and about 500 soldiers marched to the

---

[10] Historian Stephen W. Richey's analysis of Charles's dubious decision explains France's desperate situation: "After years of one humiliating defeat after another, both the military and civil leadership of France were demoralized and discredited. When the Dauphin Charles granted Joan's urgent request to be equipped for war and placed at the head of his army, his decision must have been based in large part on the knowledge that every orthodox, every rational option had been tried and had failed. Only a regime in the final straits of desperation would pay any heed to an illiterate farm girl who claimed that the voice of God was instructing her to take charge of her country's army and lead it to victory."

city, though ten times that many English sat outside of it. As per the plan, most of the French troops distracted their English counterparts long enough for Joan and the remaining soldiers to sneak into the city with some supplies. For the next few days, she toured the city streets, giving out food and raising morale. She convinced many people of her story. Within ten days, a revitalized Orléans, whose people learned that France had not given up on them—and perhaps, even better, that God has sent their savior in the form of this infectiously optimistic girl—concentrated their efforts and broke the English siege. Thousands of Englishmen lay dead, their surviving comrades retreating. It was the first substantial French victory since the disastrous events at Agincourt nearly 15 years earlier.

Joan, who became known as "The Maid of Orléans" after the victory, was clearly a wondrous inspirer of a shattered people, but she had a lot to learn about war campaigns. After breaking the siege, she met with Charles and insisted on a direct line to Reims to crown him. Military advisers disagreed and vetoed the child, wisely opting to instead take back the Loire River. Still, Joan was pivotal in securing enough volunteers to bolster French forces. She may not have been a true warrior or military genius, but there was no better standard-bearer.

The English hurried Paris-stationed reinforcements to meet and defeat Joan's insurrection, but not only did they also fail, their commanders were captured. The French then turned their sights on Reims and cut a swath to it. On July 17, 1429, at the Reims Cathedral, Charles the Dauphin finally became King Charles VII. Beaming by his side was France's 17-year-old heroine. Paris was recaptured soon after. The tide of the war had been turned.

On the face of it, such a turn of events makes little sense. France had been all but beaten. England had every ounce of momentum. How can one explain this reversal of fortune without surrendering to Joan's account of divine guidance? Was this truly one of history's miracles?

Perhaps. Leaving aside the premise that God would, for some unknowable reason, prefer a French victory over an English one, it is worth noting that Joan's ignorance of the situation was possibly her greatest asset. A reeling France had been fighting a purely defensive war for decades. As such, they only tried to slow the English attack. For example, before Joan's arrival, only once in six months did they attempt to break the siege at Orléans. Contrarily, Joan, consumed by determination and destiny rather than defeatism and despair, took the fight directly to the English. Once France realized that they could win a few battles, the French ranks swelled, making it easier to win even more. The rejuvenated army snatched away England's momentum and never gave it back, winning the war in 1453.

The end of Joan's story is a sad one. In 1430, the Burgundians captured her in battle and sold her to the English. A trial ensued in the English-occupied French town of Rouen. It was politically motivated—understandable, considering she was instrumental in crowning a rival claimant to the throne over which the entire war was fought—but was instead tried under the guise of sorcery. After all, she admitted to hearing voices.

She was charged with witchcraft, magic, impiety, and wearing men's clothes. For months she was aggressively interrogated until she finally crumbled and admitted to witchcraft. A later retraction could not save her, and the 19-year-old Joan was pronounced guilty in 1431.

She was brought to Rouen's marketplace for burning. Her final request was for a cross, so an English soldier fashioned one out of two sticks and handed it to his doomed enemy. She kissed it, held it to her chest, and called to her lord and savior no less than six times as she was burned alive.

Despite Joan's execution, France won the war and regained almost all its land. England, which held dominion over about a third of French lands on the eve of her enlistment, lost all of it but the northern port city of Calais.

The effects of this land loss cannot be overstated. England had held large chunks of French land dating back to Frenchman William the Conqueror's 1066 Norman Invasion of Britain.[11] Losing it all was, at first glance, a disaster, but later history suggests it may have been for the best.

The stripping of its continental land relegated England to an island nation. As such, England shed its European aspirations and developed a focus on naval development and seafaring. Portugal and Spain dominated the oceans in the latter part of the 1400s, but by the end of the following century it was England who claimed supremacy over the seas.[12]

---

[11] When William, the Duke of Normandy, took the English throne, he did not cede his Norman lands. The following century, before King Henry II took the English throne, he inherited more French land from his father, Geoffrey of Anjou. Henry also engineered quite the coup when he married Eleanor of Aquitaine, the ex-wife of the French King Louis VII, who brought her enormous territory in southwest France. England would lose French lands and gain some back over the subsequent centuries, but the Hundred Years' War took them away permanently.

[12] England's victory in the 1588 Battle of the Spanish Armada serves as the symbolic transition from the era of Spanish naval dominance to that of England.

As a result, the Union Jack eventually dotted lands around the globe. By the end of its run, the British Empire claimed territory on every continent, becoming the strongest power the world had ever seen. At its height, one-quarter of Earth's land and population were part of British territory, an empire on which the sun never set. Alongside its potent navy sailed and steamed a thriving merchant class that enriched Britain more than squabbling over European land ever could have.

Britain used its naval and economic might to remain the foremost global power until the early twentieth century, guiding the world's affairs and exporting British culture and rule of law to all corners of the globe. Its numerous colonies, though not without their fair share of subjugation and conflicts with the Crown (ahem), benefited from the lessons and infrastructure provided by their overlords.[13] Without Joan of Arc leading the French to victory, the English would have spent so much of its energy maintaining their European empire that they would have neither the inclination nor the resources to set sail and transform others in a way not seen since Rome.

The importance for France, meanwhile, was even greater—it survived as a nation. Without Joan of Arc, it is likely France would have ceased to exist as a sovereign state. The last five centuries without France yield a world without the influential Bourbon Dynasty, French colonization, the French Revolution, and Napoleon's conquest of Europe and his modern-

---

[13] Of the many former European colonies throughout the world, those once occupied by the British have since been, as a general rule, far more stable and successful than their Spanish and French counterparts. Does that make those places better off than if European paternalism never arrived? Perhaps not. But I do think it makes those places—America included—better off than if other empires replaced the British.

izing Napoleonic Code.[14] A world without France has no strong ally for the American colonists in their revolution against the British. A world without France cannot birth the enormously important Franco-English alliance of the last century that twice fought against expansionist German empires.[15] They have since become two separate, important nations with votes on the United Nations Security Council and NATO.

Much more difficult to assess are Joan's indirect effects, though they are still substantial. She has served as a symbol of inspiration and propaganda for centuries after her death. During the French Revolution, French monarchists used her as symbol of defending the king, while radicals used her as an icon of the French masses. In World War I, the British used her as propaganda, trying to get women to buy war bonds. When Germany occupied France during World War Two, German propaganda used her to remind the French of her corrupt English trial, while French resistance fighters used her as a symbol of struggling against foreign occupation.

Clerics have promoted her relationship with the saints, while state officials prefer her rallying to the king. Suffragettes on both sides of the Atlantic, including Elizabeth Cady Stanton, appropriated her image to champion female potential in the patriarchy. Indira Gandhi is on the record as citing Joan of Arc as her reason for getting into politics. Joan has been a character in a Shakespearean play and another by George Bernard Shaw. Voltaire wrote a poem about her. Verdi wrote an opera about her. So did Tchaikovsky. Even Leonard Cohen paid

---

[14] More about Napoleon in a later chapter.

[15] Most frightening, a world without France is a world without jokes *about* France.

tribute.[16] An inspiration across the West, she's as much the Muse as she is the Maid of Orléans.

Beyond being an inspiration, this small, young, peasant girl, in a very real way, altered the destinies of France, England, and the world. For these reasons, Joan of Arc is the 27th most influential person in Western history.

---

[16] That's when you know you're big.

#26: Peter the Great

"Ladies and gentlemen of the court caught sleeping with their boots on will be instantly decapitated."

–Tsar Peter the Great

The smallest person of this ranking is followed by the largest. In 1696, the six-foot, seven-inch, 24-year-old Peter Romanov inherited a backwards Russian kingdom that lagged far behind much of Europe. What he left his heirs, however, was an empire that rivaled those of the West. In fact, it's because of Romanov that we can even consider Russia, despite its mostly Asian geography, a "Western" nation at all. By the end of his reign, he set Russia on a trajectory that would one day fly over all other European nations.

Peter Romanov—better known as Peter the Great—is deservedly the 26th most influential person in Western history.

The seventeenth century Russia into which Peter the Great was born did not resemble the formidable Russian Empire of later days. While the European powers of Spain, Portugal, Britain, Holland, and France entered their modern age, expanded their footprints overseas, and exported Western culture to other continents, the isolated Tsardom of Russia struggled for an identity.

Centuries earlier, before the turn of the millennium, an east Slavic ethnic group known as the Rus consolidated around the city of Kiev in eastern Europe. Kieven Russia remained a sizable eastern European polity for several hundred years. By the mid-thirteenth century, however, pressure from an aggressive Asian people, the Mongols, fragmented the Rus, and they were integrated into the enormous Mongol Empire.[1] Russia—the land of the Rus—became the latest addition to an Asian composite of conquered peoples. This invasion developed into an identity crisis for the Russians. Were they still European if they were governed by an Asian people?

After 1480, the Grand Duchy of Moscow broke away from the disintegrating Mongol Empire and unified most of the Rus. The new Russian leaders had an easier time acquiring Asian territory to their east than they did the better defended European lands to their west. At the turn of the sixteenth century, with Moscow as the new capital of an expanding Russian state, Ivan the Terrible became its first "tsar,"[2] and the "Russian Tsardom" was born.

Ivan and his successors continued to push eastward. Deeper and deeper into the Asian continent they went until they became, in geo-

---

[1] The Mongol invasion was led by Bhatu Khan, a grandson of the infamous Genghis Khan.

[2] In case you're wondering, and I know you are, "tsar" is just a different spelling for czar. The word derives from "Caesar," the title of the Roman emperors. In 1453, when Muslim Ottomans captured Constantinople—capital and last vestige of the Orthodox Eastern Roman Empire—the Orthodox

graphical terms, mostly Asian. As a result, Russia absorbed more and more people who looked and sounded less and less European.

Meanwhile, major cultural differences existed between western Europeans and Russians. In fact, while Russia, in terms of its geography, seemed to be both European and Asian, in terms of its culture, it was often neither. It was a Christian Orthodox nation, whereas western Europe in 1500 was almost fully Catholic and Asia a smattering of Muslim, Daoist, Hindu, Buddhist, Confucian, and other belief systems. Additionally, Russia's unique Cyrillic script and language set it apart from the Latin alphabet of the West and the ideographs of the East.[3] And while the light skin color of western Russians said European, their unique style of dress and beards on the men's faces said no such thing. They even slept with their shoes on, a practice considered uncivilized by Westerners. In sum, before Peter the Great, Russia was neither geographically nor culturally Western. Most of it lay in Asia, as did millions of Asian Russians, and they practiced a different kind of Christianity, wore different clothes, wrote different letters, and had different social mores.

Russians considered themselves the heir to Rome. They dubbed Moscow the "Third Rome" (after Rome itself and Constantinople, which had become known as the "New Rome"), and their leaders used the Russian translation of Caesar as their title. The Russians, interestingly, weren't the only ones to appropriate this Roman moniker for their leaders. The German *kaiser* also springs from Caesar, as does a host of other titles.

[3] Cyrillic gets its name from Cyril, one of two Christian missionary brothers who taught Christianity to Slavs in central and eastern Europe. The Slavs were illiterate and had an incomparable oral language, so Cyril and his brother, Methodius, invented a written alphabet and language based on the sounds of the Slavic tongue. The product of Cyril's hard work was his eponymous language, Cyrillic. I'm not the only person who finds this stuff interesting, right?

Peter the Great

More significantly, Russia had done little to keep up with the modernizing European continent. Technologically and culturally, it fell centuries behind. It had no Renaissance, no Reformation, and no Scientific Revolution. It was as if Russia was stuck in the Middle Ages. Its army and navy lagged woefully behind. Its Orthodox clergy controlled education. There was no quality literature or art, no emphasis on mathematics or science. In western Europe, the seventeenth century was the century of Galileo and Newton, Descartes and Locke. It was a century of a rising merchant class. Rural peasants moved to growing cities for diverse employment.

But as serfdom faded away in the West, it had been increasing in the Russia inherited by Peter Romanov. And while western Europeans, with their numerous warm-water ports, sailed the seas and brought in unprecedented profits from subjugated colonies, Russia pushed eastward, finding nothing but frigid taiga, icy coasts, and the remnants of a malformed Mongol Empire that had relied more on pillaging than infrastructure. In this case, going east was the equivalent of going nowhere, and it seemed to be the only thing the Russians were doing fast.

And then came Peter the Great. In 1672, Tsar Alexis I and his second wife, Natalya, brought Peter into the world. By 1696, he inherited sole control over the Russian state. His lengthy and educated tenure as heir apparent allowed him to research and analyze everything that was right with western Europe and wrong with Russia.

He determined that the best way to catch the European powers was to become like them, so an undercover Peter traveled to western Europe to learn about the region.[4] Tsar Peter I transformed into Sergeant Peter Mikhailov and set off for Europe as part of a "Grand Embassy" of over 200 Russian diplomats ostensibly led by a trio of ambassadors who tried to form alliances with European countries. He also ordered 50 Russian nobles to scatter throughout the West to learn about, and then report on, its culture and innovations.

The Grand Embassy first stopped in Holland. As his ambassadors lobbied the Dutch government, Peter, who dreamed of a great navy for his kingdom, secured a pedestrian position as a ship carpenter.[5] For four months, "Sergeant Mikhailov" worked for the Dutch East India Company, learning the art of shipbuilding and other carpentry.[6] He then traveled to England, owners of history's greatest navy, and took a course on shipbuilding. He examined England's shipyards and artillery plants. He learned about navigation. He studied Manchester and London, learning the ebbs and flows of Western cities. He attended a session of Parliament. On his way home, he stopped in Prussia, Austria, and Poland. Throughout his trip, he visited factories, arsenals, theaters, museums, and universities. Unfortunately, as he planned a trip to Venice, the greatest seafaring city-state of the Mediterranean, an uprising in Moscow

---

[4] I am not making this up. The 6' 7" Tsar of Russia traveled undercover to western Europe. It'd make for a tremendous piece of fiction if it weren't 100 percent true.

[5] Russians later recognized this humbling act for Russia's greater good with a statue of the carpenter-king in Saint Petersburg.

[6] As you can imagine, it was difficult for the 6' 7" Tsar to remain whatever the Russian word for *incognito* is, and he was often recognized. Such is the plight of NBA superstars and gargantuan autocrats.

Peter the Great

forced Peter home—but not before his 18-month journey taught him much about the West.[7]

Then the 26-year-old, brilliant, behemoth of a man set about modernizing Russia. With gobs of money, he wooed Western technicians and scholars to brave the Russian cold and teach his people. He simultaneously sent Russians to Western schools and vocations so they could one day return as experienced Europeans ready to teach the next generation of Russians.

He also deduced that militaristic and economic strength were tied to naval might, but Russia's lack of viable coastline stymied a fleet. Russia's northern and only coast abutted the aptly named White Sea, which was frozen up to nine months a year.

So Peter let slip the dogs of war. Hoping to access the Black Sea to Russia's south, Peter attacked the Ottoman Empire. With his capture of the Ottoman fortress on the Sea of Azov, which Russians had been trying to acquire for over a century, he had his access. At nearby Taganrog, Peter built the first naval base in Russian history.

Then, in 1700, he went to war with the Empire of Sweden.[8] The war raged for 21 years. By its end, victorious Russia tacked on more land to its west, including modern-day Latvia and Estonia.

---

[7] His European tour cut annoyingly short, an irate Peter squelched the rebellion, tortured and executed over a thousand people associated with it, then ordered their mutilated bodies to be publicly displayed. Anyone who's had their vacation cut short understands his wrath.

[8] Saying "Empire of Sweden" sounds odd bordering on hilarious, but in the 17th century, Sweden was one of the stronger powers around. It controlled modern Sweden, Finland, and parts of mainland Europe in modern Germany, Latvia, Lithuania, and Estonia. It even founded a short-lived North American colony in modern Delaware. The Empire's downfall started with Peter the Great's invasion, a tangential example of his importance.

77

On this new land, Peter commissioned a massive construction project—that of an entirely new city: Saint Petersburg. He felt it useful to have a nearby city from which he could communicate with his muse, western Europe. His city plans looked just like those of the Western cities he visited during his Grand Embassy tour—wide boulevards, beautiful architecture, advanced engineering. Ten years later, he relocated the Russian seat of government from Moscow to his new Westernized city. This move had the advantage of being closer to western Europe for diplomatic relations, and it was also closer to the Baltic Sea so he could oversee the construction of a new navy. Saint Petersburg became known as Russia's "window to the west." In 1725, the Russians completed the construction of the grand Palace of Peterhof—Peter's Court—which was known as the Russian Versailles, further evidence of Russian Westernization under Peter. [9]

After defeating Sweden and taking much of its land, Russia became the dominant power of the Baltic Sea. He had officially transformed the Russian Tsardom into the Russian Empire.

Domestically, meanwhile, Peter forced his country to evolve. He had inherited a decentralized nation that was divided into many cumbersome, uneven districts, each governed by a nearby city. Peter transformed this scattered kingdom into an efficient central state around which twelve manageable *guberniya* (provinces) were administrated by able, loyal gov-

---

[9] The city remained the capital until the Soviets moved it back to Moscow in 1918. Six years after that, the name was changed to Leningrad—after the Bolshevik revolutionary Vladimir Lenin—but later, with the dissolution of the Soviet Union in 1991, the name was changed back to Saint Petersburg. You should go.

ernors. He created a Senate and cabinet to help supervise his growing empire.

He ordered new shipyards, sea fortresses, and ships, drawing the plans himself. He took an active part in the formation of a merchant fleet that grew alongside the strengthening navy. To make sure he had qualified builders and officers, Peter set up two academies: the School of Mathematical and Navigation Sciences in Moscow and the Naval Academy in Saint Petersburg.

Peter additionally promoted metallurgy as a new Russian industry, and Russia soon became the world's top maker of cast iron. This production bolstered Russian industry and the military. The Tsar designed new Russian guns and made both the army and navy professional, standing units. Government and military promotions became based on merit instead of bloodline.

Still, he wanted more than to just have western European might and industry. Inspired by what he had seen in the West, Peter felt Western innovation was tied to Western culture. Therefore, he wanted his subjects to look and behave more like western Europeans. He discouraged beards as too "Asian looking" and implemented a beard tax. He ordered the entire military, nobility, and court to lose their proud whiskers, save their mustaches, even shaving reluctant nobles himself. He required them to dress in Western clothing. He even controlled their sleeping habits; in bed, they were commanded to remove their shoes or face a mild punishment.[10] He also encouraged them to drink coffee and smoke cigarettes.[11]

---

[10] See this chapter's opening quote.

[11] Best. Tsar. Ever.

Tsar Peter also facilitated intellectualism. The first Russian newspaper, the Saint Petersburg Vedomosti, was printed under Peter's reign. Secular schools replaced Orthodox ones. Peter's encouragement of science and state-run education hastened the Orthodox Church's loss of authority. He also opened the first public museum in Russia, the Kunstkamera, which includes the Peter the Great Museum of Anthropology and Ethnology.

Peter encouraged commerce and industry, recognizing that each was essential not only to a vibrant economy, but in supporting the military. He built weaving mills and other proto-factories. He modernized means of communication and encouraged foreign and domestic trade. With a demand for skilled workers, free peasants left their farms. Villages became towns and towns became cities. A middle class grew.

Indentured serfs, however, were as subjugated as ever and forced to feed a growing population, which can speak to Peter's often questionable morality. So much of Peter reflects a persistent duality—he was at once an enlightened despot championed by the likes of Plato (#30), yet he also micromanaged his kingdom, limiting personal choices of the upper class while oppressing the lower, all to strengthen his state. He saw himself as the father of his country, guiding Russia out of its adolescence; yet, his relationship with his actual son, Alexei, became so distant that the son turned his back on his father, left the country in disgrace, and colluded with foreigners, only to later return and face a torturous inquisition that ultimately killed him.

Nevertheless, throughout Russia's transformation, Peter served as the ultimate role model for the new Russian citizen. His private life was messy, but as the public face of the country, he exuded confidence and productivity. He stayed busy, worked hard, and got things done.

Peter the Great

Perhaps no death in our Top 30 occurred more heroically.[12] Legend has it that in November of 1724, Peter was inspecting various projects along the coast of northwest Russia when he saw a group of soldiers on a sinking boat, some drowning in the frigid waters. Their Tsar rushed in to help. The giant Peter is said to have been in the ice for some time, saving everyone he could.

Afterward, fever struck. His kidneys failed. His bladder became gangrenous. He died on February 8, 1725, at the age of 52.

The Russia he left behind was transformed. The Archbishop of Novgorod eulogized him: *"We are burying Peter the Great . . . who has resuscitated Russia as if from the dead, and has raised it to great power and glory. . . . O Russia, he is your Moses! . . . Can we in a short sermon mention all his glory?"*

Perhaps a short sermon can't mention all his glory, but this lengthy chapter can try.

Peter the Great inherited an ice-and-landlocked backwater claimed by neither Europe nor Asia and retrofitted it into an intercontinental empire with a modern navy. Five tsars and 37 years later, the Empress Catherine the Great followed in the former Great's footsteps, further expanding the Empire, reducing Church authority, and promoting cultural progress. She completed Russia's eastward journey, reaching modern Alaska. Russia ultimately became the third largest empire in history.[13] Peter set Russia on the trajectory that Catherine continued.

---

[12] Apologies to Joan of Arc at number 27 and that forthcoming guy who one might say died for our sins.

[13] Bested only by the British and Mongol empires.

To wonder what might have happened to Russia without Peter, we needn't look any further than the history of the neighboring Ottoman Empire. Russia and the Ottomans, even before Peter, were archrivals, competing for control of the Black Sea and the adjoining Bosporus Strait, which linked the Black to the Mediterranean, the usage of which would allow Russia access to the Atlantic.

In the fifteenth and sixteenth centuries, while Russia was an isolated, medieval kingdom, the Ottoman Empire was the foremost regional power. It controlled northeast Africa, the Middle East, Anatolia, and it even expanded well into southeast Europe. With multiple incursions, the empire struck fear in the hearts of Austrians and Italians.[14] The empire straddled three continents and had long coastlines on the Black, Aegean, Mediterranean, and Red seas. Their glorious, ancient capital of Constantinople conjoined Europe and Asia. If one were to have predicted the futures of pitiful Russia and the flourishing Ottoman Empire, one would think that the Ottomans' was far more glorious, while Russia's fate was to again be conquered.

Peter the Great, however, had other plans. Thanks to him, Russia modernized. The Peterless Ottomans, despite far superior geography, did not. While Russia eventually joined the great powers of Europe, the Ottoman Empire steadily weakened, disintegrated, and lost land to surrounding nations, including Russia herself. The Ottoman debilitation led it to be dubbed the "sick man of Europe," and European leaders took it upon themselves to decide its fate in the events surrounding the Crimean War. After World War I, the Ottoman Empire collapsed and was forced

---

[14] And you just thought the Ottomans merely made funny foot furniture.

by the West into becoming the Republic of Turkey. The Turks, feared centuries earlier, became pawns in European games.

Thanks to the foundation Peter laid, Russia ultimately rivaled the West. Indeed, thanks to Peter's reforms, it became a *part* of the West, mirroring its culture and embroiled in its geopolitics. It is Russia (and her winter) that finally slows Napoleon in 1812 and becomes a part of the European coalitions that bring him down. From then on, Russia entered into negotiations, alliances, and treaties like any other European nation.

It should be noted that after Russia's triumph in the Napoleonic Wars, the nineteenth century was not kind to the world's largest country.[15] It seemed to have forgotten the lessons learned under Peter. While western Europe and the young United States of America steamed ahead with industrialization, Russia stalled. Still, thanks to Peter's earlier efforts, the potential was still there for a powerful Russian nation, and that potential was seized upon after the First World War, when Russia evolved into the enormous Soviet Union. By the end of World War II, the U.S.S.R. joined the United States as one of two world superpowers competing for the largest sphere of influence on and off the earth. Peter's dream was realized.

---

[15] A harsh but perfect example of this decay is the oft-forgotten Crimean War (1853-1856), the West's bloodiest conflict before the crimson twentieth century. It was history's first war between industrialized nations, though some, as it turned out, were more industrialized than others. In 30 months, the Russians lost 700,000 soldiers to the French, British, and Ottomans. Among many revelations from the war—not the least of which was that modern warfare was really, *really* bad—was that Russia had once again fallen behind the pace of Western Europe. This lesson would be retaught during World War I.

With Peter, we have an example of an innovative leader who reoriented his country to face the West. Russia's pre-Peter stagnation compared to western Europe cannot be overstated. Whereas Catherine just continued the policies of her predecessor (keeping her from this ranking), it was Peter who truly diverted Russia's future. Unlike so many other important figures of history who merely took advantage of trends better than their contemporaries did, Peter reshaped history itself. He redirected Russia from remaining a bloated blotch of Eurasia to becoming a mighty monster of the Western world.

Due to his impressive goals, effective means of achieving them, and role in creating a future world superpower, Peter the Great is the 26th most influential figure in Western history.

#25: Gregory Pincus

"After the condom came the pill—and blessed be the pill! Perhaps some future historian will hail it as our century's greatest contribution to happiness."

–author Paul Blanshard, 1973

A funny thing happened to the world population in the nineteenth century. It doubled. After taking all of humanity's existence to reach one billion people in 1804, the population neared two billion as the century closed. By 1960, it surpassed three billion. It then took a mere 14 years to eclipse four billion, another 13 years to reach five billion, and then just 11 years to reach six billion in 1999. The world's population was not only growing—it was growing faster and faster.

And then the population did a funny thing again. Its rate of increase slowed. When the world population hit seven billion in 2011, it was the first time the gap between the billion milestones was longer than the last one. Looking forward, nearly every study projects that the gaps between the billions will now get larger—that population growth will continue to slow. What was once considered an inevitable global catastrophe has since been delayed and perhaps averted altogether.

This development is important, both for the modern world and its future. There are many reasons for this significant development, but perhaps no single person is more responsible for it than the most recent figure of this Top 30 list.[1] His name was Gregory Goodwin Pincus, the inventor of the modern birth control pill and the 25th most influential figure in Western history.

It was named "Enovid," and of all the drugs ever created by medicine, it's the only one we call "the pill." Combining the estrogen mestranol and a steroidal progestin norethynodrel, Enovid was the first combined oral contraception pill in history.

Enovid, amusingly, had a father.

Unlike so many other figures in the Top 30, Gregory Pincus did not live a terribly interesting life upon which I expound for too many words before arriving at their importance. Rather, we pick up with Pincus in adulthood. His fields were physiology, which he taught at Harvard, and hormonal biology, which he studied while teaching. In 1934, his "in vitro" fertilization (later discovered to be "in vivo") of rabbits brought him mild fame. However, his controversial, ungodly work getting rabbits to asexually reproduce cost him tenure, and Pincus eventually left Harvard. In 1944, he co-founded the Worcester Foundation for Experimental Biology, a lab at which many of his ensuing breakthroughs occurred. It was a respectable career, but he received few accolades due to his obsession with hormones.[2] He was an accomplished scientist with degrees

---

[1] He was born in 1903, making him the only figure on our list born in the twentieth century, and he died in 1967, making him our most recent death.

[2] Not unlike me in high school.

from Cornell, Harvard, and Cambridge, but by no means was his résumé remarkable enough to be included anywhere near a ranking such as this one.

Then he met activist Margaret Sanger, and this duo went on to change the future of Western civilization. Before they met, Sanger was already a nationally recognized birth control trailblazer. In 1916, she opened America's first birth control clinic. Five years later, she founded the American Birth Control League which, in 1942, became the Planned Parenthood Federation of America.[3] She was a tireless champion of women's reproductive rights, a reviled enemy of social conservatives, and she campaigned across the country in an effort to open contraceptive avenues to American women.

To really promote contraception, however, more palatable options for women were badly needed. It should be noted that Pincus's birth control pill was far from the first form of contraception. Chapter 38 of Genesis notes Onan's practice of *coitus interruptus* to avoid impregnating his brother-in-law's widow.[4] The Talmud sanctions the "sponge" in certain situations. As early as 1850 BCE, the ancient Egyptians recorded their experiments with *pessaries*, including proto-spermicides, and the practice of lactational amenorrhea, which remained popular for millennia. Since those ancient examples, history is rife with humans trying to avoid

---

[3] The acronym for Planned Parenthood was PPFA, a bold theft of the far more famous Presidential Politics for America website started 90 years later. Both PPFAs are appreciated by women in all 50 states.

[4] I don't remember THAT story in church! I'd have paid more attention.

the biological imperative while still dabbling in the carnal one.[5] By the twentieth century, the most popular forms of contraception included condoms, diaphragms, and the rhythm method, but each had dissuasive properties. Men didn't like condoms, women didn't like diaphragms, and, for various reasons, the rhythm method has a high failure rate.

By 1950, Sanger knew that a simple, cheap, pleasurable, effective alternative was essential in her effort to make birth control accessible and desirable to every woman who desired it. To accomplish that goal, one would have to understand hormonal manipulation, and she was about to run into the field's foremost expert.

Pincus and Sanger met at a 1951 Planned Parenthood fundraiser. Sanger shared her vision with an interested Pincus, who assured her that contraception could be regulated. The trick was to regulate it safely and with minimal side effects. Scientists were already shooting doses of progesterone into lab animals to suppress ovulation, but regular hypodermic injections was not what Sanger (nor, I imagine, any other woman) had in mind. She secured Pincus a research grant from Planned Parenthood and asked him to work the problem.

---

[5] The Greeks, ever the lusty tinkerers, sought plants with contraceptive and abortificient properties. One plant, Silphium, was so effective and became so popular that it was said to have been worth its weight in silver. Curiously, it only grew around their colony of Cyrene (modern Libya) and could not be successfully grown anywhere else (but oh how they tried). The enormous demand bulldozed the limited crop and it went extinct by the second century BCE. The sound of every Mediterranean man slapping their foreheads at the same time is said to have been recorded by the ancient Chinese.

The brilliant Pincus solved it within months. Working with Dr. Min Chueh Chang (later instrumental in the first "test tube baby"), their trials on animals produced a successful oral contraceptive through progesterone ingestion. With this success, Sanger tapped considerably more money for Pincus than he had been given by Planned Parenthood, this time from philanthropic suffragist Katherine McCormick. By 1953, Pincus was conducting human trials via gynecologist John Rock and his infertility patients, a crucially important phase. Rock found that the right dosage of Pincus's pill usually suppressed ovulation. Unfortunately, just "usually" wasn't good enough; only about 85 percent of the time was it effective (about as effective—or ineffective—as the rhythm method), and large amounts of the drug were needed just to get it that high.

So Pincus went back to work. He surveyed chemical companies across the country for steroids that resembled progesterone. The most likely candidate, he observed, was norethynodrel, a chemical invented by Frank Colton of G.D. Searle and Company in 1952.[6] Colton had no idea that his creation resembled a piece of the oral contraception puzzle, but Pincus did. Since ingesting norethynodrel led to some minor health complications, Pincus offset that problem by synthesizing an estrogen called mestranol, which, combined with the norethynodrel, smoothed out the drug. By 1955 the first oral contraceptive pill was ready for field tests.

Since providing contraceptives of any kind was illegal in the Puritanical Commonwealth of Massachusetts and controversial throughout the country, Pincus tucked his tests away in Puerto Rico. He hired Dr. Edris

---

[6] G.D. Searle and Company has since been absorbed by our overlords at Pfizer.

Rice-Wray Carson, who worked with a network of birth control clinics made available to the island's low-income population. It took inside a year before the results revealed what Pincus already knew: they had their pill. Later tests in Haiti, Mexico, and then Los Angeles not only confirmed the results, they also showed demand from women who were finally offered an easy, painless, and less invasive alternative to their miserable birth control options.

In 1957, the Food and Drug Administration approved "Enovid," though not for the express purpose of contraception. Helpfully, another effect of Pincus's pill was that it regulated the menstrual cycle and helped treat menstrual disorders. For that reason, the FDA sanctioned the drug. This seamless integration into medical circles aided its acceptance as a contraceptive as well.

To its creators and most of its users, the pill's menstrual regulation was just a bonus. By 1960, less than one decade after Pincus met Sanger, the FDA approved Enovid to serve specifically as the first ever birth control pill.

Pincus died six years later, but his work lives on. It might have even saved the world.

I admit such a statement seems hyperbolic, but I think it must be considered. The story of world history includes tribes and civilizations competing for limited resources—with proxy fronts over competing religions, cultures, and skin tones. The premise that our population was increasing at a faster and faster rate leads to the natural conclusion that global resources would one day come up short of what was necessary to sustain our civilization. That day would have happened when we presumably had larger, deadlier, and more abundant weapons than ever. Many pessimists argued that our civilization was on an inevitable crash course with this worldwide doom; to them, it was only a matter of when this collision would occur.

But, as so many times before, science came to the rescue. In this case, it was via Gregory Pincus. Birth control in pill form must have once seemed like a foreign, futuristic concept limited to science fiction novels and movies with cheesy visual effects and v-stripe uniforms. Pincus made that future a reality. We are now a species that can safely control its population, or at least has the scientific ability to do so, if not yet the general will.

I say that because the entire world has not yet caught on to this transformative invention. Recent population studies show that while the West has experienced a sharp curbing of population growth, Latin America, Africa, and south Asia are almost totally making up for it. The world population's growth has indeed been slowing, but that's mostly because Western levels of reproduction are slowing to levels that barely replace the last generation.[7]

The causes for the West's flirtation with subfertility rates include better education and economic development, but those deviations existed before 1960, when population climbed at high speed throughout Europe and the United States. It's "the pill," and the other hormonal con-

---

[7] Many European countries (and other Westernized ones) have a jaw-droppingly low fertility rate of fewer than 1.5 children per woman. The number "2.00" is the best reference point for this statistic, as that means two children replace their biological parents. The U.S., that booming country of opportunity, three kids, and a picket fence, has slowed to 1.7 children per woman. Meanwhile, dozens of countries in Africa are north of 4.

traceptive methods it philosophically and medically inspired and allowed, that slowed the ascent and allowed this modern plateau.

Pincus's creation was important in more ways than just population figures. The FDA's 1960 approval of the pill as a contraceptive kicks off the decade most associated with sex. The Sixties birthed the sexual revolution, which broke centuries-old shackles on sexual mores. Monogamous relationships grew less common, while premarital sex did the opposite. Unlike nearly every other method of birth control available to them, the pill allowed women to be sexually spontaneous. They could be as free to engage in recreational sex as a man could.

Today, the Western world barely blinks at a couple living together before marriage. Premarital sex is a part of life in the West, accepted by just about everyone.[8] The fact that the aforementioned collapse in Western birthrates coincides with *freer* sexual relationships shows how Pincus's pill and its successors have revolutionized Western society.

With a leveling of sexual terms came a breakthrough in women's liberation. Ancient attitudes about classical gender roles were finally confronted. Women's jobs could take precedence over a family. They could avoid a pregnancy and all the difficulties that might entail for their personal career and life in general. A push for equal treatment and equal pay in the workplace followed. This momentum for women's sexual equality culminated in abortion's legalization across the West.[9]

Achieving the goal of social, political, and economic equality was never really possible until practical contraception. We now have power-

---

[8] Except by everyone's parents.

[9] The United States, in particular, experienced a revolution in its attitude toward abortion. Throughout the 1960s, many states loosened their birth

ful female athletes, entrepreneurs, and CEOs, role models who were almost exclusively male until the post-pill movement. In the last 40 years, the Western world has had its first two female Prime Ministers of the United Kingdom and a female Chancellor of Germany. The US almost had a female president, and in 2020 the country elected its first female Vice President. All of these developments came after Pincus's birth control pill allowed that discernible spike in women's liberation. One could make the case that the pill marks the most important demarcation in women's history.[10]

Of course, I'd be remiss if I didn't close this chapter without a direct acknowledgement of the important collaborators that contributed to Pincus's breakthrough. If he were solely responsible for the pill, he could have been placed into the top half of this list. Remember, however, that Sanger stimulated the idea and McCormick funded it. Pincus worked with Dr. Chang to invent it, he needed doctors Rock and Carson to field test it, and he needed Colton's drug to refine it. Pincus may have been the father of Enovid, but the pill had many midwives.

Still, Pincus's role as the linchpin cannot be ignored. Of all these contributors, he was the most responsible and indispensable. He dedicated his time and extensive knowledge to research, organize, and cre-

---

control and abortion laws, and President Johnson's Committee on the Status of Women called for a repeal of all abortion laws. In 1973, the hallmark Roe vs. Wade Supreme Court case injected the judiciary into the issue, and abortion became legal coast to coast.

[10] What would be its competitors for such a claim? Suffrage was on a nation by nation basis. Property and personal rights have evolved unevenly across regions and centuries. I don't think any one particular moment, initiative, or invention stacks up to the pill in terms of unleashing new possibilities for women.

ate, knowing exactly how to utilize the necessary resources and colleagues. From Sanger's search to Colton's chemical, Pincus was the constant.

The pill has affected Western society like few other inventions. If we predict the world's future, it's not unreasonable to assume that the pill and its descendants will eventually travel to every corner of every continent as a simple, practical strategy to plan families and control population, which would reduce poverty, hunger, crime, and the strain on the earth's precious resources. The pill can allow a reasonable allocation of Earth's resources, and that, in turn, contributes to a reasonable allocation of happiness.

When I wrap up these entries, I usually restate how much the historical figure changed the world. With Gregory Pincus, I remind you that he may have saved it. For his important role in changing Western society and its future, he is the 25th most influential figure in Western history.

#24: Thomas Jefferson

"I think this is the most extraordinary collection of talent, of human knowledge, that has ever been gathered together at the White House, with the possible exception of when Thomas Jefferson dined alone."
  -President Kennedy to a gathering of Nobel laureates, 1962

He was many things: lawyer, philosopher, naturalist, musician, geographer, inventor, agriculturalist, philologist, scientist, architect, polyglot, surveyor, slave owner, farmer, congressman, governor, ambassador, cabinet secretary, co-founder of America's two-party system, and President of the United States.

Most importantly, he was the voice of a revolution. His pen announced the separation of thirteen allied British colonies from their masters across the Atlantic. Of all these new "Americans," the revolution's leaders chose this Virginian polymath to explain to the world and their posterity why it was happening.

They chose wisely. The man they selected was Thomas Jefferson, the 24th most influential figure in Western history.

Born in 1743 on a large Shadwell, Virginia estate, young Thomas Jefferson enjoyed the good life. Slaves worked the Jeffersons' land, enriching the family. Young Thomas grew up reading thousands of books across myriad topics. He went on to study law at the colonies' southern college, William & Mary. In 1772, he married a woman, Martha, who conveyed an additional 135 slaves and 11,000 acres into his possession. It's remarkable to think that such an affluent man would want to upend his corner of the world, yet he became the primary author of the document that declared that corner's independence.

It's worth noting that Jefferson wasn't the only American colonist living the good life. Indeed, for most of British-American history, it can be argued that in no place on Earth was life so good than in Britain's American colonies. They had a growing population, endless tracts of land with slaves to work it, a high standard of living, sprouting schools and churches, considerably low taxes, and a democratic process for local leadership. They had as much freedom as anyone in the world. For most of the colonies' history with London, settlers loyally pledged themselves to the Crown.[1]

The turning point of this theretofore strong relationship was the French and Indian War, waged from 1754 to 1763. In this struggle, British redcoats and colonial militia successfully waged war against a Franco-native alliance on the frontier, and as a result the empire secured Quebec and land all the way to the Mississippi.

---

[1] Through the prism of the American Revolution, Britain looks like an oppressive tyranny and a revolution as necessary as it was inevitable. It should be noted, however, that the colonial relationship with England was strong for most of the relationship. Indeed, England was not too tyrannical. It usually broke ground on liberty's forefront. Between the thirteenth and

Thomas Jefferson

What should have signaled a new era of cooperative dominance ended up being the high-water mark for the British-Colonial relationship. After years of salutary neglect, London began to micromanage the new lands, including barring colonial settlement of it. Parliament also worked to pay off war debt through a series of fees and taxes on the colonists. Colonial resistance to these taxes led to further micromanaging and a curbing of liberties from a frustrated Parliament.

With these events as a backdrop, Thomas Jefferson rose in prominence. In 1769, the talented 26-year-old lawyer and writer had been elected to Virginia's prestigious assembly, the House of Burgesses in 1769. Five years later, after Britain issued its intolerable "Intolerable Acts," he wrote "A Summary View of the Rights of British America," a stern rebuke of what he and many Americans considered a drastic overreach by the English Parliament. "Summary View" was read all over the colonies, and the young Jefferson became a widely known colonial figure.

In 1774, colonial leaders organized a meeting of colonial representatives in Philadelphia, which history, betraying the existence of the meeting's sequel, now calls the First Continental Congress. In April 1775, after shots fired and bodies fell at Lexington and Concord, a Second Continental Congress discussed how to handle the deteriorating

eighteenth centuries, England developed such liberal ideas as a parliamentary branch and habeas corpus and liberalizing documents like the Magna Carta, the Petition of Right, and a bill of rights that predates that of the United States by a century. Indeed, like a feeding infant, many of America's ideas for government were directly siphoned from its mother. Once Parliament started withholding these rights from colonists, however, Americans felt that they were not treated like true British citizens, a sentiment which fostered rebellion.

97

relationship with the Crown. Virginia chose Jefferson as one of its delegates.[2] There, he met for the first time John Adams of Massachusetts and Benjamin Franklin of Pennsylvania.

One year and over a dozen battles later, momentum gathered for a full separation from the British Empire. In June of 1776, Congress asked a "committee of five"–Franklin, Adams, Jefferson, Roger Sherman of Connecticut, and Robert Livingston of New York–to draft a declaration of independence, just in case one was needed.[3] The elderly Franklin, a veritable celebrity and de facto leader of the committee, felt that Adams, who was, like his colony of Massachusetts, American liberty's sharpest advocate, should draft the document before the other four edited. Adams insisted, however, that Jefferson write it, as Virginia was by far the most populous colony and one with more reluctant revolutionaries than Massachusetts, and that Jefferson could write "ten times better." Jefferson accepted. In about two inspired weeks, he wrote the framework for one of history's greatest documents.

The Committee of Five made edits and presented it to the Second Continental Congress, which edited it some more. On July 4, Congress approved the wording. The Declaration of Independence was official. The "United States" announced themselves separate from the British Empire.

---

[2] In a fascinating footnote of history (and, evidently, this book), Jefferson was actually a late replacement for another Virginia delegate, Peyton Randolph. After the Second Continental Congress began, Virginia called Randolph home in order to serve as the head of the House of Burgesses. Only then was Jefferson tapped as a delegate. Close call for one of America's central founding fathers.

[3] These are the five men seen presenting the document to John Hancock in John Trumbull's famous, if misleading, painting.

Thomas Jefferson

Or so they hoped. The treasonous document intensified London's scorn. The main part of the American War of Independence raged four more years, with official peace and British recognition of U.S. legitimacy not secured until the Treaty of Paris (1783). Throughout that period, Jefferson stayed busy. After serving as Governor of Virginia during the war, Congress asked him to serve as ambassador to the new country's most important ally, France, where he arrived in 1784.[4] For the next five years, Jefferson lived abroad, interacting with members of the French court and aristocracy. He also met with French revolutionaries, helped to write their Declaration of the Rights of Man, and built relationships that influenced his later foreign policy in the American government.[5]

Jefferson stayed in touch with his compatriots when they codified and ratified a new governing document, the Constitution, in the late 1780s. He was particularly close to fellow Virginian James Madison, the document's primary author. Fearing that the Constitution would grant too much authority to the federal government, Jefferson stressed to Madison the importance of a bill of rights to protect liberties. Many "Antifederalists" agreed with him and would not ratify the Constitution without a guarantee of such protection. The document's proponents made the concession, and Madison helped steer the Bill of Rights through the new Congress and amendment ratification process.

---

[4] To pass the time on the 17-day voyage, Jefferson learned to read and write Spanish, an intellectual feat that stands in direct contrast to my seven years of Spanish leading to a decidedly *muy mal* vocabulary.

[5] Even while in France, Jefferson was felt back in America. Nearly a decade earlier, he had written the "Virginia Statute for Religious Freedom," which guaranteed freedom of religion to all faiths and later inspired this American liberty. The document languished in the Virginia legislature until it was adopted in 1786 while its author sat in the salons of France.

99

After his tenure as ambassador, Thomas Jefferson returned home just as George Washington settled in as America's first Constitutional president. Washington welcomed him home with a job offer: Secretary of State. Washington's executive branch became a sort of dream team of revolutionaries. Adams, that tireless champion of liberty, earned the vice-presidency by finishing second to Washington in the presidential Election of 1789. Jefferson, the author of the Declaration of Independence and one of the smartest men in America, guided state matters. Alexander Hamilton, Washington's right-hand man during the war and the other smartest man in America, was brought in to be the first Secretary of the Treasury.

Hamilton was a decade younger than Jefferson, a disconcerting juxtaposition for the new State Secretary, as he was used to being the youngest brilliant person of any room into which he entered. Throughout Washington's first term, Jefferson and Hamilton quarreled over the power of the federal government, including the creation of a perhaps unconstitutional National Bank. Hamilton wanted to use the new Constitution to siphon states' authority into a more efficient centralized government, while Jefferson wanted states to retain much of their sovereignty, save the federal powers expressly permitted in the Constitution. The two also had competing foreign policies, particularly when the French asked for help when they found themselves embroiled in a series of revolutionary wars against their monarchy and the rest of Europe. Jefferson wanted to defend liberty and assist his old French friends, while Hamilton saw America's success as dependent on trade with France's chief antagonist, Great Britain, and therefore wanted to avoid helping their old allies.

Hamilton, Washington's comrade in arms from the war, had the President's ear more often than did Jefferson. Consequently, Washington and Jefferson's ideologies drifted apart, as did the two men. A frustrated Jefferson eventually resigned early in President Washington's second term.

An unshackled Jefferson worked to slow Hamilton's Federalist Party, which organized to advance his ideology through elections and legislation. Jefferson worked with newspapermen and pamphleteers to hurt the reputations of his former colleagues. The old Antifederalists, ever skeptical of the kind of centralized authority advocated for by Hamilton, rallied around Jefferson as a leader of the Democratic-Republican Party, which wanted a stricter read of what the Constitution allowed the federal government to do. America's two-party system was born.

By 1796, when it became clear that President Washington would not stand for a third term, these Democratic-Republicans presented Jefferson as his successor. Federalists, meanwhile, felt that Washington's Vice President, John Adams, was the natural heir to the presidency. The Electoral College agreed, but barely; Adams won the election by three electoral votes, 71 to 68. Jefferson, as runner up, was sworn in as Adams's Vice President despite being a member of the opposite party.[6] Two decades after their dazzling collaboration writing the Declaration of Independence, these two founding fathers, as they held the highest executive offices in the land, barely spoke.

Their acrimonious rematch in 1800 tilted in the other direction. A defeated Adams returned to his Massachusetts retirement, and Jefferson

---

[6] That was an unforeseen consequence of America's initial electoral process, and it was remedied by 1804's Twelfth Amendment.

supplanted his friend-turned-rival-turned-boss to become the third President of the United States.

President Jefferson took the office in 1801 at a crossroads of American history. His victory over Adams was seen as a referendum on, and condemnation of, the Federalist ideology. Not only did Jefferson win the executive branch, but the Democratic-Republicans also swept away a Federalist majority from Congress. The turnover in both branches became known as the Revolution of 1800. Jefferson ushered in a three-decade long dominance of Democratic-Republican leadership, including 24 straight years of Virginian presidents.[7]

Despite his party's platform, Jefferson's overreach of presidential power led to the hallmark of his presidency. In 1803, he authorized the Louisiana Purchase, which doubled the size of the United States. Nowhere in the Constitution did it allow the president to negotiate the purchase of new land, especially so much of it. Jefferson had sent two ambassadors—Robert Livingston (of Committee of Five fame) and James Monroe (the future fifth President)—to Napoleonic France to negotiate the purchase of New Orleans. They were authorized to pay up to 10 million dollars for the port city, since its presence at the Mississippi's mouth could be enormously helpful for the young country's frontier. Much to Livingston and Monroe's giddy surprise, Napoleon's negotiator had a counteroffer: up the bid to $15 million (the equivalent of $342 million today) and receive not only New Orleans but the entire Louisiana territory, which stretched nearly halfway from the Mississippi to the Pacific

---

[7] Eight years of Jefferson was followed by eight years of Madison, who was followed by eight years of James Monroe. Democratic-Republican Virginians all.

Ocean. They accepted, and Jefferson later sustained the decision.[8] It remains the largest peaceful land exchange in world history.[9]

The rest of his presidency, however, shrunk the size of government (although he did keep Hamilton's National Bank). He reduced expenditures, cut taxes, and consolidated the bureaucracy.[10] He stayed out of European conflicts, save protecting American merchants in the Mediterranean from Barbary pirates. The latter part of his administration faced a deteriorating relationship with Britain, including the empire flouting agreements from the Treaty of Paris. Jefferson found himself generally unable to either bolster U.S. posture or defuse tensions through diplomacy and economic policy. His successor, James Madison, would inherit these problems, culminating in the War of 1812.

In 1809, after two terms, Jefferson followed Washington's precedent and retired from the office. In 1819, he founded the University of Virginia, which he considered one of his crowning achievements—a sur-

---

[8] I always like picturing Livingston and Monroe hearing this counter-proposal and trying to contain their excited disbelief. They quickly inhale and their eyes widen, but then they play it cool, like they weren't just offered the deal of the millennium. "Hmmm, not bad not bad," they say nonchalantly. "We have to think about it. Will you excuse us?" Then they leave the room, close the door behind them, start fist-pumping and yelling "YES! YES!" before spiraling into a series of whispered "Shut up shut up"s, taking deep breaths, and calmly walking back in. "Yeah, we guess we can do that if you really want to. No, no, we don't need to check with the boss."

[9] Shortly after the purchase, Jefferson sent Captain Meriwether Lewis and Lieutenant William Clark on an expedition across the continent to learn about the newly acquired land. You couldn't pay me enough to do that. Rumor has it there was limited Wi-Fi in the Black Hills.

[10] Or, as modern conservatives call it, "the good ol' days."

prise considered his legendary career.[11] Seven years later, at the age of 81, he passed away. The date was July 4, 1826 –the 50th anniversary of the Declaration of Independence.[12]

One could argue that no prominent figure better embodies the eighteenth century. In most interpretations of Western history, the 1700s are known for the Enlightenment and the revolutions it spawned. No figure of the century can claim to be tied to both those movements as much as Jefferson was.

The Enlightenment, in the era of autocracy and divine right, offered many progressive political ideas that were quite radical for the time, and these ideas laid the foundation of modern Western government. Despite its French fulcrum–*philosophes* like Voltaire, Jean-Jacques Rousseau, and Denis Diderot personify the movement–the Enlightenment was trans-West in scope. Great Britain had many Enlightenment thinkers, as did Prussia, Russia, and Holland. The Enlightenment also spread to the American colonies, and with no one is that more evident than with Jefferson. Like earlier "Renaissance men" Aristotle (#30) and Leonardo da

---

[11] He had his gravestone read: *"Here was buried Thomas Jefferson//Author of the Declaration of American Independence//of the Statute of Virginia for Religious Freedom//and father of the University of Virginia."* No mention of the presidency!

[12] Hours after that, John Adams, who 50 years earlier was with him in the Second Continental Congress and Committee of Five, who asked him to write the Declaration of Independence, who served with him in President Washington's executive branch, who defeated him in the Election of 1796 and lost to him four years later, proved their fates were intertwined when he, too, died 50 years to the day after they founded a new country together. It's worth knowing they resumed an increasingly warm correspondence and friendship after Jefferson left office. I'm not crying. You're crying.

Vinci, Jefferson mastered a dozen fields and philosophized with the best Europe had to offer.

But that alone wouldn't make him the century's quintessential figure. What separates him from his talented, philosophical peers across the Atlantic, many of whom were writing about revolutions before Jefferson could pick up a quill, is that Jefferson was actually part of a revolution that put the Enlightenment's ideas into practice. *Philosophes* only mused about strangling kings with priests' entrails, but Jefferson's America actually took up arms and waged a successful war for liberty. After the revolution's success, the inspired French followed in the footsteps of the Americans, but not before Jefferson served as ambassador to France, spreading more liberal ideas, leading up to France's own revolution. These two major revolutions sprung from the mind and leadership of Thomas Jefferson. He then served in post-revolution government, and with his victory over the Federalists in 1800, he furthered the cause even more.

At this point, I feel compelled to address why Jefferson isn't higher on the list. After all, if he was the hallmark figure of an important century, helped write one of world history's essential documents, and doubled the size of America, shouldn't he at least be in the top 20?

No. One might think his lower ranking stems from the reputation emphasized by his detractors—that of a hypocritical, slave-owning, racist anarchist. The charges have some merit. He wrote about equality but lived like an aristocrat. He was a voice of the people despite rubbing shoulders with American elites and French nobility. Many wonder how someone who wrote that "All men are created equal" could keep over a hundred slaves, including ones he may have fathered. As for the anarchist charge, Jefferson's ideology, however triumphant in 1800, supported the French Revolution, which seemed a referendum on a decentralized state. When the movement descended into bloody turmoil, it reflected poorly on Jefferson's ideology. More hypocrisy follows Jefferson when, as president, this ostensibly "small government, strict Constitutional interpretation" candidate continued Hamilton's National Bank and circumvented Congress when negotiating for Louisiana.

None of the above mitigates his influence, however. Rather, his ranking is limited because, to a greater degree than the entries yet to come, his most important legacies were more the acts of collaboration than inspiration.[13]

Take the Declaration of Independence, for example. First, it wasn't his idea. It was unofficially a collective proposal, and it was fellow Virginian Richard Henry Lee who formally motioned for it in Congress. Furthermore, while Jefferson was ultimately chosen as its primary author, it was thoroughly edited and re-edited by the Committee of Five and Second Continental Congress. "We hold these truths to be self-evident" was not part of his first draft, and his "inalienable rights" of "life, liberty, and the pursuit of happiness" is almost purely John Locke.[14] Only about half of Jefferson's original draft survived the editing process.

Plus, we should remember that the Declaration may have just been a formality. Lexington and Concord inaugurated the war over a year earlier. Moreover, it's not as if the Declaration was a governing document. It was merely a statement of ideas and a justification of rebellion. Even the

---

[13] Note that this circumstance also held back Jefferson's predecessor in this ranking, Gregory Pincus (#25).

[14] As we will see in a later chapter!

Thomas Jefferson

ideas weren't fresh. Locke and other thinkers of the period had been discussing these concepts for decades.

Other contributions are similarly derivative or fractional. Jefferson's push for religious freedom was a staple of both Locke and Voltaire's philosophy. As President, his promotion of small government was often betrayed by impurity. What's more, as the federal government and presidency have gained power across American history, one might wonder if Jefferson's influence was ultimately less than Hamilton's. Even the Louisiana Purchase fell into his lap when Napoleon, fighting wars in Europe, offered it to Livingston and Monroe, who themselves actually did the negotiating. Therefore, despite his well-rounded accomplishments, I must keep Jefferson behind the 23 people ahead of him.

And yet, in many ways, his legacy is safe. It cannot be a coincidence that his fingerprints are on so many important developments in early American history. He earned his brilliance through incessant study. Adams knew Jefferson should write the Declaration's first draft, Congress knew Jefferson should be sent to France, the French knew they wanted his help in writing their own famous declaration, Washington knew he needed Jefferson as State Secretary, and the Democratic-Republicans knew Jefferson had to be their candidate. Jefferson became the first to mobilize a political machine to win a contested election. Indeed, American partisanship itself stems back to he and Hamilton at each other's throats.

As President, he had the wherewithal to send ambassadors to France to see if Napoleon was interested and the foresight to quickly accept the brokered deal despite lacking the clear Constitutional authority to do so. The timing of this acquisition should not be underestimated. Without a swift purchase of Louisiana so early in American history, the cascading effects are considerable. If the land isn't bought, there's a good chance an inevitable Franco-American War erupts after the coastal American states grow overpopulated. Further, a slower American spread west delays other key moments of the nation's Manifest Destiny to reach the Pacific and transform North America along the way. Andrew Jackson has no place to march Native Americans. The Texas annexation is delayed. The Mexican-American War is delayed. The California gold rush is delayed. The Mexicans might even find gold in California before the Americans do, which then puts them in a much stronger economic position to defend against the growing United States. Indeed, if any of the above are sufficiently "delayed," they might never come to be at all. The US would never have become the formidable nation it is today. The Louisiana Purchase is that important.

Later, Jefferson stepping down after two terms should not be overlooked. If only Washington had done it, we would still remember the rather old father of our country who refused to be a king, but that wouldn't necessarily mean every president would follow in his footsteps, particularly ones younger and more vigorous. It was Jefferson who confirmed the two-term tradition, and every president not named Franklin Roosevelt emulated that affirmation.

Finally, we simply cannot ignore that while predecessors may have had the ideas before him, it's Jefferson that most famously put them into practice. He was the driving force behind religious freedom in the U.S., reversing the trend of state religions in the Western world and even American colonies. He made sure that no one forgot about a bill of rights to protect citizens from government.

Above all, the Declaration of Independence shared with the world a lasting legacy that set off a chain reaction of freedom. It remains a guidepost of American and world liberty. Not only have American leaders and citizens referenced the document for nearly 250 years, but it also became an inspiration for the world. Later nations, including colonies across the Western Hemisphere that soon threw off the yoke of their own oppressive mother countries, were inspired by the American cause, particularly Jefferson's document, and declared their own right to popular sovereignty.

Therefore, due to his diverse talents, accomplishments, and inescapable presence in one of history's most significant eras, Thomas Jefferson is the 24th most influential figure in Western history.

#23: Constantine the Great

"I believe in one God, the Father Almighty, Maker of heaven and earth, and of all things visible and invisible.

And in one Lord Jesus Christ, the only-begotten Son of God, begotten of the Father before all worlds; God of God, Light of Light, very God of very God; begotten, not made, being of one substance with the Father, by whom all things were made."

–Opening of Nicene Creed

In Dostoyevsky's "The Brothers Karamazov," Ivan Karamazov shares a parable with his brother Alyosha, hypothesizing Jesus's "second coming" during the height of the Spanish Inquisition. In the story, after Jesus establishes his identity through miracles, the "Grand Inquisitor" has him arrested. The charges—part heresy and part public disturbance—stem from the Inquisitor's belief that Jesus's reappearance endangers the

Catholic Church's authority.[1] The Inquisitor also expresses his frustration at the Lord's decision to grant man free will. Free will, it turns out, is a real nuisance to those in power.[2] The Church wanted to reign over stability and good behavior, not free thinkers. Dostoyevsky suggests that Jesus himself would not be accepted by the era's Catholic leadership.

That irony probably worked both ways. The era's ruthless Catholic Church would not have been accepted by Jesus either. Nevertheless, the Church felt justified in its show of strength. Early Christians had lacked unity and influence. A couple hundred years after Jesus's death, dozens of sects asked difficult, unanswerable questions about Jesus's ideology and nature. Those who answered those unanswerable questions taught their own interpretation of Jesus's Word. Many Christians worshiped Jesus as God Himself, some thought he was a demigod, and others even felt he lacked all divinity. Christianity mired as a decentralized religion which could not make sense of the Bible's competing voices.[3]

Then came a man who began the consolidation of Christianity into a stronger, more cohesive religion: the Roman emperor Constantine the Great. While his legalization and endorsement of Christianity make him

---

[1] *"Why hast Thou come now to hinder us?" the Inquisitor asks his Lord, Savior, and prisoner."*

[2] *"Did you forget that a tranquil mind and even death is dearer to man than a free choice in the knowledge of good and evil?"*

[3] Channeling these sects, the Inquisitor's assault on God-given free will asks Jesus, *"Did it never occur to you that [man] would at last reject and call in question even your image and your truth, if he were weighed down by so fearful a burden as freedom of choice?"*

an irreplaceable historical titan, his effects on Western civilization go much deeper. He staved off Rome's collapse, yet hastened the dark era to follow it. He also empowered Christian clergy to the point where the Church became Rome's successor as lords of the West. In the process, Constantine became the 23rd most influential figure in Western history.

In the early 300s, history's strongest civilization had never seemed so fragile. The Roman Empire's difficult third century experienced an unmanageably large territory, porous borders facing Germanic invasions, a collapsing economy, turncoat generals, deadly plagues, and depleting loyalty.

The emperor Diocletian (reigned 284-305), a great but shortsighted emperor, energetically placed bandages over Rome's gushing wounds. To better manage the bloated empire, he divided it into two halves. Each had their own co-emperor, called an "Augustus," and each co-emperor had a politically empowered heir, called a "Caesar," to help govern. Diocletian hoped the four rulers of the Tetrarchy would be better than one. He also hired fierce Germanic mercenaries to help defend the empire's lengthy borders.

Diocletian also attempted the purge of an annoying quasi-Jewish religion called Christianity, which had a stubborn history of only about 250 years. More than a few Romans, Diocletian included, noticed that Rome's turbulent third century coincided with tens of thousands of these Christians turning their backs on the Roman gods in favor of the Christian one. This correlation, they felt, could not be a coincidence.

Perhaps worse, from the emperor's perspective, was that these monotheists rejected the claim that emperors were demigods, a popular ancient tactic meant to intimidate subjects. As a result, many emperors targeted Christians for persecution. The first century's notorious Nero lit them on fire as torches to light the Roman night. Second century emperor Trajan, according to Pliny the Younger, gave Christians three chances to renounce their religion before being executed. Diocletian's predecessors in the mid-third century, including Decius and Valerian, also ordered aggressive Christian hunts and executions. Despite these efforts, Christianity continued its determined rise.

The Diocletianic Persecutions aimed to set them straight. Under Diocletian, Christian martyrs died by the thousands. They were imprisoned, tortured, fed to lions, and lit on fire, often in front of applauding arenas.

Although Diocletian's rule did indeed momentarily restore Roman strength, many of his initiatives later backfired. The Tetrarchy eventually turned on itself. Many of the Germans hired to defend Rome later betrayed their Roman generals and sided with their own kind north of the border.

And his persecutions failed. The executions, meant to terrify Christians and curb their religion's growth, actually strengthened the resolve of a determined minority. Christians believed waiting for them after agony and death was eternal happiness.[4] Worse for Diocletian, Christianity's growth had reached the army; many of the men charged with arresting and executing Christians were Christian soldiers who, of course, refused to execute, and then they, too, were persecuted.[5] All the while, Christianity grew. If ever a leader fought an uphill battle with his citizens, it was Diocletian against his Christians.

Constantine's reign began a few years after Diocletian's. He was born in 272. His father, Constantius, was a high-ranking officer in the Roman army, and he rose to become emperor of the western half of Diocletian's divided empire. When Constantius died in 306, his soldiers proclaimed the 34-year-old Constantine, a talented general, as the next Western emperor. Other generals and members of the tenuous Tetrarchy disagreed. Civil wars followed. Constantine ultimately ended these post-Diocletian wars through a series of military triumphs over numerous challengers, culminating in 312's Battle of the Milvian Bridge against the

---

[4] For many, that wasn't even a difficult decision. Many emperors, including Diocletian, often offered condemned Christians a way out of execution if they just made some token signal to the emperor or sacrifice to a pagan God. Most refused, for fear that such a gesture would derail them from their track to heaven. You can imagine the Roman leadership's frustration at trying to persecute a people whose greatest goal might have been to die as horribly as Jesus did.

[5] Some Christian soldiers faced one of the more brutal military punishments—decimation, which took the head of every tenth soldier (dec = ten) who refused to comply.

last remaining claimant, Maxentius. With his victory, Constantine became the unrivaled emperor of Western Rome.

The battle's importance, however, goes well beyond validating Constantine's ascension to co-emperor. Just as significant was to what Constantine attributed the success.

There are two popular versions of Constantine's experiences before Milvian Bridge. The first is that Jesus visited Constantine in a dream and told him to paint crosses on his soldiers' shields. The second is that before or maybe even during the battle, Constantine saw a vision in the sky: a cross and the words in hoc signo vinces—"in this sign, conquer." Neither story has historical validity, but it's historically important that Constantine at least claims that the God of the cross—Jesus—must have interfered and spurred his forces to victory.

Subsequently, Constantine went to great lengths to show his appreciation to the religion. That started the following year with the Edict of Milan, signed jointly with the emperor of Eastern Rome, Licinius, which decriminalized Christianity.

Did Constantine actually see a vision? Probably not. He had every political motivation to tolerate this growing religion—he just needed a reason to do so. He strove to reunify and strengthen the empire under his rule, and he felt that the resources spent on, and internal strife caused by, the endless effort to snuff out a growing faith seemed counterproductive. Still, he needed a reason to reverse centuries of Roman policy, and fabricating the Milvian Bridge vision served as a means to that end.

Much to Christians' delight, his fondness for them wasn't just political.[6] The stronger he grew—a decade after signing the Edict of Milan with Licinius, he defeated him in battle and became the sole emperor of Rome—the more he supported Christianity. He returned churches commandeered during the persecutions. He recognized Christianity's clerical hierarchy, including the bishop of Rome's primacy. He promoted Christians within his government at faster rates than pagans. He offered bishoprics across the empire tax exemptions and other forms of imperial patronage, including gifts and legal immunities.

All of a sudden, it became attractive and profitable to be Christian. Pagan priests felt pressure to convert themselves and their flocks. In return for his patronage, Constantine only requested loyalty, subordination, and good behavior, which Christian leadership largely provided.

But Constantine wasn't done spurring along this growing religion. He also remedied its most pressing problem.

Heading into Constantine's reign in the early fourth century, Christianity lacked clarity. It didn't know what Jesus was or what he wanted, but it seemed everyone had an opinion.

Christianity's Ante-Nicene Period—Christian history before the Nicene Creed of 325—was a mess. Scores of independent sects dotted the Mediterranean. Fourth century estimates from Christian giants Epiphanius and Augustine counted over 80 interpretations of

---

[6] His devoutly Christian mother, Helena, likely had much to do with that.

Christianity.[7] Many of these denominations disdained each other, dubbing foes as heretics. Rival bishops exchanged hateful letters. Violence erupted between Christian communities.

Problematically, Christianity spread before the New Testament codified into a solid canon in the third century. Mark, likely the earliest Gospel, didn't begin writing until three decades after Jesus's death. The latest, John, dates close to the year 100. In either case, no Gospel author had ever met Jesus nor were they working from any verifiable sources, as his deceased apostles were illiterate. Therefore, decades after his death, much of Jesus's life was based on hearsay, and it's this hearsay that the Gospels recorded. The other bulk of the New Testament, the writings of Paul of Tarsus, were similarly full of conjecture about Jesus's life, as Paul claims only to have met Christ's apparition after the crucifixion.

As a result of these multiple voices speaking after Jesus's death and the slow spread of these ideas across the Mediterranean region, his ideas evolved. Pockets of Christian communities drew their own conclusions at different times from competing texts.

The underlying disagreement between the most powerful sects involved the nature of Jesus. Was he God? Was he human? Was he somewhere in between? There were many different ideas about whom or what he was, and the Gospels held competing accounts. Some preferred John, the only book where Jesus promotes himself as a divine figure. Others

---

[7] Among the most popular were Adoptionism, Arianism, Docetism, the Ebionites, Donatism, Montanism, and several Gnostic groups, but there were many, many more.

preferred the Synoptic Gospels of Matthew, Mark, and Luke (synoptic meaning of "one eye," as they were more similar to each other than they were with John), which did not promote Jesus as fully divine.

Among those with the latter view was a popular Christian leader named Arius, leader of a sizable following of Arians throughout the empire. He argued vehemently that Jesus was only partly divine. In the early days of the thorny debate over the Holy Trinity, Arius reasoned, "If the Father begat the Son, he that was begotten had a beginning of existence: and from this it is evident, that there was a time when the Son was not." In other words, Jesus the Son didn't always exist, and therefore he cannot be God the Father, an eternal figure.

Ultimately, a wide spectrum emerged with "Jesus is God" on one end and "Jesus was but an inspired, mortal teacher" on the other, with gradations in between. Considering Jesus occupied the central place in the new religion, this crucial question tore at Christianity's poorly woven fabric. This was the discombobulated Christianity inherited by Constantine in the early fourth century.

It wouldn't do. Constantine's goal was to reign alone over a powerful, stable, unified empire. Accepting Christianity was a means to that end. Little did he know—it should be noted that he understood little about Christianity, including its theology and early divisions—that the Christian community was itself divided.

To rectify this problem, in 325 Constantine called together the Council of Nicaea, a gathering of Christian bishops. Many topics were on the docket (including how to handle lapsed Christians, when to celebrate

Easter, and when to kneel), but the largest issue was Jesus's nature. Only about a sixth of the empire's 1,800 bishops attended, many of whom were local and therefore shared similar beliefs, chiefly that Jesus was fully divine.

The Council formalized this dogma, and out came the Nicene Creed. The creed, the beginning of which was this column's epigraph, takes great pains to make it absolutely clear that Jesus was one with God and "not made." Arius and his followers, as a result of Nicaea, were henceforth labeled as heretics.[8] Jesus was officially God.

Constantine then worked to suppress all dissent. He pressured bishops to endorse the creed and withdrew the now relied-upon imperial patronage from any churches in the empire who did not adopt the freshly official version of Christianity. He faced push-back, of course, but dissenting opinions gradually faded. Within a century, Christianity not only pervaded the empire, but one particular interpretation stood much taller than the rest. This "Constantinian shift" dramatically altered Western religion.[9]

In 330, Constantine relocated the Roman capital from Rome to the ancient Greek city of Byzantium on the Bosphorus Straight. The city of Rome made for a lousy base. First, it was deep in the empire, far from

---

[8] Arianism did not go without a fight, however, as missionaries helped it thrive among Germanic tribes to Rome's north.

[9] Of course, that one interpretation would later split. What became known as Roman Catholicism eventually separated from what became known as Eastern Orthodox. Later, there were further divisions still.

spots where important military and economic decisions had to be made. Second, the eastern half of the empire had far more wealth. Byzantium sat on the trade route between Europe and Asia, and its proximity to the wealthy areas of the Middle East and Egypt made it more lucrative. Third, with water surrounding most of it, Byzantium could be more easily defended, while the Germanic tribes in the west were always within one powerful invasion of breaking through the big northern border.

Constantine therefore moved the seat of government, and Rome was no longer the capital of its eponymous empire. He renamed his new capital Constantinople–city of Constantine[10]–and made it the first major Christian city. He poured into it imperial funds, constructing beautiful churches and monuments of Jesus and himself. The Holy Land received similar constructions; he commissioned the Church of the Nativity, supposed site of Jesus's birth, and the Church of the Holy Sepulchre, supposed site of his crucifixion.

In 337, Constantine took gravely ill. Knowing death was near, he requested a baptism. Shortly before passing into eternal rest, Constantine became history's first Christian head of state.

Constantine left behind a Western culture transforming from its pagan roots to its Christian flowering. A group that once met secretly, perpetually fearful of getting snuffed out, began to proselytize. Ancient

---

[10] Oh, the humility!

polytheism came under assault from both the church and state. Money flowed from pagan temples to Christian coffers. The old temples grew endangered and eventually extinct. This fourth century process might be the largest reallocation of property and wealth in history.

By 380, in the reign of Emperor Theodosius, Nicene Christianity became the official religion of the Roman Empire. It was a remarkable evolution. Christianity came into the fourth century as a banned religion. It left the fourth century as the state's formal faith. Constantine's decriminalization of it marked the turning point.

Of course, it's never that simple. If it were, if Constantine truly took a religion from death's doorstep and catalyzed its growth into the world's largest, he could lay claim to being in this list's Top 10. However, it must be understood that Christianity gained considerable strength before Constantine even took the throne.

Sketchy population numbers cloud late antiquity, but some appraisals give us a basic picture of Christianity's growth. Historian Ian Morris, in "Why the West Rules—For Now," estimates that by the year 250, about one million Christians populated the empire, or one in every forty Romans. Morris approximates that Christianity grew at an average of three percent each year. Therefore, its slow start rapidly escalated thanks in part to what Morris cleverly describes as "compound interest." He estimates that 60 years later, in 310—essentially on the eve of Constantine's Edict of Milan—there were ten million

Christians, or one in four Romans.[11] Constantine surely perceived such a staggering upsurge, which explains why he sought a way to bring Christians into the fold. Christianity was already a runaway train; Constantine just shoveled more coal into its engine.

Still, Constantine is colossally important for other reasons. First, it's worth noting that while he did inherit an empire that was one-quarter Christian, within a century of his ascent, it was almost *fully* Christian. That doesn't happen without imperial support, or at least it doesn't happen in time for the stagnant Middle Ages, when news traveled slowly and ideas slower. Once Constantine ensured Christianity's spread to all corners of the West, the Middle Ages filled the region's remaining pagan cracks with Christian cement.[12]

Perhaps more importantly, modern mainstream Christians have his Council of Nicaea to thank for the fact that their religion even has a coherent theology. One can understand why early medieval Christians did their best to rewrite these years. An emperor with no understanding of Christianity determined what Christianity came to be, a concept later

---

[11] Christianity's intense growth of the third century is usually attributed to three factors: its proselytizing foundation (Matthew 28:19-20 asserts Jesus's desire for his apostles to "go and make disciples of all nations"); its acceptance of all people regardless of creed, knowledge, enthusiasm, or other shibboleth; and the dire circumstances of the Roman Empire during its most troubled years. When one is poor and the sky is falling, a religion confidently promising eternal happiness after death is pretty appealing. Christianity's (especially Catholicism's) continued spread after Constantine will be addressed in forthcoming chapters.

[12] Assist to Charlemagne, an imminent Top 30 figure.

known as Caesaropapism—Caesar as the pope. He helped codify what was ultimately a subjective choice made by a majority of a few hundred bishops who outvoted the minority. They said Jesus was God, and it stuck.

Furthermore, he actively worked to suppress dissent and any theological inquiry, a precedent adopted by the Catholic Church for a millennium while it controlled the West. It was a direct reversal of Greco-Roman curiosity championed by the likes of Aristotle (#30) and other classical thinkers. Constantine's policies helped usher in medieval thinking.

There's more. Recall the move of the Roman capital to Constantinople. Such a move had enormous consequences for the empire. For starters, Constantine didn't move alone. With him went large parts of the government, military, and treasury. While the eastern part of the empire strengthened, the western half deteriorated. After the two halves officially split in 395, the Western Roman Empire's days were numbered. In 476 it was gone.[13]

The move had another remarkable effect on Western civilization. While Constantine's considerable entourage included government officials and the military, it did not include the bishop of Rome, who stayed behind.

---

[13] The deprioritized West faced devastating raids from the Visigoths (410), Vandals (455), and a 476 invasion led by the Germanic king Odoacer, who deposed the last Western Roman Emperor, Romulus Augustus. The Eastern Roman Empire, buoyed by the presence of the real Roman government, survived another thousand years.

Rome's bishop was considered the preeminent bishop in all of Christendom; tradition held that Peter, to whom Jesus had passed his movement before the crucifixion, was martyred there. After Peter's death, the next Roman bishop tended to the city, and this apostolic baton-passing continued for centuries. After Constantine's move hastened the shift of political authority and personnel to the east, western bishops, all of whom looked up to the Roman bishop, filled the power vacuum. By the time of the Western Roman Empire's collapse, the bishop of Rome became the only unifying figure in western Europe. As such, many started calling him *papa*, or father. English speakers call him the pope. The absence of a strong Western ruler allowed the Catholic Church's rise to power, and Constantine's move east led to this absence.

However, as Dostoyevsky's Inquisitor suggests, Jesus would not have endorsed what the Catholic Church became. Constantine set the precedent that elite Christians determine the truth, and everyone else must follow along or face punishment, exile, and perhaps death, a policy that guided monarchs and popes for centuries. The Church governed with the institutional memory that at one time it was a scattered, persecuted group, and it therefore must show unity and strength.[14]

---

[14] "Freedom, a free mind and science will lead them into such a jungle and bring them face to face with such marvels and insoluble mysteries that some of them will destroy themselves, others will destroy one another, and the rest, weak and unhappy, will come crawling to our feet and cry aloud: 'Yes, you were right, you alone possess this mystery and we come back to you—save us from ourselves.'"

And though the Church's power has weakened since the Middle Ages, the creed laid down at Constantine's palace in Nicaea remains an assumed truth of modern Christianity. Early Christians' rival interpretations, and perhaps the true intentions of Jesus himself, were swept under history's rug. Jesus is Christians' Lord and Savior.

Due to the ramifications of Constantine's embrace of Christianity, his leadership in steering it to a coherent theology, and the long-reaching effects of his move east, he is the 23rd most influential person in Western history.

#22: Voltaire

"To hold a pen is to be at war."

–Voltaire, 1748

In each of these entries, I show how a certain historical figure upended conventional wisdom or redirected the course of Western history. What I often leave out is how some facets of history remain remarkably similar across large swaths of time.

Up until pretty recently, one of the more embarrassing constants of post-Roman history was a tripartite social order that allowed for almost no fluidity. These old groups were often described as "those who pray, those who fight, and those who work"–priests in the first group, nobility in the second, and everyone else in the third.

This old model came under sustained attack in the eighteenth century, during a period called the Enlightenment. With many converts to the new way of thinking, including from prominent political leaders, the old hierarchy began to fade. While many of the Enlightenment's philosophers contributed to these developments, their undisputed patriarch and hero was François-Marie Arouet, a courageous champion of personal

Voltaire

liberties and a devastating enemy of *le Ancien Régime*. We know him better as Voltaire, and now you should know him as the 22nd most influential figure in Western history.

François-Marie Arouet was born in 1694. His father was a successful Parisian lawyer, so François-Marie was born into the upper end of "those who work." As such, he was given a quality Jesuit education. After attempting law school on orders from his father, he discovered that the serious, strict world of law was not for him. From a young age, others found him funny, and he had a remarkable talent for writing. As a teenager, he wrote creative poetry and insightful historical analyses.

He converted these talents into a successful writing career. Essayist, historian, novelist, pamphleteer, philosopher, playwright, and poet, Arouet was the preeminent eighteenth century Western writer. At 30,000 pages, his body of work makes him the most prolific writer of this ranking.

In time, however, he learned that reasonable means, a keen intellect, and a mile-long résumé were not enough to rise into the upper crust of Western society. France had long ago formalized its three social groups into the First, Second, and Third Estates of the Estates General, a body first formed by early fourteenth century King Philip IV (#29). Though it rarely met anymore, its segregated structure loomed over France's rigid social order.

A bitter Arouet targeted the unreachable upper classes of French society. He wrote essays that took informed swipes at royalty and religion, infusing them with an accessible cleverness.[1] Unfortunately, in

---

[1] *"If God has made us in his image, we have returned him the favor."*

early eighteenth century France, cleverness did not immunize anyone with anti-monarchical or anticlerical points of view. In 1717, at 23 years of age, a jab at Duke Philippe d'Orléans[2] landed Arouet in the Bastille prison.

Making the most of his 11-month prison stint, he wrote a play, *Oedipus*, based on the Sophocles classic. He published it under a pen name, "Voltaire"—an anagram of "Arovet Li," his Latinized last name. After his release from the Bastille, *Oedipus* debuted to acclaim in 1718. It grew to be, as described by later French historians Jean-Pierre Vernant and Pierre Vidal-Naquet, "the greatest dramatic success of eighteenth century France." Only 24, Voltaire became renowned across the country, a fame he never relinquished. For the rest of his long life, he remained France's, and later Europe's, top literary persona.

After the success of *Oedipus*, Voltaire wrote extensively, eagerly accruing more celebrity and fortune in the process. It was then that this commoner began to move in aristocratic circles. Known for his sharp tongue, peerless wit, and brilliant conversational ability, he was often the life of the party. Perhaps feeling like he belonged, the flamboyant Voltaire did his best to resemble his noble hosts; he dressed like them, attended their gatherings, and, like a good aristocrat, spent showy gobs of money.

This overconfidence ultimately precipitated a turning point in Voltaire's life. His colorful behavior soon attracted negative attention. The wealthy enjoyed his company, but perhaps more as their amusement than their equal. He may have been a talented, rich commoner, but a commoner he remained.

---

[2] **Lord of the lands once liberated by Joan of Arc (#27).**

Voltaire

At no point was Voltaire's relegated status clearer to him than in 1725, when he engaged in a minor verbal spat with a haughty member of the French nobility, the Chevalier de Rohan. Voltaire, the intellectual superior of just about anyone on the continent, got the better of the exchange. Rohan took it personally and hired men to give Voltaire a beating while Rohan watched from his carriage. Worse still, Rohan, using a noble's prerogative, purchased a *lettre de cachet* from King Louis XV, which allowed him to arrest and send Voltaire back to the Bastille without cause or trial. Voltaire offered a self-imposed exile instead, which the Crown accepted.

Distraught at this insulting yet perfectly lawful development, Voltaire traveled to France's more liberal arch rival—Great Britain. He stayed for over two years and developed great respect for its constitutional monarchy, bill of rights, tolerance of free speech, and adherence to habeas corpus. While there was British nobility, an aristocrat could not legally assault and imprison a commoner. Britain's due process of law forbade it. Voltaire quickly admired English culture and history, and he immersed himself in the English titans of thought—William Shakespeare, John Locke, and Isaac Newton.[3]

When he returned to France in 1729, he published a collection of essays called "Letters Concerning the English Nation," a gushing evaluation of England's religion, economics, politics, and art. This praise was often paired with favorable comparisons to France. This glowing review of an adversary earned him another exile from Paris.

He next moved to Cirey in eastern France, allowing him a quick escape from the country if needed. Voltaire studied and wrote some more.

---

[3] All of whom make our list—and all in the top 10.

He also corresponded with Frederick the Great, King of Prussia.[4] Frederick eventually extended an invitation to Voltaire, who happily made the visit. During his two decades in Cirey and Prussia, Voltaire produced work after work, including one of the first pieces of modern science fiction, Micromégas.[5] Each publication became a must-read across the continent. He had become a European celebrity.

Resisting this upsurge in popularity was a French King and Catholic Church that despised Voltaire. They outlawed and burned many of his books.[6] This censorship, of course, spurred Voltaire all the more. Ironically, his banned works became even more valuable. They'd be printed outside France's borders then smuggled into the country. Voltaire denied many of these writings, though there was no mistaking his inimitable prose.

He lambasted the divine right of kings, which argued that the will of the king, appointed there by God Himself, is above the law. He also criticized unrealistic Biblical tales and the unthinking masses believing every

---

[4] King Frederick, though nowhere near a Top 30 influential figure of the West, is still one of the more fascinating leaders in history. He personified the "Philosopher King" promoted by Voltaire, Plato (#30), and others. He was a brilliant leader and military campaigner, but also religiously tolerant, a modernizer, a patron of the arts and sciences, and, most incredibly, an accomplished flutist and composer. I was astonished when, listening to a classical YouTube playlist, I was enjoying a symphony which turned out to be written by the former King of Prussia. Incredible.

[5] Enormous and intelligent aliens visit Earth and learn about us. They ultimately determine that we're pretty stupid because, among other reasons, we believe a god created the universe especially for humanity. Classic Voltaire.

[6] "It is dangerous to be right when the government is wrong."

Voltaire

word.[7] He attacked censorship, intolerance, and an autocratic state and Church. Most insulting to these powerful Europeans, Voltaire's main strategy was satire. The "Genius of Mockery" picked apart archaic and irrational positions supported by secular and clerical leadership. In 1758, at 64, he settled down in Ferney, again in eastern France, again allowing him a quick escape if needed, though he often toyed with the unrealistic option of returning home to Paris.

It was during this latter period where he wrote his famous "Candide, ou l'Optimisme." "Candide" criticizes the philosophy of German Gottfried Leibniz, who had done his best to explain the paradox of evil coexisting with an omnipotent and benevolent God.[8] The title character, the eponymous Candide, gradually realizes just how awful the world can be, while his straw man mentor Pangloss, who represents Leibniz's absurd rationalizations, insists that it's all for the greater good. While Pangloss comes across a fool, Candide argues for a much more pragmatic approach: the best way to forge through a scary world is to acknowledge that life isn't perfect, to work hard despite that, to accept responsibility, and to laugh. "Candide" was greeted by scandalous reviews which saw it

---

[7] *"Our [religion] is without a doubt the most ridiculous, the most absurd, and the most blood-thirsty ever to infect the world."*

[8] Leibniz argued that we live in the "best of all possible worlds." Evil and unfortunate events exist not only because of free will, which had been the blanket explanation at least since St. Augustine (354-430), but because evil can bring out of us more goodness. There is no perseverance without strife, no lesson learned without a challenge, no courage without danger. God, in His omnipotent benevolence, would never give humanity too little evil that we would not be challenged, nor would he give humanity too much evil that we could not overcome it. He therefore gave us a universe with the perfect amount of evil so we can summon the perfect amount of goodness to defeat it. The best of all possible worlds.

131

as blasphemous and a far too flippant analysis of God's goodness. Many saw it as an anti-Jesuit, anti-missionary, and anti-Inquisition[9] piece of literature. Now, however, it is not only considered Voltaire's greatest literary achievement, but potentially France's. It is regularly included in the elite canon of Western literature.

While in Ferney, he continued correspondences with the top minds across Europe. Voltaire was incensed when, in 1762, he learned of the French Protestant Jean Calas, who was wrongly sentenced to torture and death for the killing of his son who was purportedly converting to Catholicism.[10] Voltaire redoubled his efforts against religious intolerance.[11] He began ending all his letters with "*Ecrasez l'infame*"—crush the infamous. He wanted to destroy the residual medievalism found in religious fanaticism and royal tyranny.[12] He scorned the privileges of the Church, Crown, and nobility.[13] The rest of his life focused on concentrating the Enlightenment against the advantaged elite. Many rallied to his cause.

---

[9] Somehow still around in the eighteenth century.

[10] Calas was tortured in an attempt to induce a guilty plea. His arms and legs were stretched until they ripped out of their sockets. Seventeen liters of water were poured down his throat. He was tied down in a public square where his limbs were broken by iron bars. He maintained his innocence through his death, which was delivered via the merciless bludgeoning of the breaking wheel. (And how is your week going? Oh, you're kind of tired and your boss is getting under your skin? I'm so sorry.)

[11] "Every sensible man, every honorable man, must hold the Christian sect in horror."

[12] "As long as people believe in absurdities they will continue to commit atrocities."

[13] "Men are equal; it is not birth, but virtue that makes the difference."

Voltaire

Though France's leaders were never able to take him down, age eventually did. At 83, he published his final play, *Irène*. To see its March 1778 debut, Voltaire finally made his way back to Paris, the home that had not welcomed him for four decades. The bumpy five-day trip from Ferney nearly killed him.[14] Fortunately, he briefly recovered.

Word of his arrival preceded him, and throngs of Parisians welcomed their returning hero. When it came time to attend the show, he was welcomed to the theater with a sustained standing ovation that moved him to tears. For the last two months of his life, a slew of actors, writers, philosophers, and scholars, including the American Benjamin Franklin, came to pay their last respects to the legendary Voltaire, France's apostle of the Enlightenment.

Then he died and was refused a Christian burial.

In an era where French culture and ideas were the hub of Western thought, Voltaire was the hub of French culture and ideas. No other philosopher had a career as long, a voice as creative, a body of work as large, or a readership as widespread.

With such strong-minded and ubiquitous material, he was likely the most divisive figure of the era. Opposed to the divine right of kings, hereditary leadership, and the aristocracy's superiority, Voltaire was despised by the monarchs and nobility who tasted his ridicule.[15] A champion of freedom of thought and religion, he was also abhorred by the

---

[14] In fact, on February 28, fearing he was about to die, he jotted what he thought would be his last written sentence: *"I die adoring God, loving my friends, not hating my enemies, and detesting superstition."*

[15] *"In my life, I have prayed but one prayer: oh Lord, make my enemies ridiculous. And God granted it."*

Catholic Church, which suffered his scathing satire that asked people to question beliefs that had for so long been considered unassailable truths.[16] All the while, he was a hero and inspiration to countless commoners, many of whom went on to have history-altering careers of their own. Rousseau, Diderot, Montesquieu, Thomas Jefferson (#24), and many more Enlightenment thinkers were brilliant in their own right, but they all looked up to Voltaire and recognized his preeminence.

As more philosophers and political scientists embraced him, Voltaire's ideas went mainstream. They promulgated freedom of religion, thought, and speech across the West.[17] His full-throated defense of liberty and equality over mysticism and tyranny echoed off every cathedral and palace in Europe. In time, these ideas crossed the Atlantic and were used by the American founding fathers as they justified their rebellion against the British Empire and laid the framework for the later liberties found in the U.S. Bill of Rights. The new country later went on to export and defend Voltaire's cherished principles across the world.

In his own country, Voltaire died on the eve of its revolution. A decade after his death, thanks to the underpinnings laid by him for six decades, momentum had gathered enough to overthrow King Louis XVI and the archaic Estates General. The new government also strongly curtailed the strength of the Church. It was an annihilation of the *Ancien*

---

[16] "If God did not exist, it would be necessary to invent him."

[17] Disappointingly, the free-speech quote most associated with Voltaire is misattributed: "I may not agree with what you have to say, but I will defend to the death your right to say it." It's too bad that wasn't him, because the quote does sum up his speech position pretty well. Its author is actually Evelyn Beatrice Hall, who wrote it in a 1906 Voltaire biography.

Régime, Voltaire's "infamous thing" that he dedicated much of his life to crushing.

His role was recognized by the new government. He may have been denied a Christian burial, which forced his friends to bury him in a secret ceremony, but 13 years after his death, he was exhumed by revolutionary France. The new National Assembly, correctly recognizing Voltaire as a forefather of the cause, enshrined him in the Panthéon, a neoclassical mausoleum that houses notable French citizens. Voltaire's second funeral was attended by a million people who surrounded their exhumed hero. Even as a corpse, Voltaire had the last laugh over the Catholic Church.

While autocracy did not go without a fight in France or the rest of Europe, the rest of the West did eventually follow the new model. There were many revolutions for liberal reform over the next hundred years, and Western nations did eventually convert. In the twentieth century, moreover, the West's nations and international bodies have worked to instill certain liberal ideas across the world: free speech, free worship, free thought, civil liberties. Wherever these concepts exist, so, too, does Voltaire. The result has been a completely revolutionized West.

Society has changed more in the last three centuries than it had in the three millennia before. Many people are to thank, but few more than François-Marie Arouet. Because of his brave and ultimately successful crusade to liberalize the Western world, Voltaire is the 22nd most influential figure in Western history.

#21: Charlemagne

"The most famous and greatest of men."

-Einhard, "The Life of Charlemagne"

In the fifth century, Western civilization went dark. After the fall of the Western Roman Empire, infrastructure crumbled, trade slowed, schools closed, literacy dwindled, aqueducts collapsed, and voracious barbarians feasted on Rome's cold corpse. What some historians call the "Dark Ages," comprising about the first half of the Middle Ages, would last hundreds of years.[1]

But there was a bright spot. A few centuries into this dreary era, one leader reconstructed much of what was lost. He didn't just try to re-

---

[1] The "Dark Ages" as a term for the Middle Ages is problematic. It first came into use in the fourteenth century with Petrarch (he of the "Next 30" for his work with Cicero's texts and contributions to the Italian Renaissance), and it kind of stuck. Only in more recent history has further study revealed that the Middle Ages weren't without merit, particularly in the latter half. For the first half, historians now often use the term "Low" or "Early" Middle Ages. Although this earlier period, too, had its contributions, one can be excused for referring to it as a relatively dark period, as I did in the first sentence of this chapter.

Charlemagne

assemble much of Rome's land—he tried to reassemble its culture. His name was Charlemagne, King of the Franks, Emperor of the Romans, the Grandfather of Europe, and the 21st most influential figure in Western history.

Charlemagne was the greatest king of the Middle Ages. It's fair to ask, however, whether "greatest _____ of the Middle Ages" means much of anything. After all, aren't the Middle Ages rather unimpressive?

Yes and no. It is true that the Middle Ages, as the name implies, is often seen as the underappreciated middle child of Western history.[2] Its first half, the Early Middle Ages (c. 400-c. 1000), was particularly rough. Compared to antiquity and modernity, few bright minds or advancements graced the first part of the Middle Ages; there was less original literature, construction, science, and exploration. For centuries, most western Europeans were distracted by salvation and survival. The fact that no other medieval rulers even rival Charlemagne's greatness further reveals the era's relative mediocrity.

This unique stature, however, also makes Charlemagne's accomplishments all the more astounding. In a time of pervasive darkness, a lone star brightened western Europe like no time since Rome.

Before Charlemagne was Charlemagne, he was just Charles.[3] He was born in 742 to Pepin the Short, the King of the Franks, and his wife, Big

---

[2] It's a derogatory term, the "Middle Ages." Almost as an afterthought, it's in the "middle" of the great ancient and modern eras, as if we couldn't give it a better name than merely describing when it was in comparison to our beloved first child and the one on which we now dote.

[3] Truth be told it was Karl in his native German; Charles is just the Anglicized version of our history books.

Foot Bertha.⁴ The Franks were one of the many Germanic tribes that replaced the Western Roman Empire after its fall. Under their leaders of the sixth, seventh, and eighth centuries, they built a kingdom in northwest Europe, part of which was in the old Roman province of Gaul, a territory that rested about where France is now. In fact, it's the Frankish Kingdom that eventually evolved into France, the nation to which the Franks lent their name.

Pepin was the son of Charles Martel, who had led a successful Frankish defense of a Muslim invasion in 732. He then founded the Carolingian Dynasty (Charles/Karl Latinized into Carolus), a family into which both Pepin and Charlemagne were born and after which the Charlemagne-led Carolingian Renaissance was later named.⁵ Pepin and Bertha had two surviving sons, Charles and Carloman. Upon Pepin's death in 768, the two sons inherited and split the Frankish Kingdom.

The reason for the split was due to the Frankish custom of Salic Law, which decreed that inherited land be split among all male heirs.⁶ The custom predictably led to bickering between feuding brothers, acrimony

---

⁴ That's right, I said Big Foot Bertha. She was known as *"Berthe au grand pied,"* so you tell me. Of course, what makes this all the funnier is that this large, broad-footed woman married a man named Pepin "the Short."

⁵ This is not the last we hear of Martel. Stay tuned.

⁶ Salic Law began with the first king of all the Franks, Clovis, in the late fifth century. His faction of Franks, called the Salian Franks, had just consolidated rule over the other Frankish subgroups. Clovis (who French history considers the first of France's 19 Louises) decreed that upon his death, all four of his sons would share the kingdom. The Franks continued this precedent set by their unifier. No other notable medieval civilization adopted such a system, opting instead for the cleaner primogeniture—the eldest son or closest male heir inherits everything.

sometimes resolved by warfare or murder. Charles and Carloman careened toward war when, in 771, Carloman unexpectedly died.[7] Charles, then 29, assumed power over the entire kingdom and embarked on the path that earned him the nickname "Charlemagne"—Charles the Great.

Charlemagne inherited Big Foot Bertha's, not Pepin the Short's, height. It's hard to know for sure, but estimates have him as tall as 6' 3". In the modern West, someone of that height would find themselves taller than about 98 percent of the population. Among the malnourished medieval masses, such height could intimidate. Back that height with the Frankish army, and few in his kingdom dared oppose him.

He set out to build a large, organized, and, accomplished kingdom. Reigning from 768 to 814, he went on over 50 war campaigns in 45 years. From modern France, his forces spread east into modern Germany (to conquer Bavarians and Saxons), south across the Pyrenees (to fight Muslims), and southeast into modern Italy (to conquer the Lombards).[8] Thousands fell in front of his army. At the height of his empire in the early ninth century, Charlemagne controlled western Europe from the English Channel to the edge of the Balkan Peninsula, from Rome to the North Sea. In the process, he reunited much of the Western Roman Empire that had collapsed three centuries earlier (although not Iberia or

---

[7] The cause of death was said to have been a "severe nosebleed," an explanation that feels a bit empty, especially considering Carloman's wife and children then fled, were pursued by Charles's forces and never heard from again. That's some nosebleed! Quite the gusher.

[8] The Bavarians, Saxons, and Lombards lent their names to the modern areas of Bavaria and Saxony in Germany and Lombardy in Italy. Cool, right?

southern Italy), and he even added some northern European territories that Rome never controlled.

Wherever he conquered, he infused his other priorities. Foremost here is his Roman Catholicism. Thanks to King Clovis, the Franks were the first Germanic tribe to practice the faith. The other tribes were mostly Arian—a Christian sect considered heretical since the Council of Nicaea[9]—or pagan. Charlemagne felt it his duty to spread the "correct" faith practiced by the Bishop of Rome, the apostolic descendent of Peter. He forced thousands of non-Catholics, including Christians and non-Christians, to convert. Many who refused were executed.[10] Western and central Europe steadily turned Catholic at the behest of Charlemagne's sword.

His most notable defense of the Church came when Roman nobles assaulted Pope Leo III.[11] Leo pleaded with Charlemagne to restore order, and Charlemagne did so with his typical efficiency. The Franks had become the Pope's right arm, and King Charlemagne his fist.

Leo seized the opportunity. Late in 800, Charlemagne visited Rome to confer with the Pope, and Leo invited the great Frank for Christmas Mass. As Charlemagne knelt in prayer, Leo placed a crown on the King's

---

[9] Discussed in more detail in my Constantine (#23) chapter.

[10] Perhaps a quarter of all Saxons were killed by Charlemagne's wars. Many of them fled to the old Roman province of Britannia, where, with the Angle tribe, they contributed toward creating an Anglo-Saxon culture in what became known as Angleland and then, in time, England.

[11] Pope Leo III had made enemies of his predecessor's family, and a few years after Leo's ascension to the papacy, they assaulted him. His attackers attempted to gouge out his eyeballs and rip out his tongue. Guards rescued him, but not before the assailants slashed at his eyes, leaving permanent scars on both eyelids.

Charlemagne

head. The prepared clergy in attendance boomed: "*Long life and victory to Charles Augustus, crowned by God the great and pacific emperor of the Romans.*" Just like that, Charlemagne, King of the Franks, got a promotion: Charlemagne, Emperor of the Romans—an "Augustus."[12]

Charlemagne did his best to live up to the lofty title of Roman emperor. He continued working to build a centralized, reformist state. A proto-Napoleon, Charlemagne managed his empire as closely as someone in the ninth century could. Like a father of his country, he felt it was his responsibility to care for his people. He wanted a safe and cultured empire.

Adapting to an upward trend in feudalism, Charlemagne gave counts and dukes throughout his empire some autonomy, though they ultimately answered to him—and they knew it. When not at war, he made visits throughout the empire, some unannounced. However, since he couldn't cover much ground, he also sent out royal inspectors—the *missi dominici*—to ensure his orders were executed and no plots were afoot. He enacted laws, dictated new ordinances, and sent royal judges out to hear cases. He held an annual convention of clergy and nobility to hear their thoughts and give them instructions. The sum of this policy produced the largest, most efficient, and safest western European state since Rome.

---

[12] This office later evolved into Holy Roman Emperor. Leo hoped that by resuscitating an empire that had been dead for 300 years, it could rival the Greek-speaking Byzantine Empire, where the Eastern Orthodox Church had steadily been acting independently of what he thought was his own sphere of influence. However, we should not consider Charlemagne a continuance of the old Roman emperors. The Holy Roman Empire had a new line of leaders for a new territory.

But efficient and safe were not the only attributes of a great empire. Charlemagne knew his history, and he knew the wonders achieved by the Greco-Roman world, so he tried to mirror it. The fruits of this labor fueled the Carolingian Renaissance.

To help trade and travel, he built bridges. He ordered a canal that connected the Danube with the Main. He promoted architectural achievements, the product of which has been dubbed Carolingian architecture. He commissioned beautiful abbeys and churches, including the medieval wonder that was his octagonal chapel at his palace in Aachen. By the mid-ninth century, the Carolingians had commissioned 27 new cathedrals, 417 monasteries, and a hundred royal residences.

He also wanted to renew the fading Latin culture that had given way to barbaric Europe. Latin itself had already eroded into vernacular tongues, but Charlemagne, hoping to help the Church and further unify his empire, wanted to resuscitate the dying language. Carolingian scholars copied classic Latin texts. The transcribers created a new writing style—Carolingian minuscule—which standardized, among other things, differentiated capital and lowercase letters. Most modern translations of these texts derive from these Carolingian copies, and there's a chance the texts would have perished without that effort, as few original works survived the period otherwise. Charlemagne ordered new libraries to house them, too.

Meanwhile, seeing value in intelligent government officials, he promoted educational reform. He was a bright man, familiar with the ancient thinkers. He spoke his native German, had a familiarity with Latin, and also dabbled in Greek. There were no jesters at his royal dinners; instead, his court listened to someone reading from the promoted text of the day. He attracted top scholars to his palace and commissioned them to write a curriculum and texts. One of these scholars, Alcuin of York, led the creation of a curriculum that taught the trivium (grammar, rhetoric, and logic) and the quadrivium (arithmetic, geometry, music, and astronomy). Both became staples of medieval universities.

Charlemagne founded monasteries across his empire to help create a literate clergy and more teachers. As a result, some Europeans received a standardized education not seen in centuries. Charlemagne then had a new crop of literate, learned nobility and government officials for his empire.[13]

In total, his campaign for a literate and cultured upper class was more remarkable than his many war campaigns. Warfare was common in the era. Learning was not. Low European literacy levels never again returned to such a nadir. Medieval nobility perpetuated their new skill and permanently became a literate class.

Meanwhile, the rest of the population, though never formally educated, also benefited from Charlemagne's reign. Not since ancient Rome was trade more viable (Charlemagne worked to shift the continent to a single silver currency), transportation safer, or the government so fair. The inspectors sent out by Charlemagne ensured that justice was applied

---

[13] A more psychoanalytic explanation for Charlemagne's passion toward schooling was that he grew up in a time where he wasn't taught to write and lamented the fact. As he grew, he took it upon himself to learn to read, but he didn't start writing young enough to do it competently. He confided to his biographer, Einhard, who described Charlemagne hiding his frustration. The great King hid tablets under his pillow, and, at night, when no one was looking, he tried to recreate the symbols that children formed so much more easily. Alas, his mammoth hands, which wielded a sword better than a pen, failed him. The man controlled half a continent, but writing was beyond him, and he knew it.

evenly. He personified a centralized state and the "enlightened despot" dreamed about by the likes of Plato (#30).

It seems as if Charlemagne's only major mistake was his conservative approach to the Franks' myopic succession process. With only one surviving son, Louis the Pious, Charlemagne felt comfortable leaving his empire to him. In 813, the 70-year-old Charlemagne even made Louis co-emperor to help ease the transition. However, he also passed the buck on the Salic Law that later doomed his empire. Later, Louis had three surviving sons—Lothair, Louis, and Charles—each of whom inherited a third of the empire and promptly engaged in a civil war when the pious Louis died in 840. Three years after that, the Treaty of Verdun officially split into three what their grandfather had worked so hard to make one.

Once the mighty Frankish Empire split, other factors contributed to the decline of what was left of it. Invaders took advantage of the squabbling states. Islam reaffirmed its foothold in Iberia and southern Italy. Slavs and Magyars moved into the Balkans and Hungary. Most famously, the Vikings made coastal and river raids across the continent.

Charlemagne died in 814 at the age of 71. He had little idea that his empire, which he spent the better part of 45 years expanding, strengthening, and improving, would collapse just a few decades later.

Did his legacy die with him? Some of it, surely. If he had spearheaded Europe's permanent renaissance into a flourishing culture, he could hypothetically be in this ranking's top 5. However, Europe's true Renaissance was still six centuries away. Not only did Charlemagne's empire fracture with the Treaty of Verdun and ensuing invasions, but the subsequent instability in western Europe partially reintroduced the darkness

Charlemagne

that Charlemagne attempted to relegate to history. The late ninth and tenth centuries were nearly as bleak as the sixth and seventh.

The scary post-Charlemagne world could not spare the resources for education. Raiders struck at random and the Carolingian heirs were too slow to intervene. As a result, most towns and villages turned into autonomous, self-sustaining communities. The heirs of Charlemagne's former vassals did not feel nearly the loyalty to the Frankish kings that their ancestors had felt toward the great Emperor. These vassals turned into lords of their own land and went on to largely ignore their kings. They lived behind castles with moats and walls for their own protection and arranged vassals of their own to subdivide and manage their land. They secured soldiers, usually led by sons of nobles (knights), and provided protection for the many peasants who would, in exchange, work the land. With strength in numbers seen as crucial in an unsettling time, all swore loyalty, resources, or protection to someone else. Communities became entirely self-sufficient. A local parish priest provided the spirituality. It's in the post-Charlemagne West that the feudal system reached its height.

Additionally, the Carolingian Renaissance was not only short-lived, it was also not particularly creative. Carolingian scholars produced relatively few original works. Scientifically, there was little advancement. Instead, the leading thinkers of the time merely copied manuscripts, cobbled together encyclopedias, and organized curricula on existing subjects.

Still, it's remarkable that in a flood of intellectual inadequacy, someone swam so hard against the current. It was probably first necessary to build a dam before the West could begin refilling its intellectual reservoir. By preserving old texts, he made it possible for the future to benefit from them.

In addition to intellectual preservation, there were also considerable political ramifications for Europe's development. Pope Leo's crowning of Charlemagne was not well-received by the Eastern Romans, who still saw themselves as the true empire and its emperors the true leaders of it. The remaining Roman Empire maintained dreams of reconquering the old west.[14]

This position was threatened by the crowning of a new emperor of Rome. Before Charlemagne, the West had been considered, at worst, barbaric wilderness, and at best, a satellite of Constantinople. His reign partially unified a distinct region that could not be confused with a barbarous outpost of the Eastern Roman Empire. Further, Charlemagne started the shift of power from east to west. By the eleventh century, the east humbled itself and asked the west for help against invading Muslims, starting the First Crusade.

Charlemagne's conquests and priorities were ultimately a harbinger of Europe's future. The breakaway from the East was not just political. The Latin languages, threatened by the Germanization of post-Roman Europe, reasserted themselves prominently alongside the Byzantines' Greek. Western culture, including art, broke away from Byzantine influence. Charlemagne solidified a "Western" culture. Indeed, without him, I wouldn't even be able to make a top 30 tanking of Western figures.[15]

---

[14] In the mid-sixth century, their great emperor Justinian was able to reconquer some of it, including Rome itself. Though the Byzantines eventually lost these lands, they still hoped reunification could be had.

[15] You may now curse his name.

Charlemagne

Another effect of Charlemagne's coronation was that by letting the Pope crown him, he gave future popes justification for crowning future kings. Although he wasn't the first king to have received papal assent, he was the first of his colossal reputation. It was a precedent that showed that if the greatest ruler of the Middle Ages needed the pope for his crown, then surely all other kings did as well. This coronation went a long way toward the papacy's efforts to control monarchs for the rest of the Middle Ages. Not until Philip IV of France (#29) would this dynamic change.

Meanwhile, Charlemagne's mission to spread Catholicism ingrained the faith into western Europe and blocked the Orthodox Church from spreading west. The lands he conquered remained staunchly Catholic for centuries, as did the lands conquered by those lands, like Spain and Portugal during the *Reconquista*. Lands conquered by *those* lands, like South and Central America, remain Catholic today. Catholicism, the world's largest denomination at 1.2 billion adherents, makes up half of Christianity. Charlemagne is a big reason why.

He also became the idol of nearly every royal to come after him. Charlemagne was the strongest man on the continent of Europe, becoming so not only through conquest but by barking orders to all corners of his empire, keeping it together with his bare hands. His accomplishments showed what an effective administrator could do. Later autocrats emulated him, though none rivaled his empire until Napoleon a full millennium later.

His squabbling heirs impacted European political geography as well. When the Treaty of Verdun divvied up his land, it also set a course for Europe's future. His western heirs became the kings of the Western Frankish Kingdom, which evolved into France. His eastern heirs inherited the land that became the Holy Roman Empire, which later evolved into Germany.[16] In his quest to be the father of his country, he became the Grandfather of Europe.

But above all, he'll be remembered as the greatest king of the Middle Ages. An exceptional leader during unexceptional times, Charlemagne is the 21st most influential figure in Western history.

---

[16] The Holy Roman Empire lasted until 1806, when Napoleon felt there was room for only one emperor in Europe and dissolved the entity. He replaced it with the Confederation of the Rhine, which was, in turn, replaced by the post-Napoleonic German Confederation. Finally, in 1871, the German state of Prussia capped a series of wars to unify the territory into the German Empire that would go on to fight in World War I.

#20: Henry Ford

"I will build a car for the great multitude. It will be large enough for the family, but small enough for the individual to run and care for. It will be constructed of the best materials, by the best men to be hired, after the simplest designs that modern engineering can devise. But it will be so low in price that no man making a good salary will be unable to own one."

—Henry Ford

When I conceived of this list, one of the first things I did was sort about a hundred contenders by profession. For the most part, each figure was easily placed under categories like statesman, philosopher, scientist, or inventor.[1]

When I came to Henry Ford, however, I hesitated. Ford wasn't exactly a scientist, nor can we say he was primarily an inventor. He didn't invent the car, the combustion engine, the assembly line, mass production, or interchangeable parts. Though he was a tinkerer, no invention of his changed the world.

---

[1] Of those fields, the final breakdown included eleven political and military leaders, seven philosophers, six scientists, and four inventors.

Who Made the West

And yet, change the world he did. It's hard to classify Henry Ford as anything—except, perhaps, as the 20th most influential figure in Western history.

The automobile, dubbed a "horseless carriage" by contemporaries, was invented in 1885 by German inventor Karl Benz.[2] By then, Henry Ford had lived 22 years in a slow-moving world. He grew up the son of a farmer, William Ford, who had hoped that Henry would someday take over their farm in Dearborn, Michigan. If that was William's goal, then he erred when he gifted a 15-year-old Henry a pocket watch. The boy dismantled it then put it back together. After then doing the same to watches of friends and family, he felt his calling was as a machinist. He dropped out of school at 16, moved to Detroit, and worked as a machinist's apprentice and a repairman. In 1896, at the age of 33, he designed his first car, a two-cylinder, 4-horsepower vehicle he called the "Ford Quadricycle."[3] He sold it for $200, and used the money to start a business, which didn't take. Another failed business venture later, he was 40 years old and nowhere near influential.

But then he was visited by the American dream. He tried again. In 1903, with the help of Alexander Y. Malcomson, an old friend and Detroit coal dealer who was impressed by Ford's latest automobile design (which racer Barney Oldfield had driven to a racing cup's first place), they started the Ford Motor Company. Oldfield's successes helped attract investors, and Ford worked on improving his design.

---

[2] The Germans, as always, had the far more entertaining word for it: *Motorwagen*.

[3] We can't all be German.

Henry Ford

Ford's greatest gift at this early stage of his career was that of an analyst. He studied how cars were created, how they functioned, and, just as important, how their *parts* were created and functioned. By 1908, he used the industrial trends of assembly lines and interchangeable parts to assemble a car more quickly than anyone had done before. Earlier in the decade, it took nearly 13 hours to assemble his car model. By the end of the decade, his workers could follow 45 steps to manufacture an automobile in just over 90 minutes. Just five years into Ford Motor Company, he was ready to unveil the car that would change the world.[4]

Three years earlier, Ford's investors had told him that the way to increase profits was to make a car that rich consumers felt compelled to buy. The rich, after all, had the disposable income during a time where the industrialization had excelled at suppressing the wages of expendable workers.

Ford had something else in mind. He felt that the way to maximize profit wasn't to sell only to the tiny American upper class of the early 1900s. Rather, it was appealing to the millions of workers beneath them. Ford is often associated with mass production, and rightly so, but what is often overlooked is his ability to drive mass *consumption*. He didn't want to build the car loved by the rich; he wanted to build the car loved by everyone.

What's most fascinating about the original Model T is not its breakthrough affordable price; rather, it was *how* Ford was able to make its price so low and yet still make unprecedented profit. In order to make

---

[4] The tireless work ethic that bred his success has, for a century now, been pointed to as epitomizing the American dream—from farmer drop-out to richest man in America, all by working hard, innovating, and never giving up.

sure he could keep his cars affordable, he needed to cut every possible cost while still maintaining a safe and fluid environment that would not slow production.

Therefore, in addition to interchangeable parts and the assembly line, he created a sharp division of labor. Assembly line workers were not even responsible for getting parts, materials, or tools. Another worker did that for them. It was imperative not to waste a minute of a worker's time, for that would slow the belt that needed constant motion to maximize production. He even reduced the time it took to get extra parts and materials to their proper locations. Instead of sending runners, intricate systems of slides and trolleys transported whatever was needed. Ford even standardized the height of the assembly belt; its placement was where it would be easiest for workers to stand for extended periods of time, eliminating time-consuming motions like bending over, reaching up, or complaining to one's foreman about back pain.

He tirelessly analyzed the process and micromanaged his plants as if his entire life depended on that day's batch of Model Ts. If a process could be simplified to save a second, Henry Ford ordered the simplification. The result was a worker who had only one task to do throughout the day, and this task likely took little to no training. Ford confronted all possible time-wasters and promptly reduced or eliminated them.

It should be noted that none of these tactics were invented by Ford. Frederick Winslow Taylor had already preached this method of meticulous analysis, called scientific management. The assembly line had been around for a century, as had interchangeable parts, the brainchild of Eli Whitney. Still, no one before Ford had combined and scaled these ideas so effectively.

Meanwhile, Ford unleashed yet another brilliant tactic to saturate the market with his cars. He gave his workers raises. As his production rate and sales climbed in the early 1910s, Ford could afford to pay his employees more. In 1914, he more than doubled their minimum wage to five dollars a day. Imagine getting your earnings doubled now, and you can imagine what this wage hike did to their disposable income. His workers joined a growing middle class, and with this extra income, they bought more cars. This strategy also increased worker loyalty and decreased worker turnover, which kept the company humming.

These policies epitomized two core tenets of the welfare capitalism adopted by later companies. Ford and Chrysler legend Lee Iacocca nicely sums up Ford and his raises: "He figured that if he paid his factory workers a real living wage and produced more cars in less time for less money, everyone would buy them. . . . It was a virtuous circle, and he was the ring master."

Other factors contributed to Ford's success. He understood advertising, for example. He also branched out into the rubber and steel industries to further control his means of production. The Model T, therefore, was produced at the lowest possible cost, and part of this savings could be lopped off its retail price. In 1908, one could buy the earliest Model Ts for $825 each. Over the next five years, the price plummeted to $500. By 1916, it was $360, and by 1924, it reached $260. As the price dropped, the sales climbed, sometimes doubling in a year. By 1918, ten years after the car's debut, *half* the cars in the country were Model Ts. Henry Ford, drop-out son of a Dearborn farmer, became the richest man in America. The company ultimately sold 15 million Model Ts, a record for any car model until the 1970s.

By the late 1920s, after the Model T's inevitable slowing of sales, Ford came out with the Model A. Though successful, the A was no T. The Model A marked the beginning of Ford's slow decline from his two-decade long reign as America's greatest businessman. The latter part of his life was marred by a failed Senate bid, an increasingly messy relationship with workers who wished to unionize, an upstart General Motors company that surpassed Ford Motor Company's sales, a failed airline, accusations of anti-Semitism, and decreased mental acuity. The pall of the Great Depression didn't help.

When his son and successor as Ford president, Edsel Ford, died in 1943, Henry, despite his 80 years and bouts with paranoia and cardiovascular problems, re-assumed command of the company. It went on to lose 10 million dollars a month.[5] By 1945, Ford re-retired, left the company to his grandson Henry Ford II, and died two years later.

No, Henry Ford was not an inventor. He was an innovator. He didn't invent the car; he *re*invented it. By lowering costs and personifying efficiency, he was able to sell it to the common American, his employees first and foremost.

This approach to packaging and compensation ultimately rippled across the United States and Western world. The Industrial Revolution had already begun, but Ford threw industrialism into a higher gear.[6] He

---

[5] President Roosevelt considered a government takeover so as to guarantee constant production during World War II.

[6] Sorry.

Henry Ford

may have revolutionized transportation, but he brought other industries along for the ride.[7]

In 1908, when his factories produced a car every 90 minutes, that already stimulated other business sectors. By 1927, however, Ford Motor Co. was producing a car every 24 *seconds*. The secondary boons are incalculable. There are the obvious sectors of growth—car dealers and gas stations—but many other industries were happily caught up in his revolution. Car production catalyzed enormous growth in the steel, rubber, glass, and petroleum industries. Billions of dollars were poured into highway construction. In 1929, millions of American workers had the automobile to thank for their job. Ford had thrown the American economy into overdrive.[8]

Another important side effect was the rise of suburbia. Owning a car and the independent, flexible movement accompanied by one meant one could get out of the inner city and into the fresh air of a suburb. Real estate speculation benefited. When the first shopping center popped up in 1924 Kansas City, its customers used their Model Ts to get there.

A sizable middle class emerged. It was made up not only of Ford's well-compensated workers but of individuals who could use the affordable automobile to get to work at the many growing industries. Auto sales in the U.S. totaled $1.5 million in 1921. By 1929, that number had quintupled. By 1930, there was nearly one car for every five Americans, and Americans owned 80 percent(!) of the world's cars.

As wages rose during the 1920s, the middle class used its free time and excess income—both were a product of the rigid and hourly wage

---

[7] Again, I'm really sorry.

[8] They're just too easy.

system instituted by Ford and others who emulated him—to stimulate other sectors of growth. For instance, AAA estimated that in 1929, one in three Americans took vacations by car. Americans were no longer isolated from each other. They more freely left rural homes and met for social occasions, sporting events, concerts, and movies. These industries, in turn, experienced growth as well. Even if the 1930s sidetracked this economic leap forward, the U.S. emerged on the other side of World War II as an industrialized nation on wheels.

Perhaps more than any other individual, Ford helped create this consumer culture. With the rise of disposable income and freedom of mobility came a higher standard of living and desire to spend. More than anyone else of the industrial era, it's Ford that laid the foundation for a large American middle class that led to, by a long shot, the world's largest economy.

Relevantly, Ford did not keep his production methods a secret. He wrote about them. He showed them off. Seeing a chance for good publicity, he invited people into his factories. Other manufactures emulated his tactics, and "Fordism" eventually branched out into other companies and industries. The rest of the West quickly caught on, and, in the past few decades, we've seen other parts of the world use similar methods to maximize production (if not compensation). Consequently, prices fell for products in almost every industry, and more affordability meant more members of the most comfortable middle class in history.

Although the latter part of his life stalled,[9] Ford should be proud of his legacy. There's the rags-to-riches tale, but there's also his gift of automobility. He gave freedom to a people that cherish it. Almost as dear to

---

[9] Almost there.

their hearts is the innovation, individualism, and profit motive that drove Ford and the American economy to the top of the GDP rankings for the better part of a century. It's been quite the ride, and behind the wheel has been Henry Ford.[10]

For his unmatched contribution to American production and consumerism, Henry Ford is the 20th most influential figure in Western history.

---

[10] Last one. I promise.

#19: Queen Elizabeth

"I know I have the body but of a weak and feeble woman; but I have the heart and stomach of a king, and of a king of England too."

–Queen Elizabeth I of England, 1588

She's sadly just the second and final woman on our list.[1] But what a woman! It's extraordinary (though, some might argue, unsurprising) that of the 42 English monarchs since William the Conqueror started the modern lineage in 1066, the most successful of them was one of the handful of queens: Elizabeth I.[2]

Princess Elizabeth was born into a drama-filled family leading a fragile England. Elizabeth's grandfather helped end a 30-year dynastic civil war. Elizabeth's father separated the country from the Catholic Church. He desperately wanted Elizabeth to be a boy and was disappointed when

---

[1] See Joan of Arc (#27). Others considered, in chronological order: Eleanor of Aquitaine, Queen Isabella, Catherine the Great, Marie Curie, Margaret Sanger, and, of course, my mother.

[2] Of the other monarchs, only five of them were women (six if you want to count the disputed "Nine Days Queen," Lady Jane). The last of them, Helen Mirren, reigns today.

she wasn't. His anger led to her mother's beheading, and Princess Elizabeth went on to have four stepmothers. Later, Elizabeth's half-sister arrested, imprisoned, and tried to turn the country against her. Her brother-in-law tried to have her killed. So did her cousin.

Yet, she persisted. For 45 years, she transformed her kingdom into an empire. Then, the empire transformed the world. As a result, Queen Elizabeth I became the 19th most influential figure in Western history.

Elizabeth was born in 1533 during the beginning of the English Reformation. In history's most famous divorce, Henry VIII, an ardent Catholic during his youth, had just separated from his first wife, the Spanish Catherine of Aragon. Despite six pregnancies, Catherine had yet to provide a healthy son. Only one of her children survived at all—a daughter, Mary, who her parents raised as Catholic. To properly extend the Tudor line, which had begun its reign under his father, Henry needed a son, so he soured on Catherine's inability to deliver a healthy one. As she aged into her 40s, he sought a divorce.[3]

---

[3] Henry's obsession to extend the Tudor Dynasty was rooted in recent English history. His father, Henry Tudor, became King Henry VII after winning the 30-year War of the Roses, a dynastic struggle for the throne between rival Plantagenet branches. Henry's victory repaired the schism, but the permanence of that repair was in question. The elder and then the younger Henry ruled over a relatively stable kingdom, but if Henry VIII died without a son, it might have led to a succession crisis that could throw the country, which had never been ruled by a woman, back into civil unrest. Henry feared losing what his father had built and grew fixated with continuing the family line through a son. It's kind of like feeling the pressure to continue the family business, only if the business were a kingdom of a few million people.

A sixteenth century Catholic needed the Church's permission to take such action. As early as 1527, Henry pressed Pope Clement VII to allow the divorce. The Pope, chastened by the Protestant Reformation, a denominational conflict with Protestants who accused the Catholic Church of not being terribly holy, refused. In 1533, the matter took on greater urgency when Henry impregnated Anne Boleyn, one of Catherine's ladies-in-waiting. To ensure this potential son would be a legitimate successor, the baby needed to be born to a queen. Henry hurriedly separated the Church of England from the Roman Catholic Church, made himself the head of it, granted himself an annulment, then married Anne right before she gave him a second child.[4] All this for a potential son.

It was a daughter.

They named her Elizabeth. Her birth devastated King Henry. Within three years and probably as many failed pregnancies from his new Queen, Henry grew so disenchanted with Anne Boleyn that he had her beheaded on shaky charges of adultery and incest. At age 2, Elizabeth was motherless.

One day after beheading his second wife, Henry proposed to another of Catherine's maids of honor, Jane Seymour. They married ten days later, and she had a child the following year. This time it was a son, Edward, who managed to survive childbirth. The same could not be said for Jane, who

---

[4] Who needs soap operas when we have history?

died two weeks later after postnatal complications.⁵ Henry married three more times, but he would have no more children.⁶

Elizabeth, meanwhile, was raised in relative isolation. She was a disappointment to her father, unrelated to her stepmothers, and largely ignored in favor of her half-brother Edward. Third in line for the throne (after Edward and her older half-sister Mary), she was not expected to ever ascend to it, especially since Edward's potential progeny would all but ensure her permanent status as a disappointing and forgotten middle child. Nevertheless, despite her unusual childhood, she was still an English princess and given a first-rate classical education by fine teachers.⁷

When Henry died in 1547, Prince Edward, aged 9, succeeded to the throne as King Edward VI. He, like his half-sister Elizabeth, was raised by the newly Protestant royal family, and he continued the Anglicanism of the country. At 15, however, he took terminally ill. Not wanting the throne to fall to Mary, his Catholic eldest sister, his advisers and Parliament hastily arranged that his cousin, the Anglican Jane Grey, succeed him. After his death, both claimants had their advocates, but Mary, through a better claim and show of force, got the better of the dispute.

---

⁵ For those keeping track at home, Henry's three wives (so far) were Catherine, Anne, and Jane. He divorced Catherine, beheaded Anne, and Jane died. Each wife provided one child: Mary, Elizabeth, and Edward, respectively. There will be a quiz.

⁶ The other wives: Anne of Cleves (divorced for being ugly), Catherine Howard (beheaded for being slutty), and Catherine Parr (survived for being patient with Henry's final years of corpulence). The mnemonic to remember their fates: *divorced, beheaded, and died / divorced, beheaded, survived.*

⁷ One might call them Tudor tutors, but one would be careful to do so only in a footnote.

161

Lady Jane was imprisoned after nine unofficial days as monarch. Mary became Queen, and Jane was executed.

While Elizabeth stayed quiet, Mary did her best to revert the country to Catholicism. Among her more aggressive tactics were the executions of Protestants—some 300 of them—which earned her the sobriquet "Bloody Mary."[8] Paranoid and thinking Elizabeth part of a Protestant plot, Mary arrested and imprisoned her, truly unpopular acts with the English people. Meanwhile, apparently wanting to secure her unpopularity, she married a Spanish prince, the future king Philip II. This marriage worried the English that they were headed toward a long-term Spanish, Catholic reign over their kingdom.[9] Then, after Philip convinced Mary to go to war with France, the country lost Calais, the only territory it had retained in mainland Europe as a result of the Hundred Years' War.[10]

Unsurprisingly, the reign of Queen Mary was not a celebrated one, and her abrupt 1558 death, after having produced no sons with Philip, was met with few tears. At 25, the darling Princess Elizabeth—that third-in-line disappointing afterthought—became the Queen of England.

---

[8] If you want to see Bloody Mary, go to your bathroom, look in the mirror, say her name three times, then return to your computer and click on her Wikipedia page.

[9] Mary, remember, was not only Catholic, but she half Spanish, too, through her mother. The combined heirs of Philip and Mary would be three-quarters Spanish.

[10] For more on the Hundred Years' War, read up on the other woman of this list, Joan of Arc (#27).

Queen Elizabeth

Thanks to Mary's tumultuous reign, Queen Elizabeth inherited challenges. England mired far from the golden age into which she would eventually usher the country.

Domestically, England still faced the denominational question of what kind of Christianity it would practice. Henry VIII's conversion led to programs that worked to bring the kingdom with him.[11] The English were largely malleable in this regard. Historically, the island likes to distance itself from mainland Europe whenever possible.[12] Young Edward had continued his father's policies, but Mary infamously tried to return the country back to Roman Catholicism. Mary's stickiest legacy was denominational strife, and Elizabeth had to deal with the fallout.

---

[11] It's worth noting that Henry had little problem with Catholicism outside of the pope's primacy over him. Henry grew up considering the priesthood until his older brother and initial heir to Henry VII's throne, Arthur, died. In fact, Henry VIII publicly supported the Catholic Church when Martin Luther and others criticized it, earning a title which has stuck with the English monarch ever since—"Defender of the Faith." Thus, Anglicanism turned out to be pretty similar to Catholicism. Both had ornate ceremonies in massive cathedrals led by a strict and hierarchical clergy, much different than the more humble and local congregations of other fledgling Protestant sects. Anglicanism's resemblance to Catholicism soon caused a faction of "Puritans" to push for a purer interpretation of the Bible. Failed in their quest, some Puritans separated from Anglicanism, and some of those went to America on the Mayflower. Long story short, Americans have Thanksgiving because Henry VIII, nearly 500 years ago, wanted a divorce.

[12] They spoke a different tongue than Western Europe (non-Romantic). They developed a national Christian denomination. They adhered to the Magna Carta and had representatives in Parliament long before mainland European monarchies pursued similar progressive reforms. Unlike most of Europe, they successfully resisted Napoleon and Hitler. More recently, they held on to their English standard measurements long after the rest of Europe metrified. They'll give up the pound for the euro over their bloody dead bodies. All considered, Brexit shouldn't have been a surprise.

In the areas of state, Mary had bequeathed the French war triggered by Philip. Losing its last mainland territory hurt England's reputation. Mary was so focused on the religious struggle that she didn't even attempt to compensate for the loss of Calais by looking elsewhere for new land or markets. Seen as a country on the decline, the coronation of an untested 25-year-old woman did not help England's reputation on the international stage.

Elizabeth also faced challenging relationships with other European countries. To her north, Scotland's queen Mary Stuart, a cousin, became a thorn in Elizabeth's side. Unless Elizabeth had a child, Mary, Queen of Scots was actually heir to the English throne.[13] This alone would not have been a problem, but Mary was Catholic and married to the King of France, Francis II. Thus, in important ways, she resembled the unpopular Bloody Mary that preceded Elizabeth: she was problematically Catholic and married to a Catholic European king who might look to usurp power and provide a foreign, Catholic heir.[14]

And then there was Spain. When Queen Mary had died, Philip II lost not only his wife but also his chance to influence the English throne and place a Spanish Catholic heir on it. He wished to try again with Elizabeth and, like any good widower, proposed marriage to his dead wife's sister.

---

[13] Remember, Elizabeth is the last remaining child of Henry VIII. Edward, her younger brother, had his turn, as did Mary, her older sister. Mary Stuart, on the other hand, was the granddaughter of one of Henry VIII's sisters, Margaret, and therefore had Tudor blood as a great-granddaughter of Henry VII. After Lady Jane Grey's execution, no other Tudor line survived besides Margaret's. Margaret had married the king of Scotland, James Stuart (James IV), whose crown her granddaughter Mary eventually inherited through James V. Are you getting all this?

[14] And it didn't help her cause they were both named Mary.

As she would do throughout her life, Elizabeth refused a man's advances and remained England's pure "Virgin Queen." As the acrimonious relationship between these two heads of state moved forward, the scorned King was perpetually on the watch for a way to reel back England for Spain and Catholicism.

England, in sum, had no allies, a contested denomination, a power-hungry cousin to the north married to a historic enemy to the east, another historic enemy to the south, and an untested woman on the throne.

So the woman went to work. Cooperating with Parliament—a norm for her reign, which made her popular with England's increasingly powerful second branch—she immediately settled the Anglican question. After passing the Act of Supremacy and Act of Uniformity, England was once again officially Anglican and has been ever since. She did, however, allow freedom of worship for Catholics, thus easing their presence in England and quelling denominational friction.

Elizabeth was proactive in foreign affairs. Her support of Protestant movements in Europe, including one in the Spanish Netherlands, eventually earned her an excommunication from Pope Pius V. Philip of Spain and Mary, Queen of Scots took notice. Elizabeth was turning the European establishment against her, but the English people, ever so proud of their independence from Rome, loved her for it. Despite the acrimony with the Church, she still managed to secure peaceful relations with both Scotland and France with the Treaty of Edinburgh.

She also thrust England into the Age of Exploration. Spain and Portugal dominated the Atlantic, including the "New World," but that was because they were there first and the pope had allocated the land between them.[15] England, however, was no longer a Catholic nation. It could therefore ignore papal decrees at its leisure.

Elizabeth decided to send out the growing English navy, which irritated Spain and Portugal. The furthest mission was to stake a claim in the New World itself, a claim that became the Roanoke Colony in 1585.[16] She also commissioned Francis Drake to lead operations in the Caribbean, where English ships engaged Spanish ones. She hired privateers[17] to plunder Spanish and Portuguese ships of their booty. Spain, especially King Philip, grew angrier still.[18]

The final straw for Philip was when the last realistic hope for a Catholic England—Mary, Queen of Scots—was bloodily removed as the heir to the English throne. Mary had plotted to have Elizabeth assassinated, the result of which would have been Mary topping her Scottish crown with the English one, but Elizabeth found out. Elizabeth's chief

---

[15] Before and after Christopher Columbus's famous 1492 journey opened Europe's eyes to two new continents ripe for the taking, Spain and Portugal's large navies scrambled to explore as much land as they could, fanning a rivalry along the way. Pope Alexander VI wanted to avoid Catholic infighting when there were so many pagan natives to conquer and convert, so the two kingdoms were pressed into signing the Treaty of Tordesillas, which divided discovered lands along a line of longitude 370 leagues west of the Cape Verde Islands. Spain got west of the line and Portugal east. It turned out this line was drawn about halfway across South America. This division is a primary reason why most of Latin America speaks Spanish except for the eastern portion of South America, Brazil, which speaks Portuguese. Now you know.

[16] The spooky one that vanished without a trace. Well, almost without a trace.

[17] Read: pirates.

[18] Philip placed the equivalent of a $6.5 million bounty on Drake's head.

Queen Elizabeth

adviser, William Cecil, convinced her to take action. After Mary's 18-year stay in prison (during which the one-year-old son she left behind, James, grew up as a young king of Scotland), Elizabeth had her executed in 1587.[19]

Philip consequently gave up on marriages and inheritance. The way to the English throne, he determined, was through force. Philip owned the massive warships of the famous Spanish Armada, a fleet thought to have more firepower than any in history. Considered invincible, the Armada set sail for England in May of 1588. All told, 151 ships and 50,000 soldiers were to be a part of the invasion. Estimates are that they outgunned the English navy by over 50 percent.

Her Majesty's Navy showed considerably better than expected. They triumphed thanks to some smart tactics, superior technology, help from some classically British weather, and a fiery speech from their Queen. In defense of her kingdom and reign, Elizabeth inspired her soldiers and her country while challenging Philip and the rest of Europe: *"I know I have the body but of a weak and feeble woman; but I have the heart and stomach of a king, and of a king of England too, and think foul scorn that . . . any prince of Europe, should dare to invade the borders of my realm."*

Fewer than a hundred English soldiers died from the battle's engagements, and not one Spanish boot stepped on England.

---

[19] Her execution is one of history's most notorious and botched. Her executioner, likely frazzled at the idea of killing a royal who many believed served via divine right, botched the first swing of his ax. He caught more skull than neck, coaxing out Mary's understandable final words, "Sweet Jesus." More anxious still, his second swing only cut partly through her neck. He was forced to saw the rest of the way through.

Elizabeth became the stuff of legend. She was already said to be witty, charming, and fun. Her people were already attracted to her magnetic personality, assertive leadership, and pure-as-the-driven-snow sexual reputation. Then, when her mettle withstood the Spanish, her popularity exploded.

With England secure, she ushered England into a cultural renaissance—its golden age. Theater and music as mediums for cultural expression thrived. Writers and poets flourished during the latter part of her reign.[20] England blossomed with unprecedented cultural creativity. Such leadership should not be taken for granted. In 1642, the Puritan-controlled Parliament prohibited all stage plays and closed down theaters, including Shakespeare's Globe.

Meanwhile, its ships ventured into uncharted territory. Francis Drake circumnavigated the planet, earning a knighthood upon his return. The colony of Virginia was founded and named after England's Virgin Queen.[21] Elizabeth chartered five companies, including the formidable East India Company, to get England into overseas markets. The British Empire was born.

Elizabeth lived only to see that empire's infancy. In 1603, at the age of 70, she died.

Her only great failure may have been that she did not feel the need to produce and cultivate a proper heir to the throne. With no children, the

---

[20] You may have heard of one of them. In fact, I hope you'll be reading a great deal about him when we get to the top ten.

[21] There are conflicting speculations as to whether she truly remained a virgin for her whole life, but she certainly never married, nor was she ever pregnant.

Queen Elizabeth

Virgin Queen's death ended the Tudor Dynasty. Before dying, however, she did name her successor. She stuck with tradition and chose her nearest male relative. Remarkably, it was the son of the woman she had executed.[22] James, the son of Mary Stuart, became the next king of England. Raised a Protestant, he was embraced by his new kingdom.[23]

His reign, after a brief honeymoon period, was marred by considerable discord with Parliament and the English people.[24] Still, the track Elizabeth lay out for her kingdom was irreversible.

She had successfully guided the English through the dogmatic conflict that consumed other nations. The Holy Roman Empire, for example, lost a quarter of its population in the sixteenth and seventeenth centuries as Protestants and Catholics gored each other over their superior interpretation of Christianity. England hiccupped with the 300 put to death by Mary and other isolated moments of violence, but thanks to Elizabeth's policies, it emerged relatively unscathed from the Reformation's turmoil. And whereas the Holy Roman Empire further fragmented along denominational borders, England remained united.

---

[22] Bestowing the English Crown to the son of a woman she had beheaded surely ranks among history's greatest apologetic gestures.

[23] Relevantly, James Stuart was already King James VI of Scotland. When he inherited the English throne, he became King James I of England and unified the two countries under his crown. He arrived in England with three healthy children in tow, a far cry from the dramatic births, or lack thereof, of the Tudors. Thus, England celebrated the arrival of King James and the new Stuart Dynasty. Within a decade, however, they called for his head. (They had to settle for his son's.)

[24] Though largely a failure, James has two pretty sizable legacies: Jamestown, the first permanent English settlement in the New World, was named after him (and located in the Virginia named after his predecessor) as was the King James Bible, which he commissioned.

It seems as if the life of Elizabeth and the history of England followed similar paths. Both were isolated and often in danger of being caught in the orbit of a mainland European power, yet each persevered on a unique course and blossomed as a result. Her promotion of exploration and colonization catalyzed more than three centuries of British imperialism across the world. What originated in Virginia culminated with Britain patrolling five continents and three oceans. At the height of its powers, the British Empire was Rome 2.0, claiming a quarter of the world's land and population. The British used their ubiquitous navy to reign as the world's sole superpower, an empire on which the sun would not set until the twentieth century.

Of course, the British Empire's reputation is far from clean. Its influence on the world can be seen in myriad ways. Like other Western imperialists, Britain's colonial claims and new maps often ignored centuries-old racial and cultural patterns. Multiple ethnicities were often lumped together into one colonial polity, or perhaps a single culture could find itself on opposite sides of an improvised border. This considerable upheaval frequently led to sectarian conflicts, often met with the ironic finger-wagging of culpable Western nations.

Britain was also particularly good at migrating, whether it was their own settlers encroaching onto others' lands, like the British colonists in North America, or forcibly migrating laborers, like cramming Africans onto floating coffins and sending them to work those North American lands. The British triggered considerable demographical change, with ramifications on our modern world. They also forced new agricultural practices onto lands and cultures unsuited for it. Comparable processes did damage in India, Pakistan, Australia, New Zealand, and parts of Africa. These influences, though negative, are evidence of the British

Empire's impact—and therefore the impacts of its catalyzer, Queen Elizabeth, as well.

Still, the British Empire was neither uniquely nor totally awful. Other European empires did exactly what the British did, although perhaps not as effectively. Meanwhile, in many ways the British Empire helped modernize the world, exporting its physical and conceptual infrastructures. Former British colonies (the U.S., Canada, Australia, India, and an assortment of African colonies) generally fared better than did those of other European countries. England left behind superior roads, rails, farming techniques, and city plans.

Perhaps more significant, England, which had been on the forefront of liberalizing ideas dating back to the Magna Carta, deposited those ideas in its colonies as well. No country was more successful in spreading Western ideals. Due to widespread British colonialism, English became the international language of trade, commerce, and diplomacy. Accompanying the language were English ideas of limited government, personal liberty, and due process of law.

These concepts were instilled in its colonies. In fact, when the American colonies had their revolution, it was because they requested the rights of British citizens they claimed were denied to them. These same rights evolved into American ones. Later, the U.S. took it upon itself to continue spreading those British ideas. Indeed, many characteristics of what we see in America today—military might, economic domination, technological innovation, world policing, cultural exports—were first parts of the British Empire that Elizabeth started. If England had not interfered with the Spanish and Portuguese duopoly in the Americas, the last few centuries of geopolitical, social, and cultural developments would have been remarkably different.

Ultimately, it's Queen Elizabeth who stabilized England, presided over its renaissance, and began that important era of British colonialism, steering one of history's greatest countries toward its greatest era. As a result, she earns her spot as the 19th most influential figure in Western history.

#18: Thomas Edison

"Anything that won't sell, I don't want to invent. Its sale is proof of utility, and utility is success."

–Thomas Edison

When introducing my Henry Ford (#20) column, I noted the difficulty in placing Ford into a professional category. He wasn't a scientist, nor was he quite an inventor. With Thomas Edison, I have no such problem.

No man in history is more synonymous with the word "inventor." He is the archetype. His eye-popping 1,093 patents reigned supreme for a century.[1] Perhaps more important than any single patent, he set the standard for how inventions are pursued and created, birthing the idea of

---

[1] He was passed only by modern inventors. Japan's Shunpei Yamazaki and his 5,826 (and counting) patents now top the list. (When I first posted this piece on the website in March of 2018, the number was 5,083. Upon the first draft of this book in December 2020, it was 5,779. Now, in April 2021, it's 5,826. He's a machine!)

modern research and development labs across the world. While he may have stopped inventing 90 years ago, he still deserves some credit for countless inventions since his death.

Thomas Edison has earned his place as Western history's 18th most influential figure.

Born in 1847 Ohio, Thomas Alva Edison's childhood was slow and quiet. However, this leisurely society would soon experience enormous change during Edison's life—often because of it.

As young Edison grew up, no one expected genius. He had just three months of formal education. A teacher considered him mentally challenged. A reverend called him "addled." These perceived shortcomings did not position Edison as the world's most inventive brain.

But his mother, like so many mothers before and since, was his savior. She schooled him. She bought him books and let him peruse the local paper. She had faith in him, and he grew up never wanting to let her down. He read as much as possible and, as we all do at a young age, developed a fondness for qualitative analysis and experimentation. To help the household, he worked numerous jobs, including selling newspapers on the Grand Trunk Railway. His first entrepreneurial experiment came as a printer of a newspaper—the *Grand Trunk Herald*.[2] He set up a train car for printing the paper and conducting experiments.

At the age of 15, he happened onto a three-year-old child stuck on train tracks as a locomotive barreled toward him. Edison saved the boy, who turned out to be the son of the local station master. The grateful

---

[2] It was the first of his 14 businesses. You may have heard of another: General Electric.

father gave the teenager a job as a telegrapher, a job from which Edison would learn a great deal and later convert that knowledge into inventions. He quickly took to the work and wage, which allowed him time to experiment on the side.

For the next few years, he bounced around the region, working telegraph jobs by night and experimenting by day, the latter ultimately costing him the former. At 19, he was working for Western Union in Louisville on the Associated Press wire. He requested the nightshift to allow more time for experimentation. One such experiment involved battery acid which, one night, spilled, seeped through the floorboards, and landed on his boss's desk. That was his last night working for Western Union.

A fellow inventor and compassionate friend, Franklin Leonard Pope, opened up his New Jersey basement to Edison, who decided to become a professional inventor. In 1869, at 21, he had his first invention and patent. It was an electric vote recorder, which he hoped would replace the paper and manual counting ballot system. Politicians, however, had little interest, and Edison made no money from it. Edison considered the invention a failure.

Knowing there was value in telegraphy, he focused his efforts there. In 1874, his quadruplex telegraph, which could carry four separate telegraphs signals on a single wire, earned him $10,000 from Western Union. (Today's equivalent is over $200,000.) His stock ticker, another telegraphic advancement, netted him an additional $40,000.

In 1876, a 29-year-old Edison used the money to start a research laboratory in the community of Menlo Park, part of Raritan Township, New Jersey. It's now known as Edison.

Despite the impossibility of a patent for such a lab, perhaps no contribution of Edison's is more influential. The laboratory became the world's first full-time research lab dedicated to technological invention. He hired consultants and staff to work under his supervision. These white-coat assistants conducted experiments much like Henry Ford's employees would construct cars a few decades later—efficiently and relentlessly. Whereas Ford would go on to epitomize mass production, Edison was the first to use "mass intelligence." The assistants had backgrounds in science, engineering, mathematics, and other specialties, each bringing specific knowledge and skills to the lab. Edison had them working together before Ford dreamed of his first assembly line. Menlo Park, Edison's "research factory," became the epicenter of the era's technological revolution.

Within three years of founding the lab, Edison had his next breakthrough invention. His 17th patent was for a phonograph. For the first time in history, sound could be recorded and replayed.[3] With the phonograph in tow, he toured the country, even giving a demonstration to President Rutherford B. Hayes. Edison sometimes introduced himself by playing recorded sound; crowds were so astonished that some suspected magic, earning him the moniker "The Wizard of Menlo Park."

The increased fame and income allowed Edison to expand the Menlo Park lab. Over the next decade, it grew to occupy two city blocks. Edison stocked it with seemingly endless supplies and ingredients for potential

---

[3] And what were the first recorded words in history? "Mary had a little lamb." Unfortunately, the original recording perished, though Edison later reproduced it for posterity.

inventions.[4] He and his assistants went on to patent hundreds of mechanisms and processes, including a mimeograph, a microphone, and a battery for an electric car.[5] Everything they did was documented, with specifications, diagrams, and explanations at the ready, in order to apply for patents.

As the 1870s neared their end, Edison was already a productive inventor. However, he had yet to arrive at his most famous invention. On November 4, 1879, he patented an idea that later came to symbolize the very concept of an idea—the incandescent light bulb.

It's worth noting that it was not the first means of artificial light, nor was it even the first light bulb.[6] What Edison brought to the invention, however, was a way to make the light bulb practical. He promised, "We will make electricity so cheap that only the rich will burn candles."

The earlier bulbs had glaring flaws. Some couldn't last for more than a few minutes. Others were enormously expensive to create. Others still needed impractical amounts of power to run, making them impossible to distribute and operate on a large scale. Edison's genius, therefore, was not in conceiving the light bulb, but in cheaply creating an efficient,

---

[4] An Edison biography lists "eight thousand kinds of chemicals, every kind of screw made, every size of needle, every kind of cord or wire, hair of humans, horses, hogs, cows, rabbits, goats, minx, camels . . . silk in every texture, cocoons, various kinds of hoofs, shark's teeth, deer horns, tortoise shell . . . cork, resin, varnish and oil, ostrich feathers, a peacock's tail, jet, amber, rubber, all ores." Imagine working inventory week there?

[5] The majority of these patents came in the late nineteenth century. His highest single year was 1882, where he patented 106 applications. That's an average of two per week!

[6] Indeed, at least 22 prior light bulbs have been acknowledged.

long-lasting one.[7] His 48th patent did just that. His first patented bulb lasted nearly 14 hours. By the following year, further modifications had it up to 1,200 hours. Thanks to this invention, not only were the impractical light bulbs swept aside, but so, too, were the wax candle and gas, flame, and kerosene lamps. Edison's bulb turned on, and the future lit up.

Just as important as Edison's modifications to the light bulb was that Edison found a way to control the electricity going to it. With the help of financial backers (including industrial titans J.P. Morgan and the Vanderbilts), Edison founded the Edison Electric Light Company, which in 1892 evolved into General Electric. Edison then not only controlled the light bulb but its generator and feeder system as well. He oversaw the layout of history's first electric distribution grid. In 1882, for the first time ever, 59 customers in lower Manhattan had their lights turned on. What began there has since spread to an almost totally electrified Western world.

And there were still a thousand patents to go! While none of his subsequent inventions approached the level of the light bulb and electric distribution, Edison was far from finished. Still to come was the first commercially successful fluoroscope to help with x-ray machines. He also discovered the eponymous "Edison effect"—two wires that weren't touching could transmit an electric current if they existed in a near vacuum.

---

[7] Among the apparatuses that made his light bulb better: an effective incandescent material, a strong vacuum achieved by the Sprengel pump, and a high resistance that made it possible for a central electric distribution system to deliver power cheaply.

Thomas Edison

Nearly as important as inventing new things, Edison excelled at improving existing technology. The typewriter, the dictaphone, and telegraphy greatly benefited from his research lab. The audibility of the telephone was greatly improved by his carbon microphone. His kinetoscope, the first motion picture camera, was crucial in the development of films. In fact, he founded the first motion picture studio. By the turn of the twentieth century, he had more than 700 patents. Over the next three decades, he tacked on 300 more.

Throughout his impressive career, Edison was not without off-putting quirks and flaws. He had been hard of hearing since his youth, which could make him an ornery conversationalist. He could be disheveled and was known for sometimes sleeping with his clothes on.[8] He was a renowned boaster and swearer, and much of his army of assistants matched his bravado.[9]

Another fault of Edison is that this loyal army of inventors received little acclaim. Despite so much help from his lab mates, it was still Edison who received almost all of the credit and money.[10]

---

[8] That reminds me of my high school self. I had extraordinary difficulty getting up in time for my ride. At one point, desperate for a solution, I decided that on the night before I would eat late, shower, and get dressed for the next day before going to bed. I then set an alarm for three minutes before my ride arrived. My only task between the alarm and the beeping horn was brushing my teeth. This plan was, to say the least, exceedingly stupid, something else that's right in line with my high school self.

[9] George Bernard Shaw called them "profane; liars, braggarts, and hustlers." Therefore, he also called them "excellent company."

[10] Edison is a great example of what I talked about in my introduction to this series: "almost all these figures had contemporary help, too—unsung heroes working with them every day. These friends, co-workers, employees, subordinates, and acquaintances were imperative in the operation, but mostly forgotten by history."

Also disappointing is Edison's money management. His genius seemed limited to innovation. Inept socially and financially, he lost control of all 14 companies he founded, missing out on much of their future mega-profits. He was a millionaire by age of 40, yet he often found himself in debt.

Nevertheless, he remained an icon in America and across the Western world. Living into his 80s, the Wizard of Menlo Park remained a prominent American celebrity. When he died in 1931 at the age of 84, President Herbert Hoover, recognizing Edison's most famous invention, asked Americans for a one-minute dimming of their lights in his honor.

A tenable counterargument to Edison's importance has already been presented: many of "his" patents were largely developed by those who worked beneath him. Moreover, with all the innovation happening in the era, it's reasonable to conclude that many of his patents, which were often merely improvements on others' innovations, were probably imminent. The inevitability of these improvements is surely a mark against his importance, which I have considered in making the most ostensibly inventive man in Western history only its 18th most influential figure. I also consider that of his 1,093 patents, few were of any major consequence, and of those few, they grew obsolete. The phonograph, for example, was impressive, but it was eventually surpassed by the record player, tape deck, CD, and mp3 file. It meanwhile paled in comparison to other inventions of the era, like the radio or telephone.

So why do I not have Guglielmo Marconi or Alexander Graham Bell, among many other notable inventors and scientists of the late nineteenth century, on my list? Simply, no scientist of the era—or, perhaps, ever—has had such a sheer diversity of contributions across numerous fields. Marconi and Bell, while certainly having incredible genius and other ideas, were essentially, if not literally, one-hit wonders. They were important enough to make a top 100 list, but not this more exclusive one.

Edison, on the other hand, catalyzed change in numerous areas. His phonograph evolved into a hundred-billion dollar audio industry. His fluoroscope transformed the way doctors made diagnoses. His contributions to motion pictures launched one of the most popular artistic mediums in history. All told, he's thought to have the most valuable brain ever. His businesses alone generated $25 billion at his death—the equivalent of $300 billion today. Factor in all of the competitive businesses that have arisen because of his inventions, the value he has generated is incalculably large.

Although there were many helping hands at Menlo Park, we cannot forget that Edison was the one who broke through with his early inventions, which earned him funding and allowed him to assemble the Menlo Park lab. He then had the wherewithal to hire and organize the right assistants and then guide those assistants to invention. Like a head-of-state delegating to his staff, Edison was the chief executive of his laboratory. We should not overlook that he oversaw everything that happened there.

Nor should we ignore the importance of his most important invention, which by itself arguably bests the inventions of Bell and Marconi. His light bulb transformed the way the Western world conducted business. Until Edison, factories and other businesses had been chained to sunlight or the cumbersome, costly lighting alternatives. Edison's bulb, however, allowed 24/7 operation at a fraction of the previous cost. The effects of that shift, both positive and negative, are undeniable.

Plus, there was not only more time for people to work, there was also more time to read, play, socialize, or go to an increasingly electric city and enjoy sporting events, concerts, or that other Edison creation—films.

Edison therefore contributed to the creation of modern Western society and culture.

Edison's network of electric distribution is similarly crucial in our personal lives. The home and its many appliances are powered by electric distribution. Isolating the "Edison effect," moreover, led to the vacuum tube which was crucial in the development of electronics, another dominant part of the modern West.

And yet, the man with a thousand patents could not add his most important legacy to that list. At Menlo Park, Edison's organization of the first modern research and development lab was a precedent that allowed the ongoing innovation that propels inventions to this day. R&D labs are the norm for major businesses across the world. They, and those who have benefited from their creations, owe Edison a debt. It's as if he's still inventing nearly a century after his death, tacking on new unofficial patents every day.

If someone transported from the time of Edison's birth to the time of his death, they would not be able to recognize the new, wondrous place at which they arrived. So much of our society changed in those 84 years, often because of the Wizard of Menlo Park. Because of his role in modernizing our world, Thomas Edison is the 18th most influential figure in Western history.

#17: Adolf Hitler

"Try explaining Hitler to a kid."

–George Carlin

Influence is not synonymous with greatness. It means having an effect, and it can certainly be negative. Many people on my Top 30 list had negative effects. In the name of defending France, Joan of Arc (#27) extended a war that was almost over. Constantine (#23) killed heretical Christians. Ask the Swedes what they think of Peter the Great (#26) or the Saxons of Charlemagne (#21). Many criticize Gregory Pincus (#25) and his birth control pill. Philip IV (#29) had the pope—the pope!—kidnapped, leading to his death. Still to come are the controversial actions of Napoleon, Martin Luther, and Christopher Columbus. Someone can be both influential and bad.

This chapter, we arrive at the worst of them all. Adolf Hitler's rise to most powerful man in European history, coupled with his atrocities, left the world scrambling to contain his evil. Interestingly, and perhaps appropriately, his most important effects were inadvertent. As the planet reorganized around him, it grew more united than ever before.

Adolf Hitler tried to take over the world, but due to pressing the world into cooperation during and after his reign of terror, he may just have saved it instead. In the process, he became the 17th most influential figure in Western history.

Adolf Hitler was born in 1889 in Braunau am Inn, a town in the Austrian part of the Austro-Hungarian Empire. Both his parents were Austrian, and Adolf lived in the northern part of the country for nearly his entire youth. Though nominally Austrian, several factors gave Hitler a German bent from an early age. His home town in upper Austria was near Germany's lower Bavaria, which imprinted a Bavarian German dialect onto him. The proximity to Germany also allowed him to be reached by German nationalist sentiments.

Germany had only recent become a united country. In 1871, the Kingdom of Prussia, under the leadership of Kaiser Wilhelm I and his Chancellor Otto von Bismarck, capped a series of unification wars to create the German Empire. Among the wars Prussia fought was one against the Austrian Empire, with a victorious Prussia officially replacing Austria as the dominant German presence in Europe. Austria compensated for its loss by shoring up the eastern half of its empire, including elevating one of its subjugated and rebellious states, Hungary, to co-equal status in exchange for cooperation. The new Austro-Hungarian Empire subjugated neighboring ethnic groups, including in the explosive Balkan region. The multi-ethnic empire included Germans, Hungarians, Czechs, Serbs, Croats, Poles, Romanians, Slovaks, Slovenians, and Italians, each with their own languages and cultures.

To a nationalist, it was a bloated disaster. Germany's victory over the Austrian Empire seemed like proof that a united, nationalist machine would always triumph over a discombobulated, multicultural one. Under such context, young Austrian Adolf Hitler, just a stone's throw from Germany's borders, dreamed of being German through-and-through. His friends adopted the German "*Heil*" as a greeting and sang the German national anthem, *Deutschlandlied*, instead of the Austrian.

History now sees the late nineteenth and early twentieth centuries as a prelude to the First World War. During this energetic era, many Western nations experienced a combination of population growth, industrialization, militarism, imperialism, and nationalism, the result of which created unprecedentedly large and powerful militaries. Every large European state found itself stronger, and therefore more confident, than ever before. Bolstering this confidence was that each major power had other major powers as allies. Germany allied with Austria-Hungary and Italy to create the Triple Alliance in the heart of Europe. Surrounding them was the Triple Entente of Russia, France, and the United Kingdom. The imperialism of the prior centuries also linked colonies from throughout the world to each European power, meaning more manpower and resources waited on shores across the globe—yet another cause of European nations' self-assurance.

All these factors led to an overconfidence that greased the skids for war. All that was left was the excuse to wage it.

The excuse came in the form of a political assassination. In the summer of 1914, a Serbian nationalist, tired of being controlled by the Austro-Hungarian Empire, assassinated Austrian Archduke Franz Ferdinand and his pregnant wife. The killing triggered a chain reaction. Austria-Hungary threatened war against Serbia despite warnings from the Russian Empire that it would come to the defense of a fellow Slavic nation. Austria-Hungry hoped its German alliance would be enough to overcome Russian interference, but Germany calculated a war against Russia would make vulnerable its western front against the Russian ally of France. Germany therefore pre-emptively declared war on France hoping to quickly overwhelm it out of the conflict before settling in on the eastern front for a long war against heavily populated Russia. This strategy failed when Britain came to the aid of its French ally. Thus, when Austria-Hungary declared war on Serbia, Germany and Austria-Hungary quickly found itself in a two-front war against three major powers and their colonies.[1] The Great War had begun.

When the war erupted, Hitler was living in Munich. Rather than race home to join the Austro-Hungarian military, which he later claimed was too multiracial for his taste, Hitler eagerly joined the German army.[2] Germans were certain they would win the war, and their confidence was not totally misplaced. The war proved Germany had the world's strongest army, but its Central Power allies, including the dying Ottoman Empire and Austria-Hungary, were more liabilities than helpful partners.[3] Yet, for four years Germany fought the collective strength of nearly the entire

---

[1] The Italians, the third member of the Triple Alliance, didn't lift a finger. That is, they didn't for a year, at which point they joined the other side. To this day I don't trust Italian men, particularly around my wife.

[2] It's speculated that an administrative error allowed him into the German army when he should have been sent home to his own country. This was perhaps the most significant administrative error in history until my gym kept charging me fees for months after I cancelled my membership.

[3] The struggling Ottoman Empire had been called the "sick man of Europe" since the disastrous Crimean War of the 1850s. As for Austria-Hungary, one German general is thought to have said that fighting alongside it was like being "shackled to a corpse."

Adolf Hitler

planet—not just the Triple Entente and its colonies, but eventually a fresh United States as well.

During the war, Hitler served as a dispatch runner, fought in five battles, was twice wounded and hospitalized, earned official honors and praise from superiors for bravery, and suffered a mustard gas attack that temporarily blinded him. While recovering from the gas late in 1918, he learned of devastating news: an armistice had been declared and a treaty would be signed with Germany on the losing end.

A stunned German population tried to take in these developments. The war claimed nearly three million German soldiers' lives, with another four million wounded. In total, nearly 10 percent of its population was dead or injured, young men primarily among them. And they lost! After years of overconfidence, it was hard to believe.

Adding insult to injury, the Treaty of Versailles (1919) took out on Germany four years of allied frustration. The great powers forced upon Germany debilitating reparations,[4] a restricted military, and reduced land and population. Perhaps worse, the treaty's "War Guilt Clause" identified Germany as the cause of the war, the deadliest the world had ever seen.[5] An angry but depleted Germany had no choice but to accept.

---

[4] Which, by the way, they paid off only in 2010.

[5] Germans had an understandable reaction to this dubious blame. World War I started when a Serbian shot an Austrian archduke, and Austria-Hungary consequently declared war on Serbia. Germany entered only through one of the entangled alliances and executed a strategy it thought was necessary to win. However, since Germany was by far the strongest of the "Central Powers," the country outlasted its allies and killed more of their enemies. Germany's success led them to be solely blamed for World War I's 20 million deaths, which I'm sure affected Germans' collective soul.

It's impossible to sufficiently describe Germans' emotions in the years following the war. The German Empire (1871-1918) had been feared across Europe. When it lost and then carried the burden of guilt, its citizens felt some combination of depression, frustration, indignation, embarrassment, and rage. Street fights regularly broke out in German cities. Armed ex-soldiers marched in the streets looking to take out their aggressions on communists. With the abdication of Kaiser Wilhelm II and Western-style democracy forced upon the nation, dozens of political factions quarreled in an attempt to gain power. A socialist, Friedrich Ebert, became the new Weimar Republic's President, but his reduced army made up of soldiers who didn't care for the new government had little success in maintaining order. The new government faced attempted coups in 1919 (by the left wing) and 1920 (by the right).

The Weimar government also had to abide by the terms of the Versailles Treaty, which included annual payments to the victors, including industrial production to France. A few years into the Republic, however, the struggling new state had trouble meeting payments. The French responded by violating German borders with soldiers, seizing the industrial region of Ruhr for two years. Workers proceeded to go on strike, with dire economic consequences. Between hefty reparation payments and a collapsing economy, German leaders turned to printing more money to meet the demand, a myopic tactic that led to hyperinflation. Stacks of German marks were often worth less than the suitcase in which they had to be carried to purchase everyday goods. In the mid-1920s, stronger leadership and renegotiations allowed the German economy to mend, but soon the Great Depression devastated it all over again.

The post-war struggles mixed into a toxic cocktail forced down the throat of shell-shocked Germans. It didn't take long for them to miss the days when Germany was feared, its borders secure, and its economy strong. Many of them wanted to avenge themselves upon those who had put the country in such a position. Some blamed the Western powers, but some also blamed internal betrayal—the Jews, communists, and democrats who undermined the home-front. If someone could come along and articulate their anger, he could garner considerable political power.

Soon, someone fit the bill. Among Germany's angriest citizens was a decorated, wounded soldier who had earned the right to call himself German, and he had some opinions.

The ink on the Treaty of Versailles had barely dried when Hitler joined a fledgling political party—the Nationalist Socialist German Workers' Party, or *Nazis* for short.[6] He became its 55th member. He used his war experiences and rising, anger-fueled oratory to recruit more members. Within two years, he was chosen as the party's leader. The German word for leader was *fuehrer*, a title he retained until his death.

Then as now, a party's popularity was essential for political power. The Kaiser's abdication left behind an enormous power vacuum, and dozens of new political parties rushed to fill it. Each had seats in the Reichstag, Germany's legislative branch. Seating a majority, or even a strong plurality, proved difficult. The result was gridlock, inefficiency, and Germans' further frustration.

---

[6] Germans called it the *Nationalsozialistische Deutsche Arbeiterpartei*. "Nazi" stems from abbreviating the first word. It's worth noting that they weren't actually socialist, at least outside of the state providing for loyal Aryan Germans, but since socialism was increasingly popular among the struggling working class, throwing that into their name seemed good for popularity. Though the "socialist" label misleads, the first adjective in the party's name—nationalist—was completely accurate.

Hitler and his Nazis capitalized. He lambasted the Versailles Treaty, denounced the Weimar Republic, and threatened other political parties.[7] In 1923, however, a premature power grab in Munich known as the "Beer Hall Putsch" landed Hitler and conspirators in prison. While in jail, Hitler penned his notorious "*Mein Kampf*" ("My Struggle"), outlining his ideology and diagnosing Germany's new problems. His struggle mirrored that of a German people who were so starved for redemption and people to blame that they devoured his words.

Meanwhile, his Nazis continued to gain popularity with the German people. Hitler sang music to the ears of Germans who spent their childhood as a feared power but in more recent years had been treated like the West's doormat. His rousing rhetoric seduced many new members into the Nazi Party. Germans tolerated racist language (from the party's inception, Nazis proclaimed their desire for Germany to be *Judenfrei*—free of Jews), since the man seemed to embody what Germans wanted: confidence, energy, and a sense of purpose.

---

[7] "Our opponents accuse us National Socialists, and me in particular, of being intolerant and quarrelsome. They say that we don't want to work with other parties. They say the National Socialists are not German at all, because they refuse to work with other political parties. So is it typically German to have thirty parties? I have to admit one thing—these gentlemen are quite right. We are intolerant. I have given myself one goal – to sweep these thirty political parties out of Germany. They mistake us for one of them. We have one aim, and we will follow it fanatically and ruthlessly to the grave."

Adolf Hitler

Hitler championed the German cause and its destiny to be great again.[8] He said theirs was the superior race, and he pointed to two thousand years of history as evidence. In the ancient world, there was the fear that the Germanic groups cut into the heart of the Roman outpost. Then there was what Hitler framed as the First *Reich*, or "Empire," which was the thousand years when the Holy Roman Empire stretched across central Europe. More recently, there was the awesome power of the recently passed German Empire or Second Reich. With nearly every speech, Hitler foreshadowed another German Empire: a Third Reich.

By 1925, the party had grown from the 55 members it had when Hitler joined to 25,000. By the close of the decade, the party was 180,000 strong. As it increased in size, the party gained strength in the Reichstag. In the early 1930s, the Nazi Party reached its tipping point. As the depression fully set in, the party exploded in popularity. In 1932, it claimed over 10 million members. In a country of 66 million, all other parties competed for second.

In the election of 1932, the Nazis earned a 37 percent plurality in the Reichstag and pieced together a coalition of other nationalists and conservatives. This Nazi-led coalition earned the ability to elect the legislature's leader. In a surprise to no one, they chose their *fuehrer*. In January of 1933, Adolf Hitler became Chancellor of Germany.

---

[8] *"In ourselves alone lies the future of the German people. Only when we ourselves raise up our German people, through our own labor, our own industry, our own determination, our own daring and our own perseverance, only then shall we rise again. In days gone by, our Fathers, too, did not receive Germany as a gift, but created it themselves."*

One month into Hitler's chancellorship, the Reichstag building was burned down. Nazis blamed their chief political opponents, the German Communist Party, who had finished second in the last Reichstag elections, and used the crisis to consolidate power.[9] In March, Hitler's cabinet drafted the Enabling Act, which would essentially confer onto the chancellor's office the Reichstag's powers, giving him broad authority to rule by decree and execute actions swiftly. Nazi authorities successfully repressed the Communist Party's presence in the Reichstag, and enough remaining legislators were intimidated into approving the act. The only remaining step was a signature from the elderly President Paul von Hindenburg, the former general and popular war hero of the Great War. He authorized the act, knowing his own popularity bested Hitler's, that he retained the Constitutional power to dismiss the Chancellor, and that Hitler actually envisioned a similar Germany as he did—one of a united German people acting in concert.

Afterward, an empowered Hitler shrewdly deferred to von Hindenburg publicly while legislating in private. It was clear von Hindenburg was not long for the world. His 85-year-old hands had signed the Enabling Act, and cancer slowly ate away at his lungs. In August of 1934, while the President lay on his deathbed, Chancellor Hitler forced through the "Law Concerning the Highest State Office of the Reich," which combined their two offices. When von Hindenburg died the next day, Hitler announced the new decree. Two weeks later, he opened the issue to the German people through a referendum. Between voter intimidation and Hitler's popularity, the country affirmed his rise. Thus,

---

[9] There are varied theories as to who the arsonists really were. Among the theories is that it was the Nazis hoping to manufacture a crisis.

through a mixture of Constitutional and democratic processes, Adolf Hitler secured full control over Germany.

His government emulated the fascism promoted by Benito Mussolini in Italy. Hitler seized control of newspapers. He banned rival parties. He forced cultural media to promote Nazism. He allied industry, the military, and government in a symbiotic union. He co-opted clerics to toe the Nazi line. He used domestic and foreign crises to strip liberties and crystallize national unity. Most infamously, Hitler used political and ethnic scapegoats to channel German anger against those who were different from their "Aryan" race. With a Ministry of Propaganda, Hitler and his closest allies carefully crafted a cult of personality around him, convincing millions of Germans of his near infallibility.

Wind in his sails, Hitler refused payments to the Great War's victors. Unemployment fell, fortunes rose, and, whether out of devotion or fear, Germans fell in line behind Hitler's policies. He demanded strict obedience[10] and usually got it. As German industry hummed once again, he restarted the war machine and pointed its tanks toward Germany's borders. Motivating Hitler and his bitter compatriots was a desire for *Lebensraum*—living space.

At this point, one might wonder how other nations were reacting. The terms of the Versailles Treaty restricted the German military and enacted the reparations that Hitler now ignored. The Western powers—

---

[10] *"The great time has now begun. Germany is now awakened. We have won power in Germany. Now we must win over the German people. I know, my comrades, it must have been difficult at times, when you were desiring change which didn't come, so time and time again the appeal has to be made to continue the struggle – you mustn't act yourself, you must obey, you must give in, you must submit to this overwhelming need to obey."*

chiefly the U.K., France, and the United States—were the ones which had come into Germany and compelled onto it a democracy. After the war, a League of Nations had been created to foster cooperation, monitor international relations, and discourage another big war. Hitler's actions were flagrantly insubordinate, his new authority was blatantly undemocratic, and his rhetoric presaged German revenge. So where was the League? Where was the West?

The answer is that other countries had their own problems. They, too, suffered from the Great Depression. Worse, all countries were pretty war weary and suffered from a collective PTSD. Millions of young men were dead, farms were ravaged, and treasuries were emptied. War was seen as a last resort. The League of Nations itself had no standing military, relying instead on individual member states to act, and it ultimately proved toothless. Meanwhile, the U.S. had quickly returned to its isolationism after the First World War and didn't even sign at Versailles.

Hitler took advantage of the West's timidity. In March of 1936, he ordered troops into the Rhineland, a western German territory that the war's victors ordered demilitarized. The West did nothing. In October, he formed an alliance with Mussolini's Italy, creating the Axis Powers. The West still did nothing. In November, Germany entered into an alliance with the Empire of Japan. The West, again, did nothing. If its leaders and citizens had the stomach for a small conflict to avoid a larger one, action from the great powers may have averted what was to come.

In 1938, Germany marched soldiers into Austria with little resistance. Germany's success had the many ethnic Germans in Austria, like Hitler's old schoolmates, wanting to take another step toward pan-Germanism. With this annexation, the two leading antagonists of World War I were reunited. The Axis Powers controlled the heart of Europe, from the North Sea to the Mediterranean. Even skeptical Germans started to believe in the German superiority espoused by the Nazis and their considerable propaganda. The army's ranks continued to swell.

When Hitler declared his intention to reacquire the Sudetenland, a former region of Germany that had been given to the new country of Czechoslovakia as its western rim, British and French leaders took a more aggressive posture—they attended a meeting. The Munich Pact allowed Hitler to claim the Sudetenland if he promised it was his "last territorial claim." He agreed, and poor Czechoslovakia's western half was surrounded. The rest of the country was soon compelled to join the new Third Reich after Hitler reneged on the deal.

In 1939, it became clear that Hitler was playing chess as the West played checkers. That summer, to avoid a threat to the east, he signed a "non-aggression" pact with Josef Stalin and the Soviet Union. While Hitler hated Stalin and despised communists, he knew that Britain and France would only tolerate so much more. He tried to ensure that the only power to his east, the U.S.S.R., would not intervene and force Germany into another two-front war.[11] The two rivals also agreed to partition Poland between them; in September, Hitler invaded the country from the west and Stalin from the east. Poland was bifurcated in weeks.

The West had seen enough. In reaction to Germany's invasion of Poland, the U.K. and France declared war on Germany. Europe and its remaining colonies plunged into another global conflict. World War II had begun.

---

[11] Stalin, meanwhile, was trying to delay a war with Hitler. The young Soviet Union still had much modernizing to do after its poor showing in the Great War.

Hitler was eager to fight, and his appetite for living space proved insatiable. German militarists felt that it was only through war a country could meet its full potential. War could test a nation's mettle, allow the strong to rise, and invigorate an economy. It was not just revenge that motivated Hitler and other Germans, but an eagerness to prove the country's superiority on the ultimate testing ground.

The Third Reich's strength increased throughout 1940. In April, Denmark and Norway fell before Hitler's *blitzkrieg*ing military. In May, Holland, Luxembourg, and Belgium also looked up at the Nazi flag. In June, Germany had its proudest moment of the war when Paris surrendered to Nazi commanders. In nine months, Hitler did what the German Empire couldn't do in the four years of World War I. France had fallen to Germany.

In 1941, Hitler added Greece, Yugoslavia, and northern Africa to the growing Axis Powers. By the height of his power, Adolf Hitler controlled more of Europe than anyone in history, including Roman emperors, Charlemagne (#21), and Napoleon (#16).[12]

These conquests proved to be Hitler's high water mark. In June of 1941, his overzealous visions of conquest, combined with thinking a war with the Soviets inevitable, led to his betrayal of the non-aggression pact with Stalin. The Nazi army steamed into eastern Europe but could not break the Russian spirit by winter. As snow piled up on Germany's eastern front, so did Nazi casualties.

---

[12] Indeed, he often fashioned himself as the next coming of each of them. Napoleon, in particular, was an idol of his. Historians have drawn many comparisons between the two, which Hitler would love and Napoleon would detest. More on that in the next chapter.

Adolf Hitler

Worse still for Germany, its Japanese allies launched a surprise attack on the Pearl Harbor U.S. naval base in Hawaii, bringing the Americans into the war.[13] Germany had no choice but to also declare war on the Axis' new enemy. By January of 1942, the U.S. and its considerable industrial capacity sent fresh troops and arms to Britain and joined the Allied Powers in the European theater. Later that year, Germany suffered a big loss in El Alamein, Egypt. Then the disastrous six-month Battle of Stalingrad, against the Soviets, which lasted into 1943, made it clear Hitler's empire was on the decline.[14]

Ultimately, Germany met its end at the hands of Hitler's hubris and the cooperation of the civilized world. For more than two years after Stalingrad, he continued the war despite the inevitability of his country's defeat. In 1944, millions died on both fronts as the Soviets pushed from the east and the Americans, British, and others from the west and south.

Even as his country ran low on men, ammunition, and gasoline, Hitler prioritized the supplies necessary to carry out his "final solution"

---

[13] Much like Hitler saw a war with Stalin as inevitable, so too did the Japanese think a war with the U.S. assured. The two were the primary powers in the Pacific, and the U.S. had taken actions to restrict Japan's sphere of influence, including placing embargoes on an island nation desperate for resource accumulation. Knowing war was in their future, Japan determined a surprise attack on a fleet stationed in Hawaii would put itself in the strongest position possible for a war over the Pacific.

[14] Stalingrad went down as an unmitigated disaster for Germany. One of the bloodiest battles in history, it claimed nearly two million casualties. Any residual Nazi momentum was gone and they never regained footing in eastern Europe. It should never be lost to history that the heroics of the U.S.S.R. on the Eastern Front in World War II was just as important as the western Allied assault that started with D-Day.

—the annihilation of the Jewish people. As his war effort crumbled around him, he kept the extermination trains moving and the ovens lit.

By 1945, the Allies closed in on Berlin. Adolf Hitler's final victim was himself. On April 30, the 56-year-old *fuehrer* shot himself. Eight days later, the Allied Powers celebrated V-E Day—Victory in Europe.

Hitler was dead. Germany was defeated. The West was ready to begin anew.

In a strange way, much of our current world stems from Adolf Hitler's reign. His evil, while having countless negative effects, gave birth to important positive ones as well.

Negative effects first. Six million Jews—of the nine million in Europe—were killed, including one million Jewish children. Considering the current Jewish population is only about 14 million, one understands the irrevocable damage Hitler caused on the global Jewish community. We should also remember that Jews weren't the only victims of the Holocaust. Russian prisoners, Polish civilians, political opponents, gypsies, homosexuals, the disabled, Africans, and anyone else deemed inferior to the "Aryan race" joined them. Everywhere Germany went, Nazis hunted for more prey.

Motivated by revenge and racism, Nazis killed people not for their actions, but for who the people *were*. Just because they existed, a million Jewish children were murdered, and Hitler looked to find more. As early as 1933, Hitler had organized his concentration camps like a CEO oversees a business. It was the most efficient slaughter in history. He set extermination quotas. The Nazis kept records. They rifled through possessions to steal valuables, tooth fillings, and hair. These were not the acts of spontaneous war-time aggression or military strategy, popular counterarguments to indemnify history's military leaders. They were planned, systematized, and smoothly executed.

The death toll of Hitler's regime wasn't limited to the Holocaust. World War II claimed 60 million lives, or about 2.5 percent of the world's population. Millions more lost limbs, homes, and sanity. World War II was the deadliest conflict in the world's history and hopefully its future as well.

It's extraordinary that one man could instigate such misery, especially one whose background was so mundane. He originally had no special bloodline, no political connections, no money, no connections, and no substantial military rank other than what he obtained through his political rise to power. Across history, all powerful leaders had at least one of those things, but not Hitler.

And yet, it can be argued that no man had ever influenced his era more. While the people still to come on our Top 30 have had proven ramifications since their time—consequences I deem more impactful than Hitler's in the last 75 years—I don't think any of them more affected their *own* time than the man who was the driving force behind 60 million deaths and a reorganization of global geopolitics.[15]

The world's response is where Hitler's effects turn inadvertent and even positive. His evil was reminiscent of medievalism, only it was combined with modern technology. It's tragic that in a century of science offering advances in the fields of medicine, communication, food pro-

---

[15] It's worth noting that while I suspect others on this list will gradually fade from influence, Hitler will not. Assuming we don't have a conflict deadlier than the Second World War, he'll be history's last large-scale conqueror. When I update this list in two hundred years, perhaps Hitler will be ranked even higher.

duction, and so much more, a madman could rise to the heights that he did and use some of the latest technology to promote racism, bigotry, and religious persecution. It was supposed to be a more civilized era. Indeed, we almost forgive the Alexanders, Caesars, and Khans, as they were products of their time. Hitler, however, was from modern Germany, an enlightened country that had given us Bach and Beethoven, Kant and Goethe. Germany raised Adolf Hitler near the same time it groomed Albert Einstein. Despite this progressive home, Hitler had tapped into the kind of base tribalism we hoped we had shed centuries earlier.

His malevolence demanded a question be asked of our civilization, then and now: how far removed from the Dark Ages are we really? Was the next Hitler waiting around the corner? Might he still be? Is there still a subconscious racism simmering beneath us, one that's waiting to be unleashed with the right mixture of context and rhetoric?

The world feared the answers. Therefore, at the height of the war, countries across the globe summed up their collective courage, resolving to contain and eliminate him. It is still the greatest example of geopolitical heroism and teamwork in history.

Just as important, however, is how that collaboration created momentum for post-war cooperation. The subsequent creation of the United Nations, which began in October of 1945, might be the most important development since World War II.[16] A millennium from now, it could very well be considered the most important step ever taken by mankind.

---

[16] It should be noted that it was not the first international body whose purpose was to maintain stability and peace. The Congress of Vienna of the early nineteenth century and the League of Nations of the period between the world wars each showed European cooperation. Neither, however, were as long-lasting or effective as the U.N. has been.

Adolf Hitler

Before the U.N., wars were getting bloodier and deadlier—the Napoleonic Wars, the Crimean, the Russo-Japanese, and then each of the world wars. Thanks to burgeoning industrial technology and production, each war was worse than the last, and the last introduced the atomic bomb. The trend was terrifying, and with the introduction of nuclear weapons, many expected a Third World War inevitable and possibly apocalyptic.

But the U.N., formed by 51 countries just a few months after World War II, now includes 193 nations. Though far from a perfect body, the U.N. monitors the world's security, trade, human rights, and much more. Never before has there been such international cooperation, friendship, and stability. Our weapons are deadlier than ever, but most motivations or means to use them internationally are squashed early enough that they don't become major concerns or earn much attention. Speaking volumes for its effectiveness is that since its inception we haven't had a global conflict.

And we haven't had another Hitler either. The long tradition of a warmonger bent on conquering the world died with him. The world was so horrified—ashamed even—that countries took measures to ensure that another Hitler would be nearly impossible. Potential sequels—Pol Pot, Slobodan Milošević, and Saddam Hussein, for examples—were up to the barbaric task, but international teamwork, whether economic or military, contained their atrocities.

A final argument for his importance, although I usually avoid its kind, is that his acts seemed neither inevitable nor expected. It seems like so many other figures on this list did something that was either imminent or bound to happen eventually.[17] Hitler, however, seemed uniquely driven to commit these atrocities and was talented enough to convince a country to follow him. Things weren't just bad in Germany; they were bad *everywhere*. Yet there was only one Hitler.

Think about the popularity of other major worldviews—like capitalism, democracy, and socialism—over the last 150 years. They've been around the world, are still practiced today, and have had lots of people to thank for their rise and endurance. But Nazism? Not only was it isolated to Germany's empire, but, with the exception of recent sects who either claim or are accused of Neo-Nazism, it scaled and fell from its peak with one man—Adolf Hitler. German laws and traditions since 1945 tightly manage the discussion of Hitler and the Holocaust, and many Germans remain embarrassed of that era in their history. A collective guilt has guided the country for decades, manifesting in its crucial role powering the European Union and bailing out other E.U. nations.

In the end, Hitler had incredible success in accomplishing many of his objectives, but significant miscalculations cost him all his goals. The contrived War Guilt Clause at the end of World War I animated him and the German people, but since World War II a collective guilt naturally replaced it. Hitler wanted to give Germany living space and then to rule

---

[17] The birth control pill from Gregory Pincus (#25) was due. If Thomas Jefferson (#24) didn't write the Declaration of Independence or purchase Louisiana, someone else would have. Henry Ford (#20) was the first to capitalize on mass production and scientific management, but surely that was bound to happen as well. Almost all of the inventions of Thomas Edison (#18) were imminent and took place in an explosion of innovation. Still to come on our list, the actions of people like Darwin, Pasteur, Luther, and Columbus were probably all inevitable. That being said, this list rewards those who did important things, no matter how inevitable those achievements were.

the world, but the country was partitioned for 45 years after the war and ended up with less land than it had before him. Hitler abhorred democracy, but Germany has become democratic and a champion of liberalism. He hated communism, but communism continued to strengthen in the Soviet Union and then China, each of whom became major world powers while Germans couldn't even govern their own nation. He wanted to exterminate the scattered Jewish population, but the Jews were soon given a state of their own. It can be argued, quite pleasingly, that Adolf Hitler is among history's greatest failures.

Like evil, however, even failures can change the world. He is evidence of both. Between his rise to madman of Europe and the progress the world has experienced because of him, Adolf Hitler is the 17th most influential person in Western history.

#16: Napoleon Bonaparte

"I used to say of him that his presence on the field made the difference of forty thousand men."

–Arthur Wellesley, 1st Duke of Wellington, 1831

Last chapter, I wrote about a man who grabbed control of his country, conquered a continent, turned the great powers against him, and inadvertently redirected the West's destiny. That man was Adolf Hitler. Over a century earlier, however, someone else had also roared to leadership, established hegemony over Europe, forced coalitions to contain him, and ushered in a reorganization of Western geopolitics. That man was Napoleon Bonaparte.

As the last two emperors of Europe, Hitler and Napoleon are often compared. Though Hitler loved that, Napoleon would have detested it. While there are obvious parallels between these two dictators' careers, these similarities are mostly superficial. Whereas Hitler's vision hearkened back to the Dark Ages, Napoleon's looked toward the future. His drive helped him become the 16th most influential figure in Western history.

Napoleon Bonaparte

Napoleone Buonaparte was born on the newly French island of Corsica in 1769.[1] Raised in an affluent home of low nobility, at age 10 he entered a military academy in mainland France. His stay was not enjoyable. While he was technically French, his Italian accent earned him thorough teasing. Most of his classmates were much wealthier, providing mockery another target. Napoleon quickly hardened and later recalled these moments as part of his origin story.[2] After five years of intense study, he was accepted into Paris's prestigious *École Militaire*. Although students ordinarily completed this academy in two years, financial straits pressed Napoleon to do it in one. Upon graduation in 1785, the 16-year-old *Italiano Corso* became a second lieutenant and artillery officer in a French regiment.

Four years later, revolution broke out in France. Calls for *Liberté*, *égalité*, and *fraternité* started in France and were soon echoed by hopeful castes across Europe. The Bourbon monarchy was overthrown, Louis XVI was guillotined, terror reigned, governments replaced governments, and France defended itself as nervous European monarchs, very much attached to their heads, declared war on liberalism.

---

[1] The island had just lost its sovereignty after only 14 years of independence. Before that, the Genoese Republic controlled it for about five centuries. Nevertheless, despite the island having an Italian feel, Napoleon was born a French citizen.

[2] The memoirs of his first wife, Joséphine, mentions that he once told her, "I kept aloof from my schoolfellows. I had chosen a little corner in the school grounds, where I would sit and dream at my ease; for I have always liked reverie. When my companions tried to usurp possession of this corner, I defended it with all my might. I already knew by instinct that my will was to override that of others, and that what pleased me was to belong to me."

It was in these wars where young Napoleon distinguished himself. In the Siege of Toulon, where the republican French army battled a royalist counter-rebellion in late 1793, the relatively unknown, 24-year old Captain Napoleon was put in charge of the artillery and showed remarkable skill.[3] With his success, he was promoted to brigadier general, becoming the youngest general in French history. In 1795, his leadership protected the revolution at the "13 Vendemiaire" skirmish with royalist forces.[4] He received another promotion, this time to division general.

Meanwhile, the new French government, the "National Convention," failed. France switched to the five-man Directory (1795-1799), the most prominent member of which both respected and feared Napoleon.[5] Napoleon's success at 13 Vendemiaire had made him

---

[3] The general in command at Toulon, Jacques François Dugommier, heeded Napoleon's attack strategy over that of more senior officers. He later noted: "I have no words to describe Bonaparte's merit: much technical skill, an equal degree of intelligence, and too much gallantry." Nailed it.

[4] The French revolutionaries created a new calendar based around the Enlightenment ideals of "Christianity, mythology, and other things that don't make sense must go." To that end, the years restarted so as not to be tied to the birth of Jesus, with the French Revolution occurring in Year I. Their new calendar had 12 months of an elegant 30 days, with an extra 5 or 6 called "Complementary Days." Each month began on what we would now call the 21st, 22nd, 23rd, or 24th of each month, allowing the seasons to begin on the first of a month. Further, each month's name was tied to terms associated with the seasons. Winter had a month called Nivôse (winter), spring had a month called Floréal (flower), summer had a month called Thermidor (heat), and autumn had a month called Vendémiaire (vintage). On the 13th of that last month was the battle of 13 Vendémiaire. I'm deeply sorry it took me so long to get to the point.

[5] That man, the extensively named Paul François Jean Nicolas, vicomte de Barras, was once paired with Napoleon's wife, so there was likely more than just political jealousy between the two.

a hero to the troops under his command and republican France. Fearing Napoleon's ambition and popularity during its early days of leadership, the Directory needed to relocate Napoleon while also not angering him.[6] In March of 1796, Napoleon was promoted again, this time to army general, and he was given command of a campaigning army across the Southern Alps. For the moment, the threat was distracted.

While in Italy, Napoleon again thrived. Though sometimes outnumbered, he won battle after battle, almost always killing and capturing many more soldiers than he lost. Soldiers who had been embroiled in three-year conflicts found themselves, after Napoleon's arrival, winning in a matter of weeks. They quickly learned to adore their rescuer.

After securing victory in Italy despite facing a coalition of European countries, the tactician in Napoleon deduced that the greatest threat to French dominance was the British Empire. Despite recently losing 13 of its American colonies, Britain remained Europe's top military power and possessed the world's largest navy. Napoleon considered an invasion of Britain, but France's navy was too weak by comparison. Instead, in 1798, he determined the best way to weaken his foe was by first severing Britain's trade with its Indian colony, followed by working with local Indian leaders in a rebellion against British rule. The first step in this plan meant securing the Isthmus of Suez in Egypt, and the Directory approved the plan.[7]

---

[6] Barras purportedly told his colleagues, "Advance this man or he will advance himself without you."

[7] More privately, Napoleon wished to walk in the footsteps of former conqueror of Egypt Alexander the Great, who he expected was his only historical rival on the battlefield.

Though he excelled on the Egyptian battlefield, Britain's navy decimated his. In the calamitous Battle of the Nile, 13 French ships squared off against 15 from Britain led by the iconic Admiral Horatio Nelson. The French lost all but two ships, while the English fleet came away whole. Whereas there were about 9,000 French casualties and prisoners, British losses numbered one-tenth of that. The campaign a disaster, Napoleon left his troops under a lesser general's command and raced back to Paris, where another coalition of European nations threatened France.

Despite the loss in Egypt, Napoleon remained a hero back home. In his absence, the Directory had lost popularity as European forces threatened to wipe away the revolution. Napoleon seized the moment and engineered a coup d'état. In the Directory's place, Napoleon and two others formed the "Consulate," with Napoleon acting as "First Consul." The transition was affirmed by an overwhelmingly supportive plebiscite of French citizens[8] who were attracted to stable, competent leadership after a decade of revolutions and coups that ripped up a few constitutions and pieced them back together in different forms. Napoleon seemed to offer that stability. The Consulate (1799-1804), while republican in theory, quickly evolved into a military dictatorship. The other two consuls were weak and, living up to their titles, merely consultative. Napoleon, only 30 years old, controlled France with unchecked power.

The French got the decisive leader they wanted. Under the Consulate, Napoleon instituted a series of long-lasting reforms—first for France, later for much of Europe and beyond.

---

[8] The final, shady tally was over three million in favor and 1,567 opposed.

Among his initiatives was the divestment of North American holdings. The decade-long Haitian Revolution had cost France lives and treasure as it fought to maintain its slave colony. Though the French Revolution had abolished slavery in the empire, Napoleon, after initial reluctance, reinstituted it in an amoral attempt to regain order over the colony. The brutality of his generals galvanized the Haitian resistance all the more. Further slave revolts and yellow fever ultimately made Haiti too costly to govern. With Europe again ready to go to war with France, Napoleon decided to leave the colonial game altogether. He gave up on Haiti and sold the massive Louisiana territory to President Thomas Jefferson (#24) and the Americans for just $15 million ($342 million today).

Domestically, though First Consul Napoleon re-centralized the French state with power in one man's hands, he still framed himself as a progressive leader. In his view, a well-managed state, even an autocratic one, could lead to liberty and prosperity. Under his leadership, there was stability and fortune in France through his nationalization of banks and education, modernization of the government's judicial and financial systems, creation of a national university, promotion of science, and a new civil legal system which bore his name—the Napoleonic Code.

With these reforms, Napoleon eradicated the remnants of feudalism and defended the legal equality of men. He outlawed privileges based on birth, ensured religious freedom, and reorganized government and military positions to ensure that promotions occurred based on merit instead of familial connections. Most reforms survived him and continue to this day. It was a code for the future, and Napoleon took it wherever he conquered.

Who Made the West

And conquer he did. The brilliant tactics and sense of timing that so impressed his teachers at the academy and commanders on the battlefield followed him throughout his political career. He sped up war's pace with faster marches. He had a knack for positioning artillery, cavalry, and reserves to capitalize on superior numbers or make up for inferior ones. His daring flanking maneuvers ripped apart defenses. It was as if he had retrained the dogs of war.[9]

Toward the Consulate's end, the War of the Third Coalition erupted. As Napoleon battled Britain, Austria, and Russia, he sealed his dictatorship back home by forcing Pope Pius VII to crown him "Emperor of France" in 1804.[10] This ascension marked the first time France had a papal coronation of an emperor since Charlemagne (#21) just over a thousand years earlier.[11]

France went on to defeat his opponents' combined might, including a hallmark achievement against a Russo-Austrian force led by Tsar Alexander I at the Battle of Austerlitz. Despite French forces being outnumbered by 20 percent, there were 12 Russians and Austrians killed for every French soldier.

---

[9] If this were Risk, he'd be the guy rolling far too many sixes.

[10] After learning of Napoleon's crowning, Ludwig van Beethoven, whom had thus far been a huge fan of Napoleon's progressive management and was dedicating his Third Symphony to him, is said to have scratched off the dedication. The surviving title, "Eroica," still conjures Beethoven's disappointing hero.

[11] It should be noted, however, that while Charlemagne's crowning at the hands of Pope Leo III solidified an era of papal dominance, Napoleon took the crown from Pius's hands and crowned himself, showing that not even the Church was above his state.

Napoleon Bonaparte

In contrast, Emperor Napoleon still couldn't handle Admiral Nelson and the British navy, which handed him a devastating loss at Trafalgar. With this latest failure to subdue the United Kingdom (to which Great Britain had transitioned in 1801), Napoleon enacted the "continental system" across Europe, hoping to weaken the U.K. economically by forbidding any European country from trading with it.

By war's end in 1806, Napoleon had pushed into central Europe and dissolved the Holy Roman Empire.[12] Prussia took note as France encroached into its sphere of influence, and soon another war began as Prussia aligned with Britain, Russia, and Sweden in the War of the Fourth Coalition. Despite the four opponents, Napoleon won in about a year. To protect this new border, Napoleon reached out to Tsar Alexander, and the two entered into a friendship agreement in the Treaty of Tilsit.

Napoleon's grasp stretched further. In 1809, Napoleon's *Grande Armée* defeated yet another coalition—the Fifth, which included Britain, Austria, and Bavaria. For the next few years, the Napoleonic Empire remained at its height. Though directly controlled French land was only about twice its normal size, Napoleon's satellite states (including Spain, the Holy Roman Empire's remnants, southern Italy, and modern Poland) and forced alliances (Denmark, Prussia, and Austria) extended his power over almost all of Europe. Any monarchs he didn't trust he replaced with family members.

---

[12] Napoleon removed Holy Roman Emperor Francis II from the throne before dissolving the empire altogether. His reasoning: there should only be one emperor of Europe.

Napoleon, the teased Corsican son of a low noble, was not yet 40 years old and controlled more of Europe than anyone in the continent's storied history.

Inevitably, a man who swings as hard as Napoleon sometimes misses with such a flourish that he nearly falls down. The two significant mainland European holdouts—Portugal and Russia—beckoned him. In his attempt to conquer Portugal and subdue Spanish opposition, Napoleon became stuck in the frustrating Peninsular War (1807-1814). Year after year, this war for Iberian control drained French resources as Portuguese and Spanish resistance fighters fought for independence.[13]

Napoleon's other large failure is the far more remembered debacle. In the summer of 1812, after Tsar Alexander began ignoring the continental system and resumed trading with the U.K., Napoleon backed out of the Tilsit Treaty and invaded Russia.

Never had his thirst for domination cost him more.[14] For the invasion of the world's biggest country, Napoleon amassed the largest army in European history. Napoleon led about 600,000 soldiers into Russian territory. In defense, the Russians only mustered a professional army of about 200,000. Napoleon, who had regularly won battles while outnumbered, ostensibly had a huge advantage. With this overwhelming com-

---

[13] In his defense, the French army dominated the Peninsular War during the conflict's middle portion when Napoleon personally led the campaign. Before and after his presence, however, the French had steady losses dotted with Pyrrhic victories.

[14] The following should be read while listening to Tchaikovsky's "1812 Overture." In 1880, the great Russian composer wrote the piece to commemorate the Russian resistance.

mitment of resources, Napoleon counted on Russia realizing resistance was futile.

What he did not count on, however, was Russia's ingenuity, her desperation, or her winter. Russian commanders knew that pitched battles against Napoleon would be hopeless. The defense therefore largely avoided direct conflict with the invaders. Instead, it coupled minor skirmishes with a gradual retreat into the endless tracts of Russian land. As Napoleon and the French army pursued the Russian retreat, Russian leadership ordered towns and farms evacuated and burned. This strategy, called "scorched-earth," effectively reduced or eliminated the supplies that the massive French army needed to sustain itself. A large invading force usually lived off the land, but Russia denied Napoleon this option.

Napoleon determined that the only way to secure Russian surrender must be an outright assault on Moscow. He would not only force the capitulation of Russia's most populous city,[15] but his famished and freezing army could use its resources for food, rest, and shelter. The army arrived in Moscow on September 14, just as summer gave way to autumn. What the soldiers found astonished them: like the Russian countryside, Moscow was evacuated and burned to the ground.[16]

He lingered in Moscow, hoping the Russians would realize that its largest city being in flames should compel them to surrender, but they did no such thing. After a month of waiting, Napoleon moved southwest

---

[15] Note that Moscow was not the Russian capital ever since Peter the Great (#26) moved it to Saint Petersburg. Moscow became the capital again after 1917's Bolshevik Revolution.

[16] The extreme to which the Muscovites went is extraordinary. Before their evacuation, they disassembled fire engines, kept fuses lit, and packed the homes with anything flammable. In a wooden city, 80 percent of it was destroyed. All self-inflicted.

to again battle a Russian army, and again Russian commanders avoided a direct engagement. By the middle of October, Napoleon realized it was no use. He ordered a retreat.

This withdrawal, however, turned out to be more ruinous than the invasion. The no longer grand *Armée* returned along the same barren route on which it had traveled into Russia. With no grass for the dying horses, the entire army resorted to walking hundreds of miles. Carts and wagons could no longer be pulled, so more supplies were lost. December arrived before Napoleon's army escaped Russian territory. Frostbite and disease took their toll on the soldiers more than the Russians ever had.

The Moscow campaign inflicted devastating damage on the French army. Of the approximately 600,000 invading troops, only about a hundred thousand returned to France. Of those hungry and frostbitten survivors, perhaps 30,000 were still able to fight. The largest force in European history returned at five percent of its strength.

European countries quickly pounced on the declawed emperor. A massive Sixth Coalition of Austria, Russia, Britain, Portugal, Sweden, Spain, Prussia and old Holy Roman states ganged up on the hollowed out army. It still took 16 months and the Battle of Leipzig—the largest battle in European history to that point (not topped until World War I)—but Europe finally vanquished its great antagonist. In April 1814, Napoleon abdicated.

The victors exiled him to the island of Elba, just off Tuscany's coast. In a cruel jest, he was allowed to serve as the tiny island's governor. The triumphant coalition then restored the Bourbon Dynasty. Louis XVIII, brother of the king beheaded two decades earlier, took the French throne.

Incredibly, Napoleon's story does not end there. After a failed suicide attempt robbed him of alternatives, he started to work within his new situation. Ever the leader and problem solver, his nine months on Elba were spent governing the island, including instituting social and economic reforms. Through newspapers, he was kept abreast of the situation in France. Louis XVIII grew unpopular as land from the French Empire was stripped and returned to European countries while reparations were assigned to the nation. France had gone from continental power to a country manhandled by foreigners and a complicit king who owed them his crown. The French people and military pined for the glory days of Napoleon.

To their excitement, in February of 1815 Napoleon escaped from Elba. A week later, he came ashore in France. Louis sent soldiers to intercept Napoleon's return. When they arrived, Napoleon bellowed to them, "Here I am. Kill your Emperor, if you wish." Without much of a pause, the soldiers began responding "*Vive L'Empereur!*" They lined up behind him and entered Paris together.

With the army's support, he resumed the emperorship for what became known as his "Hundred Days." It took a Seventh Coalition of just about every European country (including Austria, Prussia, Britain, and Russia, each of which promised 150,000 soldiers to the effort) to again unseat him, with their efforts culminating in the Battle of Waterloo. The defeated Napoleon was again exiled, this time to the island of St. Helena in the middle of the south Atlantic.

There, he lived out his final six years. Napoleon Bonaparte's final battle was with stomach cancer, an ailment that conquered him in 1821. He was only 51.

But what a 51 years it was! There are few more incredible biographies in our Top 30. Born an outsider, Napoleon showed peerless talent and drive to eventually become the most powerful person in European history.

As I've said before, however, this list isn't about greatness. It's about influence. So what was his? Estimates are that about five million people died from the Napoleonic Wars. Beyond the death toll, his wars destroyed European economies, farms, and infrastructure.

These were necessary requirements for industrializing, thus hindering the process across the continent. Yet, while mainland Europe was torn apart by two decades of war, the United Kingdom remained relatively stable. True, it constantly fought with Napoleon, but the island itself, thanks to Admiral Nelson and the gallant British navy, remained safe. As a result, the Industrial Revolution steamed ahead in Britain while mainland Europe did not have the requisite advantages in land, labor, and capital to keep up. The British pulled far away from the rest of Europe in industrialization, and only late in the nineteenth century would others rival it.

Politically, his reign precipitated the Congress of Vienna, where states across Europe sent representatives to discuss how to contain the impacts of Napoleon and the French Revolution. This group guided European affairs in the post-Napoleonic years. It was the largest show of European cooperation in its long, divisive history. It became a precursor to bodies such as the League of Nations, United Nations, and European Union. While its conservative, even reactionary policies worked to undo the French Revolution and Napoleon's "damage," many progressive ideas were too popular and entrenched after a decade of Napoleonic rule.

Napoleon also instilled a new sense of nationalism in European countries. The Holy Roman Empire had hundreds of states for much of its thousand years in central Europe. When Napoleon disbanded it in 1806, he replaced it with the less complicated Confederation of the Rhine, which came to have only 36 states. The Congress of Vienna didn't mind it too much and converted into the similar German Confederation. Each was a step toward fewer German states and more unity. A half-century later, the German kingdom of Prussia, through war and diplomacy, consolidated many of these states into what we now call Germany.

The Italian states were also fused under Napoleon and began their own march toward unification, achieving it at almost the same time as Germany. These two new nations soon allied with each other and became primary players in the twentieth century's world wars.

Socially, the Napoleonic Code diffused throughout Europe. Enlightenment ideas promoted by the likes of Voltaire (#22) and Jean-Jacques Rousseau (near miss) were spread by Napoleon through his reforms to European legal systems. Nobility had been dealt one of its final blows as liberalism continued its march, this time alongside General Napoleon.[17] Napoleon may have been a feared and hated occupant, but European citizens did not want to roll back his more favorable changes.[18]

European colonies, with their mother countries occupied by Napoleon, also began the transition to Napoleonic modernity. Not only

---

[17] Napoleon seemed to recognize the importance of the Napoleonic Code: "Waterloo will wipe out the memory of my forty victories; but that which nothing can wipe out is my Civil Code. That will live forever."

[18] The Revolutions of 1848 are perhaps the greatest manifestations of this resistance to post-Napoleonic leaders' reactionary policies.

did some of them import the Napoleonic Code, but Spanish colonies were able to use his occupation of Spain as a means to escape from underneath the empire's thumb, which had been pressing down on them in the centuries since Christopher Columbus. Starting in the early nineteenth century, with Spain too distracted and then too weakened by Napoleon to stop them, Spanish colonies from Mexico to Tierra del Fuego began declaring their independence. We now know these colonies as the countries of Central and South America. Napoleon's disruption of Iberia hastened Brazil's independence from Portugal as well.

Another former European colony, the United States of America, also benefited from Napoleon's reign, as shown with the Louisiana Purchase. Almost overnight, the U.S. doubled its size and took a leap toward its other shining sea and destiny as a world power.[19]

It's worth noting at this point that many of Napoleon's effects were inadvertent, which brings us back to this column's hook—Napoleon Bonaparte and Adolf Hitler have some remarkable similarities. Like Hitler, Napoleon was born into obscurity and became the master of Europe. As with Hitler, Napoleon's downfall was overextending his empire. (Incredibly, both did so by invading Russia and being defeated as much by its winter as its army.) Finally, like Hitler, Napoleon was so strong that he forced the West to gather its collective strength to contain and then eliminate him, which clearly wasn't part of the plan. The victorious allies then did all they could to reduce the impacts of their beaten rival.

However, we mustn't forget some important distinctions between these two men. Whereas Napoleon was motivated by ambition and a de-

---

[19] The consequences of this transaction were more deeply explored in my chapter on Thomas Jefferson (#24).

sire to socially (if not politically) modernize a continent, Hitler's motivation was a repugnant worldview that more resembled medievalism than any progress advocated by Napoleon. Although Napoleon inexcusably resurrected slavery in the French West Indies, he did so grudgingly and only after the island had been difficult to govern without it, which distracted him from European geopolitics. He ultimately landed on a different solution, which was to allow the island to break away altogether and sell off North American land.

For the most prominent example of a contrast, consider that Hitler wanted to exterminate the Jewish population, but Napoleon welcomed them and even lifted anti-Semitic laws. Napoleon's emancipation of the Jews removed laws that restricted them to ghettos. He allowed them property, freedom of worship, and entrance into careers of their choosing. He then withstood anti-Semitic reactions from officials who wanted them deported. He vowed, "I will never accept any proposals that will obligate the Jewish people to leave France, because to me the Jews are the same as any other citizen in our country."

Napoleon abolished the Spanish Inquisition, which was somehow still around in the 1800s, whereas Hitler instigated something even worse. Although both men were largely motivated by ambition and a quest to make their country's great, Napoleon also made an effort to move Europe forward. Hitler felt compelled to kill those who were different because they were different, a considerably backward concept.

These differences explain why Napoleon outranks Hitler on this list. Hitler spread Nazism beyond German borders and Napoleon spread the French Revolution's liberal ideas beyond France. Which ideology remains more dominant today? It's liberalism—hopefully permanently.

If both men saw modern Western culture, Hitler would recognize his failure, while Napoleon would probably congratulate himself. Therefore, Napoleon Bonaparte edges Adolf Hitler to become the 16th most influential figure in Western history.

#15: Charles Darwin

"It has often and confidently been asserted, that man's origin can never be known: but ignorance more frequently begets confidence than does knowledge: it is those who know little, and not those who know much, who so positively assert that this or that problem will never be solved by science."

-Charles Darwin, "The Descent of Man," 1871

The opening quote from my Nicolaus Copernicus (#28) chapter came from the German philosopher Goethe, who said of Copernicus's heliocentric theory:

"Of all discoveries and opinions, none may have exerted a greater effect on the human spirit than the doctrine of Copernicus. The world had scarcely become known as round and complete in itself when it was asked to waive the tremendous privilege of being the center of the universe. Never, perhaps, was a greater demand made on mankind."

Goethe was right. Copernicus had challenged mankind's "tremendous privilege"–the one that assumed we were literally the central part of God's plan—which indeed had a "greater effect on the human spirit" than any idea up until Goethe's lifetime.

However, Goethe was right only because he died shortly before an idea rivaled heliocentrism's audacity. A generation after the philosopher's 1832 death, a new proposal once again humbled humanity. This new idea came from Charles Robert Darwin, a naturalist who is now the 15th most influential figure in Western history.

February 12, 1809 marked the births of two historical titans. One was Abraham Lincoln, who didn't make this Top 30, and the other was Charles Darwin, who now lands in the top half of it.[1] Born in the English town of Shrewsbury to an upper-middle class family headed by a successful doctor, young Charles was meant to follow in his father's footsteps. As a 16-year-old, he reluctantly enrolled in the University of Edinburgh to study medicine. His courses acquainted him with anatomy and surgery, but, finding the former dull and the latter gross, he put little effort into either. His father thought sending him to Cambridge to become a priest would set him straight, but once Charles was surrounded by the bright young minds of that prestigious university, their hobbies became his. While at Cambridge, his apathy toward schooling contrasted with curiosity elsewhere. Among these interests was natural history, a field he would soon transform.

A professor took notice and recruited Darwin to fill an opening on a ship that was about to set sail for a circumnavigation. The ship was the *HMS Beagle*, and the opening was for a naturalist. Darwin, much to the

---

[1] Lincoln, of course, is near the top of a "most influential Americans" ranking. I'd share with you the rest of that list, but why spoil a potential sequel?

Charles Darwin

chagrin of his father, immediately accepted the adventure of a lifetime. He hopped aboard accompanied by an ironic choice of reading material—Milton's "Paradise Lost." The ship departed England in 1831 and played host to one of the most revealing voyages in world history.

The *Beagle*'s five-year voyage was a naturalist's dream. The ship made stops on Atlantic islands and both coasts of South America. It then crossed the Pacific Ocean, landed in New Zealand and Australia, traversed the Indian Ocean, landed in South Africa, and then hit South America again for good measure before returning home. At each stop, while the *Beagle* charted the coast, its naturalist, like a reborn Aristotle (#30), studied and categorized every living thing he found. Most remarkably, it was a low-tech venture. He had no laboratory, no microscope, no telescope, no scope of any kind. It was only Darwin and his copious notes that formed the foundation for his later species-altering proposals.

His most famous stop was at the Galápagos Islands off the northwest coast of South America. Aside from Darwin's celebrated visit, these isolated islands are mostly known for their endemic species—that is, species that can't be found anywhere else. Darwin was in heaven. He studied species unknown to Europe—mammals, insects, reptiles, birds—each with tremendous variety. He identified 12 different types of finches across the islands, and he observed tortoises so big he thought their species predated the Biblical flood.[2] Only later did Darwin assign mean-

---

[2] Just how big are Galapagos tortoises? Upwards of 900 pounds! They'd have enjoyed this heft more if it hadn't made them, in the words of Darwin, "capital soup." Darwin also ate roast armadillo and rhea on this trip. Animals must have swam, run, and flown for cover when they spotted the *Beagle* coming over the horizon.

ing to the Galapagos Governor's offhand comment that he could look at a tortoise and know precisely from which island it came.

When Darwin returned home at age 27, he started publishing his work, though his hallmark ideas wouldn't get proposed until his 50s. In between, his newfound work ethic made him a prolific author and an accomplished naturalist biologist. Meanwhile, he began what's now called the inception of Darwin's theory, followed by its development.[3]

Within a few years of his return home, he started to juxtapose his discoveries with the recent evolutionary premise from Jean-Baptiste Lamarck (1744-1829). Lamarck was the first prominent advocate of species changing over time rather than remaining fixed across history and prehistory. He believed that species had evolved from fewer in number and simpler in structure to more numerous and complex. Lamarck often erred with big ideas—most prominently that acquired traits during one's life can be passed on, meaning a species could choose to evolve its genetics with decision-making.[4] Nonetheless, the notion of evolution itself was a foundational idea that Darwin, supported by observations around the world, built on and refined.

Darwin agreed with Lamarck that all species—not just animals but also plants—did not remain static over time. However, Lamarck had not correctly determined why they changed. After reading Thomas Malthus's "An Essay on the Principle of Population," which proposed that over-

---

[3] You know his idea is a big deal when its inception, development, and then publication get separate Wikipedia articles. No one else has that, right?

[4] Lamarck used the example of a giraffe stretching its neck more and more to reach food, and this longer neck could be passed on to its offspring. If we were to apply that to humans, it would mean that someone who lifts weights or runs marathons could pass along strength or endurance to their child.

population led to death and a return to a manageable number,[5] Darwin determined that those most adapted to their environments—those who were fastest or strongest or had the longest neck or sharpest beak, depending on what was most environmentally useful—would more likely survive such catastrophes and pass their traits along to the next generation. Those less adapted would be less likely to survive, and therefore less likely to reproduce, and therefore more likely to die out as a species. This "natural selection," as he called it, would not only weed out certain species, but it would cause surviving species to change over time as their favorable traits became more pronounced while less favorable traits faded. Though catastrophes might speed up the process of natural selection, the same process occurs over longer periods in the face of less aggressive extinction processes.

This phenomenon explained the differences in the Galapagos tortoises and finches noted by the governor and Darwin. Over generations, the animals had evolved based on their specific island's habitat. "The result," his "Autobiography" later notes, "would be the formation of new species." *New* species!

Darwin knew his theory of evolution, which congealed around 1840, would face fanatical resistance, so he held off publishing it for nearly two decades as he prepared his thesis, organized his research, and shored up supporting evidence and arguments. It was not until 1859

---

[5] See: Malthusian catastrophe or, more significantly, the importance of Gregory Pincus (#25).

that the 50-year-old Darwin felt comfortable publishing his theory. He called his book "On the Origin of Species."[6]

Darwin made it a pretty accessible work, allowing it to be consumed by all sectors of society. Pulling from history, anatomy, biology, geology, geography, morphology, and embryology, he marshaled diverse evidence, showed how the puzzle pieces fit together, and led any open-minded reader toward one inescapable conclusion: evolution by means of natural selection is real.

The widely discussed book generated debate across the Western world. Traditionalists and older naturalists resisted the idea, but younger scientists embraced its increasingly obvious truth. Still, as acrimonious as this discourse was, the discussion was relatively civil compared to what was to follow.

There was an idea Darwin had merely implied in the "Origin of Species" that he would explicitly propose in his next major work. "Origin" had concluded quite provocatively:

"There is grandeur in this view of life, with its several powers, having been originally breathed into a few forms or into one; and that, whilst this planet has gone cycling on according to the fixed law of gravity, from so simple a beginning endless forms most beautiful and most wonderful have been, and are being, evolved."

In other words, all life came from one or a very limited group of ancestors. Many wondered if Darwin included mankind in this theory.

---

[6] Well, it was actually called, "On the Origin of Species by Means of Natural Selection, or the Preservation of Favored Races in the Struggle for Life." Now you know why I relegated the full title to a footnote.

Twelve years after "Origin," the wondering was over. In 1871, about a week after his 62nd birthday, he published "The Descent of Man." In it, he put forth the most controversial idea of his—and perhaps anyone's—career.

It took three paragraphs into the book's introduction to show he was playing with Prometheus's fire: "*The sole object of this work is to consider, firstly, whether man, like every other species, is descended from some pre-existing form.*" His answer, eventually, was yes, we are. Mankind descends from prehistoric apes, and apes descend from earlier species as well.

Mankind was not pleased with this news.

You can't blame people for bristling at the idea. To many Westerners, the Bible was, as the saying implies, Gospel. Even Copernicus, whose displacement of the earth from the universe's center called into question some Biblical passages, didn't directly contradict the Good Book. "The Descent of Man," however, refuted "Genesis"—the Bible's *very first story*. And if Genesis fell, so would the books that come after it, one invalidated domino after another.

Darwin's sacrilegious thesis not only dethroned man, it exiled God Himself from the traditional story of our creation. Darwin was challenging creationist premises that dated back to at least the very beginning of recorded history—and surely further back than that. People didn't want to hear they evolved from damned, dirty apes. Apes were nasty, inferior creatures with no master plan in place. That's more than humbling—it's traumatic. And the mind will go to great lengths to ignore trauma.

Though detractors abhorred the idea of being related to feces-throwing primates, they had little problem slinging some mud at Darwin, who feared, "I shall soon be viewed as the most despicable of men." Much of the subsequent ridicule, like an editorial drawing from an 1871 magazine that spliced Darwin with an ape, confirmed his suspicions. Despite all the ensuing public debates, formal and informal, Darwin himself rarely appeared publicly to defend himself. He left it to proponents and opponents to hash out what he already spent decades studying.[7]

Still, so irrefutable was the evidence and logic that, by the time he died in 1882 at the age of 73, his ideas were mostly accepted. He expected to be buried at a local churchyard, but his colleagues and the U.K. government would have none of that. Charles Robert Darwin, the kid who dropped out of school and hopped aboard the adventure of a lifetime, was buried in Westminster Abbey, near Sir Isaac Newton, at a funeral attended by thousands.

The acceptance of his ideas waxed and waned in the decades following his death.[8] Today, however, it's almost universally accepted by credible scientists and thinkers. In fact, "On the Origin of Species" has been called the most influential book of the nineteenth century and the most influential academic book ever written. *Scientific American* identified Darwin as humanity's foremost influence on modern thought.

Darwinism's remaining objectors come almost invariably from religious groups and those funded by them. Though most major denominations now accept the premise of evolution (allowing for God's intervention), there are some whose heels are dug in just as deeply as they were in

---

[7] He was also constantly in poor health, likely a result of something contracted while on the Beagle's voyage. (Maybe eating roast armadillos isn't such a good idea after all.)

[8] See: "Eclipse of Darwinism."

Darwin's day. These holdouts would likely object to Darwin's placement on this list.

So, too, might those who think Darwin's role in the theory of evolution is overvalued. True enough, Lamarck's evolutionary proposal beat Darwin's by a half-century. Darwin's own grandfather, Erasmus Darwin, also wrote about evolution as an explanation for species' variety. Earlier still we find eighteenth century Scottish polymath James Burnett, whose evolutionary thoughts preceded them all.

However, though Erasmus Darwin and James Burnett believed in evolution, they did little scientific work to advance the idea, and though Lamarck did some scientific work, his deeply flawed understanding of genetic mutations limited his impact. It's Darwin who not only assembled a cogent theory of evolution by means of natural selection, but he also discovered, archived, and organized an incontrovertible body of evidence before publishing the material in two of history's most important scientific works. Evolution's progenitors may have been ahead of their time, but they lacked the evidence and analysis that makes science *science*. Darwin lacked neither.

Nevertheless, one might ask about evolution's importance. Why does it matter? It's a good question, and evolution's relative lack of applicability and clear effect on the West's development keep him down at number 15.

Still, his ranking is just relative to the 14 people ahead of him. Darwinism is enormously important. For starters, his impact on broader science is not inconsiderable. Darwinism transformed not only biology, anatomy, zoology, and botany, but its ideas have altered our approach to anthropology, sociology, and psychology as well. There have been many applications of evolution across scientific fields, including medicine, agriculture, and artificial selection.

In addition, Darwin's effects on the human condition are almost without parallel. He altered the way we think of ourselves and the world around us. He challenged religion's long-held creationist beliefs. For too long, questions about life were asked to holy leaders who referenced holy texts while guessing at holy answers. Darwin offered competition in this arena, and he, along with his successors, have unearthed more evidence about our origins in the last 150 years than organized religion had in its entire history.

Darwinism itself evolved—from unthinkable to the mainstream. To remain realistic, most organized religions have accepted evolution, grafting it onto their belief system in some way. Here we see a successful infiltration of science into religion, when for most of history it was the other way around. Darwin helped remove the clergy from the scientific establishment, a key that has unshackled scientists ever since, allowing more scientific studies and breakthroughs.

We must wonder just how much Darwin's success in using science to give us practicable theories has played a role in the observable weakening of Western religions' popularity. Evolution's success reinforced the progress of the Scientific Revolution in helping science gain people's trust. In Darwin we have a sequel to Galileo.[9] Both showed us that science and its innate skepticism can better tackle questions about the material world than can religion and its innate confidence.

Ultimately, Darwin toppled preconceptions that went back to the beginning of mankind, and his ideas, thanks to sustained scientific sup-

---

[9] We'll be visiting the original shortly.

port despite an onslaught of attacks from threatened dissenters, have stood the test of time. Like Copernicus's proposal, Darwin's theory challenges our dangerous vanity. Not only is this planet not at the center of the universe, but all species on this displaced planet are related to us, and we to them. There has perhaps never been a more contextualizing notion for humanity.

More than anyone in history, he contributed to the timeless question of where we came from. Charles Darwin earns his spot as the 15th most influential figure in Western history.

#14: George Washington

"The time is now near at hand which must probably determine whether Americans are to be freemen or slaves."

–George Washington[1]

Imagine the last century without the United States. Would there be Union Jacks erected across North America? Might swastikas still cast shadows over Europe? Could hammers and sickles hover over not only our oceans but the Sea of Tranquility as well?

Because of George Washington, we never found out the answers to those questions. Thomas Jefferson wrote, John Adams hollered, and Alexander Hamilton schemed, but George Washington led. At critical points throughout America's War for Independence and its subsequent republic, Washington provided a desperately needed steady hand to steer America through choppy waters. More than any of America's "founding fathers," it's Washington to whom history owes the American Revolution's success.

The father of the United States earns his spot as the 14th most influential figure in Western history.

---

[1] Slave owner.

George Washington

George Washington was born in 1732 as a fourth generation Virginian.[2] His father, Augustine Washington, was a wealthy planter, and this gentry life gave his son every advantage, including security, slave labor, education, and connections. Dead when George was 11, Augustine bequeathed most of his estate to George's older half-brother, Lawrence, a 25-year-old adjunct general in the Virginia militia. Lawrence left his legacy by renaming their plantation Mount Vernon (after his former commanding officer, Edward Vernon), but he died nine years after inheriting it. His death left 20-year-old George the Mount Vernon plantation, its slaves, and one-quarter of Lawrence's militia responsibilities. Virginia's governor soon granted him the rank of major.

In 1754, as Washington arrived in his twenties, the British and French empires found themselves in their latest squabble over North American land claims. Major Washington marched part of the Virginia militia to the most hotly contested area, the Ohio Valley, and he soon found himself inaugurating the French and Indian War.[3] Deploying daring (if costly) tactics, Washington quickly earned respect from his militiamen and Virginia leadership. Within two years, he was leading a thousand men from the Virginia militia. This experience allowed the young Washington to cut his false teeth (he lost his first real one at just

---

[2] His great-grandfather emigrated from England in 1656. Virginia, by the way, was named after the "Virgin Queen" Elizabeth, the 19th most influential figure in Western history.

[3] Ask someone "Who fought whom in the French and Indian War?" and you'll almost certainly be answered with, "The French and the Indians!" Then throw your head back and laugh. This struggle, which lasted from 1754 to 1763 as part of a broader territorial rivalry between Britain and France, pitted the French and many Indian tribes against the British Empire,

24) on military organization, strategy, training, discipline, and inspiration. Two decades later, these qualities would serve him well in a more noteworthy war.

In one of those sneakily fragile moments of history, Washington had hoped that his success would earn him a commission in the British professional military, but no such respect was given.[4] Consequently, the bruised young leader left the militia in the middle of the war to return home. From 1758 until the outbreak of the Revolutionary War 17 years later, he contently managed Mount Vernon. A 1759 marriage to wealthy widow Martha Dandridge Curtis brought more money, land, and slaves. Washington planted himself in the southern gentry, became one of the richest men in the colonies. He agreed to stand for office in Virginia's colonial legislature, the hallowed House of Burgesses,[5] where he served in the early 1760s. Wealthy, experienced, proper, and tall, he was among the body's most respected members. By 1775, Mount Vernon had grown to 6,500 acres worked by over a hundred slaves, and their owner was practically Virginian royalty.

During this period, political philosophy and European affairs were not Washington's priorities. Unlike other revolutionary thinkers, he

---

including their American colonists. This specific front of the war was over land east of the Mississippi River, which both sides claimed. The English had been spreading west from the Atlantic Ocean for over a century, while the French had sailed down the Mississippi and spread from there. The two sides collided just west of the Appalachian Mountains, starting in the Ohio Valley. This conflict eventually dragged in colonies and European allies, evolving into what is known as the Seven Years' War (1756-1763). With combatants across five continents, some call it the true first world war.

[4] How history might be different if they recognized his talent!
[5] Founded in 1619!

preferred books about manure and soil, not metaphysics and science. Whereas Jefferson spoke five languages, Washington was content with the one. Many famous early Americans traveled extensively in Europe, among them Jefferson, Adams, Benjamin Franklin, and James Monroe. Washington, with the exception of an excursion to Barbados as a teenager, never left the country. Why cross the Atlantic, he wondered, when it would just take him away from Mount Vernon?

Still, he felt it his duty to serve whenever called upon, an obligation exploited by others throughout his adult life. This selflessness was true in the French and Indian War, it was true in the House of Burgesses after that, and it was about to be true on the greatest scale yet.

When the British Empire and their colonists had won the French and Indian War, the Treaty of Paris (1763) gave them all land east of the Mississippi. Despite this success, tensions between the American colonists and London rose almost immediately after their victory.

Colonial westward expansion onto the newly acquired land was met by a Native American revolt led by Pontiac. Over 2000 British were killed or wounded, leaving London to think they should delay its westward push and at least momentarily placate hostile tribes. Parliament therefore passed the Proclamation of 1763, which forbade American colonists from settling west of Appalachia. This act enraged many colonists who felt they had spilled blood for that land and it was now their right to settle it. Meanwhile, Britain had accrued a large debt from the war and felt it reasonable that those they helped protect should pay it back. In 1764, Parliament's Sugar Act attempted to squeeze revenue from the colonists, as did the Stamp Act one year after that.

While the British believed that pacified natives and colonial restitution justified these laws, the colonists saw them as micromanaging local affairs. Colonists, though loyal to the Crown, had long resented intrusion from across the Atlantic, particularly at the height of the Age of Enlightenment, when writers championed the ideals of limited government and popular sovereignty. Arguing they could not be fairly taxed and micromanaged without representation in Parliament, which was considered a right of British citizens back in England, many colonists resisted nearly every step of the way. In turn, the Townsend Acts (1767), the occupation of Boston, the ensuing Boston Massacre (1768), the Boston Tea Party (1773), and the Intolerable Acts (1774), among other developments, pushed the two sides down the slippery slope toward schism.

By the mid-1770s, some citizens of the 13 American colonies were openly discussing independence. In 1774, leaders of 12 of the colonies picked representatives to attend a congress in Philadelphia.[6] Of the 56 delegates that convened, seven were from Virginia, and one of those was George Washington.[7] Among the resolutions from this "Continental Congress" was to use boycotts to pressure the British to secure what they considered were their rights as British citizens. The body also pressed colonies to organize militia, just in case the relationship further deteriorated.

---

[6] Underpopulated Georgia, experiencing problems with Native Americans on the southern frontier, relied on royal support and therefore avoided angering the Crown. Still, it eventually became a late addition to the new confederation of colonies.

[7] Other colonial delegates included the cousins John and Samuel Adams from Massachusetts, future Chief Justice John Jay from New York, and Virginia's Patrick Henry (he of "Give me liberty or give me death" fame).

George Washington

Hopeful their grievances would be redressed, Washington and his fellow delegates returned to their home colonies. Fewer than six months after the congress adjourned, however, deadly skirmishes broke out between British redcoats and colonial militia in the Massachusetts towns of Lexington and Concord. One month later, the Second Continental Congress met with Washington again in attendance.[8] This time he showed up in his military uniform, which convinced John Adams of Massachusetts to nominate the Virginian to be commander-in-chief of a "Continental Army."

Washington, of course, accepted. A year later, fellow Virginian Thomas Jefferson (#24) proclaimed the United States of America were independent of British rule.

For eight years, Washington led the United States through their earliest, darkest hours, and he did it without pay. Interestingly, what makes his tenure as general successful is not his record in battles. Few historians place Washington among the all-time great generals.[9] Instead, his brilliance stemmed from his ability to hold an amateurish, inexperienced, largely volunteer force together in the most trying of circumstances.[10]

---

[8] A veritable "who's who" of colonial titans, Washington was again joined by John Adams. With them was young Virginian Thomas Jefferson (a last-minute replacement) and old Pennsylvanian Benjamin Franklin.

[9] Though Washington's face is on the actual Mount Rushmore, he comes nowhere close to the proverbial Mount Rushmore of generals. The most common faces carved into it are Napoleon (#16) and Alexander the Great. I'd say the next tier of contenders includes Genghis Khan, Julius Caesar, Hannibal, Attila, Saladin, and Cyrus the Great. Man, I wish I got paid for making lists.

[10] Valley Forge!

The colonists were outgunned and outmanned by the professional British military. The British also controlled the coasts with its dominant navy. By 1777, the Americans had lost their three biggest cities—Philadelphia, Boston, and New York—and Norfolk was burned to the ground in Washington's home colony. The Continental Congress was chased from the capital and saddled with debilitating financial and political problems, and many felt the war was a hopeless cause. And yet, General Washington's soldiers kept fighting.

Tactically, his greatest strength was knowing when to retreat. He refused to overcommit his forces, which allowed the army under his direct command—by far the largest colonial force—to survive to fight another day. As long as his army stayed together, the war could continue. He knew the goal of the colonies was not to obliterate the British forces; instead, not unlike modern insurgents, his aim was just to harass them to the point where they'd give up the occupation. To that end, he approved guerilla tactics that bothered the more traditional British style.

His flawless victory at the Battle of Trenton on Christmas morning, 1776 (the one before which he famously crossed the Delaware to sneak-attack Hessian mercenaries) resulted in zero American deaths from combat and a huge morale boost for the American cause. After the American victory at 1777's Battle of Saratoga convinced France to join, momentum was firmly in the American camp.[11] At 1781's Battle of Yorktown, Washington, his soldiers, and their French allies surrounded Britain's largest North American army and forced its surrender, effectively ending the war. In 1783, Franklin and Adams led a negotiating

---

[11] A colonial victory there convinced the French to join the war efforts, and other European countries also seized the opportunity to knock big bad Britain down a peg by bankrolling the underfunded American cause.

team to Paris to finalize peace terms. Washington was finally allowed to retire back home to Mount Vernon.

It's worth noting here that although Adams's voice, Jefferson's quill, and Franklin's diplomacy were valuable in the independence movement, their roles might easily have been replaced by other patriots. If not for Washington, however, it's unclear who could have pulled off the upset for the American cause. This accomplishment alone would land Washington near the top of the list of influential Americans. Considering America's later importance on the modern world stage, it might have also qualified him for the outskirts of this Top 30 list.

Washington, however, wasn't nearly done guiding the new country. Or, rather, the new country wasn't nearly done with Washington's guidance.

During much of the war and throughout most of the 1780s, the American colonies-turned-united-states were governed by what they called the Articles of Confederation. Infamously, the Articles set up what amounted to 13 almost sovereign states joined in more of a military alliance than a unified country. Such decentralization stemmed from these states' fear of a faraway government telling them what to do. Exchanging a distant ruler in London for a moderately less distant one in Philadelphia was not considered that much of an upgrade. Therefore, the Confederation's weak national government could not even tax.[12] It had no chief executive, no court system, and no uniform trading or commercial policies. It really did seem like 13 different "states," a term most of the world uses

---

[12] It could, however, *ask* states for taxes. What would your answer be?

to describe nations.[13] It proved to be a weak, impractical, inefficient system that needed fixing, so, in the summer of 1787, representatives of 12 states came together to amend it.[14]

Since many Americans shared a collective paranoia about rejiggering a system that had purposefully limited the type of central government against which they had fought, a collective skepticism hovered around this meeting. Its delegates, wanting to legitimize their efforts, invited General Washington out of retirement to chair the gathering. He, of course, accepted.

His presence galvanized the delegates, who ultimately went beyond merely amending the Articles and instead drafted a new national government. Soon, this meeting brandished a brilliant document that has stood the test of time—the Constitution of the United States. Though largely the brainchild of James Madison and Alexander Hamilton, among other Constitutional Convention delegates, it was George Washington's presence that made it possible. By the following summer, enough states had ratified the document, and the Constitution became the new law of the land.

---

[13] Even when the Articles were replaced with the Constitution, states made sure to maintain some level of sovereignty, which explains American states having their own legislatures, executives, courts, and laws.

[14] Now it's Rhode Island as the odd state out. Under the Articles, each of the 13 states, no matter its population, had the same power in the national government—one vote. As a result, Virginia, with ten times more people than Rhode Island, had no more of a say at the national level despite representing so many more people. The tiny state with the long name (the State of Rhode Island and Providence Plantations) loved this system and did not want to endorse a change by its presence at the convention.

George Washington

Among the problems fixed by the Constitution was the creation of a presiding executive officer—a president—to serve as a single point-person to run the government. The president would be just one person (some considered making it a multi-person branch), independent of the legislative branch (some colony's executive was tied to the colonial legislatures), elected (but not by the people), with veto power over that legislative branch (barely negated by a difficult override process), and he would be commander-in-chief of the military.

At the time, these extensive executive powers were considered surprisingly broad for states that just a few years earlier were fighting a war for liberty against a monarchy and then drafted the Articles of Confederation, which had no executive whatsoever. Why were Americans acquiescent to giving so much power to one person?

Though the failures of the Articles and an economic recession had softened the ground for change, it helped that they all knew exactly who the first chief executive would be. Though Washington never asked or campaigned for the office, he unanimously won the first presidential election. Still the only person ever to sweep the Electoral College, he reluctantly repeated the feat in 1792. Though he did not seek the office, once called upon to serve, he, of course, accepted.

With John Adams as his Vice President,[15] President Washington went to work. He admirably helped navigate the turbulent challenges of fledgling nationhood. A military man more than a politician, he rose

---

[15] Adams was runner-up in those elections, an accomplishment the original Constitution awarded the vice-presidency. It made sense at the time—the ostensibly second most popular person in the country should naturally be next-in-line behind the most popular. However, with the rise of political parties in the 1790s, two problems presented themselves. First was that the runner up could be a member of the opposite party, meaning an entire

above bickering foreign and domestic. As Europe went to war thanks to the politically charged French Revolution, Washington vowed to stay out of it. When violence erupted on the western frontier, Washington handled it. When a rebellion tested the new government in Massachusetts, Washington put it down with minimal casualties.

Knowing his limitations, President Washington surrounded himself with top minds of the period and created the first presidential cabinet. Included in it were Thomas Jefferson as Secretary of State and Alexander Hamilton as Secretary of the Treasury. Unfortunately, thanks to those two cabinet members and the inevitabilities of a democratic republic, political parties, much to the President's frustration, gradually coalesced.

Throughout it all, he stayed the only unifying force in the country. When reading about Washington, one will always come across the same descriptions: graceful, sensible, patient, soft-spoken and beyond reproach. All attributes were essential during America's wobbly first steps.

party switch in the White House was one heartbeat way, and in the meantime teamwork was unlikely. An opposing party might even resort to underhanded maneuvering to remove the president and replace him with the vice president. Second, the Constitution instructed each elector in the Electoral College to cast two ballots for two separate people. A party wanted to finish in the top two spots to secure both elected executive offices, so it behooved partisan electors to vote for the same two people across their ballots. (This was all before electors were tied to the popular vote of their home state, a shift of the democratic 1820s and 30s.) That plan was executed too well in the Election of 1800, leading to a tie between Democratic-Republicans Thomas Jefferson and Aaron Burr. With many such ties likely in the future, the Twelfth Amendment of 1804 addressed these problems by asking electors to cast separate ballots for the president and vice president, thereby allowing the rise of the modern presidential ticket. This has nothing to do with George Washington but everything to do with history, politics, and the Constitution (three of my favorite things), so I couldn't resist.

George Washington

Even Vice President Adams, electorally the country's second most popular statesman, had few friends in the south. In the many natural growing pains of the new nation, Washington's strong hands held the country together.

Among his most important legacies was his decision to not stand for a third term in the Election of 1796. In fact, he had wanted to step down after one term, but Hamilton and Jefferson, who otherwise agreed on so little, insisted he must run for a second term or watch sectionalism break apart the brittle country. Still, after acquiescing once, he could not sacrifice again. Feeling each of his 64 years, he informed his country he'd again be returning home. Vice President Adams stood for the presidency and succeeded him in March of 1797.

On December 14, 1799, a 67-year-old George Washington died at Mount Vernon from illness compounded by bloodletting. Amazingly, one year earlier, while President Adams was in the midst of the quasi-war with France, the new President asked the old one if he would consider coming out of retirement yet again to lead the army in case of an all-out war.

He, of course, accepted.[16]

Aside from German-born Albert Einstein, no American will be ranked higher on this list. That's because no American is as crucial to the nation's existence.

---

[16] Fortunately, he was never needed, as Adams ultimately soothed Franco-American relations.

One of the rare unflattering legacies of George Washington was that he was the intellectual inferior of the other great founding fathers. Franklin, Adams, Jefferson, Madison, and Hamilton were authors, inventors, scientists, philosophers, musicians, architects, and fierce intellectuals. When reading early American history, one gets the impression that these were the nerds of the revolution and Washington the jock.

It's not a bad analogy. During the revolutionary period and debate over the new governments, it's the Adamses and Hamiltons who fueled the fire of discourse. When generating our founding documents and ideals, the great well-read minds of the revolution considered ancient Greco-Roman ideas, modern Enlightenment ones, and everything in between. These founding fathers were among the most learned persons in the world—and they were eager to prove it. Meanwhile, the taciturn Washington almost always kept to himself, only weighing in on the most pressing of issues. Yet, when he did speak, everyone listened.[17]

Still, he earned everyone's respect by more than just the infrequency of his words. He may not have been a man of philosophy, but he was a man of action. While he wasn't as philosophically brilliant or well-read as other founding fathers, perhaps the fact that there were so *many* of those types made those men just a tad redundant. Washington was uniquely qualified to lead the nation during war, legitimize the Constitutional Convention, and then run the new government created by it. At each of these pivotal stages, he calmly exercised responsibilities that would have overwhelmed most of his colleagues. These same brilliant founding fathers recognized his greatness and created an entire branch of govern-

---

[17] Therein lies an advantage of rarely speaking, a talent of mine at social gatherings.

ment for the skills he embodied. Of all the great early Americans, no one was as indispensable.

Furthermore, he modeled the presidency for all his successors. A cabinet is not in the Constitution, but he made it the norm. On multiple occasions he exercised his role as commander-in-chief. His self-imposed two-term limit has only once been surpassed, even though such a restriction wasn't law until 1951.[18]

His effect on America beyond dispute, the only argument to make against Washington's place on a list of influential Westerners is that his effects might be localized to just America. Indeed, unlike other Americans on this list, he didn't advance science for the planet (as did Pincus), he wasn't an international figure (as was Jefferson), he wasn't a visionary who revolutionized daily life (as was Ford), and he didn't invent anything that was used outside of the country (as did Edison). Should we then argue that his influence was on America and America only?

We should not. The American Revolution was a turning point not just for American history, but world history as well. It's a line of demarcation between the old regimes of the Western world and the republican democracies that were about to replace them. It's after the successful Revolutionary War that other colonies in the Americas steadily declared their own independence and became countries. It's after the successful implementation of the Constitution where liberating constitutions sprang up across the West. If the American War of Independence or its subsequent experiment with government were failures, it's unclear when, or if, that turning point would have happened. The failure of

---

[18] Franklin D. Roosevelt successfully won a third and fourth term in the 1940s. Ulysses S. Grant, elected in 1868 and 1872, left the job after two complete terms, but he attempted another run in 1880. That's the list.

Washington in the war or early republic would have seriously threatened the American chances in both. The birth of modern Western government hinges upon his success.

Similarly, his decision to step down from office is one of humility's most consequential moments. Some expected he could have been King George I of the United States. Before Washington, Western leaders almost without exception left their position in one of two ways—they were killed by someone or had a natural death. In either case, they went out flat on their back. Washington not only walked out, but he set the precedent that American commanders-in-chief should not seek to usurp power or get elected in perpetuity. Since the great George Washington didn't overstay his welcome, nearly every president after him emulated that decision. Further, after Washington, the concept of term limits moved from ancient idealism to something practiced throughout the world. Though he didn't have to, he showed that a leader wasn't superior to the people—he was one of them.

Consider how many revolutions in other parts of the world eventually experienced a new tyrant rise to power. It was the far more likely scenario. Even the enlightened Napoleon (#16) across the Atlantic, just a few years after Washington's presidency, showed what usually happens—when a talented general's popularity goes to his head, so does a crown.

And yet, without strong and quality leaders, revolutions cannot succeed in the first place. George Washington had the perfect combination of strength and selflessness necessary for the successful start of the United States. He had the exact amount of ambition required to rise to his position, but not so much ambition that he took advantage of it. As impressive as traversing the Delaware was, walking this tightrope was his greatest crossing.

George Washington

In the long term, America's importance grew with time. In the nineteenth century, the United States acted as a counterbalance to the British Empire in North America. In World War I, it broke a stalemate and helped democracy turn back the autocratic Central Powers. In World War II, it saved Europe and the Pacific from the Third Reich and Japanese Empire. The U.S. then led Western capitalism in the Cold War against the communist Eastern bloc. Countless technological and scientific breakthroughs have occurred in its many universities, labs, and spaceships. Without the United States, we probably have a dramatically different modern period. Without George Washington, we probably don't have the United States.

Thus, for his essential role in creating this important country and serving as the model figure in modern government's transformation, George Washington is the 14th most influential figure in Western history.

#13: Charles Martel

"From the hammer of Charles Martel to the sword of Sobieski, Christianity owed its safety in Europe to the fact that it was able to show that it could and would fight as well as the Mohammedan aggressor. . . . The civilization of Europe, America and Australia exists today at all only because of the victories of civilized man over the enemies of civilization."
    –President Theodore Roosevelt[1]

It was among the most fragile moments in Western history. The year: 732. The location: southwest France, somewhere on the road between Tours and Poitiers. The combatants: Christian Europeans and Muslim Arabs.

If the battle were a boxing match, Christianity hobbled in as the declining veteran, far from its heyday as Master of the Mediterranean. In contrast, Islam, just one century removed from its founder, bounded into the ring as the hungry up-and-comer, indomitable in its spread across west Asia, north Africa, and into the Iberian Peninsula. An Arab victory

---

[1] His description of Muslims is not necessarily endorsed by me, New London Librarium, or just about anyone else today.

on this random patch of French land, Europe's last realistic choke-point of defense, would likely precipitate the whole of Europe falling. Islam, it seemed, was the fate of the Western world.

It should come as no surprise that fate was thwarted that day. Christianity has been the world's largest religion for some time. If, however, the Battle of Tours had resolved differently, that would almost certainly not be the case.

Yet, few people have heard of this battle, nor do many know of the man who led the victorious Christian defense. His name was Charles of Herstal. Chroniclers gave him the nickname Martel—"the Hammer." He's the man who saved Christianity, and in the process he became the 13th most influential figure in Western history.

Nailing down all the details of Charles Martel and his hallmark achievement is difficult. Let's not forget what Europe was like in the early eighth century. It was the dimmest point of Europe's so-called "Dark Ages"— three centuries removed from the fall of Western Rome but still three decades short of the mini-renaissance led by Charlemagne (#21). A collection of barbaric, Germanic tribes scattered across the continent, filling the vacuum left behind by Rome's implosion. Descendants of the old empire lived in isolated communities led by castled nobles and protected by armored knights, most of whom relied on peasants to work their land and provide their food. All political and social energy focused on survival and earning salvation through the Roman Catholic Church. The result was a dearth of education and technological progress.

Christianity barely united these scattered communities, but the type of Christianity varied from tribe to tribe. Only the Franks were Catholic.

Many others were Arian.[2] Others still were pagan. The West's peak, the ancient Greco-Roman world, existed only in history books, which almost no one wrote or read.

The Muslim world, meanwhile, was in the midst of a rapid expansion. Mohammed had founded the faith in 610 CE. By his death in 632, Muslim warriors were on the march, a Koran in one hand, a sword in the other. Islam quickly secured the Arabian peninsula and, by 661, had spread from the Middle East, as far east as the Indus River and as far west as modern Libya. The Arabs then continued pushing west across northern Africa with little difficulty, killing, plundering, enslaving, and ruling.

After reaching the Atlantic, they turned north, crossed the Strait of Gibraltar and entered the Iberian Peninsula. There waiting for them was one of the old Roman Empire's most feared enemies, the vicious and hardened Visigoths. These rugged warriors quickly fell in front of Allah's army, which then continued its push north across the Pyrenees and toward the heart of Europe as a seemingly invincible force of destiny.

Charles Martel cared little for destiny. Born in 688, he was the bastard son of a Frankish noble, Pepin of Herstal, and a mistress. The Franks had settled into the former Roman province of Gaul and established a kingdom under the Merovingian Dynasty. Pepin served as what we would now describe as the king's chief of staff, a title known as "Mayor of the Palace." Over time, this hereditary position had secured as much and even more de facto power than the king himself. Mayor Pepin and his wife, the seductively named Plectrude, had two legitimate sons. Though both boys predeceased their parents, the elder son, Grimoald,

---

[2] For more on the widespread Arians, who disagreed with Catholics regarding the nature of Jesus, you should brush up on Constantine (#23).

first had a son of his own, Theudoald.[3] A jealous Plectrude wanted to void the illegitimate Charles from inheritance, especially Pepin's position as Mayor, so she convinced Pepin to anoint their grandson Theudoald as heir.

Charles had other plans.[4] An accomplished military leader under his father, he had many allies in the Frankish kingdom. Helping his cause was the death of Pepin in 714. Theudoald was only eight years old. Few lords felt comfortable deferring to the child. Many of them instead recognized the 26-year-old Charles as the true heir and backed his claim as Mayor of the Palace. Over the subsequent decade, he beat back challengers and helped grow Frankish territory. In 720, he brought the office to its height and handpicked the next king of the Franks, Theuderic IV.

The Frankish kingdom had become Martel's in all but name. Meanwhile, his next great challenge inched closer.

In 730, hearing rumors of fearsome conquerors from Africa, Martel turned his attention to the encroaching Muslim menace which had by then crossed the Pyrenees and twice decimated a southern Frankish defense under Duke Odo of Aquitaine, who then begged Martel for help.[5] Martel answered the call.

---

[3] There will be a quiz.

[4] What a bastard.

[5] Interestingly, up until the previous year, Odo was a rival of the Franks. Martel himself had fought against him to bring the nominally Frankish duchy back into the kingdom's direct possession. When the Muslims

Numbers for the battle remain unconfirmed, but most estimates have at least 15,000 soldiers to each side, with as many as 50,000 for either or both. The Arab invaders almost certainly boasted more cavalry, a unit for which they were renowned, while the Franks had mostly infantry. We know that Martel's counterpart on the Muslim side was Abdul Rahman Al Ghafiqi.[6] Abdul Rahman had already defeated Duke Odo in battle twice, the second conflict with a death toll that, according to a Western chronicler, "God alone knew."

Arab foreign intelligence surmised that European kingdoms would quickly capitulate. Merely a collection of scattered barbarian farmers, they would not be any more difficult to conquer than the collection of west Asian and north African civilizations through which Islam had carved so easily.

The shrewd Martel, however, prepared for the clash. News of the advancing Arabs preceded the encounters with Duke Odo. Martel felt that to successfully stand up to this great foreign foe, he would need to

---

arrived, Odo swallowed his pride to call upon his former vanquisher for help. Better to serve under a fellow Christian than risk what a Muslim leader might have in store for him. He had already heard that his captured daughter was sent to a harem in Damascus—for any father a punishment worse than death.

[6] That, believe it or not, is his abbreviated name. His full name was Abu Said Abdul Rahman ibn Abdullah ibn Bishr ibn Al Sarem Al 'Aki Al Ghafiqi. Introducing himself took several minutes and a break for water.

train a full-time army.[7] To pay soldiers for over a year, he reacquired land and money that he had, for the better part of a decade, donated to the Catholic Church.[8] In addition to the conscripts, he brought with him his most proven warriors, whose relationship with Martel dated back to his controversial ascendancy to Mayor of the Palace. By battle's eve, flanking him were loyal, battle-hardened comrades and eager, trained infantry. We can conclude Martel's organized defense, including its organization, experience, and leadership, caught the invaders off guard as they marched from Poitiers.

As the Arabs approached Tours, Martel positioned his soldiers on high ground. He also hid much of his army in the forest to obscure his numbers. The situation flummoxed the Muslims, who were not even expecting a real conflict. For a week, both sides avoided a large engagement. But then, an October day in 732 hosted the battle for Europe's future. The West calls it the Battle of Tours or Poitiers. Arabs call it the Battle of the Highway of the Martyrs.

On brand for the Middle Ages, the details of what transpired on that fall day are unclear. Two oft-cited sources were released decades later: the

---

[7] Normally, most Europeans were available for combat only after planting and before the harvest, and few would have any real experience or training. Standing armies evaporated with the Roman Empire and wouldn't be brought back on any large scale until toward the end of the Middle Ages. The famed knights of the period were rarer than you were probably taught; their total European number is probably measured in the thousands across a continent measured in the tens of millions.

[8] "Reacquire" is just a fancy way of saying "stole." The Church was by no means happy about it and threatened excommunication. This threat was justly withdrawn after Martel pried Catholicism from the jaws of extinction.

"Chronicle of Bishop Isidorus Pacensis," often referred to as the "Chronicle of 754," and the "Chronicle of Fredegar," completed in 768. The former has the Muslims attacking first and Martel's valiant Franks defending "like an immovable wall." The latter contends that it was the Franks who first attacked the invaders, "scattering them like stubble before the fury of his onslaught."

In either case, the battle was seemingly won inside of a day. Among those killed was Abdul Rahman, who fell trying to rally his men.[9] By the next morning, the invaders withdrew. They had grown accustomed to uncommitted Christian "armies" dispersing after the opening clash, but this one barely budged. Thus, while the sources disagree on the details, most historians conclude it was a dominant victory for Charles Martel and the Franks.

Over the next few years, Martel acquired more land for the Frankish kingdom before his leadership was again required. In 736, the Franks' Mayor of the Palace once more protected Christians from invading Arabs, now at Narbonne. It was the last Arab incursion into France.

In 737, King Theuderic died. Rather than appoint another king or claim the throne himself, Martel let it sit vacant. His heirs, however, claimed it and much more. His son, Pepin the Short, cajoled Pope Stephen II, who was beholden to the family for past heroics and newer challenges, into crowning him King of the Franks in 752. Later, Pepin the Short's son, named Charles after his heroic grandfather, inherited the kingdom and expanded it into an empire that spread across western

---

[9] Some Franks had circled around the battle front and attacked the rear of the Arab forces, where families and booty vulnerably sat. When some warriors learned of this development, they broke ranks and galloped backward, leaving Abdul Rahman unexpectedly lonely and quickly dead.

Europe. That grandson became known as Charles the Great. We know him better as Charlemagne (#21).

Charles Martel died in 741, but he had started a new dynasty: the Carolingians.[10] They reigned over western Europe into the ninth century. As discussed in my chapter on Charlemagne, the accomplishments of Martel's grandson, who, among other feats, ingrained the Franks' Catholicism across the lands he conquered, make him the most accomplished figure of the Middle Ages.

However, without his grandfather—without Charles Martel—not only is there no Charlemagne, there might not *be* Catholicism, or even Christianity, today.

Is there a hint of hyperbole in that conclusion, one might wonder? How can the world's largest religion—by many estimates it has around 2.5 billion adherents, or about one-third of the world's population, practicing it—be fragile enough that one battle decided its fate?

The leading voice on this issue is, as usual, Edward Gibbon, the venerated eighteenth century English historian.[11] He noted the Muslims had advanced "a thousand miles" into Europe, and "the repetition of an equal space" would have brought them into Poland.[12] The Londoner feared "the Arabian fleet might have sailed without a naval combat into

---

[10] Carolus is the Latinized version of Charles. (For example, the later American "Carolina" colony was named after England's King Charles.)

[11] His supreme *The History of the Decline and Fall of the Roman Empire* might be the most respected work on any historical topic... that is, until this epic Top 30 hits the market!

[12] "The Rhine" Gibbon points out, "is not more impassable than the Nile or Euphrates," two rivers already taken by the Islamic conquerors.

the mouth of the Thames" and that Oxford might now be teaching the "interpretation of the Koran" and "the sanctity and truth of the revelation of Mahomet."

Other historians chime in: Belgian Godefroid Kurth said that the battle "must ever remain one of the great events in the history of the world, as upon its issue depended whether Christian Civilization should continue or Islam prevail throughout Europe." German Hans Delbruck states plainly that there is "no more important battle in the history of the world."

Counterarguments to the battle's importance include the size of Abd Al-Rahman's invading force as not large enough to occupy Europe. True enough, the Arab forces who fought between Poitiers and Tours that day were more marauders than occupiers. They had no hope to advance much further. Revisionists, therefore, chalk up Tours as one of history's many Christian-Islam battles, with both sides alternating victories and defeats.

Still, we should not overlook the analysis of Louis Gustave and Charles Strauss, whose book on the battle concludes that "The victory gained was decisive and final. . . . The torrent of Arab conquest was rolled back and Europe was rescued." In other words, Tours was the tipping point. After thousands of miles of Arab conquest, it's difficult to believe that Muslim expansion *coincidentally* stopped when an opponent had finally thwarted them so convincingly. If Abd Al-Rahman and his men yet again steamrolled over a Christian battlefield, taking more land and treasure, it stands to reason that their European incursion would have continued into much broader areas more difficult to defend, and in their wake would be the spread of Islam not unlike what happened in Northern

Africa. Southern France was the last bottleneck; Martel had to succeed there, or it would likely have been too late.

The next question we must then answer is: would Christianity have survived if the Muslims did indeed charge into Europe? Probably. While the majority may have steadily been converted or killed, scattered groups of survivors could have eked out a living in tiny, maybe illegal, enclaves with considerably different interpretations of their endangered religion. However, without the unifying conquests of Charlemagne, it would likely resemble the early Christianity of the two centuries before Constantine (#23). While that's technically survival, the culture of the continent would have developed quite differently.

But Martel *did* win, and the momentum of the religions soon reversed. The subsequent centuries saw the Christian *Reconquista* of Spain and Portugal. By the close of the fifteenth century, western Europe was fully Christian (and predominantly Catholic) again. Christian Europe then took to the seas, with Christopher Columbus's monumental 1492 voyage occurring in the same year as the eradication of Islam's last Iberian holdout, Granada. In the centuries to follow, Christianity spread across the Americas and Oceania. If Europe were Muslim during the Age of Exploration, it's Islam that spreads to these new continents. Instead, Christianity's place as the world's largest religion was secured.

Still, even if we grant the significance of the battle in the context of Christianity surviving and spreading, ranking the influence of Martel and Tours still depends on one's opinion of the practical importance of these religions. This topic is much trickier to navigate. Just how important is religion in the development of a society, or an individual? What concrete applications are there? To what extent are morality, culture, and technology tied to a society's religion? In other words, does it matter whether

Europe stayed Christian or became Muslim? Your answers to those questions determine whether Martel should be on this list at all, or if he should be ranked near the top, or if he should fall somewhere in between.

To answer these questions, we must consider *why* the Western world ultimately pulled ahead of the Arab world in science, technology, and liberalism. Was it due to religion? I'm not so sure. Remember that during Europe's "Dark Ages," it was in fact the Arab world that was the beacon of civilization. For the centuries surrounding 1000 CE, it was actually Christian Europe that played the role of the slow-moving, theocratic region, while Muslim Europe was the more advanced, vibrant area. It took centuries before one can make the case that the Western world outstripped the Arab world in cultural and scientific arenas. What's more, one of the catalysts behind the Renaissance was an influx of advanced culture from the Middle East following the Crusades.

How, then, could religion be the relevant factor of the West's triumph as the dominant region? Clearly, Christianity wasn't automatically better for progress, and Islam wasn't automatically worse. Frankly, it's reasonable to ponder whether Muslim control over Europe may have prompted the European Renaissance six centuries before it actually happened. Imagine where the human race would be today if that took place!

Nevertheless, in the long run, the Arab world did not scientifically or politically modernize like the West did. Instead, the West eventually caught and surpassed the Middle East in myriad areas that made the modern world possible. Was the Arab world's eventual stagnancy because of Islam, or was it due to other factors?

Charles Martel

I told you it was tricky.[13] My ranking of Martel at just inside the top half of this list hints at my thoughts on those questions, some of which will be explored later when I arrive at Jesus's chapter. For now, Charles Martel, the savior of Christianity and hero of Europe, is the 13th most influential figure in Western history.

---

[13] Excuse this lengthy footnote, but since this information is non-Western it doesn't feel well placed in the main body. Among the primary factors why the Muslim world stagnated is the mid-thirteenth century Mongol invasion of Arabia. The invasion ended the Abbasid Caliphate, which had overseen the Golden Age of Islam before the Mongols sacked Baghdad and executed the last Abbasid Caliph, Al-Musta'sim Billah. (They did so creatively; not wanting to spill royal blood, they instead wrapped him in a rug and had horses trample him. Not good times for Al-Musta'sim.)

The fall of Baghdad and the Abbasids led to the decline of Islamic culture. New Sunni Islam leaders recentered Islam, striving for social and religious consensus based on the Koran rather than freedom of inquiry and a marketplace of ideas, hallmarks of the prior centuries. The decline of scientific output soon followed.

These developments mirror the impact of fourth century Christian homogenization spearheaded by Constantine (#23), which, as discussed in his chapter, similarly set the stage for the decline of Western culture, bringing Europe to its own "Dark Ages." History doesn't always repeat, but it sure does rhyme.

#12: Galileo

"I do not feel obliged to believe that the same God who has endowed us with senses, reason, and intellect has intended us to forgo their use and by some other means to give us knowledge which we can attain by them."
–Galileo Galilei, 1615

Despite the paradigm-shifting idea of Nicolaus Copernicus (#28), his heliocentric theory twisted in the solar wind for nearly a century afterward. It took another man to layer incontrovertible evidence onto Copernicus's daring proposal. That alone would make this other man an all-time great contributor to Western science, but he gifted us so much more than merely enhancing someone else's idea. He had a series of inventions, discoveries, and theories in astronomy and mechanics that helped modernize science. Perhaps most importantly, he embodied, furthered, and inspired a growing sentiment that truth is a slave to science and facts, not authority and dogma.

This man was Galileo Galilei, and he's the 12th most influential person in Western history.

Galileo

Galileo was born in 1564 Pisa, Italy—21 years after Nicolaus Copernicus's friends published the dying astronomer's major work on heliocentrism.[1] Galileo benefitted from an Italy that had been experiencing renewed intellectualism for quite some time. It was in Italy that the Renaissance began more than a century earlier. By the time of Galileo's birth, the printing press had aided literacy levels across western Europe. The Scientific Revolution followed on the heels of Copernicus, and Galileo took full advantage.

As a young man, he identified the tautochronic curve that explains why the pendulum behaves as it does.[2] This discovery laid the groundwork for Christiaan Huygens to create the world's first pendulum clock, which became the most accurate method of time-keeping until the twentieth century. The precocious Galileo may have also invented the thermoscope (though there are alternative inventors proposed), a forerunner to the thermometer. At just 22, he published a booklet on hydrostatic balance, giving him his first bit of fame.

He attended medical school but dropped out to work as a tutor and switch tracks to mathematics. He eventually became chair of the mathematics department at the University of Pisa. A few years later, he moved to the University of Padua to teach geometry, math, and astronomy.[3] It

---

[1] Before reading any further, I recommend first looking over, if you haven't already, my chapter on Copernicus (#28). It's an essential prequel to Galileo's story. Isaac Newton will later finish the trilogy. (I just hope the Newton chapter is better than "Return of the Jedi.")

[2] You know... pendulumy. (I could pretend to teach you about the isochronal principle, but you'd be able tell I was making it up.)

[3] The University of Padua was founded in 1222! That is OLD. In fact, it's the fifth oldest surviving university in the world. Next year it'll celebrate its 800th anniversary. *Meravigliosa!*

was a promising start. He taught at Padua for nearly 20 years, and by the end of his tenure there, he turned from reasonably well-known Galileo Galilei to *Galileo*. Like the great Italian artists of his age, he became so talented and renowned that eventually just his first name sufficed.

It's difficult to organize a pure chronology of Galileo's accomplishments. Throughout his career, from teaching to house arrest, he made accomplishments across several fields at different times. There were no neat phases of discoveries like those had by a Gregory Pincus (#25) or Charles Darwin (#15), nor is there a suspenseful narrative like the ones that accompany the lives of a Peter the Great (#26) or Napoleon (#16). Instead, rather than chronologically, I'm forced to organize his career categorically.

We'll start with mechanics, a branch of physics that studies motion, forces, and friction. The field had been around since, as usual, the ancient Greeks, with Archimedes and Aristotle (#30) among the early experts. Also as usual, Aristotle was sometimes right and sometimes wrong. He felt objects fall because their natural place is at the center of the earth, which is in fact toward where objects fall. Unfortunately, he also theorized that heavier objects fell faster than lighter ones. Observing a light feather fall slower than a rock suggests such a conclusion.

Galileo disagreed. He posited that balls of similar substance but different mass fell at the same rate. He theorized that a feather falls slower than a rock not because of the contrasting weight but because of the extra friction caused by the displacement of Earth's atmosphere on the flat-

Galileo

ter object.[4] The most famous confirmation of Galileo's theory was done by Apollo 15 astronaut David Scott, who, while standing on the moon, dropped a hammer and feather simultaneously and watched them hit the lunar surface at the same time.[5]

Galileo built on this foundation a mathematical formula that showed the rate of acceleration for falling objects on Earth. Tying math to physics, he helped lay the groundwork for later studies of inertia. These mechanical discoveries provided a firm foundation for Isaac Newton's further modernization of the field.

---

[4] Unfortunately, the story of him dropping objects from the Leaning Tower of Pisa is likely apocryphal.

[5] Of the 11 manned Apollo missions to blast off, Apollo 15 is my fourth favorite. If you don't think I've ranked at least a Top 5, then you don't know me that well:

Apollo 13 secures the top spot for the heroism and problem-solving on the spacecraft and on the ground.

In second is Apollo 11, our first moon landing. Yes, I watched "First Man," and yes, it was awesome.

Earning the bronze is Apollo 8 for being the first manned mission to leave Earth's orbit, circle the moon, and shoot the best photograph ever—that of the precious earth from the angle of the moon.

Now we arrive at Apollo 15 for its confirmation of Galileo and being the first lunar mission to bring—wait for it—a rover, delightfully known as the "moon buggy." Leave it to the middle-aged guys at NASA to fly a quarter of a million miles then use a car to drive a couple more. If you don't think the astronauts' elbows stuck out of their moon buggy a few extra inches, you don't know many middle-aged guys.

Speaking of middle-aged guys doing middle-aged guy things on the moon, coming in fifth is Apollo 14. American legend Alan Shepard made his long overdue return to space ten years after he became the first American to voyage into it. As the mission's commander, he smuggled on board a makeshift 6-iron and a couple of golf balls to hit in the low lunar gravity. With characteristic golfer embellishment, he claimed he hit the ball for "miles and miles."

Though his contributions to mechanics and physics are considerable, Galileo is most famous for his astronomical accomplishments. While conventional wisdom is wrong about his supposed invention of the telescope, his astronomical résumé is far broader than just one invention.

In the early 1600s, despite Copernicus's elegant (if flawed, as discussed in #28) heliocentric model of the solar system having debuted more than a half-century earlier, skeptics remained. Indeed, there was an ongoing divide among astronomers; some favored the Copernican model while others clung to the traditional Ptolemaic premise adopted by the Catholic Church, which put the earth at the universe's center. Even Tycho Brahe, a leading post-Copernican astronomer, favored geocentrism, though his Tychonic system did make some allowances for Copernicus's less controversial ideas. Brahe's position helped him avoid the fate of heliocentrist Giordano Bruno, who was burned at the stake by the Catholic Inquisition in 1600.[6] This heated astronomical climate awaited Galileo.

Like Bruno, Galileo knew Copernicus was right, and he set out to prove it. Early in the seventeenth century, he received word about a new invention created by the German-Dutch spectacle-maker Hans Lippershey.[7] In 1608, Lippershey used his knowledge of lenses to make a re-

---

[6] In truth, Bruno's fate had probably less to do with heliocentrism and more to do with an extensive list of heretical beliefs, including splitting with the Church on eternal damnation, the Trinity, the divinity of Christ, the virginity of Mary, and transubstantiation. Bruno was also a pantheist. Next to such positions, his advocacy of heliocentrism was like a murderer also stealing some mail.

[7] If I ever make a Top 30 list of best names in Western history, Hans Lippershey is in the conversation.

fracting telescope, which could magnify objects to make them appear three times larger. Galileo, though he may have never seen a telescope in person nor even designs of one, heard a basic description of it, checked the information against his brain's sizable database, realized it could work, and built one of his own. A better one.

With his improved telescope he could magnify objects nine times—and later models twenty and thirty times. He pointed it to the once unknowable heavens and observed what was once unobservable.

For example, it was assumed that the moon, like all the heavenly spheres, was perfectly smooth. Galileo observed craters and mountains. He inferred, accurately, that all celestial objects had blemishes of their own.

Galileo also discovered that Venus, like the moon, has phases (crescent/quarter/half, waxing/waning, etc.). This step was monumental toward confirming Copernicus's theory, as Venusian phases require certain angles of sunlight that a geocentric model does not allow.

He aimed his telescope further. Though Jupiter had been observed since the ancient world, what Galileo was the first to discover was satellites orbiting around it—the Jovian System. In other words, a planet other than the Earth had stuff orbiting it. It was another voice in Copernicus's symphony singing "We're not that important."

Pointing his telescope at the sun, Galileo observed sunspots. Though the Chinese first discovered them in 800 BCE, as Westerners did five hundred years later, no one had seen or sketched them as clearly as Galileo had. It was another argument against the perfection of the spheres in our sky.

Furthest of all, the observable hub of the Milky Way galaxy was assumed to be, just as it looks to us, a big, milky cloud. Galileo discovered it was not a cloud, but a huge cluster of stars. We now know it numbers in the billions.

Though others at the time also pointed rudimentary telescopes toward heavenly bodies, Galileo's accuracy was unsurpassed and he beat them to publishing. In the process, he not only bolstered Copernicus's heliocentric theory, he allowed the likes of Johannes Kepler to more accurately plot out the planets' orbits, Isaac Newton to explain how it was happening, and Albert Einstein to explain why.[8] Telescopic images were such a colossal step forward in the observation of the universe that some people didn't even believe what they were seeing, electing to instead remain skeptical of Galileo's "sorcery."

Ever the watchdog on sorcery, it was time for the Catholic Church to guard its territory. Protective of geocentrism and its right to teach us about the heavens, the Church had some suggestions about exactly where the astronomer could stick his telescope. In 1616, under the leadership of Pope Paul V, heliocentrism was deemed officially off limits, and Galileo was instructed "henceforth not to hold, teach, or defend it in any way."

A few years later, an inconsistent stretch of papal leadership got Galileo into some trouble. In 1623, Pope Urban VIII took a shine to Galileo and encouraged his studies, asking him to write a book summarizing both theories—geo and heliocentric. A grateful Galileo assembled more ideas into his largest work, 1632's "Dialogue Concerning the Two Chief World Systems." Though he was instructed to give the geocentric model equal weight, Galileo found ways to show the superiority of the

---

[8] Two of those guys are still to come on this list. (Sorry, Kepler. Love your telescope.)

heliocentric model. The following year, almost as if a trap were set, the Catholic Inquisition responded with a formal condemnation and trial, charging him with violating the earlier 1616 decree. *Dialogue* was placed on the Church's *Index of Prohibited Books*.

Galileo's popularity endangered him in some ways but protected him in others. The Church had to make an example of him, but it also limited his punishment to a public retraction and house arrest for his remaining days. At nearly 70, he didn't have the strength to resist. Old, tired, and losing his vision after years of repeatedly pointing a telescope at the brightest object in the solar system, he accepted his sentence.[9] Blind and condemned, his final years were mostly spent dictating "Two New Sciences," which summarized his 30 years of studying physics.

Though keen and curious until the end, his body gradually failed him. In 1642, it gave up. His long, fascinating life came to an end at the age of 77.

I must admit, despite his ranking near the middle of this Top 30, Galileo put together a top five résumé. Save only Newton, Galileo is probably the most diversely accomplished scientist on this list. Since I've clearly eval-

---

[9] The most famous iteration of his trial has him ending on a defiant tone. After being forced to acknowledge that the earth is immobile at the universe's center, he is said to have muttered under his breath, "E pur si muove"—"And yet it moves." It's probably his most famous quote, even if he didn't say it. Another famous Galilean quote opines that the purpose of the Church "is to teach us how one goes to heaven, not how heaven goes," but even then he was quoting someone else. Between these misattributions and the apocryphal Leaning Tower story, my high school education feels like one big lie. (No offense, Mr. Rourke.)

uated scientists as enormously important in Western development,[10] why, then, have I ranked him just 12th?

It's because Galileo, despite his amazing career, falls comparatively short in the key requirement for this list's historical figures: *influence*. Don't get me wrong – he's hugely influential. Still, he's less influential, I think, than the 11 names still to come.

The broadest argument for his influence comes from his several historical titles, including the "founder of modern astronomy" and the several mentioned by his Wikipedia entry: "the father of modern physics," "the father of scientific method," and even the "father of science." It's an impressive array.

With each of them, however, I must disagree. The "father of modern astronomy" label is surely worn by Copernicus. Switching from geocentrism to heliocentrism is the clearest demarcation in astronomical history. There is no more important turning point in advancing the field. Galileo should be commended for offering supportive evidence and expanding on it, but Copernicus was its founder. Indeed, google the phrase "founder of modern astronomy"–it's Copernicus that dominates the results. Though Copernicus doesn't have the breadth of Galileo's contributions, hence the former's lower ranking, his hallmark accomplishment pushes back against Galileo's astronomical paternity.

Similarly, "founder of physics" is much more appropriate for Isaac Newton, whose hallmark laws of motion and gravity formalized the field. Meanwhile, "father of *modern* physics" turns up Einstein. For those reasons and more, we'll see they're ranked higher than Galileo.

---

[10] The ten scientists and inventors of this ranking comprise a third of the list.

Galileo

The final two monikers we can lump together: the "father of the scientific method" and the "father of science." In both cases, there are more appropriate choices. The father of the scientific method in the West, as discussed in my #30 entry, is Aristotle.[11] Admittedly, one might reasonably choose to dismiss Aristotle due to his many errors or the fact that science was largely lost to the West during the early part of the Middle Ages; these opponents might elect to relegate him to "grandfather" status.[12] Even granting that, the modern scientific method is more often attributed to Sir Francis Bacon. Furthermore, if we identify the turning point of modern science, we again return to Copernicus and his contemporary, anatomist Andreus Vesalius. Two decades before Galileo was born, they each published a seminal work in 1543. Copernicus's "On the Revolutions of the Heavenly Spheres" transformed astronomy. One month later (amazing, if you think about it), Vesalius's "On the Fabric of the Human Body" laid the foundation of modern anatomy. Thus, 1543 traditionally marks the beginning of the Scientific Revolution, a period that allowed Galileo to flourish.

Even during Galileo's time, other astronomers were having similar accomplishments. Hans Lippershey's earlier telescope was noted, and he beat Galileo toward observing the starry hub of the Milky Way. Thomas Harriot had moon sketches four months before Galileo. Simon Marius noted the Jovian system shortly before Galileo. Johannes Fabricius sketched sunspots independently of Galileo. Harriot, Marius,

---

[11] Or, perhaps, Thales before him.

[12] I'd like to note that my sons' grandfathers are hall-of-famers, so no disrespect is meant toward the fraternity of grandfathers.

Paulo Lembo, and Galileo all seemed to recognize Venus's phases around the same time. It was quite the era for astronomy. With Galileo so often joined by these other scientists, it's fair to question Galileo's placement this high on the list.

However, it was Galileo, not the others, who became the embodiment of this modernizing movement, and he advanced it in crucial ways. He tied science to math. His meticulous quantitative measurements became the standard for all scientists to come after him. His relentless empiricism across multiple fields made him the foremost scientist of the era.

Galileo's successes were symbolic of a cornerstone in modern science. His struggle against the Church embodied the argument that truth comes from experience, experiments, and the facts—not dogma. Just because one wants something to be true does not make it so, even if someone more powerful tells us that it is. Galileo reminds us authority and knowledge are not interchangeable. Though the Inquisitors silenced him in 1633, his discoveries, works, and ideas outlived them.[13]

For centuries, he has stood as an inspiration for free thinkers wrestling against ignorant authority. Incredibly, Galileo is now used as an example by scientists who want religion kept out of scientific decisions *and* by those who know little about science when they stand up to

---

[13] Inexcusably, Galileo's "Dialogue" was not removed from the *Index* until 1835. An apology from the Church, where it finally admitted that it was wrong to treat Galileo as it had, did not come until Pope John Paul II mea culpa'd in 1992. Some might consider 359 years a bit overdue, but the Church has always made an art form out of moving at a glacial place.

the mainstream opinion of scientists. When one's struggle can be appropriated by two oppositional positions, that's influence.

For all these contributions toward science, he has my gratitude. He also earns my spot as the 12th most influential figure in Western history.

#11: Albert Einstein

"Ptolemy made a universe, which lasted 1400 years. Newton also made a universe, which has lasted 300 years. Einstein has made a universe, and I can't tell you how long that will last."
  -George Bernard Shaw at an event in Einstein's honor in 1930

"Way to go, Einstein."
-My father to me, on many occasions

This one's going to be hard. I know when he lived. I know that he had a couple theories of relativity. I know that modern scientists worship him. I know that his ideas led to the atomic age. And I know he was affable, pacifistic, and among history's smartest individuals. When it comes to Albert Einstein, I know a lot.

But do I *understand*?

No. Look at his areas of scientific accomplishment organized by Wikipedia:

Galileo

2 Scientific career
    2.1 1905 – *Annus Mirabilis* papers
    2.2 Statistical mechanics
        2.2.1 Thermodynamic fluctuations and statistical physics
        2.2.2 Theory of critical opalescence
    2.3 Special relativity
    2.4 General relativity
        2.4.1 General relativity and the equivalence principle
        2.4.2 Gravitational waves
        2.4.3 Hole argument and Entwurf theory
        2.4.4 Physical cosmology
        2.4.5 Energy momentum pseudotensor
        2.4.6 Wormholes
        2.4.7 Einstein–Cartan theory
        2.4.8 Equations of motion
    2.5 Old quantum theory
        2.5.1 Photons and energy quanta
        2.5.2 Quantized atomic vibrations
        2.5.3 Adiabatic principle and action-angle variables
        2.5.4 Bose–Einstein statistics
        2.5.5 Wave–particle duality
        2.5.6 Zero-point energy
        2.5.7 Stimulated emission
        2.5.8 Matter waves
    2.6 Quantum mechanics
        2.6.1 Einstein's objections to quantum mechanics
        2.6.2 Bohr versus Einstein
        2.6.3 Einstein–Podolsky–Rosen paradox
    2.7 Unified field theory [1]

---

[1] I mean the "adiabatic principle" is just a Wikipedia editor making something up to see if we notice, right?

Damnit, Jim, I'm a high school history teacher, not a theoretical physicist. I don't understand most of that stuff.

Admittedly, there's a chance that the main reason he's kept from a deserved spot in my top ten is because neither I, nor you, nor the smartest person you know fully understands what Einstein understood. It is perhaps my ignorance that slots him as just the 11th most influential figure in Western history.

Albert Einstein was born in Ulm, Germany on March 14, 1879.[2] From age 5 to 15 he attended German schools, but then his father's work as an engineer migrated the family to Italy. Young Einstein stayed behind to finish school, but the intense German education, particularly its emphasis on rote learning, repelled him. He cut classes, earned bad grades, and eventually dropped out to join his family south of the Alps. At 16, he looked to Switzerland's respected Federal Polytechnic school, but he failed the entrance exam despite high marks in physics and math. The school's principal suggested finishing secondary school to broaden his education before reapplying, which he successfully did one year later. That same year, sensing war ahead for his Kaiser's German Empire, Einstein renounced his German citizenship and eventually became a Swiss citizen. By century's end, the college graduate was about to embark on a successful run at a PhD, but there were few signs of the genius that stirred inside the man whose name would one day be synonymous with it.

---

[2] To math nerds, March 14, written out as 3.14, is whimsically known as Pi Day. I'm genuinely amused that Albert Einstein was born on Pi Day. I really hoped he was born on 3.14 at 1:59, but it looks like a disappointing 11:30.

That is until 1905. After earning his doctorate from the University of Zurich, he tried to find an academic teaching position, but no one hired him. Quite fortuitously, his unemployment gave him time to write. That year he published papers on the photoelectric effect and Brownian motion.[3] He also published the first part of an idea called the theory of relativity and a related paper about the equivalence of mass and energy. In the last of these he revealed history's most famous equation: "e," it turned out, equals "m c" squared.[4]

These papers came between June and November. It was soon called his *annus mirabilis*—a "miraculous year"—and it made Albert Einstein, at just 26 years old, a bona fide celebrity in scientific circles. He never again had trouble finding work.

Examples of such work included guest lectures at several European schools and professorships at the universities of Berlin and Prague. After positive experiences in the latter, he became an Austrian citizen—his third citizenship, after German and Swiss. He then moved back to Germany to become the director of the prestigious Kaiser Wilheim Institute of Physics.

During these years of migration, he constantly studied. This stretch's most famous idea was a second theory of relativity. The first, generated back in his miracle year, was thereafter known as his "special" theory of relativity. The second, in 1915, became his "general" theory of

---

[3] Did you look at this footnote to learn more about those ideas? You came to the wrong place.

[4] "e = mc2" written out: Energy (e) = Mass (m) times the speed of light (c) multiplied by itself. ("C" is the first letter of *celeritas*, the Latin word for speed, a root for our word accelerate.) The speed of light times itself is a colossally large number. If one could find a way to convert a small amount of mass into energy, it would yield a huge amount of it.

relativity, and its mind-and-space-bending proposal theorized that gravity caused curvatures in space, that gravity could curve light itself, and that people traveling at different speeds experienced time differently. These were crazy ideas ridiculed by many contemporaries—until they turned out to be right.

A Nobel Prize in Physics followed, and soon the entire world demanded its most famous scientist. In the 1920s, he gave lectures in Britain, America, Singapore, the Middle East, and Japan. Along the way he met scientists, politicians, nobility, and an emperor. A second visit to the U.S. in the early 1930s made him feel particularly welcome, a warmth that contrasted with developments back in his birthplace of Germany, where Adolf Hitler (#17) and his Nazi Party steadily consolidated their power. Upon hearing his German cottage was seized (and then used for a Hitler Youth school), Einstein, a non-practicing Jew and a pacifist moreover, renounced his German citizenship a second time. He then spent years traveling Europe, warning leaders of Hitler's rise and working to rescue Jewish scientists from Germany. In 1935, he settled on his final home—the United States. By decade's end, he added "American" to his list of citizenships. He became a member of Princeton's Institute for Advanced Study, where he worked for the rest of his life.

His new country adored him. In addition to his peerless brilliance, he personified magnanimity. Charmingly, he often appeared silly, informal, modest, poorly dressed, and full of good humor. A refugee himself, he helped found the International Relief Association and its American arm, the International Rescue Committee, one of the largest refugee and humanitarian aid organizations in the world. He endeared himself to every generation, particularly children. He was also a proto-Civil Rights

Movement warrior. In 1946, he gave a speech on the topic of racism at the historic Lincoln University, and he later joined the NAACP. He described racism as America's "worst disease" that was "handed down from one generation to the next." Meanwhile, he pushed for a Jewish state that would welcome all Jews, particularly those affected by Hitler's Holocaust. This push was, of course, successful.[5]

Once World War II erupted, this beloved and newly minted American citizen who abhorred tyranny and racism signed a letter to his president, Franklin Delano Roosevelt, urging him to beat Hitler to the development of the atomic bomb. The letter to the President many attribute to Einstein was actually penned by Hungarian physicist Leo Szilard. Eight months before the August 1939 memo was written, German physicists discovered nuclear fission and published a paper on the topic. It was Szilard who first realized that harnessing nuclear fission could create a nuclear chain reaction. The work done by the Germans and by Szilard both worked off Einstein's earlier discovery of mass and energy's relationship. Einstein had provided the bedrock of this process by theorizing that splitting open even one atom released a great amount of energy. Thus, for better or worse, Einstein had helped usher in the "Atomic Age." Szilard approached Einstein with this terrifying potential consequence of his equation, and Einstein replied, for probably the only time in his adult life: "*Daran habe ich gar nicht gedacht*"—"I did not even think about that."

Einstein eagerly signed Szilard's letter to the President, providing it much needed weight. Roosevelt took heed and prioritized uranium and

---

[5] In fact, in 1952, Israel asked him to be its second president, a moving offer he had to decline.

nuclear research. This urgency manifested in the Manhattan Project, which armed the U.S. with nuclear weapons before the Axis and allowed the Allied Powers to win World War II.

There is some tragedy here. Considered by many to be the father of the nuclear age, Einstein guiltily spent much of his remaining years working against the proliferation of the worst weapons in human history. He deeply regretted his role in the production of atomic weaponry, lamenting in 1954: "I made one great mistake in my life—when I signed the letter to President Roosevelt recommending that atom bombs be made." In 1955, he signed an appeal spearheaded by the British philosopher Bertrand Russell, a paper henceforth known as the Russell-Einstein Manifesto, which pleaded with world leaders to curb the development of nuclear weapons, to rely on diplomacy to secure peace, and to stop toying with humanity's fate.

Then, just a few days after signing Russell's letter, Albert Einstein, the world's most beloved citizen, suffered an abdominal rupture and died. He was 76.

What a career. What a life! The greatest scientist of the twentieth century, Einstein remains the latest addition to the Mount Rushmore of history's greatest scientists: Aristotle (#30), Galileo (#12), Newton (#You'll See), and Einstein. That's the list.[6]

Each of his papers from his *annus mirabilis* played massive roles in science. The photoelectric effect was a crucial discovery in the develop-

---

[6] Maybe we chisel Stephen Hawking as a fifth face? Incidentally, Newton, Einstein, and Hawking once played poker with Lt. Commander Data on an episode of *Star Trek: The Next Generation*. You should really know these things.

ment of quantum theory, while Brownian motion did the same in atomic theory. He even found time that year to publish a revolutionary paper on light being comprised of photons.[7] Then, relativity changed the face of physics.

What's perhaps most remarkable about his proposals was that they were almost all theoretical. It was all in his head and on the pieces of paper and chalkboards in front of him. Often, it was only later when his ideas proved valid. For example, his theory that gravity bent light—a process now known as gravitational lensing—was formed in 1911. It took a solar eclipse eight years later to prove it, when the apparent position of stars behind the sun revealed themselves to be slightly moved by its gravity. Another theory—that massive enough gravitational waves ripple out and affect space-time—was just proven in the last few years after astronomers witnessed the collision of two neutron stars 130 million light years away.

He didn't need to experiment to be right, which frustrated short-lived critics who found his ideas too controversial or outrageous to believe. The concept of gravity-induced curvatures in space sounded preposterous, but it was correct. It seemed insane that at high speeds mass increases and time slows down, but he was spot on. He knew his ideas sounded paradoxical, but he also knew he was right. With mathematical formulas and logic, Einstein showed how the physics of the universe worked. Einstein helping us better understand the universe's physics has allowed many practical advances, including the cathode ray television

---

[7] These photons, of course, were later deployed in the Starship Enterprise's torpedoes.

sets that entertained us and the Global Positioning System that guides us.

Relativity dramatically evolved our ideas of space and time. Isaac Newton's mechanistic vision of the universe was the triumph of physics for two centuries, but once Einstein came along, Newtonian mechanics became known as *classical* mechanics, which needed to be distinguished from, and some might even say relegated by, Einstein's *quantum* mechanics. In a rare instance of Isaac Newton's science falling short, his laws of motion and gravity did not correctly predict the behavior of the universe's tiniest or fastest objects. Quantum mechanics did.

When relativity was proven, *The Times* of London seized on the drama:

REVOLUTION IN SCIENCE.
NEW THEORY OF THE UNIVERSE.
NEWTONIAN IDEAS OVERTHROWN.

"Newtonian ideas overthrown." It's hard to now fully capture how big of a deal that was, but *it was a huge deal*. As we will see in his chapter, Isaac Newton's ranking as history's great scientist is considerably supported. Yet, in this case, Einstein trumped him.

Just as impressive, no one has since been able to trump Einstein. His theories have survived every assault by every skeptic. Thanks to him, we continue to know that everything is, in fact, relative.

In the end, Einstein believed "nobody understands me" but "everybody likes me." The latter ensures his indelible reputation, but the former might be the reason he's limited to just the 11th most influential figure in Western history.

#10: William Shakespeare

"What point of morals, of manners, of economy, of philosophy, of religion, of taste, of the conduct of life, has he not settled? What mystery has he not signified his knowledge of? . . . What lover has he not outloved? What sage has he not outseen? What gentleman has he not instructed in the rudeness of his behavior?"

–Ralph Waldo Emerson on Shakespeare

As we arrive in the Top 10, it's clear this ranking has bent toward scientists and statesmen, professions I felt most directly impacted the development of Western civilization. Artists did not receive as much attention. When writing the introduction to this series, I acknowledged as much, and I did my best to explain my reasoning. Here's what I said, with new bolded emphasis added:

"I had enormous difficulty weighing the importance of artists, musicians, and authors. Ultimately, no artists or musicians made the list. **Aside from one exception,** *no authors made the cut unless that vocation was not their primary one. . . . While I have enormous appreciation for the arts and adore classical music, I simply could not make the case that any* one *artist*

or musician changed the West's development more than those who made this ranking. Perhaps the best way to look at it is that these cultural icons were superb reflections of an era; when studying a period, it's good to study the titans of music and art, much like an archaeologist unearths artifacts to draw conclusions about a past culture. Yet, they do not shape their era or future ones as much as others on this list."

Today, we get to that "one exception." This chapter, instead of science, war, or government, we focus on the human spirit and a man who connected with it better than anyone. That man was William Shakespeare, the 10th most influential figure in Western history.[1]

William Shakespeare was born in April 1564, two months after Michelangelo died. Perhaps that's how long it takes for the essence of creative genius to float from Rome to Stratford-upon-Avon. Despite being born into an illiterate family, Shakespeare was nonetheless given a strong education thanks to a typically strong English school system. He became literate not only in his native English, but he was also taught Latin and learned from classical texts as well. At 18 he married Anne Hathaway, and in the next three years they had three children—daughters

---

[1] This chapter will proceed with the assumption that there is nothing fishy about Shakespeare's historicity. Alternative theories, many of which can't comprehend that someone of Shakespeare's genius lived so unremarkably, comprise the "Shakespeare authorship question." Some believe, for example, that the person named Shakespeare was just used as a cover story for the actual author who wanted to remain anonymous. Others believe it had to have been a collection of writers that created such prolific prose. In total, conspiracies have proposed up to 80 men and women as the true author of "Shakespeare's" works. The scholarly consensus, however, is that these conspiracy theories, unlike Ophelia's lungs, hold little water.

William Shakespeare

Susanna and Judith, son Hamnet—and moved to London. From 1585 to 1592, he left little historical record (a period known as his "lost years") as he probably tried to scratch out a living through writing, directing, and acting.

Inspired by the Italian Renaissance, Shakespeare's early, optimistic period of the 1590s produced his most romantic, funny, and Italian works, including *The Comedy of Errors, A Midsummer's Night Dream, A Merchant of Venice, and Romeo and Juliet*. He was not well received, however. Though some recognized him as a bit of an unrefined genius, he was nonetheless perceived as too rough around the edges. The only company to perform his plays, The Lord Chamberlain's Men, was the one he co-owned. In 1599, this company built a theater on the south bank of the River Thames and called it the Globe.

The Globe's architecture allowed it to entertain a variety of people. Indeed, Shakespeare's plays were attended by a broad, albeit segregated, spectrum of social classes. In the Globe Theater, while the upper classes enjoyed great views from locations that mirrored their social standing in society, the lower class—or the "groundlings"—found themselves at the base of the stage in the appropriately named "pit," where they stood on dirt, garbage, and nutshells. Shakespeare wrote plenty of crass lines to play to this colorful crowd.

When tragedy struck Shakespeare, his plays took a different tone. In 1596, his son died at just 11 years old. Shakespeare's father passed a few years later. As a result, the late 1590s and first decade of the 1600s hosted his most sobering histories—the *Henry IVs, Henry V*, and *Julius Caesar*—in addition to his greatest dramas and tragedies—*Othello, Macbeth, King Lear*, and *Hamlet*. Unlike his early, Italian-based works, this period usually moved the setting to more dreary northern Europe—most prominently England and Denmark—a relocation that was later seen as part of the Northern Renaissance. These works rival the best of da Vinci, Newton, Mozart, and Einstein (#11) as the greatest concentrated flourish of creativity in human history.

His final period of plays began after the death of his adored elderly mother. Her death seemed to remind him of his younger, happier days, and he tried to channel her kindness into his works. Reflecting this impression on him were *Cymbeline*, *The Winter's Tale*, and *The Tempest*. Though they're not quite as lighthearted as his early comedies—his midlife tragedies very much left an indelible mark on his creative process—their resolutions were lighter than anything from his more tragic period. Unlike the dire fates of Julius Caesar, Macbeth, and Hamlet, the bulk of his last great works culminated in reconciliation and forgiveness.

Aided by an English Golden Age inaugurated by Queen Elizabeth (#19), Shakespeare's creative talents allowed him to gain modest prosperity. Though he enjoyed nowhere near the success one might assume he must have had, Shakespeare did well enough to buy the second biggest house back in Stratford before moving there for semi-retirement around 1610. Six years later, he died relatively young, just 52, from unknown causes. His passing, beyond his family and circle of friends, went unnoticed.

Considering William Shakespeare is history's greatest writer, perhaps no one has ever had a greater gap between their reputation at death and

William Shakespeare

reputation in modern times.[2] In his career he wrote 38 plays,[3] 154 sonnets, and an assortment of other works. His main failure was that he prioritized working over fame. He did not seem particularly adept at projecting a reputation. Since he did not publish his works, they made few impacts on England's flourishing culture. It was not until a decade after his death that friends canonized the *First Folio*, a collection of nearly all his plays. It's an assemblage now hailed as one of the most important books ever published in English.[4]

In fact, if we consider the impact on the English language itself, the *First Folio* is probably the language's most influential work. English had been in flux before Shakespeare. It was a slowly evolving hodgepodge of Anglo-Saxon German, Scandinavian, Latin, and even some Greek. The rules of spelling and grammar were far from standardized. However, by the time Shakespeare's reputation caught up with his talent about a century after his death, just about every literate person in England was reading him. He deftly wove together England's source languages into a considerable canon. As a result, his phrases and spellings gradually became English norms.

---

[2] Other contenders include Jesus, Vincent van Gogh, and, one can only assume, the author of the book you're reading.

[3] An average of nearly two per year!

[4] Most of his plays have been translated and printed from this single source and might not have survived otherwise. How fragile! They printed only 750 original copies of it, and 235 are still known. In 1623, one could buy a copy of the First Folio for one English pound. In October 2020, one copy was sold for nearly $10 million, making it the most valuable piece of literature ever auctioned. Not a terrible investment.

Just as relevant, about 10 percent of the 17 thousand words he used were of his own creation. Some estimates put the number of words he contributed to the language as high as several thousand.[5]

Why all the inventive wording? English hadn't matured as a language as much as Greek and Latin had. It was still shedding its basic, Germanic routes by the time of the Renaissance. The most educated among the English had long used Latin or French, since these more aged and refined languages had more specific words and phrases for more complex ideas and situations. Rather than borrow from another language too often, Shakespeare adapted English words (perhaps modifying a word to change its part of speech, or adding a suffix or prefix), or he even invented them out of whole cloth. As Plato (#30) told us, necessity was the mother of invention.

After more than a millennium of being a mishmash of constantly changing dialects, Shakespeare's words combined with English speakers' desire to read them formalized the language. This accelerated evolution occurred in time for English to be exported around the globe during the rise and height of the mighty British Empire. Accompanying joint-stock companies and His Majesty's Navy were officers *Hamlet*, *Othello*, and *Lear*.

Hurting the argument for Shakespeare's influence is that it's hard to say in any tangible sense how else Shakespeare directly influenced West-

---

[5] These new words include accommodation, amazement, apostrophe, assassination, bloody, castigate, countless, critic, dishearten, dislocate, dwindle, eventful, frugal, generous, gloomy, hurry, impartial, inauspicious, indistinguishable, laughable, lonely, majestic, monumental, obscene, premeditated, reliance, sanctimonious, submerge, and suspicious.

ern history. Again, that's the problem with which I earnestly grappled when considering the West's cultural titans.

Nevertheless, despite my evaluation of scientists and leaders as the more influential professions, I still acknowledge the importance played by art. We spend a good chunk of our lives consuming art through our various preferred entertainment—movies, TV, books, and more. The consumption of these creative works, from the lowest form of reality TV to obscure foreign films, from pulp novels to timeless ones, affects our personalities, feelings, and souls in a meaningful way. We react. We develop animosity. We emote. We develop empathy. We get inspired. *We get influenced*. Indeed, for most people, art touches their soul more than cold science ever has, and therefore perhaps the soul of mankind matters just as much as its politics and technology.[6]

No one seemed to understand that soul like Shakespeare. Even if there are rivals to such a claim, earlier writers—from Homer and Virgil to Dante and Chaucer—are nowhere near as read and performed as Shakespeare is today. And even if he was inspired by and borrowed from earlier authors and works, what he did with that inspiration modernized every genre he touched. He has in fact superseded every writer in the Western catalog, and second place is so small in his rear view mirror that he can't even see it anymore.

Modern critic Harold Bloom believes that Shakespeare isn't just the most important part of the Western canon—Shakespeare *is* the canon. Bloom argues Shakespeare "sets the standard and the limits of literature." His ubiquitous works grace Western stages, ballets, screens,

---

[6] This dynamic connects to what I previewed about Western history when discussing the two earliest entries on this list—Plato and Aristotle (tied for #30).

and classrooms. He is the earliest author read by just about everyone in the Western world, and he's still the almost singular source of inspiration for modern comedies, dramas, and tragedies. He has totally defied time.

It's as if his characters speak to us from our own heart. Contemporary Ben Jonson called him the "soul of the age" and "wonder of our stage." Modern hero Nelson Mandela, who kept a volume of Shakespeare's works while in prison, believed "Shakespeare always seems to have something to say to us." In between, writer and critic John Dryden told us, "He was the man who of all modern, and perhaps ancient poets, had the largest and most comprehensive soul."

Shakespeare fashioned a mirror into which we've since stared. Even among all his polysyllabic creativity, he could still connect with us using the simplest of phrases: "To be, or not to be?" It is the deepest question we can ask of ourselves, and no one asked it any simpler or more profoundly.[7]

"When he describes anything," says Dryden, "you more than see it, you feel it too." He can touch our souls and leave a lasting mark. In *Hamlet* we recognize the self-absorbed youth grappling with maturity, responsibility, torturous decisions, the stark realities of the world, and wondering if it's all worth it. In *Romeo and Juliet* we feel what it's like to be more controlled by love than family, logic, and life itself. In *King Lear* we feel what it's like to grow old, to lose friends and relatives, and to wonder if this is the end and what it all meant.

---

[7] Quite appropriate for a play with a first line that doubles as the ultimate introspection: "Who's there?"

William Shakespeare

Thus, where I found it hard to rank Bach, Mozart, and Michelangelo above any of the people on this list, Shakespeare seemed the best fitting cultural ambassador. His narratives and their spiritual descendants permeate high and popular culture more than Mozart's music or Michelangelo's art.[8]

He has inspired countless modern works. He's invaded our consciousness so deeply that it is now exceedingly difficult not to be derivative of Shakespeare. We think we're only now in the unimaginative era of sequels, adaptations, and spin-offs, but we've actually been living in that era ever since the *First Folio*. The characters mentioned above, along with, Lady Macbeth, Othello, Iago, Beatrice, Shylock, Cordelia, Falstaff, and so many more, have become the ultimate archetypes of modern entertainment.[9] He so clearly modeled how we think and how we behave across the genres that his plots not only invite imitation, they make imitation inescapable. If something isn't Shakespearean, we say it doesn't make sense.

It's nothing short of wondrous that, four centuries later, his plays still feel modern. They still work theatrically and visually, and they still connect personally. We can't say the same for any writer before him. It's as if he birthed modern entertainment, and he'll be forever enshrined as its founder.

Though the likes of Michelangelo and Bach missed this list due to the comparatively limited impact of art and music on the development of

---

[8] Recall the varied consumers of his work. He had something for all of them —and therefore all of us.

[9] A Shakespeare nut can watch the first act of a TV series episode and by the first commercial break say, "Oh, so they're doing *The Tempest* in this one."

Western civilization, Shakespeare's mastery of the written word very much affected it. When Ben Jonson eulogized him by calling Shakespeare the soul of the age, he later corrected himself, stating he "was not of an age, but for all time." Quite right.

No artist, musician, or writer so gently held the human heart and told us why the beats were worth it. His colossal contributions to the West's dominant language and its artistic output make him our leading cultural inspiration—and the 10th most influential figure in Western history.

#9: Karl Marx

"The philosophers have only interpreted the world, in various ways. The point, however, is to change it."

–Karl Marx, 1845

He is probably this ranking's most divisive figure. Just about all of us line up against Hitler (#17). We celebrate the heroism of Joan of Arc (#27), the science of Galileo (#12), and the canon of Shakespeare (#10). We embrace the genius of Ford (#20), Edison (#18), and Einstein (#11). Enough time has passed for us to ignore the deaths caused by Peter the Great (#26), Constantine (#23), and Charlemagne (#21).

But Karl Marx? Though it's grown increasingly negative, his is a mixed reputation. As the primary theorist behind modern communism, atrocities have been committed in the name of his ideology. Yet, he neither took a life nor ordered subordinates to do so, and many of his ideas catalyzed social modernization. He's recent enough to cause a visceral reaction, but early enough to give us over a century to objectify our position.¹ I'd guess that of those who manage to finish this chapter on his influence, left-leaners will think me too critical and right-leaners too lenient.

He also remains divisive because even though he was wrong about a lot, he was right about a lot, too. In both cases, he left his mark on society, politics, and economics. Love him or hate him, Karl Marx is undeniably influential. In fact, he's the ninth most influential figure in Western history.

Karl Marx was from Trier, part of the Prussian Kingdom in modern Germany. He was born in 1818—about the halfway point between the French Revolution, which helped inform his ideology, and the Revolutions of 1848, which his ideology helped inform. His lawyer-led family provided young Karl a full education. He studied law at the University of Bonn before receiving a Ph.D. in philosophy at the University of Jena. In between, he married Jenny von Westphalen. They went on to have seven children, though poor living conditions helped send four to early graves.

His studies waded deeply into social, political, and economic history. The patterns he noticed—those of a working class's perpetual subjugation at the hands of a wealthy, landed elite—turned him radically liberal. Still in his 20s, he edited Cologne's liberal *Rheinische Zeitung* newspaper, but his controversial political opinions—particularly against

---

¹ Writing that paragraph, I realized Marx does have one rival for "Most Divisive." Appropriately, it's a man who seemed to be everyone's rival: Napoleon (#16). Still, I think Napoleon, who began his rise in the late eighteenth century, is just early enough to be romanticized despite some controversial actions. Marx feels more modern and therefore still despised by his ideological opponents.

Karl Marx

Prussian King Frederick William IV and his autocratic government—attracted political pressure.

Marx's dealings as the *Rheinische Zeitung*'s editor during his formative years proved to be consequential. The newspaper criticized Frederick William and his aggressive Prussian government. Despite warnings, the newspaper persisted. Marx and the paper's other leaders hoped that writing liberal editorials for a like-minded population would galvanize Prussia's citizens into forcing a change in the government. The result would be the government's peaceful, if slow, move from absolute monarchy to something more constitutional—perhaps even a democratic-republic. Prussian leadership resisted and undermined the paper at every turn, leading Marx to the conclusion that only through aggressive means —like in the American and French revolutions—will the status quo be upended. Consequently, in 1843 he fled to the home of the first modern European revolution: Paris.[2]

There he met Friedrich Engels, his longest lasting and most prominent intellectual partner.[3] The two were kindred spirits; both lamented the burden of the common man whose arduous labor provided the most succulent fruit to a fat few. While in France, a fanatical Marx could not

---

[2] By then, France had two notable revolutions: the famous French Revolution of 1789 which led to Louis XVI's beheading, and then the July Revolution of 1830, which led to the abdication of Louis's youngest brother, King Charles X. Two years later a smaller rebellion broke out in June, though it left few impacts besides a few hundred casualties and an obscure novel which later turned into an unknown musical titled "Les Misérables."

[3] Engels was never really considered for this competitive list. While Engels co-wrote major works with Marx and the two were often inseparable (with Engels frequently a financial backer of Marx and his family), it was Marx who conjured and animated most of their revolutionary work.

hold his tongue and openly expressed these controversial ideas to Parisians. He founded another paper, *Vorwärts*, which he published for local Germans. Assuming he was safe in the heart of France, he lobbed more criticisms over the border at Prussian leadership until Frederick William asked French King Louis Philippe to silence the annoying expat. Two years into his stay, Karl Marx was expelled from his new home.

Home number three was Brussels, where Engels joined him. Feeling more comfortable in Belgium, they organized their thoughts and unleashed a series of influential works. Written from 1845 to 1846, "The German Ideology" was the first attempt to codify the ideas that later battered Western capitalism. Marx and Engels built an entire philosophy out of the premises laid out in "Ideology," but the book could not find a publisher. Two years later, they injected its ideas into a pamphlet and produced one of the most famous works in the Western canon.

In February, 1848, Marx and Engels published "The Communist Manifesto." Though small in size—it amounted to only 23-pages—the work eventually became the standard bearer for communist ideology. Though the "Manifesto" did not cause the many "Revolutions of 1848," it captured the *zeitgeist* of that year better than any other work. Belgium expelled him for his troubles.[4]

With newfound name recognition, he returned to his native Cologne to help its struggle against authoritarianism and poor living conditions. He set up a workers club and published a handbill to circulate demands on the Prussian government. Again, Marx was expelled.

---

[4] All his expulsions/exiles/fleeing as a result of radical ideas should remind you of Voltaire (#22). Surprisingly, anti-elite ideas are not well received by the elite.

Karl Marx

For his final move, in 1849 a 31-year-old Marx settled into London, home for the last 34 years of his life. He continued to spend most of his time researching and writing about social, political, and economic history. Among his work was as a correspondent with the *New-York Daily Tribune*, founded by editor Horace Greeley, a co-founder of the Republican Party and future presidential nominee. Its considerable readership of working class Americans lapped up Marx's take on European affairs until the considerably distracting American Civil War broke out in 1861.

Marx's career in London led to many more published works, culminating in one that even surpassed the status of "The Communist Manifesto." In 1867, he published the first volume of his masterwork, "Das Kapital," a culmination of many themes in Marx's now considerable bibliography.

Favoring chronology before analysis, I've mostly ignored those themes so far, so let's get into them now.

They start with a premise. Chapter 1, Line 1 of "The Communist Manifesto" proposes that "The history of all hitherto existing society is the history of class struggles." These struggles pitted those who owned the means of production—that is, land and capital—against a labor force they employed to procure themselves more land and capital. For the landed elite, Marx used the term *bourgeoisie*; the oppressed working class he labeled the *proletariat*.⁵ Of all the shortcomings of this system, Marx thought, the greatest was that the bourgeoisie got to enjoy most of the wealth, even though it was the proletariat that actually created it. Whereas the farm laborer or factory worker actually tended the field or worked the machine, it was the plantation and factory owners that saw the profit.

The laborers, moreover, were stuck in their lower class, since their impoverished nature lacked the requisite land and capital to take advantage of the system. Countless generations bequeathed their social status, whether bourgeois or proletarian, to their children, and the cycle fed itself. With many examples, from ancient Rome through the feudal medieval era and into the modern industrial world, Marx and Engels noted how consistently this haves-and-have-nots paradigm flowed across history.⁶ This approach to the field became known as a "materialist conception of history," or historical materialism.

---

⁵ The term bourgeoisie came from "those who lived in the borough," or in the cities, where the economic action was. Proletariat derives from an old Latin phrase "proletarius," which is connected to the ability to produce offspring. Ancient Romans used that term for people without land and money, whose only contribution to the state was the children they provided.

⁶ "In the earlier epochs of history, we find almost everywhere a complicated arrangement of society into various orders, a manifold gradation of social rank. In ancient Rome we have patricians, knights, plebians, slaves; in the Middle Ages, feudal lords, vassals, guild-masters, journeymen, apprentices, serfs; in almost all of these classes, again, subordinate gradations. The modern bourgeois society that has sprouted from the ruins of feudal society has not done away with class antagonisms. It has but established new classes, new conditions of oppression, new forms of struggle in place of the old ones."

Though only in the 1893 preface to a new "Manifesto" edition does Engels use the word "capitalism" to describe the prevailing economic model, Marx's original pamphlet does frequently reference the bourgeoisie as "capitalists" who wanted to protect the system. These capitalists prioritized their own wealth over the well-being of their workers. They would pay workers just enough to keep them working, a historical pattern called the "iron laws of wages." Moreover, the bourgeoisie, having a vested interest in perpetuating the system from which it benefited, was either a part of political and cultural leadership or controlled them. It could therefore use its economic, political, and cultural power to promote and continue the capitalist model. Even religion, Christianity included, served only to distract and control the exploited proletariat.[7]

Marx and Engels felt this system was not only unfair, it was unsustainable. They thought laborers would eventually discern the relationship was one-sided. Capitalists, according to the "Manifesto," were therefore sowing the seeds of their own doom. They were their "own grave-diggers." Inevitably, there would be an international revolution—international because members of the proletariat across countries had

---

[7] The Manifesto writes that capitalism is "veiled by religious and political illusions." Later, it suggests man will one day outgrow this distraction, and communism can help: "All religions so far have been the expression of historical stages of development of individual peoples or groups of peoples. But communism is the stage of historical development which makes all existing religions superfluous and brings about their disappearance." Perhaps most famously, Marx, in another work, calls religion *"das Opium des Volkes"*—the opium of the people. When we should be mad as hell, religion, by design, calms us with false peace.

more in common with each other than they did with the upper class of their own nation—that would destroy capitalism.[8]

In its place, Marx and Engels wanted the revolutionaries to create a system where the means of production—the land, capital, and labor that elites had controlled for centuries—were owned and shared collectively in communes. Each person would contribute what they could and consume what they required, which in 1875 Marx famously phrased, "From each according to his ability, to each according to his needs." In the end, with all this cooperation in communities, there would be no more poverty, hunger, or homelessness. Instead, there would only be this collective of classless communes. In a word: communism.

The "Manifesto," though it quickly became the most prominent promoter of this vision, wasn't the first work to do so. Communism's cousin, socialism, had also been around, both in concept and by name, for some time.[9] Marx, however, gradually drifted from most contempo-

---

[8] Marx called the proletariat to action in the closing lines of "The Communist Manifesto": "Workers of the world, unite! You have nothing to lose but your chains!" Notably, this sentiment fit perfectly with 1848's international movement of the proletariat against the powers that controlled them.

[9] Marx can alternatively be viewed as a "socialist," a "communist," or both. He promoted each at various times for various purposes, and he's considered the modern world's foremost ambassador of each. Most broadly we can say he embraced socialism—which aims to reduce inequality through a redistribution of wealth and free access to benefits like health care and education—and recognized it as a pivotal step toward arriving at the ultimate goal of communism, which would have no social classes or private property. Meanwhile, he was of course "Marxist," which overlaps with each but more focuses on the premise of the aforementioned historical materialism, class struggle, and inevitable revolution of the proletariat.

rary socialists.[10] These contemporaries—who Marxists derisively dubbed "utopian socialists"—agreed that the common man was taken advantage of by the landed class, but their approach to solving the problem was too moderate for Marx's liking. They advocated educating people about socialism. Then, as society learned about this superior alternative to capitalism, it would democratically and peacefully convert. Marx considered this approach naïve. Voting rights in Europe were considerably limited, and beyond that he knew those in power would never allow society to destroy the conventional economic patterns from which they benefited so much and for so long.

To Marx, mere ideology did not make a revolution. Action did.[11] He therefore advocated for a more aggressive, violent proletariat revolution. That was the only way workers could seize the means of production, destroy the bourgeoisie, and create a "dictatorship of the proletariat." Since he saw it as an inevitable event once workers realized they were being taken advantage of, distinctive from utopian socialism was Marx's "scientific socialism." He saw capitalism as a transient, shortsighted problem, socialism as the natural fix, and a revolution as the necessary pivot to get from the inferior to the superior.

Indeed, Marx felt his economic philosophy was grounded in a scientific approach. "Das Kapital," perhaps his most scathing rebuke of the capitalistic model, described capitalism as concerned only with maximizing profit and not at all about the worker's long-term well-being. Marx thought the dense, meticulous analysis of capitalism classified "Kapital"

---

[10] Picture bearded, disheveled men gathered in the revolutionary salons of Europe, sharing and debating controversial ideas and sometimes coming to inebriated blows.

[11] Note this chapter's epigraph.

as a scientific text. He even described what he called capitalism's "laws of motion," including where and how it began and where and how it would meet its inescapable, self-inflicted demise.[12]

He had two more volumes planned for "Das Kapital," but he wouldn't live to see them through. (Engels cobbled together his notes to publish the work posthumously.) His health deteriorated in the 1870s. He continued to research and write, but never with the vigor of his younger days. After his wife died in 1881, he developed catarrhal inflammation, which triggered bronchitis and pleurisy, ailments that dogged him for the last year of his life.

In 1883, shortly after his oldest daughter became his fifth child to predecease him, the fiery Karl Marx finally gave up the fight. He died at the age of 64. His funeral was attended by no more than a dozen mourners. Those in attendance were the first to see his final instructions in the form of the tomb's epitaph: "*Workers of all lands unite.*"

Marx died not knowing his ideas would one day form the heart of the following century's communist movement, which spread those ideas across much of the world. At the time of his death, he was known in some socialist circles, but he had no reputation beyond them. Soon, however, "The Communist Manifesto" gained traction. After that, as socialism gathered momentum, Marx's reputation did as well.

The tipping point came 35 years after his death, when Marxophile Vladimir Lenin spearheaded the Bolshevik Revolution, which deposed Russian Tsar Nicolas II and installed what it claimed was a Marxist

---

[12] *"Capitalist production begets its own negation."*

state.[13] Russia gave Marxism its first national backing, and the country quickly worked to spread the revolution by controlling surrounding countries and exporting Marxist ideas to them. This Union of Soviet Socialist Republics gradually enveloped much of the northern part of the Eastern Hemisphere. Each of its countries translated into their mottos Marx's famous plea and epitaph. For 70 years the Communist Party controlled the Soviet Union's governments, and "The Communist Manifesto" was practically required reading for its early leaders.

In addition to securing the U.S.S.R., the world's largest country by area, communism in time took the world's most populous country as well. In 1949, China fell to communist leaders. Naturally, all territories in these two massive countries' spheres of influences, including parts of Africa and faraway islands in the Western hemisphere (like Cuba), converted with them as well. In each place Marx's ideas were used to meet the local problems of each nation. Joseph Stalin, Mao Zedong, Pol Pot, Fidel Castro, and others each imported Marxist ideas, though always modified. Still, in common was the Marxist legacy of overthrowing the established leadership to begin the conversion to communism. The result: by the centennial of Marx's death, communist governments controlled a colossal amount of land.

---

[13] Lenin, like a good scientific socialist, saw the Russian revolution as inescapable: a massive nation of factory workers and peasant farmers getting taken advantage of by a narrow circle of tsarist elites could only last so long. After the Bolsheviks seized power, the country's new flag represented the worker and the farmer with the hammer and sickle. Not coincidentally, "Das Kapital" had sold better in Russian than in any other country. Marx lived long enough to observe that in Russia, the book "was read and valued more than anywhere."

This growth was not without its opposition. For the 50 years after World War II, "First World" powers represented by the United States, United Kingdom, France, and others worked to contain the "Second World" collection of communist allies.[14] Thankfully, these two sides never plunged us into a catastrophic conflict, but this Cold War was still the main rivalry of the post-World War II era. With it came nuclear proliferation, the U.S. Marshall Plan, the partition of Germany, NATO, the Space Race, red scares, and more. In essence, the First World had become primarily motivated by, and redirected much of its resources to, containing and defeating the economic and political philosophies of Karl Marx. The man with fewer than a dozen mourners at his funeral had his ideas, nominally at least, worm their way into the lives of over a billion people, with another billion resisting.[15]

However, I do say nominally. Truth be told, no governments arrived at Marx's final communist utopia. Communist parties enacted some socialist reforms and were meant to work toward communism. However, either from bribery, incompetence, a lack of desire, or all three, they had little success in doing so. Instead, they usually moved directly from revolution to dictatorship and seemed to forget about the democratic and utopian components. Though they did have a socialist approach, their corruption usually undermined it.

Still, while Marx's ideas were misunderstood or misinterpreted, the same could be said for others in this ranking. Previous entries Plato (#30) and Jefferson (#24), among others, had some of their ideas cor-

---

[14] Underdeveloped "Third World" countries became pawns in their game.

[15] Interestingly, his once lonely London burial plot has since become a veritable pilgrimage site for aspiring socialists across the world . . . and they have to pay to see it!

Karl Marx

rupted, as did Jesus and Martin Luther, entries still to come. Even when modified, however, the DNA of those ideas is undeniably impactful.

Also working against Marx is what seem to be his philosophical missteps. At best, his utopian vision for a society has proved unrealistic; at worst, it's been an utter failure with catastrophic consequences. He thought capitalism would inevitably be replaced. That hasn't happened. Instead, it's been the communist regimes that have regularly fallen, flailed, or grafted onto themselves elements of capitalism to survive in the modern world. Most notably, the Soviet Union's collapse in 1991 is heralded as a triumph for Western capitalism, and China has implemented considerable modernization to blend capitalism with its communist aspirations.[16]

Worse yet, communist countries' penchant for wide scale atrocities is a sizable demerit for its viability. Communist leaders have used communism as a justification for many horrors—not the least of which include rebellions, wars, assassinations, and repression—that have caused upwards of a hundred million deaths. Is Marx the cause of all that tragedy? Not directly. If he were, he'd be ranked even higher than number 9 on the list. However, the diffused responsibility for the crimson twentieth century insulates him from too much blame. Still, he did endorse revolutions, and his advocates must wrestle with the pattern of deadly communist regimes.

Marx was also wrong about some of capitalism's negative effects over the long term. He suggested that those in the lower tiers of society would grow gradually poorer as their wealthier employers hungrily gobbled

---

[16] I do wonder where I would have ranked Marx a few decades ago. Perhaps top five. If socialism makes a big comeback this century, perhaps this list's 100th anniversary edition will put him there.

more of the pie, and he said that the middle class would gradually disappear as nearly all its members were relegated to the proletariat. Despite modern rhetoric from the left, though the 1 percent are indeed wealthier than ever and the Western middle class has seen sluggish growth of late, almost all of the 99 percent has gradually seen, among many improvements, our standard of living increase, our life expectancy grow, and our literacy climb, among many other gains. Most Westerners today have more comfortable lifestyles than the wealthiest of Marx's time. Perhaps the 1 percent owns half the pie, but the pie has never been larger or more delicious.

Nevertheless, although Marx may have erred on some specific predictions, so did Aristotle (#30). So did Copernicus (#28). So did Darwin (#15). Many irreplaceable scientists and thinkers had imperfect theories.

Influence, however, is not merely a reflection of exactitude. Even with his errors, Marx's effects are considerable. He struck a nerve that continues to reverberate. As a philosopher and social analyst, he ranks among the most influential figures in political, social, and economic thought. "The Communist Manifesto" continues to be one of the most influential and referenced political works of all time, and it continues to inspire modern socialists, however misguided one might think they are. "Das Kapital," meanwhile, ranks as the most cited pre-1950 work in modern social science.

Consider what he got right. His analysis of the relationship between elites and laborers and his interpretation of history allow many to still paint him as a champion of the underclass. As he described, a working class still seeks employment from those that control the means of production. The landed class still has an outsized role in government and culture. Marx also wrote about capitalism burning through resources for short-term wealth—relevant as ever in a world depleting its nonrenewable resources.

He vociferously promoted labor unions, noting how imperative they were in the quest for livable wages. Practicing what he preached, in 1864 he co-founded the International Workingmen's Association, which at its height included millions of Europeans. Three years later, he published the first volume of "Das Kapital." Soon after, Britain, France, and Germany each legalized unions.

He railed against the flaws of capitalism, particularly its tendency to encourage cost-saving measures to the detriment of employees' safety and pay, and the post-Marx years boast more frequent factory safety laws and steeply climbing wages.

It's impressive that the logic he used then is still used today. His argument that the capitalist model is unsustainable gets reintroduced every time there's a financial crisis. He anticipated Occupy Wall Street and the like by 150 years, and such movements pressure political and economic leaders to tighten the system.[17]

Further haunting the modern political standard is Marx's advocacy for international movements. Though nationalism guided most nineteenth century Westerners, Marxists pushed in the other direction. Wanting workers of all lands to unite, Marx lamented the borders erected by the bourgeoisie to separate them and hamstring their collective strength. In more recent history, this ideological strand exists in proponents of globalization and more open borders.

---

[17] In fact, during the great recession at the end of the last decade, Marx's writings, particularly "Das Kapital," saw a spike in demand and sales.

Marx also wrote about how mechanization dehumanized workers as the bourgeoisie raked in unprecedented profits. Though life for the average Westerner could be demeaning even before the industrial period, the industrialization process—with its brutal factories, strict foremen, and greedy owners—seemed to add injuries to the insult.[18] In response, "The Communist Manifesto" made a series of demands aimed at any leaders who wanted to stave off the imminent violent rebellion of the proletariat. Included in these demands were a progressive income tax, abolition of child labor, and free public education. All were heeded. Balancing capitalism with a bit of socialism, these ideas contributed to the progress of the last century. Our children aren't forced to work, we're more educated, and we live longer and more comfortably. There have been few more relevant changes to our lives.

Thus, perhaps Marx's greatest legacy was not as a torpedo into capitalism's hull, but as a warning shot across its bow. Communism may have failed, but Marxism continues to loom. The specter of his ideology continues to haunt capitalism as a counterbalance, ensuring it doesn't run amok.

Therefore, the divisive, controversial, and enormously important Karl Marx is the ninth most influential figure in Western history.

---

[18] And boy, were there injuries.

#8: Louis Pasteur

"I am on the edge of mysteries and the veil is getting thinner and thinner."

–Louis Pasteur, 1851

Before we get into #8, let's first take a look at this chart:[1]

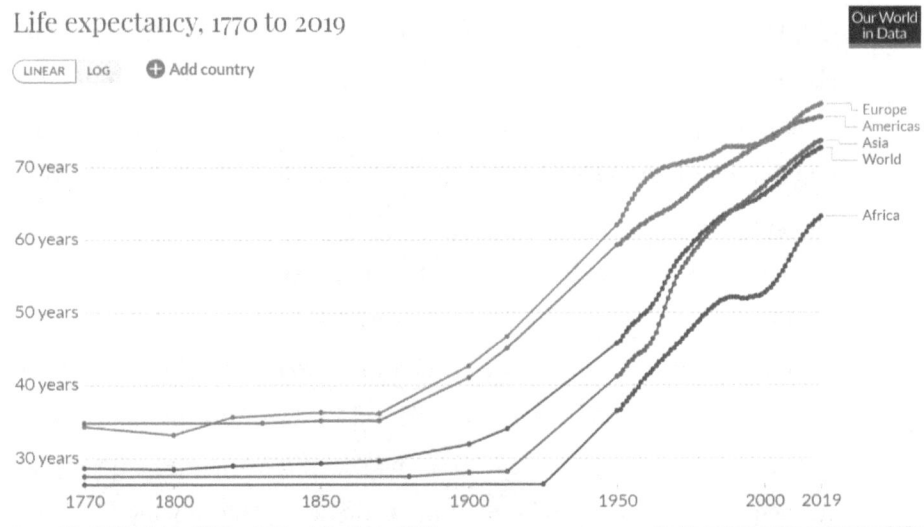

[1] Max Roser, Esteban Ortiz-Ospina and Hannah Ritchie; First published in 2013; last revised in October 2019.   https://ourworldindata.org/life-expectancy

There's a point, right around 1870, where the average life expectancy of a Westerner was just 36 years. For the world, it was less than 30. That's about where the number had been for centuries. Millennia even.

Soon after, however, the average length of a human's life rapidly climbed. Now, a Westerner's average life expectancy is around 80 years. So what happened?

Louis Pasteur happened. We owe our long lives to the eighth most influential figure in Western history.

Louis Pasteur was born in 1822 Dole, France. Not a bright student in primary or secondary school, he made up for it with a strong work ethic and a repetitive, almost obsessive-compulsive approach to everything he did. His academic disappointments not only taught him persistence, but also the process of testing approaches, failing, and then re-testing until he found something that worked. Unbeknownst to history's most important doctor, he had been developing a tolerance for the tedious scientific method.

His drive eventually got him into college (where he failed his first exam), and he eventually earned a general science degree despite struggling in chemistry. He barely qualified for graduate school after a poor entrance examination, though he insisted on re-taking the test a year later to improve his score. By 1845, he secured his master's degree in science. He became a professor at the Collège de Tournon and a lab assistant at the prestigious École Normale Supérieure (ENS). In his next few years, he earned a doctorate, became a University of Strasbourg professor of chemistry, then the chair of its department, then the dean of science at Lille University. In 1857, at only 35, he finally returned to ENS as director of scientific studies.[2]

It was there that Pasteur made many of his breakthroughs. It was also there where his fanatical work ethic and undiagnosed OCD made Pasteur his fair share of enemies.

He was obsessed with improving science itself—the approach to it, the respect for it, and the insistence on perfectly and repetitively run experiments. As director of the ENS, his rules for students were so stringent—"quasi-militant," as biographer Patrice Debra describes it—that he faced two walkouts. (After enforcing a purportedly inedible mutton dinner every Monday, he faced, I kid you not, a "bean revolt."[3]) Offenses included talking in class, dawdling, and tardiness. He enacted a rigid schedule planned down to the minute, and to be late was to resign one's place from the academy. He even once threatened expulsion to any student caught smoking—a habit as much a part of nineteenth century French culture as the language of French itself—prompting all but seven of his eighty students to withdraw from the school.

But he was tolerated. Part and parcel with his maddening quirks was his passion for discovery, which in time turned Pasteur into France's

---

[2] I identify with Pasteur's academic struggles. I had a disappointing 2.2 high school GPA, barely got into a state university, and then struggled to a 1.9 first semester GPA. This performance earned a formal letter from the dean, who allowed only one more semester of that nonsense before it'd be suggested that I go work outdoors for a living. I kept working at it, and I eventually earned my B.A., M.A., and a teaching position. And now look at me—at only 38, I'm writing a book that might be read by nearly one-third of my family! I'm basically Pasteur.

[3] I really wanted to include a date, like "the Great Bean Revolt of 1865," but I couldn't find one. Every great revolt needs a year attached to it, don't you think?

foremost scientist. He became the leading Western mind in biology, physiology, chemistry, and medicine. The world-renowned Sorbonne even offered him the chair of the organic chemistry department, which he declined. Instead, he founded a laboratory at ENS and directed it for 20 years.

I've gone too long without talking about what he actually did that lengthened our lives. Let's first consider the world of medicine before Pasteur.

It wasn't pretty. The miasma theory—which held that disease came from bad air—was still largely accepted. So was the spontaneous generation of germs, a theory that refers not just to bacteria, but to any type of disease-causing microorganism such as viruses, fungi, protists, and prions. If someone got sick or infected, it was often seen as chance or divine interference, as if the germs randomly appeared in people's bodies or the food and drink they consumed.

In other words, the most important piece of knowledge in the field of medicine—how the microscopic stuff that hurts us spreads—was stuck in the Middle Ages. Overall, we knew preciously little about the source and transmission of germs.

Pasteur's work, as well as later contributions from Robert Koch, replaced the prevailing miasma and spontaneous generation theories with the currently accepted theory of disease: germ theory. It's not that Pasteur was the first to propose the concept of germs, but he did show that they weren't a result of foul air or chance.[4] Through the use of a microscope and his trademark experimentation and careful data collection, he proved that covered and sterilized containers did not lead to festering bacterial growth, whereas open containers of the same material did.

This discovery was paradigm-shifting. All that was left to do was prevent bacteria from spreading. That's not an easy task, but at least it was a task—a clear objective on the way to avoiding disease. It certainly beat merely hoping for the best.

Pasteur's realization encouraged many new practices that worked to control the spread of bacteria. Wash your hands before eating. Cover your mouth when you cough. Bathe regularly. Disinfect surfaces.[5] These are post-Pasteur trends. So, too, are sterilization techniques for surgeries. As a result of Pasteur's discovery, Joseph Lister revolutionized surgery by using antisepsis to reduce the likelihood of infection. Whereas people were once just as likely to die from infection after surgery as they were from whatever the surgery was trying to prevent, surgeries became safe procedures used successfully by millions.

As part of his studies, in the 1860s Pasteur identified the most common way germs such as bacteria entered the body: ingestion. He

---

[4] That honor went to Girolamo Fracastoro three centuries earlier. Fracastoro was the first to propose that infections can spread through passing on certain infected items, like clothes, linen, or cups. He called infected items *"fomes,"* the Latin for tinder. Coincidentally, today's Tinder also passes on infections.

[5] And socially distance during pandemics! That was not a part of the initial entry online, but now I'm editing during COVID-19. I've left social distancing out of the main body for posterity. I'm thinking those other hygienic recommendations will still exist decades from now, but socially distancing will be as weird to people in the future as it was to us before 2020. (I hope the same will be said about toilet paper shortages.)

therefore determined that it'd be best if we made our best effort to kill germs in liquids and food before we consume them. From that idea we get his most famous contribution to medicine, a process that nearly every milk carton now assures us has cleansed the milk inside of it. The process bears his name: pasteurization.

Pasteurization is usually the process of heating liquid—though it can also be food—to the point where almost all pathogenic microbes inside are killed. It almost totally eliminates the possibility of passing on disease, and it also aids food preservation.[6] Before pasteurization, 25 percent of all food-borne illness was caused by cow milk, but these days that's exceedingly rare.

Pasteur's quest to prevent the spread of disease did not end with pasteurization. In the 1870s, he standardized the practice of vaccination. Edward Jenner (1749-1823) had invented the first vaccination by infecting patients with a mild strain of cowpox to create immunity against the more deadly smallpox.[7] Jenner's contribution, however important in eradicating a prominent killer, was limited to just the one disease. Pasteur extended Jenner's findings and applied it to much more, including chicken cholera, rabies, and anthrax, the last of which ravaged the cow population.

---

[6] We usually associate it with milk because it was a common carrier of dangerous, disease-carrying microbes. Milk poisoned and even killed thousands of people per year. To combat this threat, urban areas kept their own cows in order to shorten the time between the milking and the consuming. Pasteurization allowed cows to be isolated to rural areas. I love pasteurized milk as much as the next guy, but frankly it'd be a lot of fun if cows randomly strolled down Fifth Avenue and the Champs-Élysées. Thanks a lot, Pasteur.

[7] It's from the Latin for cow, *vacca*, that we get the word vaccination.

Louis Pasteur

Pasteur also trumped Jenner's vaccination and other age-old inoculations (a practice that had been around for centuries) by artificially weakening the injected strain. Traditional inoculation, including the smallpox vaccine, was usually the transference of some cells from a sick host to a healthy one in order to build up immunization. This strategy often led to unpredictable results, the scariest of which was activating the disease one had hoped to avoid.

Pasteur, through a variety of strategies like heating bacteria or combining it with certain chemicals (such as potassium dichromate), made sure the strain was sufficiently weakened first. The modern widespread and successful use of vaccinations, which have saved countless lives and improved quality of life, has him to thank. The World Health Organization estimates that two to three million lives are saved annually from vaccination.[8] Ultimately, not only did Pasteur's rabies and anthrax vaccines directly prevent disease, but he also made possible the later eradication of polio, typhoid, and many other devastating diseases.[9]

He spent his final years securing a legacy. In 1887, he established and began directing the Pasteur Institute. Pasteur was active there until nearly the end of his life. Much earlier (in 1868, when he was 46), a stroke paralyzed the left part of his body. In typical Pasteur form, he worked toward recovery until he had his full faculties again. In 1894, however, he had another stroke, and he died the following year. France

---

[8] Sadly, according to the WHO, 1.5 million unvaccinated children die from preventable diseases. Again, that's 1.5 million children. Nearly 30 percent of children worldwide who die between one month and five years old could have been saved with vaccination. I'd rather not weigh in on the vax vs. anti-vax debate, so I'll let these statistics speak for themselves.

[9] He also furthered research on mirror-image isomers of tartaric acid, which, of course, needs no explanation.

honored him with a state funeral at Notre-Dame cathedral. His body was then interred underneath the world-renowned laboratory that still bears his name.

Quite deservedly, Louis Pasteur is generally considered the most important person in the history of medicine. He truly transformed the field.

This success was not without its controversy, however. He rarely gave credit to scientists that had laid the groundwork for his breakthroughs. It was also later discovered that he sometimes faked results or experiments in order to secure further support for his work.

His personality also left a lot to be desired. Just as his body of scientific achievement was without rival, so was his arrogance and inflexibility. His obsession with science detracted from myriad other areas of his life. He was cantankerous toward his contemporaries. His obsessive-compulsive tendencies and experience studying germ prevention infected his life. He avoided shaking hands, wiped down all his silverware before using it, and was frequently observed taking apart his food in a preemptive search and destroy mission against potential contaminants. In other words, he was annoying.

Nonetheless, tolerating such a man was a small price to pay for his gifts to humanity. Though his breakthroughs came at a time when the Industrial Revolution propelled many discoveries across diverse fields, including ones that made us healthier and live longer, no one matches the sum of his contributions to medicine.[10]

---

[10] Apologies to Alexander Fleming, who was part of this ranking's "Next 10."

Louis Pasteur

The Pasteur Institute survives to this day as one of the most important medical research institutions in the world. Its breakthroughs have helped humanity's struggle against malaria, diphtheria, tetanus, tuberculosis, the flu, yellow fever, and plague. In 1983, the Pasteur Institute became the first to discover HIV. More than a century after its namesake's death, the Pasteur Institute continues one of the greatest scientific careers in history.

Thanks to Pasteur more than anyone else, our life expectancy has more than doubled since he first gazed into a microscope. That's twice as long to do everything—to learn, to love, to experience, and to create. It's more time to enjoy our lives, our children's lives, and our grandchildren's lives. He made it common for grandparents to even meet their grandchildren, and for the grandchildren to know, appreciate, and learn from their grandparents.

The effects of this longer lifespan helped enable the wondrous advancements of the last century. Modern innovators and scientists have had that much more time to work, gain experience, collaborate, and achieve all the marvelous scientific and technological accomplishments we've enjoyed over the last hundred years.

Thanks to these literally life-changing contributions from Louis Pasteur, he is the eighth most influential figure in Western history.

#7: Jesus

"Go and make disciples of all nations, baptizing them in the name of the Father and of the Son and of the Holy Spirit, and teaching them to obey everything I have commanded you. And surely I am with you always, to the very end of the age."

—Matthew 28: 19-20

That's right, I said it. He—He!—is only number 7.

Of all the entries on this list, I dreaded this one the most. This fear was not caused by the divisiveness surrounding the topic of organized religion. Instead, my dread resulted from the fact that although the adherents of the world's largest religion are fairly quantifiable, the influence of Christianity on its adherents is not. Considering Jesus's teachings comprise half the world's most ubiquitous moral text, he is surely a top-tier historical figure. At the same time, however, the religion has been used as a justification for actions across the moral spectrum, an ethical flexibility that demands scrutiny. Has Jesus had as much impact as one might assume?

Jesus

After reflecting on this question, I now propose that Jesus of Nazareth, the inspiration for the planet's most widespread faith, is only the seventh most influential figure in Western history.

Before starting his biography, let's get one thing out of the way: his last name was not Christ. Christ is more of a label, a posthumously-awarded title given to him by the Christians he inspired to start a new religion. It came from the Greek *christós*, meaning "anointed one" or "messiah," a figure that Judaism had prophesied as the savior of Israel. The Jews who believed he fulfilled the prophecy became the first Christians, or followers of the Christ, while those who did not see him as the fulfillment of their messiah remained Jewish and continued to wait.

Speaking of the Jews, Jesus was one of them. He was born Jewish (perhaps in Bethlehem), lived Jewish (likely in Nazareth), and died Jewish (certainly in Jerusalem). While his interpretation drifted from that of contemporary Jewish leadership, his theology, he argued, more clarified Judaism than rebelled against it. Remaining misconceptions include his birthday (probably not in December), birth year (embarrassingly a few years "Before Christ"), and his actual first name (Yeshua).

Though there is little doubt of his "historicity," or existence, the difficult task of knowing much more than those facts results from his status as a common carpenter of the first century who left no writing behind, nor did his generally illiterate following. Moreover, the chief sources on his life, the Gospels, were written well after Jesus died, one factor among many that casts doubt on their historical reliability.[1] The only two things about the "historical Jesus" we seem to know with reasonable certainty are his baptism by John the Baptist and his crucifixion by the Roman state. The rest is varying degrees of reliable.

Nonetheless, even if history can't endorse the Biblical Jesus narrative, at least a paragraph should be spent summarizing it, as Jesus's importance is tied to billions of people across history believing it to be the truth.

In the year later called "AD 1" (though history now suggests 4 BCE), the Christian Jesus, thanks to the intervention of the Holy Spirit, was born of the virgin Mary in the little town of Bethlehem, part of the Roman Empire's Judea province. Raised by Mary and her betrothed, the carpenter Joseph, Jesus grew into his adopted father's occupation. As an adult, he performed a series of miracles, including healings. In the meantime, he taught a growing ministry about his version of Judaism, which most notably differed from mainstream interpretations by believing in a more loving, understanding, and welcoming God than the jealous, angry, and egomaniacal Creator of what would later be called the Old Testament. His God's more accepting nature aided in Jesus's popularity (and, later, Christianity's popularity as well). The charismatic Jesus saw his following grow, which worried a combination of Jewish leaders (who resented his indirect challenge to their leadership) and the Roman state

---

[1] Aside from their considerably posthumous nature, working against the Gospels' reliability are the tens of thousands of textual variants of the New Testament, the unknowable sources from which the Gospels worked, internal inconsistencies between the Gospels, external inconsistencies between the Gospels and what we know of history and geography, and finally their authorship, particularly the motivations of the authors themselves. (Hey, don't shoot the messenger. Jesus wouldn't want that.)

Jesus

(which worried about a potential insurrection). He was charged with blasphemy and treason, and he was punished by execution via crucifixion, a death that Christians believe atoned for humanity's sins. His body was then buried, but on the third day of his ostensible death he resurrected, made appearances for 40 days, and then ascended into heaven. The end.

But the end was only the beginning.

After Jesus's death, his disciples spread his Word throughout the region. Importantly, the contemporary most responsible for the proliferation of Christianity never met him at all—at least, not in the material sense. His name was Saul of Tarsus (c. 5 CE – c. 67 CE), better known as Saint Paul.

Paul barely missed my Top 30,[2] but he is nevertheless a critically important figure. No one else in the first couple centuries after Jesus is more responsible for Christianity's growth. According to Christian tradition, Saul, a Jew from the Roman city of Tarsus (in modern Turkey), was actually a persecutor of early Christian disciples. Sometime in the mid-30s, however, while on his way to Damascus to retrieve some followers of this runaway sect and return them to Jerusalem for trial, he was intercepted by Jesus's apparition. Saul claims this awe-inspiring moment struck him blind, but three days later he was healed by Christian disciple Ananias of Damascus. An overwhelmed Saul converted and was baptized with the name Paul. He spent the last three decades of his life traveling across the Mediterranean, spreading Jesus's Word and founding churches dedicated to him.

---

[2] He was "Next 10."

Paul also wrote letters to believers throughout the region, including to Romans, Corinthians, Galatians, Ephesians, Philippians, Colossians, and Thessalonians. These letters survived history and today make up much of the New Testament. In all, Paul authored as many as 14 of the 27 books of the New Testament—about half. Naturally, Paul injected much of his own ideology into these writings, giving us, for better or worse, what historians call a "Pauline" bent to much of Christian theology. Most notably, he asserted Jesus as the long-awaited Christ and the son of God, an idea that gradually caught on.

Eventually, biographers arrived in Judea to learn and write about Jesus's life. Of the many "gospels" to come from this process, four were eventually canonized into the Christian Church and added to the fledgling New Testament. Matthew, Mark, Luke, and John wrote these texts between 65 and 110 CE, or 35 to 80 years after Jesus's death. Their scriptures gradually came together as Christianity took shape in the second and third century, and Paul's letters were added to them. Most Christian interpreters of these texts eventually determined that Christ was of "dual nature"—that he was both man and God in one hypostatic union; God took human form to teach charity, modesty, and love, and Jesus's reported miracles evidenced His divinity.

While these beliefs were in their nascent stages, it wasn't a good time to be Christian. The Roman state, led by emperors who framed themselves as demigods, resisted this new monotheistic religion that refused to recognize the emperor's divinity. For the first couple centuries of their religion's existence, thousands of Christians were martyred by the Roman government. It was not until Emperor Constantine (#23) in 313 CE that Christianity became legal. Only then could Christians emerge, proselytize, and recruit. Constantine himself patronized the growing faith, and by the end of the fourth century Emperor Theodosius made it the empire's official religion. Christianity spread across the continent in time for Rome's fall in the late 400s, allowing the religion to saturate most of Europe before the Early Medieval period slowed travel and communication across western Europe.

In time, Christianity spread further, much in thanks to the work of political leaders. The religion's last vulnerable moment came in the early 700s, when expansionist Muslims stormed across the Iberian Peninsula and into southern France. This invasion threatened the Christian continent of Europe before a Germanic leader, Charles Martel (#13) of the Franks, saw to Europe's defense. Martel's grandson, Charlemagne (#21), spread Christianity, particularly his Roman Catholicism, across western Europe and even into northern European areas, like Germania, that ancient Rome had not conquered. He also started the *Reconquista* into Iberia, a process which lasted for the next seven centuries, culminating in a totally reclaimed Spain and Portugal for Catholicism. Spain and Portugal also inaugurated the Age of Exploration, ingraining their Catholicism into South and Central America. Soon after, Britain and France colonized North America, spreading Christianity some more. Britain then made its way to Australia and did it again. By the 1800s, as Europeans carved up Africa and made Asian inroads, Christianity was global.

Concurrent with its spread, Christianity's growth was aided by potent emotional motivators: fear and hope. From the medieval Catholic Church to the *conquistadors* in the Americas, forced conversion—and forced retention—was the norm. Wars were often religiously justified. Heretics faced exile, excommunication, and execution, punishments rarely preceded by what we now consider due process. Fear of coming out as anything other than Christian closeted any nonbelievers and perpetuated Christian domination of Western culture, society, and government.

Alongside that fear existed a genuine hope and universal acceptance to all that professed the faith. Christianity separated itself from most other religions by accepting everyone. There was no genetic requirement. There was no memorization of text. Indeed, there was no shibboleth whatsoever. All who sought salvation through Jesus were welcome. Those most desperate for salvation were the impoverished commoners of the Roman Empire, particularly when the empire faced the struggles of late antiquity.

Subsequently, during the so-called "Dark" Ages, the scared, destitute population turned to the hope of a perfect, eternal afterlife where they'd enjoy reunification with dead family and friends. Perhaps no greater motivator could exist. With Christian leadership enjoying the loyalty of the flock, even those more affluent and powerful during the period fell under the spell of a Catholic Church that could strip that affluence and power by turning the flock against them.[3]

The confluence of conquest, conversion, hope, and fear turned a persecuted religion into the world's largest. Most modern estimates of its population report that between 2.2 and 2.5 billion people—about a third of the planet—are Christian today.

Here is when we must ask the question: considering Christianity's billions of historical and current adherents claim Jesus as some combina-

---

[3] My chapter on Philip IV (#29) expands on this paragraph's ideas.

tion of their religious, spiritual, intellectual, or moral guide, shouldn't he be at the top of this list?

I think not. I settled Jesus at number seven for a few reasons.

First, the Paul factor. It sounds paradoxical, but Jesus Christ was not the founder of Christianity. Again: he was born, lived, and died Jewish. He also didn't write anything down to truly codify his theology. In both crucial steps—the founding and the codifying—Paul deserves more credit. It's his writings that make up the earliest parts of the New Testament. At the very least we can say Paul co-founded the religion.

Furthermore, we cannot overlook Paul's infiltrative impact on Christian theology, or the aforementioned "Pauline" effect. Much of Christianity is tied to Paul's interpretation, amplification, and expansion of Jesus's ideology. As the primary proselytizer of Christianity in its first century, Paul's own ideas very much shaped the religion, including its practices.[4] One way to summarize each man's contribution to the religion is that Jesus provided the spirituality and morality of Christianity, while Paul was responsible for the rigidity and dogma.[5]

All that said, before you get the impression that Paul is the more influential of the two, I believe Jesus is the dominant partner. Jesus's personality and purported healings had already started the spread of his worldview before Paul traveled the road to Damascus. The subsequent centuries leading to Constantine's decriminalization of the religion support the idea of an almost unstoppable ideology spreading across the

---

[4] As one would expect, there have been criticisms of Paul's potential corruption of Jesus's vision.

[5] In other words, I'd argue that Jesus represents what's good about religion, while Paul represents what's annoying about it.

Mediterranean world. Did Paul help? Absolutely. But he may have merely sped up an inevitable process.

It's also worth noting the perhaps overrated condemnations of Pauline critics. In the most critical stages of Christianity's congealment—the Christological and Trinitarian debates of the third and fourth centuries that tried to determine the nature of Jesus[6]—Paul's writings played almost no role. Meanwhile and later, the many sects of Christianity, most notably after the Protestant Reformation, took it upon themselves to use as much or as little Pauline theology as they wished. While the Gospels have always been taken as gospel, the role of Paul has been comparatively less critical to Christianity.

A related argument works against Paul's placement in the top 30 and Jesus's placement any higher than number seven. Christianity and the man upon whom it is based are malleable subjects. How one interprets Christianity is deeply affected by the cultural, social, and political lens through which it is viewed. The religion has been used as a motivation for innumerable acts of generosity and love across history—charity, hospitals, orphanages, food, shelter, and so much more. Yet, it has also been used as a justification for atrocities—the Crusades, massacres of Jews and Muslims, executions of heretics, the bloody conquest of the Americas, and the Inquisition, among other examples. Christians have even turned their weapons on each other to defend or propagate their superior interpretation of Christ's Word. Sectarian conflict tore apart Europe in the century after the Protestant Reformation, and we've even seen such examples in more modern history.

---

[6] Elaborated in my Constantine (#23) chapter.

Billions of people have seen him in thousands of ways. He's been alternatively seen as a messiah, just a man, a war god, a pacifist, a knight, a king, a hippie, a conservative, a liberal, a socialist, a libertarian, a lord, and a savior. Even Islam, decidedly non-Christian, sees him as a prophet. In his name, people donate to charity and help the homeless. In his name, people bomb abortion clinics and condemn homosexuality. American Republicans, who advocate for social values and against government overreach, think he would be one of them. Yet, so do American Democrats, who push for expanding the social safety net and government-funded healthcare for the sick and poor.[7]

With this wide range of interpretations of what Jesus would want, it seems to me that people's morality, politics, and actions are frequently determined *personally*, not religiously, and the interpretation is then tailored to justify those actions. And if that's the case, the impact of Jesus, even as the inspiration for the world's largest religion, is not as paramount as we thought. People might be doing exactly what they would have done otherwise, which could mostly neutralize Jesus's influence.

Even his "Golden Rule"—Matthew 7:12's "all things whatsoever ye would that men should do to you: do ye even so to them"—is not as consequential as one might think. Leaving aside the countless Christians who have not followed that rule, it's actually one of the more ubiquitous moral underpinnings of world religions. It existed before Jesus in ancient Egypt, Greece, Persia, and Rome. It existed in Judaism, which in fact informed Jesus's ideology in the first place. Islam embraces the

---

[7] I propose that he would be neither. If you agree, consider that next time you ask "What Jesus would do?"

Golden Rule. So do Hinduism and Buddhism, Confucianism and Taoism. It's not a uniquely Christian value. It's a universal one. Of course, just like in Christianity, these religions' adherents often fail at practicing the Golden Rule, but that further speaks to the issue of personal choice over religious influence.

Though the Golden Rule's ubiquity is a mark against the influence of Jesus, he did have a more unique message regarding self-defense. A pacifist, Jesus rejected an "eye for an eye" punishment, instead advising, through Matthew 5:38-9, "if anyone slaps you on the right cheek, turn to him the other also." This "turn the other cheek" message is reinforced by Luke 6:27-8, which asks for us to "Love your enemies, do good to those who hate you, bless those who curse you," and "pray for those who abuse you." Quite unlike the Golden Rule, this peace-at-all-costs philosophy is actually not that common among other belief systems.

And yet, this unique worldview is also counteracted by the many Christians who have ignored it in the name of the day's cause. Though many early Christians followed the peaceful principle to their martyrdom, no powerful Christians since then—particularly heads of state—have matched that pacifistic extremism. Modern Western society accepts and sometimes encourages justified wars, violent self-defense, or capital punishment. Those actions might be advisable—and even congruent with the Old Testament—but Christian they are not. I again must conclude that being "Christian" carries less influence than one might think.

Finally and most importantly, though Judeo-Christianity has played a substantial role in the development of Western culture, it did not do so peerlessly. The start of Western culture predates Jesus. Its traditional starting point is with the Greeks: Pericles, Hippocrates, Socrates, Aristotle (#30), Euclid, Archimedes, and so many others. Western liberalism's seeds were planted in the Athenian democracy and Roman republic. Each began five centuries before Jesus. After Rome's fall almost eradicated these principles, Christianity's greatest dominance over Western thought experienced its zenith in the Middle Ages, a period that for the most part is antithetical to modern Western values like democracy, due process, the rule of law, the promotion of science and education, and the freedoms of speech and worship.[8]

What truly helped the West turn the corner were the Renaissance, a movement more informed by those ancient Greeks and Romans than the Old and New Testaments; the Scientific Revolution, which relied on a scientific method that cast aside the mysticism and Biblical reliance of the previous age; the Enlightenment, including its deist leaders who proudly broke from organized religion; and the Industrial Revolution, which was motivated by profit more than prayer, genius more than genuflection. These movements, not the rise of Judeo-Christianity, helped dig the West out of its doldrums and gave us, for better or worse, the modern world in which we now live. For that reason, key players in those movements will make up nearly all of my top six.

I acknowledge that for the first and only time on this list, I've made a case against a historical figure's influence more than for it. In conversations

---

[8] I'm not saying Christianity was the cause of darkness. We can more attribute that to the larger, inescapable effects of ineffective governments and extended climactic problems. Most members of the Christian clergy were uncorrupted and played a selfless role in maintaining some semblance of civilization in the absence of stable government. Many of them also preserved copies of ancient texts, and some monks wrote in earnest to create new copies. Yet, despite the ubiquitous faith of the period, progress was slowed and even reversed.

about this ranking, Jesus was the person about whom I'm most asked. No other figure comes close. Nearly every person with whom I've engaged on the topic has either assumed Jesus is number one or at least "in the top three." I felt it important, therefore, to downplay that preconceived significance.

Nevertheless, my counterarguments should not totally detract from Jesus's importance. There is something undeniably relevant about a third of the world and most of the West calling itself "Christian." Many of those Christians now and across history went to a church every Sunday, some more frequently, to worship him and learn what He wanted of them. No book has been more read or referenced by humanity than the Bible. In times of joy, sadness, desire, curiosity, and terror, more people have looked to that book than any other work in human history. More than any single person in that book, it's to Jesus that Christians look for guidance, morality, and salvation. They might not always agree about what Jesus would do, but they do ask the question.

For all of the above reasons, I slot Jesus of Nazareth as the seventh most influential figure in Western history.

#6: Martin Luther

"The true Gospel has it that we are justified by faith alone."
–Martin Luther, 1535

I know what you're thinking. You're thinking: "Luther ranked higher than Jesus? You're crazy." Maybe I am, dear reader. Maybe I am.

Martin Luther, after all, began the Protestant Reformation, a movement that aimed to purify western Europe's Christianity, a religion predicated on the teachings of Jesus of Nazareth (#7). Since Luther's religion is based on Jesus, logic presumably dictates that any subsequent clarification(s) of it, like the ones offered by Luther, are less important than the religion itself, especially if most adherents of the religion did not go along with these new refinements.

When put that way, it does sound crazy. I hope to prove, however, that Luther's actions were far more consequential than merely reforming the West's main religion for a minority of its adherents. More so than even his Lord and Savior, Luther made possible our modern world. For that reason, Martin Luther is the West's sixth most influential figure in history.

Martin Luther was born in 1483 to his parents Hans and Margarethe. His family lived in Eisleben, Saxony, part of the Holy Roman Empire in modern Germany.

Significant to our story is a joke among historians since Voltaire (#22) first uttered it: the Holy Roman Empire was neither Holy, nor Roman, nor an Empire. Though seen as an arm of the Roman Catholic Church, the empire did not behave in a particularly Christian manner. It also rarely counted Rome as part of its empire; it only briefly held the city early in its long history, which dates from before the turn of the millennium until Napoleon (#16) dissolved it in 1806.

Most importantly for Luther's rise to prominence, it was not a cohesive empire. Unlike other western European kingdoms of the period, the Holy Roman Empire resisted the forces of centralization. The result was a rather disheveled heart of Europe. The prince of Luther's Saxony, in the far north, retained considerable sovereignty.

Luther's father, a disciplinarian who wanted his son to become a lawyer, pushed him into academics. The young Luther learned Latin and the trivium: grammar, rhetoric, and logic. At 17 he began attending the University of Erfurt, which mandated a 4:00 a.m. wake-up for a day of rote learning. He earned a Master's degree at 22, but compared his educational process to hell.[1] He attempted law school but felt uncomfortable with the ambiguity and constant evolution of law and government. Seeking certitude, he turned, much to the chagrin of his father, to theology.

It was right around that time that he was hit by an epiphany—and perhaps by God Himself. Luther claims that while riding his horse home

---

[1] These frustrations with the intense German education system would later also frustrate Albert Einstein (#11).

from university during a raging storm, a lightning bolt struck next to him. Galloping the rest of the way, he begged the heavens for mercy and promised to become a monk if he survived, which he gratefully did. In his mid-20s, he became ordained, earned a degree in Biblical studies, and was hired by the University of Wittenberg (now named after him) to teach theology, a field where he earned his doctorate in 1512, aged just 29. He chaired the department for the rest of his life.

Toward the latter part of these formative years, Luther began to form an ideology that ultimately put him at odds with Europe's most powerful organization—an organization to which he belonged: the Roman Catholic Church.[2] In 1510, he had been excited to make a pilgrimage to Rome. It was the city where the Pope lived, where St. Peter and other early Christians had been martyred, and it housed innumerable relics of ancient Christian history. What the young monk found, however, deeply disturbed him: Rome was a hotbed of corruption, greed, and other worldly desires. Worse, not only did the Catholic Church not stop such sinfulness, it was a key player in it. Around him, ignorant Catholics prayed to the supposed bones of martyrs, usually paying the Church for the privilege.

During this period, the single practice that most bothered Luther gained popularity: the selling of indulgences. Indulgences were (and

---

[2] Have you noticed how there are fewer explanatory footnotes in these pieces the further along we go in the ranking? Here is a good example of why: In the earlier days of this list, this is about where I'd get into how the Church got and remained so powerful. But if you've been paying attention, you don't need to be told again. It came up in the #30, #29, #28, #23, #22, and #21, with the amount of context tapering until it's now unnecessary. I hope.

sometimes still are) a way for Catholics to reduce sinning's impact on their chances at salvation. The Church awards indulgences when Catholics earn them through certain actions, whether pilgrimages, specific prayers, or any number of "good works." Most controversially, particularly in Luther's time, one could donate money to the Church and receive an indulgence.

On the face of it, this practice sounded reasonable. We think it's nice, after all, to donate to one's church. However, in the Late Middle Ages and early Renaissance period, indulgences were abused by the Church in order to maximize revenue. They soon became commercialized. Skilled salesmen—most infamously Johann Tetzel—scared poor Christians into emptying their pockets for fear of eternal damnation. The public perception was that the Church was raising money for the construction of the magnificent St. Peter's Basilica, but in truth much of it was diverted directly to the private coffers of corrupt clergy.

Even if these indulgences truly were solely used for the Basilica, critics raised questions. Could giving money as a form of good works replace actually performing good works? Would Jesus have wanted money siphoned from poorer Europeans and redirected toward the wealthiest organization in Europe? Would He not instead have wanted the poor to keep their money and the wealthy class to redirect its money toward the impoverished? And does the Church even have the ability to remit sins in the first place?

After his Roman pilgrimage, Martin Luther began asking these questions and more. In the years that followed, a horrified Luther heard from Christians who felt they no longer needed to repent for their sins since they bought indulgences. Luther steadily realized this expensive practice actually cheapened true grace. Someone had broken his Catholic Church.

So, with the mind of a lawyer, the faith of a monk, and the knowledge of a theologian, Martin Luther set out to fix it. In 1517, knowing his Bible cover to cover and verse for verse, he organized a list of propositions and complaints about contemporary Catholic practices, including how they contradicted the Bible. Themes include an attack on indulgences and clarifying the true way to earn salvation. His stance was that no priest, not even the pope, had true control over anyone's soul or prospects for getting into heaven. Instead, one's salvation depended on true repentance and, above all, faith in Christ. These propositions, which coupled Biblical support with logic, numbered 95. The result was the Christendom-shattering *Ninety-Five Theses*.

Luther sent a copy to his local high cleric, the Archbishop of Mainz, and legend says he also nailed a copy into the Wittenberg church's door.[3] Traditionally, if not officially, this moment marks the beginning of the Protestant Reformation, which forever altered the Christian Church.

Luther didn't just mail his *Theses* to a high-ranking Catholic. He began preaching his ideas and used the recently invented printing press to better spread them. This invention—first modernized by fellow German Johannes Gutenberg about a generation before Luther was born—gave Luther an ability that earlier potential reformers did not possess: mass production of written ideas.

---

[3] In truth, he probably just posted his ideas on the equivalent of the church's bulletin board and other locations in the area. The legend, however, makes for the much better story, which partly explains its longevity. Luther literally nailing into a church a list of problems with *the* Church makes for powerful symbolism.

It's worth noting here that Luther was not the first Christian to be critical of Church practices. Notably, another dissident of the Holy Roman Empire, the Czech Jan Hus, condemned the clergy's corruption and immorality a full century before Luther, even going so far as singling out the papacy itself. He was branded a heretic and burned at the stake, his Hussite movement thereafter contained. A bit earlier, Oxford professor John Wycliffe had also pleaded for reforming the corrupt institution. Though tolerable in England, the few writings that escaped the island were destroyed in the mainland. Indeed, the pattern for a millennium was that if the Church disagreed with a person's book or pamphlet, the Church or its surrogates burned the work (like Wycliffe's). If one kept pressing the issue, they burned the person (like Hus). Though the laws of England protected Wycliffe's life, his ideas were mostly confined by fourteenth-century constraints.

In the sixteenth century, however, Luther's access to the printing press accomplished what Wycliffe and Hus could not. As he built a following in northern Germany, those followers turned to the press to spread his teachings. In the subsequent months and years, with popularity serving as a tailwind, his teachings evolved and grew even more pointed. He rejected some of the Church's sacraments, the clergy meddling in the affairs of the state, the idea of purgatory, and mandatory celibacy for men of the cloth.

Most notable was his clarification of how one earned salvation, which was the primary motivation of most Christians—and perhaps most mortals—across history. He argued that all one needed to earn God's grace was faith, a requirement he called *sola fide*, or "faith alone." This stance contradicted a key tenet of the Catholic Church: that faith needed to be combined with "good works" to earn salvation. It was upon this plank of the Church's platform that the sale of indulgences stood. It was a "good work" to donate to the Church.

Importantly, Luther's *sola fide* doctrine removed the Church as a middleman between man and God. God's grace was completely free and available in abundance and perpetuity to everyone who had faith. *Sola fide* proposes that no member of the clergy could affect another's chances of getting into heaven. Essentially, Luther called into question the most basic role of the Church. That included the relevance of the pope himself, purportedly the Vicar of Christ, mediator between Christ and man.

Needless to say, the monk's teachings caught the papacy's omniscient eye. Summoned on several occasions, Luther met with higher ranking clerics that hoped to rein him in. He seemed willing to change his mind if anyone could point out his error in reasoning or Biblical interpretation, but no one succeeded. For too long, simply being an authority figure invested that figure with the ability to say what was right and wrong. Luther disagreed.

His stubbornness placed him on a track toward Jan Hus's fate. Even fellow critic Desiderius Erasmus, for whom Luther had the utmost admiration, warned Luther against pressing the issue. Erasmus ultimately broke with Luther as the former veered toward safety while the latter careened toward his assured demise.

By 1520, that demise seemed imminent. Shortly after Luther controversially declared that popes were fallible, Pope Leo X issued a papal bull ordering Luther to recant his teachings or face excommunication, an expulsion from the Church that included the loss of access to sacraments and likely secured an eventual spot in hell. Excommunication had been the most aggressive weapon of the papacy for centuries; its threat had on countless occasions intimidated more powerful opponents into submission. Luther not only ignored this threat, he publicly burned a copy of the papal command. In that moment, it seemed certain Luther would share its fate.[4]

With Luther's continued audacity, the Pope instructed the Holy Roman Emperor, Charles V, to take care of the annoying monk from Wittenberg. The Emperor called for a hearing at the German city of Worms during an imperial diet.

Luther's trial at 1521's Diet of Worms was expected to be his undoing.[5] As the trial unfolded, Luther was faced with a final opportunity to recant or he would be branded a heretic and lose all rights and protections in the empire. Looming over such a punishment was a near certainty that he would be killed, either by the state or a random, vengeful Catholic who would face no repercussions.

At this moment, when he was given a last chance to withdraw his position and save his own life, one could imagine everyone in Europe holding their breath to hear Luther's response. In just a few years, his revolutionary ideas had made him the first common celebrity in modern history. He had quickly grown popular in the northern reaches of Europe. After all, his ideas on salvation democratized the path toward heaven. No longer did the wealthy have the advantage because they could more easily fill Church coffers than could the peasantry. If all one needed was faith,

---

[4] Almost every step of the way, Leo badly misread Luther. The Pope relied upon the premise that the papacy had the ability to deny one's place in the Catholic Church (while alive) and affect one's soul in the afterlife (when dead). Once Luther rejected the pope's authority to do these things, the threat of withholding sacraments or heaven was rendered toothless.

[5] As you can imagine, I've rarely been able to get through mentioning the "Diet of Worms" in my classroom without a student saying, "Eww."

then everyone became equally eligible for God's grace. Luther's answer at his trial could potentially turn his back on this fledgling movement and reassert the status quo, including the Church's grip over the whole of Christendom. One could argue that this was not just the "trial of the century," but the trial of the millennium.

Thus, when Luther was asked whether he would recant, it was as if the whole continent leaned in during his pregnant pause, wondering if the feisty monk from Saxony would continue to defy the undefiable.

He defied it all right. Luther responded that only "Scripture or clear reason" could force him to recant his words. Tradition, perhaps legend, holds that he finished his reply with the ultimate defense of one's own conscience: "Here I stand. I can do no other."

After his refusal, he was found guilty of heresy, and the Emperor issued the equivalent of a death sentence.[6] Luther, who had been guaranteed safe passage to and from the trial, quickly boarded a carriage back to Wittenberg. Fearing for Luther, his allies staged a fake kidnapping on his trip home, leaving many to believe a group of angry Catholics had ended his life. However, he instead went into hiding in Wartburg Castle for a year.[7]

---

[6] *"For this reason we forbid anyone from this time forward to dare, either by words or by deeds, to receive, defend, sustain, or favor the said Martin Luther. On the contrary, we want him to be apprehended and punished as a notorious heretic, as he deserves, to be brought personally before us, or to be securely guarded until those who have captured him inform us, whereupon we will order the appropriate manner of proceeding against the said Luther. Those who will help in his capture will be rewarded generously for their good work."*

[7] *Is this real life or a movie script?!*

While safely tucked out of sight, he translated the Bible into German. Soon, common Germans would be able understand the Good Book for themselves instead of relying on a clergyman to interpret it for them. Of note, most Germans, despite their many dialects, wanted to understand Luther's Saxon tongue in order to read his Bible and many other works. As a result, Luther's Saxon German, complete with his personal prose, gradually became the standardized version of the German language.[8]

Word soon got out that Luther had survived. Still, once he resurfaced, he had become so popular in northern Europe that he was fairly untouchable and avoided punishment.[9] Since local princes had local authority in the decentralized empire, Luther only needed their support for his survival. These princes, particularly Frederick the Wise of Saxony, mostly embraced Luther, either to ride his popularity, stick it to the emperor, or both.

---

[8] A century later, the writings of William Shakespeare (#10) had a similar impact on English.

[9] It helped that a distracted Emperor Charles V had a full plate. He had inherited a bunch of disparate crowns, and his discombobulated empire had diverse demands for his attention. For examples, Muslims encroached into southeast Europe, and as Holy Roman Emperor it was his duty to defend Christendom. Charles was also King of Spain, which meant he was also emperor of the Americas. These pressing duties only scratch the surface of his many responsibilities. Between these concerns and Luther's budding Reformation, Charles was both one of the most powerful people in European history and one of the most shackled by his circumstances. He ultimately abdicated both crowns and divided them between his brother, Ferdinand, and his son, Philip II (husband of the English Queen Mary and therefore brother-in-law to the 19th most influential figure in Western history, Queen Elizabeth), so neither would be saddled with such burdens. Charles himself retreated to a monastery to live out his days as a monk. Life can be hard sometimes.

Martin Luther

In the subsequent years, Luther kept busy. He churned out thousands of pages of pamphlets and sermons clarifying and promoting his interpretation of Christianity. This interpretation started the Lutheran Church. A music enthusiast, he wrote dozens of hymns, believing they could help develop and confirm one's faith. Many of these hymns have since been sung in churches. He also married a nun, Katherine von Bora, and they had six children.

By the time he died from illness in 1546, the 62-year-old Luther had lived a surprisingly full life, one that deeply affected Western civilization.

Luther's impact on Western society is colossal. As discussed last chapter, Jesus's teachings were profound and inspired billions of Christians since his death, but the extent to which those teachings tangibly affected Westerners is difficult to gauge. Acts on nearly the entire moral spectrum have been justified, correctly or not, in His name. With Luther, however, not only do we see clearer effects, but we also see his impact spread beyond religion and morality.

Let us nevertheless start with the theological effects. Luther would have loved if all Christians saw the light and joined his Lutheran movement, but that was not the case. Most Christians, particularly in southern Europe, remained Catholic. Others partly agreed with Luther, but not on every last word of his theology. Therefore, though they, too, split from Catholicism, they did not become Lutheran. They became something else.[10] There are countless "something elses" that have sprung up since

---

[10] Most famous here are John Calvin's Calvinists, who propagated many modern offshoots in the form of Reformed churches, and Henry VIII's Anglicans, last discussed in my chapter on Queen Elizabeth [#19].

this movement. Nonetheless, since they agree with Luther's protest against the Catholic Church, they are all called "Protestants."

These Protestants subdivided into their more specific sects, or denominations, like Lutherans, Baptists, Anglicans, Presbyterians, Methodists, and many, many more. All are Christian, but each has at least once disagreement important enough to separate them.[11] Some studies estimate tens of thousands of these Christian sects. Nonetheless, the billion or so Protestants today trace their branch of Christianity, if not their specific denomination, back to Martin Luther. Were it not a part of Christianity, Protestantism alone would be the world's fourth largest religion.[12] Protestants also make up one half of the modern U.S. and can claim all but two of its presidents.[13]

Though no two sects are identical, there are broad patterns in Protestantism, and many of those patterns were started by Luther. Protestants reject papal authority and most Catholic sacraments. They deny ordained priests have exclusive powers to administer baptism or the Lord's Supper. They do not believe communion's bread and wine are literally the body and blood of Christ. They look only to the Bible, not clerics or Church traditions, as the source of Christian authority. They emphasize the importance of faith for salvation as opposed to faith and

---

[11] This ambiguity in Christianity can be seen as an added mark against the influence of Jesus himself. It's yet another case of people drawing considerably different conclusions about Christianity, conclusions determined more by the interpreter than the original source.

[12] It would rank after Islam's 1.8 billion, Christianity-minus-Protestantism's 1.3 billion, and Hinduism's 1.1 billion. It would double fifth place Buddhism's 500 million.

[13] In the initial publication of this entry online, I noted the one exception: JFK, a Catholic. A second exception, Joe Biden, has since been sworn in.

good works. They do not pray to saints and angels. Protestants, like Luther, sing hymns in their Congregations. Protestants, priests, like Luther, can marry. In sum, Luther is huge in Protestantism, even with non-Lutherans.

His theological effects, however, are not limited to Protestantism. The Catholic Church, which had for so long ignored criticisms, experienced throngs of Christians fleeing its towering cathedrals for Protestantism's humble churches. Once considered too big to fail, the Church realized it must reform or risk descending from omnipotence to endangered minority in a matter of decades.

Thus, in reaction to the Protestant Reformation, the Church conducted its own Catholic, or Counter, Reformation. The Catholic Reformation began the long process of curbing abuses and reprioritizing spirituality in the Church. Without Luther, there's no telling how much longer the Church would have continued its medieval, indulgent ways. This internal reformation successfully wrapped a tourniquet around Catholicism's hemorrhaging numbers.

The evolution of Christianity was not without strife. In the 150 years following Luther's initial protest, a series of wars between Catholics and Protestants tried to settle the matter, making the fourth-century doctrinal struggles that Constantine (#23) tried to solve look mild by comparison. The estimated death toll from these conflicts is as high as seventeen million, mostly from the Thirty Years' War (1618-1648). Such chaos should come as no surprise. For over a millennium, the Church brought order and some semblance of unity to the continent. Once Luther fractured that unity, Christendom didn't know what to do with itself.

At the same time, Luther's displacement of the Church as the central authority in Europe allowed a political, economic, and intellectual evolution in the West. The Reformation, for example, hastened the rise of nationalism. Many western Europeans had felt stronger loyalty to the Roman Catholic Church, which they believed controlled the fate of their souls, than they did to their kings and princes, whose reach was only temporary. However, after Luther, the papacy—wounded, if not mortally so—was much weaker by comparison, allowing state leaders to earn more loyalty from their citizens.

Meanwhile, Luther's *sola fide* doctrine returned agency to Westerners. Salvation's democratization—that is, leveling the playing field by denying the power of indulgences and clerics—empowered Christians with individualism. We can each be our own priest, and our local community can be its own church. We can make our own Biblical interpretation. Since it's demonstrably difficult to agree on Biblical interpretations, that reinforces the will of the individual. Luther replaced papal authority with the Bible's, but soon the Bible's authority was replaced with that of our own conscience.

What followed was the liberalization of Western thought. Western culture now cherishes individuality, free thinking, and the equality of humankind. When the Church controlled Western thought and labeled dissenters as heretics, such circumstances discouraged debate, speculation, and innovation, whether philosophical or otherwise. However, once independent and competing faiths emerged, so, too, did independent, competing ideas of all kinds. It is no coincidence that following the Reformation was the Scientific Revolution, which set the foundation for modern science. Then arrived the Enlightenment, which envisioned modern liberalism and republicanism, and the breakthrough of capitalism, which guides the modern economy. Each gained traction after the Reformation helped loosen medievalism, and their ideals now dominate

Western civilization. It is too easy to imagine a world where the Church retained its omnipotence, stifled individualism, and denied modernity. Although it's worth considering if, on balance, trading in a unifying Church and agrarian economy for competitive states and industrial capitalism has yielded a more positive modern world, the influence of those developments is undeniable.

At this point, Luther may sound like quite the hero of Western history. With considerable courage, he stood up to Europe's most powerful organization, one that had swiftly punished dissenters, and defended his convictions. He started a movement that changed the composition of the world's largest religion, forced the Catholic Church itself to reform, and helped the West turn the corner toward the modern world.

But it's never that simple. First, he was no role model. Most disappointingly, he was an outspoken anti-Semite, and his many anti-Semitic writings contributed to German hatred toward Jews, allowing the likes of Adolf Hitler (#17) to convert that underlying animosity into the Holocaust. Luther had an ironic intolerance of dissenters. He stood up to the Church not because people should stand up to authority, but because he was right and it was wrong. Since he was right, he was hoping everyone would realize his righteousness and follow him. When that didn't happen, his frustration turned him bitter.[14]

Moreover, one might argue the spread of Luther's ideas is overstated. Indeed, only about a third of the world practices Christianity, and

---

[14] *"There are almost as many sects and beliefs as there are heads; this one will not admit baptism; that one rejects the Sacrament of the altar; another places another world between the present one and the day of judgment; some teach that Jesus Christ is not God. There is not an individual, however clownish he may be, who does not claim to be inspired by the Holy Ghost, and who does not put forth as prophecies his ravings and dreams."*

Protestants make up a minority of worldwide Christians. Lutherans, in particular, only number about 80 million, barely one percent of the planet and only a few percent of Western civilization. Meanwhile, the strength of religion declines across Western culture. Considering those numbers, perhaps Lutheranism isn't that relevant after all.

However, these counterarguments, unlike Luther at Worms, cannot stand. I reject the idea that Western civilization would be a better place without the Reformation. This chapter and others on this list have made clear that, thanks to the unleashing of individualism, liberty, and science, we live in a comparatively more organized, free, and comfortable world than if that unleashing never took place.[15] As for the limited impact of Protestantism and declining importance of religion in Western culture, one should remember that, though one billion Protestants isn't too shabby, that's not the point. In fact, the declining importance of religion is an argument for, not against Luther's importance. The ability of people to distance themselves from religion and pursue other priorities is surely correlated to the weakening of the Church.

Perhaps the greatest, almost paradoxical irony of Luther is that he was an extreme conservative who helped catalyze Western liberalism. To Luther, Christianity needed to return to its Biblical roots, which he thought would lead all Christians to break free of the Church and ultimately share his correct originalist interpretation. That's a decidedly conservative ideology. And yet, this approach shattered Christendom by encouraging people to think and make decisions for themselves, a liber-

---

[15] And even if, on balance, the world has transformed for the worse, that is not an argument against Luther's role in the transformative change.

ating result that freed Western civilization from the shackles of medieval culture.

Nevertheless, whether deliberate or not, Martin Luther played a huge role in forming the modern Western world, even more than the man who inspired his religion. As a result, he surpasses his Lord and Savior to become the sixth most influential figure in Western history.

#5: James Watt

> *"If the steam-engine be the most powerful instrument in the hands of man to alter the face of the physical world, it operates at the same time as a powerful moral lever in forwarding the great cause of civilization."*
> –William Huskisson, British statesman, 1824

Coming on the heels of Jesus (#7) and Martin Luther (#6), a name like James Watt might seem like a stretch. Can Watt really be more influential than *Jesus*? Or even other household names like Einstein (#11) and Shakespeare (#10)?

You bet he can.

James Watt *is* a household name, actually. Every machine and device you own relies on the unit of power named after him—the watt. And for good reason, too. More than any other individual, Watt is responsible for modernizing power, which propelled the most important technological and economic shift in history: the Industrial Revolution. For that reason, he has earned his spot as the fifth most influential figure in Western history.

James Watt

In 1736, the Scottish James Watt was born into a world that would, by the time of his death, be unrecognizable to those who delivered him. Though this change is true about most people's lifespans since then, rarely could we have said that about anyone who lived before. It very much feels like history and change have unfolded faster and more dramatically in the last two centuries than in the two millennia before. Watt is a primary reason why.

Before Watt, the history of civilization moved at a glacial place. Let's pick 2000 BCE as a nice round number that's early enough for an assortment of cultures to be "civilized." By about that time, we had full-fledged civilizations across a handful of locations; they recorded information, built palaces, erected monuments, charted stars, constructed public works, worked with metals, and marched into battle on the orders of dynastic governments. It was early, but it was unmistakably civilization.

Most relevant for daily life, almost every man farmed or herded. With the exception of some small cities and towns, society was agrarian and largely immobile. Some think it was right around 2000 BCE that we may have had the first cities reach 100,000 people, but most people lived outside of them. The world's population approached 30 million.

Fast-forward through most of history to the mid-eighteenth century, when James Watt entered adulthood. The world's largest cities were still only measured in the hundreds of thousands. We still used "million" to count the world's population. More than 90 percent of the world still lived in rural areas. Almost everyone still farmed or herded. Almost everyone was still closely tethered to their local area. All labor and travel were powered by people, animal, water, and wind. Most jobs were at the mercy of the seasons. Life expectancy had only barely improved.[1] In a macro sense, for nearly four thousand years, not much about society had changed.

Then the Industrial Revolution changed everything. And it was James Watt who changed the Industrial Revolution.

Water plus heat equals steam. Steam equals power.

Though Watt pushed the limits of those equations, he wasn't the first to realize them. That honor goes to, of course, an ancient Greek,[2] and several inventions used those premises in the subsequent centuries. It wasn't until Thomas Newcomen in 1712, about 50 years before Watt's breakthrough, that we had the first practicable steam engine.

In Newcomen's steam engine, the steam piston, also called a steam cylinder, is where the atmospheric magic happened: boiled water created a vacuum on one side of the piston, which resulted in a pressure difference to push the piston down, which in turn created the power to operate something on the other end, like a pump.[3] Meanwhile, little water was lost during the process since it was continually recycled through the sys-

---

[1] To that point in history, the average life span bounced around between the late 20s and mid-30s. Those with means, however, could expect to live to their 60s.

[2] Hero of Alexandria (10-70 CE). I love that the first person who realized the potential of the human race to transcend our assumed limitations was named Hero. Only Prometheus would feel more on the nose.

[3] Please don't ask me questions about this. It doesn't make sense to me. While this list hopefully reflects that I recognize science's importance to civilization, it never made as much sense to me as politics and philosophy, and even those confuse me all the time. I'm about to move on as quickly as possible. Forgive me.

tem. Even if someone lived away from a natural water supply, as long as they could somehow acquire an initial volume of water via ground transportation or plumbing, they could have power via a steam engine that would rarely need refilling.

Though a wondrous invention, Newcomen's steam engine was extremely inefficient. The piston had to be repeatedly cooled and reheated, which required energy and created thermal stress, shortening the machine's lifespan. For decades its main purpose was merely to pump water out of coal mines, a useful but narrow application.

Enter James Watt. As a child, he loved tinkering in a corner of his father's shipbuilding workshop. Already a clever engineer in his 20s, in 1765 he had his world-changing idea. After working to fix one of Newcomen's engines, he found a way to improve it. Watt increased its efficiency by adding parts and making modifications. Most importantly, he included a separate "condenser" apart from the steam cylinder. This separate chamber would be surrounded by a "steam jacket" to keep it at a hot but consistent temperature, saving a great deal of energy and stress on the hardware. The result was a much more efficient and durable machine.

It was such a dramatic improvement over Newcomen's invention that many now mistake Watt as the actual inventor of the steam engine. Newcomen's engine just wasn't that useful or realistic to most people. Watt's was considerably more efficient and practical, and as a result it became commercially viable.

Though Watt's brilliance helped him develop this device, he quickly found that his genius did not extend to business. He wasn't sure how to convert his technical expertise into financial success. He also didn't have the capital to invest in all his experiments or a large-scale model.

Watt wisely sought benefactors, and in industrialist John Roebuck he found one. In exchange for a majority share of the patent, Roebuck paid Watt's debts and funded his work. However, Roebuck himself soon went bankrupt, which paved the way for Watt's ultimate business partner. A local factory owner, Matthew Boulton, acquired Roebuck's patents in exchange for paying Roebuck's debts. Soon, the firm of Boulton & Watt cranked out steam engines that transformed the world. A shrewd Boulton seemed to anticipate the possibilities of Watt's invention, boasting, "I have at my disposal what the whole world demands, something which will uplift civilization more than ever by relieving man of all undignified drudgery. I have steam power."

This claim wasn't just hot air. In fact, not only did the steam engine's hot air convert into power—it was *cheap* power. Let's remember that before steam, everything had been powered by people, animals, wind, or water, all of which had either natural or costly limitations. It's why society remained at a leisurely pace in an agrarian setting for several millennia. Watt's steam engine, on the other hand, transcended the limitations of old energy.

Since it allowed unprecedented sustained power, Watt struggled to explain the almost incomprehensible energy released by his steam engine. To make others understand, he coined a new term: horsepower. Watt's earliest steam engine had what he called "10 horsepower"; in other words, it could, for example, turn a wheel as well as 10 horses. Even better than horses, moreover, it wouldn't need food or rest.

Meanwhile, since any location could enjoy this kind of power, one no longer needed to live on expensive real estate next to a river or on the coast to use water mills. Watt freed industries from having to build manufacturing facilities next to waterways and allowed them to be put any-

James Watt

where, which led to the building of many more factories. New industries soon spread across his native Great Britain, then throughout the West, and then the world. By the time the 83-year-old Watt died in 1819, his steam engine had unleashed the Industrial Revolution. The world was changing.

The Industrial Revolution is arguably the most important development in Western history, and James Watt is its most important contributor. Though there's a long list of industrial titans we could consider for this list, some even predating Watt's contributions, most of them gave us more specific inventions or improvements that transformed few fields.[4] As important as they were, none of them were as crucial to the broader Industrial Revolution as was Watt's steam engine. In addition to facilitating the energy boom, the steam engine made possible or improved many other inventors' contributions.

With enormous, mobile energy, the Western world experienced an explosion of manufacturing and business. Steam-powered, indefatigable machines powered increasingly productive factories.

The old way of powering things had restricted the productivity of industries. Laborers had to sleep and get paid, animals had to rest and

---

[4] An incomplete list of examples follows: the aforementioned Newcomen, Roebuck, and Bolton; Thomas Savery (who actually had a cruder, pre-Newcomen steam engine), Charles Townshend, the Abraham Darbys (I, II, III, and, IV), John Kay, James Hargreaves, Richard Arkwright, Eli Whitney, George Stephenson, Lewis Paul, Samuel Crompton, Thomas Highs, John Lombe, John Wilkinson, John Smeaton, James Beaumont Neilson, Benjamin Huntsman, Nicolas LeBlanc, Charles Tennant, Joseph Aspdin, the gloriously named Humphry Davy, Robert Fulton, Michael Faraday, Allesandro Volta, Henry Bessemer, Alfred Nobel, Gugliemo Marconi, Joseph Lister, Nikola Tesla, Thomas Edison (#18), and, of course, the rock band Jethro Tull.

eat, wind was unreliable, and water power was localized in costly locations. However, the steam engine circumvented those restrictions. Unimaginable amounts of consistent energy became available for production and transportation. In time, Watt's steam engine triggered once inconceivable economic growth not just for the duration of the Industrial Revolution, which lasted through the 1800s, but beyond it into our modern world.

To get a clearer idea of how the steam engine could lead to such revolutionary effects, let's take a look at one industry: textiles. It was a pre-existing trade that had grown even before the steam engine, but it was severely hampered by its own business model. Textile mills were located on waterways in order to utilize water to power a wheel or turbine that drove the mechanics of the mill. However, the fabric necessary to make the clothes, primarily wool, was on the skin of sheep controlled by herders out in the country. Sheared wool had to therefore be transported to the water by mules and horses. That's a long, slow process that required the expensive upkeep and fitness of animals. Plus, the more wool someone wanted to transport, the heavier the load for their pack, either slowing down and fatiguing the pack or requiring more animals which is therefore more costly. This frustrating system hindered the growth of the textile industry.

Then, with one invention, the entire process was immediately made more efficient. One could build a textile mill closer to—or perhaps even in!—the countryside, install a steam engine inside of it, and then operate it with costs and time saved in countless ways. Numerous industries could set up shop where it made sense, saving time and costs accordingly. Profit and economic growth naturally followed.

James Watt

Concurrently with industrialization—and often aided by it—an agricultural revolution pushed population growth. Better farming techniques combined with new agricultural inventions produced record crop yields, which helped grow the population. Soon, medicinal advances of the industrial world—most notably the contributions of Louis Pasteur (#8)—further lengthened life expectancy, which led to even more population growth when fewer early graves were filled. This growth demanded more food, clothing, and all the other new products created by steam-powered machines in factories, which created a feedback loop.

Another major area of modernization was transportation. In the slow pace of the old world, transportation, like energy of all kinds, relied on people, animals, ocean currents, and wind. No longer. By the early 1800s, Watt's improved steam engines became small enough to be released from factories and onto vehicles. As a result, the world had its first steam-powered ships. What could easily be a month-long journey across the Atlantic powered by wind and man sped up to under 10 days with the steam engine, a length of time that was nearly halved by the end of the nineteenth century.

The steamship's land-based cousin was the steam locomotive. Railroads allowed rapid travel across a country along something other than rivers (with their annoyingly specific routes) and roads (with their annoyingly fragile conditions). Railroads allowed the building of even more towns, cities, and factories in new locations. For the first time ever, people and goods were moved by something other than what was naturally given to humanity. Steamships and railroads then gave people access to a new diversity of goods from a diversity of places.

All combined, not only did Watt's steam engine help produce all this new food, clothing, and medicine, but it also helped distribute it faster and to more places than ever before. After 10,000 years of humanity's slow-paced population growth, the two centuries since industrialization sent Western economic production and population skyrocketing. It took civilization thousands of years to reach one billion living people in 1804. It then took only 123 years to reach two billion in 1927. In the nearly hundred years since, we've climbed nearly six billion more. The turning point was the Industrial Revolution powered by Watt's steam engine.

The effects were felt first in Watt's Britain and then the rest of the West. The United Kingdom's manufacturing output quickly leapt far in front of all others, a lead that allowed it to economically and militarily dominate most of the following century. Other Western nations soon followed. Paul Kennedy's "The Rise and Fall of the Great Powers" charts the escalation of Western output during the industrial era. He finds that in 1750, Europe accounted for only 23 percent of the world's manufacturing output, with the colonies that became the United States contributing only a tenth of a percent. By the end of the nineteenth century, however, Europe's share accounted for 62 percent of global manufacturing output, while the U.S., by itself, put out another 24 percent. In tandem, the combined European and American share grew from 23 to *86 percent*. In the same period, non-industrialized India and China fell from a combined 57 percent of the world's manufacturing to just 8 percent. Western GDP correspondingly skyrocketed. The result was a collection of Western powers that came to dominate the world's economy and its geopolitics.

Of course, all this progress was not without negative consequences. As people moved to the new factories to work, towns and cities were built in areas that were once totally rural. Those who lived in the rural areas grew from annoyed to evicted. Meanwhile, the agricultural advancements of the period meant less labor was needed to grow food. Farmers rich enough to invest in agricultural inventions soon claimed more and more of a dwindling supply of land as they bought out or bullied poorer farmers who couldn't compete. These farmers were forced to move to the cities to find low-paying work in the factories that manufactured the very products that helped take their land. Thus, the growing population overall coupled with a massive migration from rural to urban areas soon overpacked unprepared cities.

It's been quite the shift from the days where just about everyone lived in rural areas. For example, in the first United States census (1790), only 5 percent of the American population lived in urban areas, with the other 95 percent living in rural areas. By 1900 it was up to 40 percent. In the 2010 census, the figure was up over 80 percent. Numbers in Europe are nearly as high–right around 75 percent.

Awaiting the new city-dwellers of the industrial period was a dramatically different lifestyle. Ripped from lives of fresh air and freer toil, Westerners were introduced to the working day: clock in, clock out; hourly wages; do what the boss says; keep your head down and don't complain; do one task over and over every day. In earlier human history, people created tools that accommodated to humans. In the Industrial Revolution, we entered into an era where we had to accommodate to the tools—in this case, the machines we had invented.

In the name of profit, ambitious factory owners frequently prioritized these machines over workers. Industrial workplaces were extremely dangerous, and a day's work could easily be sun up to sun down with barely enough time to sleep and see one's family in between. The family often went to work in the factory as well; that included children who lost limbs reaching their usefully small hands into frequently broken machines, often with devastating results upon dislodgement. Although inequality was nothing new—nobility and peasantry are as old as history itself—the dangers associated with being in the lowest classes certainly were.

Worse, perhaps, than industrialization's physical dangers were the more psychological costs. Before the Industrial Revolution, artisans could take pride in their work. Every gun, for example, could be specially made. A gun maker could take pride in that gun, injecting their own style and flair. The same could be said for makers of tables and clothes, tools and decor.

The Industrial Revolution, however, gave us interchangeable parts, promoted by Eli Whitney, and the assembly line, mastered by Henry Ford (#20). Before, a broken gun could need a sizable overhaul if not a total replacement, but now only a relatively cheap part needed to be fixed or replaced. It limited one's creativity and reputation in a community. By creating a machine to do the work of a person, it took something away from the person.

The laborer's new job was helping to assemble those interchangeable parts. The new job likely entailed one simplistic task done repeatedly in order to contribute to making a larger product. There had never been a more abrupt change to how a population made its living.

This living has been threatened by something perhaps more existential than anything mentioned so far. Industrialization caused skyrocketing pollution. Industrialists' insatiable demand for power, first from coal and then from oil and gas, has depleted natural resources and infected our air. So, too, has our own demand for power, products, and automobility. The byproducts of manufacturers and consumers have created mountainous landfills on our land and state-sized garbage patches in our oceans. Many ubiquitous plastic products will take centuries to biodegrade, one of many problems our descendants will inherit.

At the same time, the Industrial Revolution enhanced by Watt's steam engine modernized and made accessible innumerable things we now take for granted. Mass production lowered prices on just about everything, making just about everything more affordable to workers. Workers then purchased these goods, which was a boon to businesses. It was yet another feedback loop first made possible by the steam engine.

As a result, the bland lives of the once-rural workers were spiced up by consumerism. Though at first most workers lived in overcrowded slums and tenements, in time, as labor movements earned better pay, shorter hours, and safer work conditions, a strong middle class steadily emerged. Since there was plenty of work in a growing economy—countless industries emerged alongside all the new inventions—just about everyone was making some money and, reinforcing the system, spending it. Meanwhile, tied to a clock, the end of the new urbanite's shift at work allowed them to take to their growing city to fuel the rise of sports, popular music, theater, and so much more. The contrast to earlier eras of feudalism and serfdom, which should not be glorified by opponents of industrialism, could not be starker.

What I've described for the last few paragraphs, of course, is the modern economy and modern world.[5] It's the Industrial Revolution that made them possible. Look at how some historians describe the era:

- Deidre McCloskey: *"[The Industrial Revolution] is certainly the most important event in the history of humanity since the*

---

[5] And I can only imagine how it would have been written differently by Karl Marx (#9) and his advocates.

domestication of animals and plants, perhaps the most important since the invention of language."

- Gregory Clarke: *"The Industrial Revolution . . . represents the single great event of world economic history, the change between two fundamentally different economic systems. . . . The Industrial Revolution thus seems to represent a singularity. A unique break in world history."*
- Robert E. Lucas: *"During the last 200 years, both production and population growth have accelerated dramatically. . . . The novelty of the discovery that a human society has this potential for generating sustained improvement in the material aspects of the lives of all of its members, not just of a ruling elite, cannot be overstressed. We have entered an entirely new phase in our economic history."*
- Leif van Neuss: *"The industrial revolution, which started in Britain before sweeping through Europe and the USA, is traditionally viewed as the deepest mutation ever known to have affected men since Neolithic times. . . . Historians have often used and abused the word revolution to mean a radical change, but no revolution has been as dramatically revolutionary as the Industrial Revolution."*

I rest my case on industrialization's importance. As for Watt, was he solely responsible for it? No. In fact, some industrialization began before him, and the crowded gathering at a recent footnote shows that industrialization had many people to thank. These factors, in fact, kept Watt out of my top four—my Mount Rushmore of history's most influential Westerners, if you will.

James Watt

Yet, the Industrial Revolution is so important that it needs an ambassador high on this list, and Watt's contribution to the movement is peerless. Watt's steam engine grew the Industrial Revolution many times over. It catalyzed a remarkably rapid transition from rural life to an urban one; from slow living to our fast-paced world; from an ancient level of technology to the splendorous, problematic world we live in today. So much of modernity was made possible by Watt: cars, trains, planes, space travel, phones, satellites, tablets, pollution, the houses we live in, and everything we buy to put inside of them.

Never forget that every time you plug in, it's the watt running your world. His name, appropriately, represents the fundamental unit of power today. He is that significant, and he's earned his spot as the fifth most influential figure in Western history.

#4: John Locke

"In the world of thought, it was a political philosophy which made rights the foundation of the social order. . . . The first famous exponent of this philosophy was Locke, in whom the dominant conception is the indefeasibility of private rights."

—R. H. Tawney

This ranking's "top six" captures the most important individual in each of Western history's six most important eras and movements. Martin Luther (#6) catalyzed the Reformation, and James Watt (#5) powered the Industrial Revolution. Representing the four remaining movements is what we can call my "Mount Rushmore" of Western history—the West's four most influential people ever. Like the 26 names that came before them, each of these figures contributed essential components to some leap forward. Still, compared to the previous 26, the top four played an even more consequential role as a part of their respective eras.

Today's historical figure was a part of the Enlightenment, an intellectual movement that, among its many ideas, modernized our approach to government. During this "Age of Reason," Western philosophers analyzed preconceived notions about government with such relentless rhetoric and logic that they inspired permanent political change. Of the many who did so, one man stands more impactful than the rest. His name was John Locke, and he's now chiseled on our historical Mount Rushmore as the fourth most influential figure in Western history.

Our knowledge and beliefs are handed down by prior generations, often despite these beliefs' accuracy or reasonability; we believe things because we were told to believe them by someone who seemed to know what they were talking about. In the seventeenth and eighteenth centuries, however, a new movement prided itself on challenging these preconceptions. For philosophers of this movement, nothing (not even Christianity) was off limits. The Enlightenment challenged *everything*.

Nowhere was this furious attack on traditional knowledge more relevant than government. In order to determine the best approach to governing, Enlightened philosophers asked some of the most fundamental political questions one can ponder: Do we need government? Why do we have it? From where do governments derive their power? How powerful should governments be? To what extent should a government's citizens have influence over it?

We know how these questions were answered for most of history. Indeed, these answers offer sobering reminders of our subjugated past. In almost every historical civilization, autocrats and oligarchs had total control over their people. That power was justified either because their fathers had total control before them, or because they had soldiers at their side and/or priests in their corner. Frequently tied to this paradigm was a belief in a higher power that authorized these successions and power dynamics. With few exceptions, the people's historical authority over the government was almost non-existent.

Heading into the Enlightenment, the West was still entrenched in an age of absolutism. The prevailing Western political premise—the "divine right of kings"—insisted that God, not wanting to be bothered with micromanaging each kingdom's day-to-day governing, delegated authority to monarchs to do it for Him. The proof of this belief was the typically flawless logic of theocrats; if God, in His infinite wisdom, did not want a certain king in power, then God had the power to remove him. This widespread belief justified unchecked authority for most of Western Europe's powerful sovereigns.

Thinkers from the Enlightenment disagreed. The Age of Reason's philosophers didn't think tradition or preconceptions were good reasons to believe in old ideas. Instead, as converts to the Scientific Revolution due to its success in identifying natural laws and predictable outcomes, they worked to determine the natural laws of men in order to determine the best way to govern them.

During the Enlightenment's century-plus of inspiring ideas, many philosophers offered different answers to the foundational questions of government, formulated new arguments, published their thoughts, and convinced many Westerners to upend conventional wisdom. The result was history's most important political pivot.

Before we get into the philosophical specifics, let's first interrogate a common American phrase, an interrogation that can serve as a gateway into the mind of some Enlightenment thinkers: *"It's a free country."*

John Locke

What does that mean? Usually, people say it as a flippant response to someone who asks to do something they're clearly allowed to do. *"It's a free country,"* we say. *"You can do whatever you want."*

But that's not true, is it? We can't do whatever we want. We're not allowed to kill, assault, or steal. We can't drive while drunk, or at a hundred miles per hour on our way to work, or park wherever we want when we get there. There are hundreds of restrictions placed on us in this supposedly "free country." None of the above actions break any natural laws like the ones outlined by Galileo (#12) and Einstein (#11). They do, however, break political ones.

Many of these restrictions are probably for the best. Consider some of those limits: don't kill, don't assault, don't drive recklessly. While these laws do, in fact, curtail our freedom of choice, they also mean our freedom of choice does not overrule others' right to safety. I don't have the right to kill you because you have the right to not be killed. Those two rights cannot coexist, and we thankfully choose to prioritize the latter.

But who protects that right to live or not get assaulted? Enter the government. It creates and enforces laws. Despite our deep political differences today, we usually come together on wanting the government to protect us from being killed.[1] Where we're not as united, however, is when we consider how far the government should go to provide or ensure things like order, prosperity, health, and any number of other benefits. How one evaluates the extent to which government should protect

---

[1] Usually.

and intervene in its citizens' lives goes a long way toward determining one's political ideology.[2]

We're now primed enough to examine the first notable attempt in modern history to answer the earlier basic questions about government. Before Locke, many of those fundamental questions were well explored by Englishman Thomas Hobbes (1588-1679).[3] The messy English Civil War of the 1640s deeply affected his political ideology. He reacted with one of political history's greatest works, 1651's "Leviathan." Hobbes tackles the above questions and dilemmas with a series of premises that justify an extremely powerful government—though with one critical limitation.

Hobbes first determines the necessity of government by addressing an important term in moral and political philosophy—our "state of na-

---

[2] How one responds to the above determines how a person or group would structure a government and its relationship with the governed, because how one responds reveals their "first principles," and these first principles justify one's politics. That's important to keep in mind when considering modern political discourse. For example, if someone thinks people's behavior and decision-making can be trusted more than the government, or if they generally think life is fair, they're more likely to bend libertarian, allow unrestricted gun ownership, advocate lower taxes, and hold other small-government positions. If someone thinks individuals don't do what's best for the group and government can be an agent of good, or that life isn't fair and there should be efforts to equalize the playing field, they'll likely develop opposite political positions. From the premise sprung logical conclusions. If you can't identify and change someone's premise, you have little chance to change their stance on a political issue. Change the premise, change the conclusion.

[3] Hobbes didn't make the Top 30, but he did make a showing in the "Next 30."

ture." In other words, Hobbes pondered the natural state of people without the refining force of society. If there were no government to protect and civilize us from cradle to grave, what would mankind be like?

In such a scenario, Hobbes has low hopes for mankind. He foresees chaos. Without what he called a "common power," we'd have "no arts; no letters; no society; and which is worst of all, continual fear, and danger of violent death." In other words, we'd have no civilization at all. He theorizes that without this strong government, "the life of man" would be "solitary, poor, nasty, brutish and short."

That's our state of nature, says Hobbes. We're innately greedy. We'd selfishly kill, harm, and steal from each other in order to improve our own lives. His work's title revealed *us* as the Biblical "Leviathan"—an unruly monster.

Therefore, to control our basest instincts, Hobbes proposed that we need a strong government with broad power. Here's where Hobbes introduces another fundamental phrase of political philosophy: the social contract.[4] Social contract theory suggests there's an unwritten agreement between the state and its people—the government and the governed—that helps maintain the order craved by Hobbesian philosophy. In the agreement, the people cede rights to the state—for example, our natural abilities to kill, harm, and drive a hundred miles per hour—in exchange for the state protecting us from each other. And, since we are not to be trusted, the government should be empowered with considerable authority to most effectively ensure this protection.

---

[4] Though the concept of a social contract predates Hobbes (all the way back to, of course, the ancient Greeks), Hobbes formalizes the term for the modern world.

Though this concept predated Hobbes, he added a progressive idea. His model government, though nearly absolutist, was not, unlike most governments throughout history, all-powerful. Hobbes felt that the government, too, must have a limit. He said that part of the government's social contract responsibility is protecting a certain "natural right," or a right with which we're born. There's only one natural right, according to Hobbes, but it's a big one: the right to life. Not only must the government protect our right to live from others that might want to infringe upon it, the government itself must also respect that right. If it doesn't, it has failed. It has broken the social contract. Short of that, Hobbes gives the state wide latitude to control its people so they do not bend toward their chaotic state of nature.

By modern standards, Hobbesian government sounds wildly conservative.[5] For the period, however, it was a rather liberal step. In an era when the "divine right of kings" propped up monarchs, Hobbes was the first to invert this power structure and elevate man's "natural" right to live. Essentially, it wasn't that God delegated his omnipotent authority to kings; it was that God gave *us* a natural right while the king was given power with the express purpose of protecting it. In other words, the state was *subservient* to our right to live. Though not nearly as liberating as the ideas of subsequent philosophers, we can call this a critical moment in

---

[5] A note on "liberal" and "conservative" because modern politicians and talking heads have effectively mangled their traditional meanings. Keep in mind that for most of world history, "liberal"—from the Greek *libertas*, or "freedom"—meant instilling political change to provide more power and freedom to the people, while "conservatives" aimed to maintain traditional, top-down politics in the name of order and consistency.

John Locke

Western political theory.[6] More relevant to this Top 30 entry, Hobbes placed a cornerstone around which John Locke built his towering ideology.

When Hobbes published "Leviathan" in 1651, John Locke was a 19-year-old Puritan raised by an educated family just outside Bristol. He attended Oxford, earned bachelor's and master's degrees, and eventually earned a degree in medicine in 1675. Already aged 43, it seemed history's most important political philosopher was instead going to live out his life a talented but forgettable doctor.

Then, thank goodness, one of Locke's patients became gravely ill. This illness redirected Locke's life. The man's name was Lord Anthony Ashley Cooper, the prestigious Earl of Shaftesbury, a founder of England's famous Whig Party, and one of the most influential members in Parliament. A liver infection convinced him to seek medical help at Oxford, and it's there he met Locke. Cooper quickly appreciated Locke's sharp mind—and his lifesaving surgery. A grateful Lord Cooper invited Locke to be his personal physician and soon after his personal secretary.

For Locke, this relationship was formative. Cooper's Whig Party was a burgeoning liberal faction which had congealed around an anti-absolutist ideology. Locke's philosophy became deeply colored by his experiences with Cooper and the Whigs. Their greatest victory came in 1688, when Parliament's pressure campaign against the unpopular (read: Catholic) King James II convinced him to step down in favor of his daughter Mary and her husband William of Orange. This

---

[6] Wow, Hobbes was pretty important. Wait a minute... should he have been in the top 30 after all? WHAT HAVE I DONE?!

Glorious Revolution was dubbed the "bloodless revolution," as it was a successful nonviolent rebellion against a king who had lost the people's mandate to lead, followed by replacing his government with another. Unlike Hobbes, whose ideology was informed by England's bloody civil war, it is the noble Glorious Revolution that primarily molded Locke's worldview. Locke's experiences with Lord Cooper and the revolution, combined with his own agile mind, led him to organize his thoughts onto paper.

An inspired Locke, already 56, finally wrote his first major published work, a book now hailed among the most important in Western history: the "Two Treatises of Government."[7] The "First Treatise" rebuts "Patriarcha Non Monarcha," an earlier book from philosopher Robert Filmer that defended absolute monarchy and divine right. The "Second Treatise" outlines Locke's ideal political system—a system under which the entire Western world operates today.

To understand Locke's political ideas, we must first understand his positions on the aforementioned Hobbesian concepts. Regarding man's "state of nature," Locke disagreed with Hobbes's pessimistic take on our natural, evil inclinations. Starting with a different premise, Locke

---

[7] Full title: "Two Treatises of Government: In the Former, The False Principles, and Foundation of Sir Robert Filmer, and His Followers, Are Detected and Overthrown. The Latter Is an Essay Concerning The True Original, Extent, and End of Civil Government." I assure you what he lacked in titling skills he made up in political insight.

believed we were born as a "*tabula rasa*," or blank slate.[8] All our knowledge and beliefs develop not as a result of innate tendencies, as Hobbes believed, but from experience.[9]

Locke, therefore, had much more faith in humanity than did Hobbes. His view of human nature appeals to the best of us. He thinks that under the right circumstances, individuals can be reasonable, fair, and decent. We can therefore be trusted to problem-solve, to come up with the best answers to fit certain situations. We can be *good*.

For that reason, Locke believes Hobbes's nearly absolutist state is unnecessary. In fact, it can lead to more problems than it solves. Much like the absence of government, the common man's historical struggle against tyranny also led to bloodshed.[10] That struggle may even embitter the common man and turn him cruel. It's that cruelty which Hobbes says requires a strong state to control a people, but Locke suggests that it can be the government itself that soured the people's disposition in the first place. Indeed, the English Civil War that drove Hobbes to his pessimistic take on humanity pitted Parliament against a tyrannical king.

Thinking Hobbes's premise flawed and his conclusion self-fulfilling, Locke amended the social contract. Whereas Hobbes only granted to man a single natural right—the right to life—Locke believed natural law granted people *three* rights: life, liberty, and property.

---

[8] It's actually in a concurrent work to the "Two Treatises," "An Essay Concerning Human Understanding," where Locke laid out this epistemological position. It blends well with the more major publication, and using its ideas here helps us understand Locke's reasoning.

[9] In psychology's popular "nature versus nurture" debate, Locke would have very much sided with nurture and Hobbes with nature.

[10] That's an observation later shared by Karl Marx (#9), although the political recommendations of the two men were miles apart.

These broad new rights were considerably more liberal. "Liberty," for example, could entail any number of evolving freedoms. Meanwhile, "property" included all possessions. Locke believed a person's labor was infused with inherent value to a state, and a laborer worked in order to have a home and possessions. If the government could violate one's property, one's motivation to work decreased, which then hurt the strength of a nation.

Rarely had the masses been treated with such respect. Locke believed common people had a role to play in a successful state, and they should therefore be treated like valued citizens. The state's reason for being was not merely to maintain order; it also should oversee its citizens' welfare by safeguarding their natural rights. The best way to do that was not only by protecting the people through laws, but also by not overreaching into its people's lives. In other words, the power of the government should be *limited*.

Just as important, Locke also outlined what should occur if the government breached its end of the social contract, which would mean it did not protect citizens' rights to life, liberty, and property. Such a violation triggers a fourth right: the right to rebel, or the right of revolution. In essence, if the government failed the people, the people should get a new government.

It's perhaps the most important principle in political science. Hobbes had fallen short of explicitly stating such a proposal. Though both men placed the divine right within us instead of within kings, Locke went further and rejected the hereditary, near-absolutist model altogether. The state doesn't have inherent authority. Authority is loaned to it by the people. The social contract is revocable.

John Locke

Locke's other ideas in "Two Treatises" and various works over the next 15 years now read as a veritable wellspring of modern political theory. His model government had branches with separated powers and checks and balances. Like a good Whig, he promoted a legislative branch comprised of the people's representatives. He blasted hereditary rule. In "A Letter Concerning Toleration," he pushes back against another Hobbesian belief—that government should promote religious uniformity to create an efficient society—by insisting on a separation of church and state. Channeling yet another natural right—the right to one's conscience—he wanted faiths, even non-Christians, treated equally under the law.[11] All of his arguments supported his main thesis—that the best kind of government is a limited one.

In 1704, John Locke died at 72 having never had a wife or children. Yet, he soon became the grandfather of a revolution.

Locke's political ideology is now called classical liberalism. It's founded on the premise that government gets its legitimacy not from divine right, hereditary authority, or military strength, but instead from the consent of the governed for the purposes of safeguarding our inalienable rights.

That probably sounds familiar to you—not because you've read Locke, but because, at some point in your life, your most boring history teacher made you read the U.S. Declaration of Independence. The following italicized text comes from its second paragraph:

---

[11] Exception: Catholics. The persistent anti-Catholic sentiments of Anglo-American culture stem from the fear of Catholics being more dedicated to a foreign leader (the pope) than their local state. It's not the faith itself that bothered Locke and other non-Catholics—it was the split loyalties. Britain's American colonies-turned-republic had similar anti-Catholic bias. Still, judged against his era, Locke's toleration to everyone else was progressive.

"*We hold these truths to be self-evident, that all men are created equal...*" Locke said of man that he is "by nature free, equal, and independent." He believed we're all born a "tabula rasa" and with the same natural rights.

"*... that they are endowed by their Creator with certain unalienable Rights, that among these are Life, Liberty and the pursuit of Happiness.*" Though the founding fathers swapped in the last bit, this sentiment is clearly lifted from Locke, who noted that the reason man needed government was "to preserve himself, his liberty, and property."

"*That to secure these rights, Governments are instituted among Men, deriving their just powers from the consent of the governed...*" Locke believed that the point of government is to protect our natural rights, a power made possible "by the will and determination of the majority."

"*... that whenever any Form of Government becomes destructive of these ends, it is the Right of the People to alter or to abolish it, and to institute new Government.*" Locke asserted "the people shall be the judge" of a government and its efficacy, and they have a right and obligation to rebel against a government that's not doing its job and replace it with one that will.

Relevantly, in the years leading up to the American Revolution, many of the colonial complaints—taxation without representation, security in one's homes and possessions, due process of law—echoed often close to verbatim the greatest philosopher of the empire from which they would soon separate. Though it was not until 70 years after Locke's death that Thomas Jefferson (#24) and the rest of the Continental Congress wrote the Declaration of Independence, we could be forgiven for calling Locke its co-author.

The revolutionary period at the end of the eighteenth century can be seen as the culmination of the Enlightenment, as it was the Enlightenment that offered justification for the revolution. The American founding fathers were each well-read, and nothing more inspired their words and actions than did the Enlightenment's ideals. The colonial rebels were the first to put into action the sentiments of a movement that, to that point, was mostly just an intellectual exercise. America's founding fathers received political ideas from other Enlightenment philosophers—Hobbes, Jean-Jacques Rousseau, the Baron de Montesquieu, and Voltaire (#22), to name a few—but none of them rivaled Locke's influence.

The impact of Locke didn't end when the United States secured their independence. After victory in their Revolutionary War, it was then time for the Americans to govern. They eventually settled on a document that has guided the United States government ever since: the U.S. Constitution.

Look closely enough at its parchment, and once again we find John Locke's fingerprints. As advocated by Locke's social contract, the U.S. created a government to protect citizens' natural rights, as expressly indicated in the preamble, which explained the Constitution was written in order to "establish Justice, insure domestic Tranquility, provide for the common defence, promote the general Welfare, and secure the Blessings of Liberty." The first three articles of the Constitution go on to create three branches of government, each with their own powers and the ability to check the others. Moreover, the most powerful of the three, the legislative, contained elected representatives.[12] Shortly after the states ratified the Constitution, the Bill of Rights was added to it, protecting Americans' freedom of life, liberty, property, and worship from the federal government—Lockean ideas all.

Meanwhile, the Americans built into their government elections and ways to amend their governing document. If the people did not like their government, no longer would they have to rise up in a violent rebellion and slay the sovereign; they merely had to wait until the next election and vote out who they didn't like.[13] They could also work to gain enough consensus to modify the government itself through amendments. Thus, woven into the country's governing document was a peaceful "right to rebel" if the government or its laws did not have the consent of the gov-

---

[12] Yes, Congress is more powerful than the president. Imagine if the power of all 535 members of Congress were condensed into an individual. That person could pass any law they wanted and, if necessary, override the president's veto. The Legislator could declare war on whomever he wanted, and he could deny any high-ranking executive appointee, including judges, and he would even have a chance to amend the Constitution itself if enough states were on board. The president cannot initiate legislation, and the process of amending the Constitution does not go through the executive branch. The legislative branch is immensely powerful, even if its cumbersome structure cedes leadership to the chief executive.

[13] Although the U.S. Senate and president were initially insulated from voters, those voters elected the state legislatures who picked a state's senators and its members of the Electoral College. In that way, members of the government could be influenced by members of the public, albeit indirectly.

John Locke

erned.[14] The weapon of revolution used to be bullets, but then it was ballots.

Locke's impact, of course, was not limited to the United States. Locke and the American cause soon inspired others. The subsequent French Revolution's Declaration of the Rights of Man mirrors the American ideals inspired by Locke.[15] These ideas steadily spread until the entire Western world followed Locke's lead. Representative democracies and constitutionally limited monarchies are now the norm across the West and much of the world.

In a remarkable and consequential paradigm shift, Locke's classical liberalism overturned the traditional power structure of Western government. Before him, most countries were governed by an almost omnipotent state controlling the people and doing whatever it wanted in the process. The implementation of Locke's ideas meant that governments, imbued with limited authority, were subordinate to us. Now we aren't the only ones who have rules we must follow; the government does as well. A radical idea at the time has become commonplace today.

The influence of such a reversal is profound. With a government that is expected to be responsive to the governed, we contribute to that gov-

---

[14] Though we sometimes are frustrated with how slowly government acts on an important issue, the cause of that slow reaction almost always stems from a considerable fraction of the population disagreeing with what we want to do. That's the blessing and curse of democratically-based governments. Other people besides you get a say, even if they are in the minority.

[15] Of course, the French experiment eventually went berserk. Excessive revolutionary leaders soon stopped protecting life, liberty, and property in a paranoid counterrevolutionary purge. The French Revolution's failure was a result of being inspired by Locke's liberalism when rebelling but not when operating their new government. The Americans did a cleaner job of it.

erning. We influence and can even control the government's agenda. We tell it what to prioritize. What a colossal change in the way we live and get things done compared to just a short time ago. Through this process, we can affect our civilization's politics, economy, culture, society, science, and every other area in which the government can affect our lives. Relative to most of history, these new, far-reaching abilities further justify Locke's high ranking on this list.

Therefore, feeling more secure in our lives, liberty, and property, we can call John Locke the fourth most influential figure in Western history.

#3: Isaac Newton

"Here is buried Isaac Newton, Knight, who by a strength of mind almost divine, and mathematical principles peculiarly his own, explored the course and figures of the planets, the paths of comets, the tides of the sea, the dissimilarities in rays of light, and, what no other scholar has previously imagined, the properties of the colours thus produced. . . . Mortals rejoice that there has existed such and so great an ornament of the human race!"

-Inscription on the gravesite and monument of Isaac Newton, Westminster Abbey

He once wrote that his accomplishments were only made possible by peering from the shoulders of giants that came before him. Betraying his faux humility is not only his supreme confidence, but the fact that he towers above every other scientist our species has produced. No one before or since has contributed as much to our understanding of how the universe works.

This ranking has been heavily populated by scientists. None were as important as Isaac Newton, the third most influential figure in Western history.

American founding father John Adams said John Locke (#4) and Isaac Newton were "examples of the deep sagacity which may be acquired by long habits of thinking and study."[1] At birth, however, it appeared Newton wouldn't have the chance to develop a habit of anything. The universe almost didn't host the man who made sense of it.

Newton was born in the hamlet of Woolsthorpe, England on Christmas Day, 1642.[2] He was a premature baby so small that his mother, Hannah, claimed he could fit in a quart mug. Widowed three months before Isaac's birth, Hannah was solely responsible for the unlikely survival of her child. He lived, but it was not an easy upbringing. When he was three, his mother remarried and left to live with her new husband, leaving young Isaac with his grandmother. He grew up feeling abandoned by his mother, whose lifesaving dedication he couldn't remember, and resentful of his stepfather, whose house he threatened to burn down. Newton started his life angry at the world, and that stuck with him. For most of his life he was considered an arrogant but insecure man, a brilliant but bitter scientist.[3]

From a family of farmers, Newton had to be sent away for schooling, ultimately becoming the first literate person in his family. He lived with an educated man, William Clarke, who watched over him as he attended

---

[1] I had to look up sagacity because, as should be clear by now, I don't have much of it.

[2] Earlier in 1642, Galileo (#12) died. If ever there were a reason to believe in reincarnation, this is it.

[3] Indeed, if he's reading this from Scientist Heaven, he's surely insulted at this lowly ranking of 3. Since it came up, what do you think Scientist Heaven is like? I picture crazy experiments, disheveled hair, broken beakers, and constant guffawing. It'd be like teenagers when parents are away on vacation, only with fewer girls and more accidental explosions.

Isaac Newton

The King's School in the nearby city of Grantham.[4] However, though he displayed a precocious capacity for mechanics and tinkering, he struggled with formal education.[5] His mother eventually pulled him from school and resolved to make him a farmer. Perhaps it was the possibility of working manual labor outside for the rest of his life that motivated Newton to study.[6] Fortunately for him, the school's headmaster recognized Newton's considerable potential and persuaded his mother to let him return. A reinvigorated Newton graduated from The King's School in 1661 and was accepted to the prestigious University of Cambridge at Trinity College.

Before Cambridge's greatest alumnus could make his mark on the world, the world made a mark on Cambridge. After a few years of voracious reading acquainted Newton with the era's leading mathematical and scientific ideas, the Great Plague of 1665 visited itself upon England. In response, Trinity College closed its doors and suspended its classes. Newton, consequently, had time to spare, and he began converting what he had learned into new ideas and experiments of his own.[7] It

---

[4] Just over a century earlier, this school was attended by William Cecil, a young man who as an older man went on to recommend that Queen Elizabeth (#19) execute the meddlesome Mary, Queen of Scots.

[5] Not unlike Darwin (#15), Einstein (#11), and the author writing these words.

[6] Also not unlike the author writing these words.

[7] It's a fortunate coincidence, frankly. He had spent his early years at Cambridge writing his "Quaestiones," a series of questions about mechanical philosophy, including the nature of gravity, motion, inertia, light, and color. His busy schedule meant he never had the time to answer his questions—in other words, to formulate his monumental theories—until the plague afforded him a break to revolutionize each of those fields. So, sure, a hundred thousand Londoners had to die miserably, but humanity got a lot out of it thanks to Newton. If you want to make an omelet, am I right?

quickly became clear that he was inspired with history's foremost combination of curiosity and brilliance, a pairing that allowed him to divine the laws of nature.

His talents effected modernizing change across diverse areas. For example, he advanced the burgeoning field of optics, the study of light's behavior and interaction with matter. Aided by his reflecting telescope—the 26-year-old Newton invented it in 1668, and it's still the telescope of choice by astronomers today—he founded the subfield of physical optics. He discovered that sunlight is comprised of particles and corpuscles. Through his work with prisms, he helped establish the nature of color itself, including that white light is the combination of all the colors of the rainbow. Before he was 30, these advancements earned him a presentation at the prestigious British Royal Society—an organization of which he would soon become a member and eventually president.

And that's just optics! His accomplishments in mathematics were just as far-reaching. He's considered the co-founder of calculus,[8] which is but the most prominent of an impressive series of arithmetical ad-

---

[8] The other co-founder, Gottfried Leibniz, established calculus concurrently in Germany, and the two men seemingly had little influence on each other as they developed it. Who came up with it first is not without its controversy; calling them "co"-founders seems the easiest way to resolve it, if one can even call that a resolution. (I am proudly #TeamNewton.) Still, even his rival recognized Newton's place as an all-time great. Leibniz once remarked that "taking mathematicians from the beginning of the world to the time when Sir Isaac lived, what he had done was much the better half."

Isaac Newton

vances.⁹ The principle of calculus likely came to him at an absurdly young age—perhaps 23 or 24.

And that's just mathematics! Even more important, he applied this new calculus to the most consequential contributions in the history of science.

Aristotle (#30) told us that although no one ever uncovers the whole truth of the universe, we can all contribute our bit of knowledge until "a considerable amount is amassed." It's as if we all can shade in a fraction of a pie chart, contributing to the sum of human knowledge, and over time the shaded area grows.

No one has ever identified a greater fraction of the universe's truths than Isaac Newton. Perhaps the poet Alexander Pope said it best: *"Nature and Nature's laws lay hid in night/God said, Let Newton be! And all was light."* When Newton developed his thoughts on mechanics, he decoded a universe that had puzzled humankind since well before we had anything resembling science.

Mechanics—the science of how physical bodies behave, react to forces, and affect their environment—governs how and why things move. Newton didn't "invent" mechanics, nor did he inaugurate its study. The inaugurators were, of course, the ancient Greeks. More recent, nine

---

[9] The following comes from his Wikipedia page's overview of just his mathematical discoveries. Tell me if this stuff makes sense to you: "Newton is generally credited with the generalized binomial theorem, valid for any exponent. He discovered Newton's identities, Newton's method, classified cubic plane curves (polynomials of degree three in two variables), made substantial contributions to the theory of finite differences, and was the first to use fractional indices and to employ coordinate geometry to derive solutions to Diophantine equations. He approximated partial sums of the harmonic series by logarithms (a precursor to Euler's summation formula) and was the first to use power series with confidence and to revert power series." In the words of my six-year-old... "Wait, what?"

chapters ago I discussed the many contributions of Galileo (#12) to the field. In fact, Galileo beat Newton to his first law of motion (see below), which, fairly enough, earned the former credit from the latter. Nevertheless, Newton defined mechanics for the modern age.

Was his idea inspired by an apple falling from a tree? Perhaps, although it didn't land on his head.[10] Regardless, it's a helpful image. Newton wondered why things fell straight down, as if falling objects had plotted a course toward the center of Earth before being denied entry by its surface. He wondered if all motion could be as predictable as an apple falling straight down.

In time, he discovered that it could. To explain, he developed his three hallmark laws of motion:

"Every body persists in its state of being at rest or of moving uniformly straight forward, except insofar as it is compelled to change its state by force impressed."

"The alteration of motion is ever proportional to the motive force impressed; and is made in the direction of the right line in which that force is impressed."

"To every action there is always opposed an equal reaction: or the mutual actions of two bodies upon each other are always equal, and directed to contrary parts."

In other words, due to inertia, an object at rest or moving in one direction stays that way unless acted upon by an external force (the first law). To move or predict the motion of anything, one needs to know that the acceleration and direction of an object in motion depends on the force or action applied to it (the second law). Finally, once the action is

---

[10] Who do we have to thank for the propagation of the apple story? None other than the 22nd most influential figure in Western history, Voltaire! (A vociferous anti-Leibnizian, by the way).

applied, one must also consider that for every action there's an equal and opposite reaction (the third law).[11]

Newton not only explained that these laws existed, but he also paired with them useful equations. His second law, for example, teaches us that $F = ma$, or force equals mass times acceleration. If one knows how massive something is and how fast one wants to move it, then one knows the amount of force that is necessary to do the moving.

The laws of motion alone would have placed him among the few most relevant scientists in history. These discoveries have since been endlessly applicable to what we do on this planet. Newton, however, was not satisfied with just figuring out how our planet's mechanics work. He assumed his laws could apply everywhere in the universe.

Building off the astronomical work of Galileo and Johannes Kepler, he deduced his law of universal gravitation. Just like the massive Earth pulls the tiny apple, Newton believed all objects in the universe pull toward each other, and the amount they pull toward each other is inversely proportional to their mass and distance.

Once again, he developed an equation to explain his law and apply its findings:

[12]
$$F = G\frac{m_1 m_2}{r^2}$$

---

[11] Wikipedia helps us understand these laws by asking us to imagine two standing ice skaters, one of which pushes the other, presumably because the two are rivals for a medal at the Lillehammer Winter Olympics. The first skater pushes the second so that the second starts sliding on the ice (the first law). The direction and speed of the second skater depend on the force and direction that the first skater applied to her (second law). Finally, the first skater is also affected by her pushing of the second skater; she'll feel force in the opposite direction and at a predictable speed (the third law).

[12] Obviously.

To find the gravitational "Force" one body has on another, we must multiply the masses of each object (**m1** and **m2**) and divide that number by the square of the distance (**r², or r squared**) between the centers of the objects, before then multiplying that number by Newton's **Gravitational constant**.[13] The equation revealed that the more mass an object had, the more it would pull at all other objects in the universe—with a greater effect on objects that were closer and/or smaller.

Together, Newton's calculus, laws of motion, and gravitational equation not only explained but *predicted* the motion of bodies in the solar system, including the moon, comets, other planets, the earth, and any apple that plummets to its surface. It was a cohesive theory of why and how things move, and it all acted like clockwork. His findings would later be applied to everything man would create for the purpose of moving, from cars to planes to rockets.

Two decades after the Great Plague shut Cambridge's doors and allowed Newton time to think, he put all these ideas into history's most important scientific work—1687's "Philosophiæ Naturalis Principia Mathematica," usually called "the Principia."[14] With its publication, physics finally arrived in modernity.

The above ideas were the highlights of his illustrious career, but in his decades as the world's principal scientist Newton contributed in a host of more minor ways. He was the first to compute a nearly accurate speed of

---

[13] You can play along at home: the value of "G" is 6.674×10^{-11} N·kg^{-2}·m^{2}. Have fun, kids!

[14] He was aided and funded by English astronomer Edmund Halley, who a few years later predicted the return of our solar system's most famous comet. Of Newton's book, French physicist Pierre-Simon Laplace, sometimes called "the Newton of France," opined: "The Principia is preeminent above any other production of human genius."

Isaac Newton

sound (falling short only because no one knew sound waves affect and are affected by temperature); he correctly inferred that Earth was an oblate sphere; his laws helped him predict the tides, the slow precession of Earth's axis, and the trajectory of comets; he advanced acoustics and the binomial theorem; he organized a law of cooling; and so much more. A fantastic number of terms in science and math are named after him. It felt like he could figure out anything, an assumption acknowledged by Italian-French philosopher Joseph-Louis Lagrance when he offered, "Newton was the greatest genius that ever existed, and the most fortunate, for we cannot find more than once a system of the world to establish."

Newton also dabbled in the affairs of the state. Late in the 1600s, he served two terms as a member of Parliament. At the turn of the century, he was made Master of the Royal Mint. In 1705, Queen Anne recognized this lifetime of contribution with a knighthood. About a century after Sir Francis Bacon received the honor, Sir Isaac Newton became only the second scientist to be knighted.

Newton never had a wife, partly because he was married to science and partly because he was, by all accounts, a difficult man. Traditionalists predictably pushed back on his new theories. Some even believed that his proposition that an unseen force acted upon and between all things was mystical heresy. Newton combatively defended his work, solidifying his cantankerous reputation. He may have even suffered a nervous breakdown by the end his life, a condition perhaps hastened by mercury poisoning via his hobby of alchemy. Regardless of the cause, his condition deteriorated in his old age, a period when he experienced constant abdominal agony and digestive problems.

Finally, on March 31, 1727, death relieved the pain of history's greatest scientist at the age of 84. Sir Isaac Newton, the infant who could fit in a quart mug, the boy from an illiterate farmer family, the young man who almost failed out of school, was buried alongside kings and queens in Westminster Abbey.

We can call him the founder of modern science, math, and physics. He had inherited a smattering of disjointed, often inaccurate, and generally inapplicable theories about how the world and universe worked and bequeathed to us a grand unified theory of predictable, universal mechanics, including workable ways to create the machines and vehicles that could help us understand even more about everything around us. He not only set off revolutions in optics, mathematics, mechanics, and gravity, he showed the interplay between those fields as if they were a single arithmetical system. No one else had approached that level of scientific contribution.[15]

These discoveries unleashed what science, which was still stubbornly perceived by some to be merely theoretical, could actually *do*. Without Newton, Henry Ford (#20) wouldn't have created an efficient assembly line or the world's most popular automobile. Thomas Edison (#18) wouldn't have harnessed light, or James Watt (#5) steam. Without Newton, the Wright brothers don't take to the sky, astronauts don't take to space, and we don't have geosynchronous satellites allowing you to conveniently purchase a book on the 30 most influential figures in Western history.[16] Almost all of today's engineering and physics are built on the foundation of Newton's models. No person in history is more important to our modern scientific era.

And yet, he's only ranked third. Third! Can I justify that without fully revealing my top two?

---

[15] Recognizing Newton's unique genius, William Wordsworth, the English poet, described him as *"a mind forever/voyaging through strange seas alone."*

[16] Perish the thought!

Isaac Newton

I can try. Over the last few chapters, my entries have made clear that I most value the impact a figure has on setting up our modern world. That explained why someone like Martin Luther (#6) could be ranked above Jesus of Nazareth (#7), the man around which Luther's religion was based. I told you I had determined the six most important movements in the West's development, and essentially selected each period's most important ambassador for my top six. Martin Luther represents the Reformation, James Watt (#5) the Industrial Revolution, and John Locke (#4) the Enlightenment. In this chapter, Isaac Newton represents the culmination of the Scientific Revolution.

Still, when it comes to these all-time influential figures, I had to find some criteria to rank them against each other. Part of the equation is ranking the importance of a movement. Though few things are more important than the Protestant Reformation, I believe the Industrial Revolution is one of them, so Luther fell in a head-to-head against Watt. At the same time, I also had to factor in the degree to which a figure's contributions were fundamental to that era. I see the Enlightenment as nearly on par with the Industrial Revolution in giving us our modern world, but Locke's effects on his movement were more significant than Watt's on his, so Locke made my Top 4 (my historical "Mount Rushmore") while Watt had to settle for number 5.

As for Newton's Scientific Revolution, it made both the Industrial Revolution and Enlightenment possible. Newton boiling everything down to equations made it much more accessible. He mainstreamed science unlike anyone had done before him, which directly made possible the Industrial Revolution. Furthermore, Newton's explanation of natural laws inspired the Enlightenment, where natural laws and the attempt to predict everything lay central to the philosophers' worldviews. Newton's revelation that the entire universe was organized and subject to rationality and predictability inspired philosophers to apply his approach to everything, including political science. Both movements were founded on an objective approach to solving problems, essentially injecting the effective scientific method into industry and philosophy.

Therefore, as the greatest ambassador of this era of great import, Newton leaps ahead of Watt and Locke and into the top three. His ranking outside the top two, however, should lead you to a conclusion: either I've determined our top two figures' movements to be more impactful on Western history than even the Scientific Revolution, or I've determined they are more paramount to comparably important eras than the figures that came before them, or both.

That brings me to where Newton falls just a bit short of wearing the Top 30 crown. Not only did Newton not start the Scientific Revolution, he wasn't even close. The truest catalyst to the era is Nicolaus Copernicus (#28), who published his major work on heliocentricity nearly 150 years before Newton published "the Principia."

Dozens of influential scientists came between Copernicus and Newton. Many of them have been mentioned in this book. There's that Englishman who earned a knighthood before Newton—Sir Francis Bacon—who a century before Newton formalized the scientific method for the modern West. There's Galileo and his role as a sort of proto-Newton. We should also remember that while Newton developed calculus, Gottfried Leibniz independently did the same. As Newton developed his law of gravitation, fellow English scientist Robert Hooke made strides in the field as well. The 1600s was that kind of century.

It's relevant that Newton rose in an era when science was already accepted and embraced by European intellectuals. Thus, though Copernicus had feared publishing his heliocentric theory and waited until the year he died, and Galileo was put on trial for heresy and condemned to house arrest, Newton was lauded across the West as a celebrity genius. He was clearly aided by a sociopolitical acceptance of science made possible by his predecessors, which eased his path toward greatness.

Meanwhile, an even stronger counterargument might actually reside not with those that came before him, but with someone who came after. Newton may have had the advantages Copernicus and Galileo did not, but at least he became the greatest scientist who had ever lived. It's hard to ask for much more than that. The problem, however, is that two centuries later someone rivaled him for that title. Albert Einstein (#11) pointed out that Newton's laws don't quite work all the time, particularly when dealing with objects that are very small or moving very fast. He also seemed to better understand gravitation not as an attraction between two forces but the result of mass actually curving space-time, which creates a kind of well that pulls in other objects. Indeed, thanks to Einstein, an entirely new subset of mechanics—quantum mechanics—was created in order to transcend Newton's. Sir Isaac's version was thereafter relegated to a term that implies a measure of archaism: "classical" mechanics.

Combined, these two counterarguments—that Newton was but the greatest of many scientists from his progressive era and Einstein ultimately superseded him in some ways—keep Newton from the top two.

They won't, however, lower him any further. In both cases, the practicability of Newton's laws mostly acquits him of the charges. Einstein was hugely important, of course—after all, I ranked him as the 11th most influential figure in Western history—but much of his work was either theoretical or its relevance was limited to people in white lab coats who work at MIT or CERN. The applicability of quantum theory is limited, especially in comparison to the almost universal usefulness of Newton's laws.

Though Copernicus and others trail-blazed Newton's path, no scientist had yet offered the kind of real-world relevance on the scale of Newton. Copernicus, for instance, told us the sun was at the center of the solar system, but there was little to be done with that information. Before

Newton, science was still a field reserved for the most educated or wealthy intellectuals of the West.

Newton, with his colossal contributions to optics, math, physics, and gravity, helped transition science from a potentially temporary fad enjoyed by a small circle of elites to a permanent and widespread centerpiece of Western culture. Copernicus and Galileo may have ushered in modern science, but it is Newton who centered it. After Newton conjured, diagrammed, and proved his laws, no serious Western thinker could attack science as pointless, immoral, or wrong. He helped us comprehend our universe, and he even brought us closer to traveling into it. It is Newton's laws that made it possible for us to expand humanity's horizon. Indeed, we have a spacecraft that has departed our solar system for interstellar space, and it's as if Newton sits in the cockpit.

Ultimately, Isaac Newton pushed us in a particular direction, and then inertia brought us to our modern world. How appropriate. For these reasons, the man that literally taught us what makes the world go round is the third most influential figure in Western history.

#2: Johannes Gutenberg

"The discovery of the art of printing unbarred afresh the gates of Heaven, and let in that flood of light, of knowledge, and of wisdom, which enabled men to emancipate themselves again from the slavery of superstition—to take their proper place in the ranks of created beings—and in ennobling themselves, in gradually exalting their understandings and amending their hearts, to pay at length the worthiest homage to the goodness of their common Parent, and prove themselves to be—as the Almighty himself originally formed them—inferior only to the Angels."

—Sir William Hamilton

L et's do something fun. Let's plot on a timeline the lifespans of those ranked on this nearly finished Top 30 list.

Who Made the West

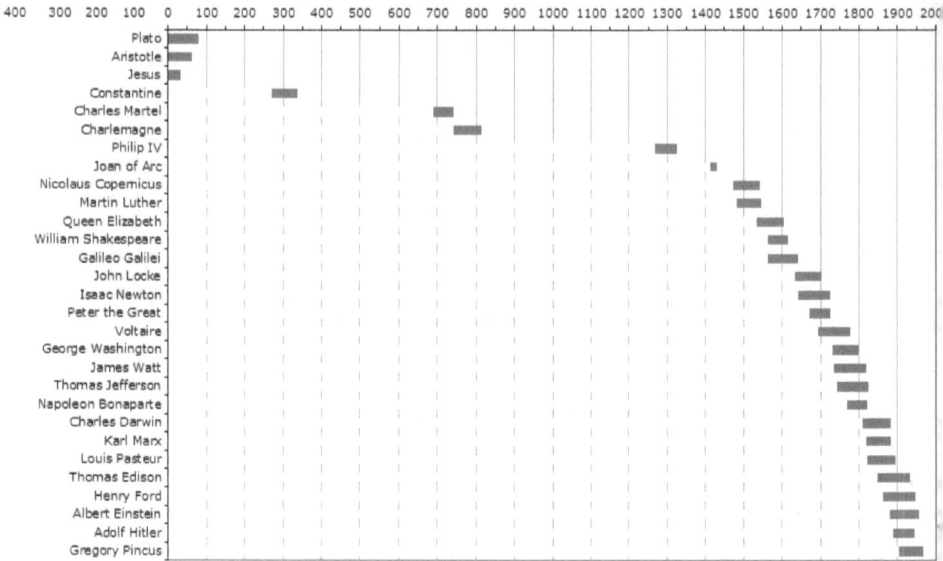

Fascinating. Of the 29 people discussed so far, only seven dot the two thousand years between 500 BCE and 1500 CE. In the five hundred years since, however, 22 figures crowd the timeline. What can we infer from this sudden explosion of influential figures?

Something important happened in the 1400s, and this something changed everything else. This something was modern history's most important invention: the printing press. Its inventor was Johannes Gutenberg, the second most influential figure in Western history.

To best understand the magnitude of Gutenberg's importance, one must first understand what the Western world was like before his contribution. For a thousand years, the West had been mired in the Middle

Johannes Gutenberg

Ages. As many entries have discussed, the Middle Ages, though not totally without contributions, was not our proudest historical hour.

Among the reasons for its intellectual stagnancy was rampant illiteracy. This illiteracy resulted from books only being written and copied by hand. Those who did so were usually monks—a sliver of the population.

The copying process was a slow, painstaking one. For example, history's most popular book, the Bible, took a year or two to copy by hand. This inefficiency severely limited the number of available books. Across all of Europe, it's estimated there were only 30,000 copies of books.[1] That figure combines works of philosophy, science, literature, law, and everything else. Books were *rare*.

Due to their scarcity, accessing books was almost impossible, and there were intellectually devastating consequences. One cannot learn to read if one cannot practice reading, and with so few written sources, practice was impractical. Clergy were literate, but, with some exceptions—thank you, Charlemagne (#21)—laymen generally were not. Few people could learn to read on their own, so few people got that smart, so few people wrote new ideas into books or other written materials. Any potential authors couldn't make much money if copying was difficult and literate consumers were rare. All these factors resulted in books being rare, which, of course, was also the initial cause of all these limitations. Thus, what plagued Europe for centuries was a perpetuated cycle of ignorance:

---

[1] In comparison, the library in the Connecticut high school in which I work, which serves about 800 students, has approximately 10,000 books, or about one-third of the total books in western Europe before Gutenberg. The largest medieval library (in Paris) housed about a thousand books, a *tenth* of what my high school brandishes on its metallic shelves.

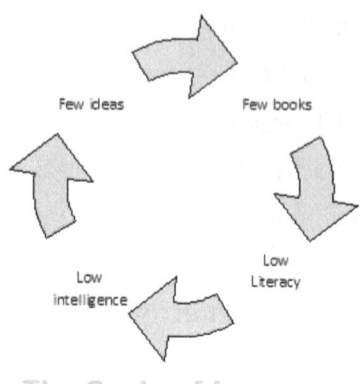

The Cycle of Ignorance

Then along came Johannes Gutenberg.

Despite his place as one of history's most important people, no one on this list was less well known during their lifetime. We can't narrow down the date of his birth—it came sometime between 1394 and 1404—but we do know it occurred in the town of Mainz, part of the German Holy Roman Empire. His father was a merchant and possibly a goldsmith for the bishop of Mainz. After Gutenberg's birth, a question mark hovers over the early part of his biography.[2] Little is known about his life until he

---

[2] It's a dark spot that symbolizes historical records' rarity before Gutenberg transformed the production and consumption of the written word.

Johannes Gutenberg

resurfaces historically with a letter from 1434 Strasbourg.[3] He remained there for at least the next decade, during which he unveiled, to characteristically little fanfare, a new invention.

In perhaps 1439, he finished work on his printing press. Converting a machine typically used for pressing grapes or olives, Gutenberg placed in it metal casts of letters that could be arranged into any order.[4] Onto them he'd put oil-based ink before pressing absorbent paper onto that. The paper then peels up with the letters stamped onto it. The printer could quickly create many copies of a page before rearranging the casts and moving on to the next page. When he finished all the copies of as many pages as he needed, he could bind pages in the right order and make as many leaflets, pamphlets, or books as he needed. It was arduous, but it was hundreds of times faster than quilling a hand-written copy.

A few years after finishing this invention, he moved back to Mainz with the hopes of converting his creation into a profitable business. In 1448, he apparently took out a loan from his brother-in-law for that purpose. By 1450, he began printing commercially. The first Western printed material to ever be sold was likely a German poem.

---

[3] Historians' best theories at this interim period wonder if his family fled Mainz with other upper-middle class folk after an uprising; that he attended the University of Erfurt; and that he became an accomplished tinkerer who earned a living as a smith (gold and black). These are educated guesses, but guesses nonetheless. Considering his importance, it really is rather remarkable how little we know about him.

[4] Fun fact: early printers stored capital letters in a shelf above the little letters, which sat in a case. With the capital letters above and the smaller letters below, they earned the nickname "upper case" and "lower case." Isn't history the best?

Still looking to scale upward, Gutenberg took out yet another loan—this time from wealthy investor and future printer himself, Johann Faust—before then taking on printing's first apprentice, Peter Schöffer. They were soon joined by as many as 25 craftsmen for the labor. With financial backing and many pairs of hands, he was ready to assemble 180 copies of history's greatest printed treasure—the 42-lined Gutenberg Bible.[5] It quickly sold out and became a sensation. The book was discussed even at the highest levels of the clergy.[6] It seemed the hardworking smith from Mainz was on the verge of wealth and fame.

He wasn't. His genius, insofar as the most important invention since the earliest days of civilization is a work of genius, did not expand to two crucial areas. First, he did not know how to become wealthy and famous. For example, he didn't write his name anywhere on the Gutenberg Bible or anything else he printed, so he had a weak claim that the press was his intellectual property. He never took advantage of having literally the best invention ever for getting his name out to consumers.

Similarly, though he was the best at copying books, he never quite learned how to balance them. Money frequently went unaccounted for. When his investors came looking for their annual principle plus interest, they grew increasingly impatient with Gutenberg's squandering. Faust

---

[5] Only 21 complete copies remain. None have been sold since 1978, when a copy auctioned for $2.2 million. If one were to be sold today, estimates have their worth at between $25 and $35 million each. You should get one.

[6] While still a bishop, the future Pope Pius II wrote to a cardinal: *"All that has been written to me about that marvelous man seen at Frankfurt [sic] is true. I have not seen complete Bibles but only a number of quires of various books of the Bible. The script was very neat and legible, not at all difficult to follow—your grace would be able to read it without effort, and indeed without glasses."* I smell a dust jacket blurb!

Johannes Gutenberg

took him to court, and, insult to injury, apprentice Schöffer testified against his teacher.[7] Faust won, and Gutenberg turned over his Bible profits, machinery, and supplies to pay off the debt. Worse yet, Faust and Schöffer began replicating Gutenberg's invention and did a much better job of promoting themselves and monetizing the process.

Gutenberg, now bankrupted and in his 60s, had little hope for a second career. Historians think he cobbled together a humble shop for some small printing jobs, but since he still didn't mark anything with his name, we can't be sure. As Faust and Schöffer enjoyed the fruits of Gutenberg's labor, he plunged back into anonymity. A late recognition from Mainz's archbishop netted him a title and stipend, but it was too little too late.

Perhaps 70 years old in 1468, Gutenberg died from old age and obscurity. It would take four decades before a historian correctly identified him as the inventor of modern printing. He was buried by a church that, along with its cemetery, was later demolished. His remains are lost.

Though history tried hard to forget Johannes Gutenberg, it was forever changed by him. He had given birth to a "printing revolution" that reverberated across every intellectual field in the West. From science to philosophy, government to religion, it was a turning point in Western civilization.

In my most recent entries, I've noted how each of my top six represents what I consider the most important eras of Western history: Martin Luther (#6) the Reformation, James Watt (#5) the Industrial Revolution,

---

[7] It was right around this time that Schöffer married Faust's daughter, which might explain the betrayal. At the very least we've got a sufficient "B Plot" to a Gutenberg biopic. Really, Spielberg, I'm right here.

John Locke (#4) the Enlightenment, and Isaac Newton (#3) the Scientific Revolution. Before each of them, as printers erected presses across Europe, the Renaissance spread across the continent. Though the return of Greco-Roman appreciation pre-dated the printing press, the invention allowed more Europeans than ever to acquire, peruse, and be stimulated by Greek and Roman texts. More importantly, as news of technology, politics, religion, science, and the arts spread through printed newspapers and books, education rose. Ideas spread across the West and survived long enough to be built upon by the next great minds. Europe's intellectual rebirth allowed each of the aforementioned movements to begin and thrive, and the modern world was made possible.

To be fair, some kinds of printing predated Gutenberg. The Chinese invented woodblock printing as early as the third century, and the Koreans and Japanese had the ability to print books a few centuries after that. The earliest printed book dates from 868 Tang Dynasty China. Near the turn of the millennium, historians think Bì Shēng, using porcelain ceramic for his letter casts, was the first to invent movable type. Much of this technology had even arrived in Europe before Gutenberg's invention. For some, these forerunners might cast doubt on Gutenberg's importance.

But they shouldn't. All of these predecessors were severely limited, and none could have unleashed what the Gutenberg press did. Whether using wood or porcelain, the process used by the East was difficult and the machine delicate. For example, entirely new woodblocks had to be created for new books, a big disincentive for mass production. Meanwhile, wood and ceramic letters regularly broke. Indeed, the technology was rarely even used for books; instead, cloth design, mostly on silk, was the principle purpose of Asian printing. The existing technology had

Johannes Gutenberg

neither the capacity nor the intent to create the kind of literary change Gutenberg catalyzed.

Gutenberg was the first to combine metal casts for movable letters (instead of fragile wood and ceramics), oil-based ink (more durable than traditional water-based ink), soft and absorbent paper (for clarity and the express purpose of reading rather than wearing), and an innovative idea to repurpose the era's screw presses to print mechanically for the first time in history.

With these modifications, his new invention became more than the sum of its upgraded parts. Gutenberg's mechanical press was orders of magnitude better than all of its ancestors. It was the sturdiest ever, the fastest ever, and it copied the clearest writing ever—all by a wide margin over earlier presses. As a result, it made possible the mass production of pamphlets, leaflets, journals, and books.

It's hard to know where to begin describing the printing press's importance, because it so dramatically revolutionized the Western world in countless ways. History itself is the study of recorded material, and part of what made eras like Europe's "Dark Ages" so "dark" was because of the lack of written material left behind. With the printing press, however, we've since had increasingly copious amounts of written material with which we can record events and from which we can learn about them. The field of history is more indebted to him than anyone since the anonymous Sumerian and Phoenician creators of writing itself.

Furthermore, recall the "cycle of ignorance" I described earlier: the lack of written materials hindered the process of learning to read, which meant few people learned much and therefore did not conjure new ideas of their own to write about.

399

Gutenberg smashed this sluggish cycle. Because printed books and other materials were easier to produce, they could also be sold cheaper, and their prices steadily dropped as the practice of printing improved. Affordability meant accessibility, and accessibility meant Europeans were on the verge of an intellectual revolution. By speeding up the copying of books several hundred fold (a pace which would gradually quicken over the ensuing decades and centuries), it allowed many more people to learn to read works on all topics, become smarter, and build new ideas on top of old ones.

And what did they do with those new ideas? They published them! Gutenberg didn't just break the cycle of ignorance. He replaced it with a new cycle—the cycle of intelligence:

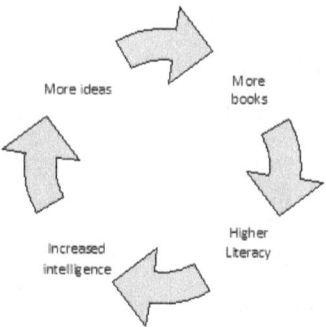

The Cycle of Intelligence

As a result, by the end of the fifteenth century, Europe went from having about 30,000 copies of books to about 30,000 different *titles* numbering 20 *million* copies. A century later, the number was ten times that much. By the dawn of the nineteenth century, Europeans had a billion books at their disposal.

Johannes Gutenberg

This printing revolution quickly produced mammoth change. The change in how we acquired information, for example, was profound. Before Gutenberg, an illiterate population hardly ever received "news." Not only were there few day-to-day developments that we would consider newsworthy, but to receive news someone usually needed someone else to directly tell it to them. Word-of-mouth news spread at a crawling pace. Most medieval Europeans were isolated in villages and small towns, and they might not receive important news for years.

The printing press marked a turning point in how news and ideas spread. They had never been passed on so easily. Soon, pamphlets, newspapers, and books could spread ideas more efficiently and make them more ubiquitous than ever before. Additionally, though the invention of writing already allowed one's ideas to survive one's lifetime, it's not until the printing press where that became commonplace. Human consciousness had never been so extended, its ideas so immortal.

As a literate middle class gradually filled out alongside clergy, royalty, and nobility, the upper class's monopoly on information—which had been only sporadically allowed to others, and only when it suited their purpose—shattered into a thousand pieces. Knowledge is power, and both began to steadily slip away from the grips of elites. As information grew relatively unrestricted, it became increasingly difficult to keep people in the dark. Mysticism and authoritarianism steadily faded as revolutionary scientific and political ideas formulated by educated writers took hold. The Church and strong-man governments continued censoring, but after the printing press it became exceedingly difficult to do so. The information revolution was underway; alongside the printing press eventually came newspapers, radio, television, and the internet. The era of mass communication was born, and it was Gutenberg who had birthed it.

Gutenberg's liberation of knowledge allowed the masses to become progressively more informed.

As they did so, they recognized their collective power, which allowed our democratic age. Few things are more central to Western culture than a liberated society with a free press educating it, and none of that would have been possible without the printing press. Some may complain about bad press, biased media, muckraking, or fake news, but the alternative to free press is downright dystopian.

Another way to compare the importance of Gutenberg with the importance of Bì Shēng and the other early east Asian printers is to consider the impacts their printing had on each region's destiny. China, which at the time was the more advanced region, continued printing in its traditional, limited ways. However, it didn't fully adopt the new European-style printing until the nineteenth century. By that time, of course, the West had far surpassed the East's science and technology. That incredible Western charge was made possible by Gutenberg's press, which sparked Western innovation and, thanks to more rapid communication, brought the West under the same cultural umbrella. Due to the printing press, we consolidated from a collection of isolated villages and cities to a broader, communicative Western civilization that shares news, collectively enjoys breakthroughs, celebrates together when news is good, and consoles each other when it's bad.

Put another way, Gutenberg was instrumental in creating modern Western history. If one accepts the conventional divvying of Western history into its three eras, ancient Greece and Rome comprised our admirable classical period before Rome's fall allowed the regressive and fragmented Middle Ages. The modern era followed as a sort of course correction.

Johannes Gutenberg

It was Gutenberg who plotted that new course, one on which we've cruised for the last five centuries. Eventually, most people on this ranking—22 of the 29 so far listed, remember—reaped the benefits of Gutenberg's invention. Of note, many of the important inventions of the Industrial Revolution were imminent whether or not Marconi invented the radio or Bell the telephone. Other planes were being worked on during the Wright brothers' time. Daguerre was one of several fathers of photography. But as far as we can tell, Gutenberg was the only Westerner even considering a device such as his. We could be decades or even centuries behind without him.

It's as if he's the trunk of a tree, and nearly all of the influential figures since Gutenberg are its branches. Luther's fiery Reformation, for example, would have been snuffed out before it burned down the Church's hegemony. The birth of modern individualism was therefore fathered by Gutenberg; Christianity and the route to salvation would never have been personalized without a literate population that could read plenty of Bibles.

Soon after Luther, Copernicus (#28) published his book on the heliocentric theory, inaugurating the Scientific Revolution. This scientific awakening made possible the likes of Galileo (#12) and Newton (#3), both of whom set up Einstein (#11). The Scientific Revolution then made possible the Enlightenment, where Voltaire (#22) and Locke (#4) posited new theories on government, which in turn inspired Jefferson (#24) and Washington (#14) to lead the American Revolution, which itself inspired similar revolutions across the West, including the one that allowed the rise of Napoleon (#16).

Like these other areas, the Industrial Revolution—catalyzed by Watt (#5) before later culminating with figures like Edison (#18) and Ford

(#20)—was another productive movement of world-changing ideas made possible by the Western world's literate, forward-looking, newfound intelligence.

Without the printing press, Pincus (#25) and Pasteur (#8) would not have had laboratories to make discoveries to help humanity thrive. Darwin (#15) could not have humbled us, Hitler (#17) could not have threatened us, and Marx (#9) could not have rallied half the planet to his ideology. Shakespeare (#10) would have neither the background to understand our souls nor the means with which to move them.

Without Gutenberg, none of these figures would have been inspired by people before them nor could they inspire others after. He's that important. As history moves forward, more influential figures will come and go, some of whom will elbow their way onto rankings such as these. Those figures, too, will be but branches and leaves on Gutenberg's tree.

The man almost forgotten by time is now timeless. For making possible the incredible advancement of the last five centuries, Johannes Gutenberg is the second most influential figure in Western history.[8]

---

[8] Who could possibly beat that? You're about to find out.

#1: Christopher Columbus

"He gave the world another world."
—George Santayana on Christopher Columbus, *Poems*

A long time ago, in an Arctic region far away, Earth looked a bit different than it does today. Around 15 to 20 thousand years ago, as much of the planet shivered in its last ice age, large polar ice caps soaked up some of Earth's oceans. As a result, global sea levels dropped by over a hundred meters. These retreating oceans revealed land normally topped by shallow water.

For the next few millennia, humanity's original diaspora—out of Africa to Asia and Europe—was no longer contained to its original continents. Thousands of nomadic migrants were able to travel over a temporary land bridge under what is now the shallow Bering Strait between modern Russia and Alaska.

These nomads gradually spread across two new land masses. In the process, they became the first immigrants to this new part of the world. We now know them as the first Americans.

Then, about 12 thousand years ago, the ice age ended. The warmer climate re-melted some of each ice cap. Sea levels rose, our familiar coastlines formed, and oceans again isolated the two halves of the world. With no written history, all knowledge of the world's other half was lost within a generation of the last people to cross over the Arctic pass.

In the millennia to follow, the peoples on the separated hemispheres diverged in countless cultural ways. Coastal dwellers on each half of the planet stared over endless water, clueless of what was on the other side. Unbeknownst to them, their long-lost cousins stared back.

And then, after all those thousands of years, someone organized a family reunion. His name was Christopher Columbus, the most influential figure in Western history.

In 1451, right around the time Germany's Johannes Gutenberg (#2) began work on history's first mass-produced book, about 500 miles south of him, in the Italian city-state of Genoa, a future explorer was born—Cristoforo Colombo. As the Middle Ages gradually gave way to the modern period, his family eked out a living as part of the growing middle class. His father, Domenico Colombo, was a Genoese weaver, cheese maker, and tavern keeper. He worked all these jobs to provide for his family. It was a stressful, claustrophobic living that partially explains why Cristoforo left home as a young man and took to the Mediterranean.

He first climbed aboard a boat at age 10 and quickly fell in love with the open water. By 19 he had secured his first commission; the teenage Columbus manned a Genoese warship headed toward the Kingdom of

Naples in an attempt to support René of Anjou's claim to its throne.[1] During his 20s he boarded any ship that would take him. The young Columbus docked at ports from Greece to Ireland to Guinea. In 1477, sensing Portugal as the future of seafaring, he moved to Lisbon, where he lived for the next seven years.

He was wise to trust his senses. Portugal's navy was ascendant. Fifteenth century Portuguese seamen enjoyed a prominent patron in the kingdom's royal family—Prince Henry the Navigator (1394-1460). Henry promoted Portuguese exploration for decades. He encouraged Portuguese exploration along the West African coast, and each expedition pushed further south. With an ultimate goal of sailing around Africa to India and China, Portuguese explorers inched closer and closer to Africa's southern tip. Even after Henry's death, momentum carried Portugal further. By 1462, Portugal had reached modern Sierra Leone.

An efficient trade route to East Asia was the dream of European leaders and traders. Though the Far East was little more than rumor to most Westerners, some Eastern commodities had traveled between the two extremes of the Old World. Ancient trading routes—most notably the Royal Road of the Persian Empire and the Silk Road that linked China to the Romans—served as sufficient if arduous pathways of material exchange. Closer to Columbus's time, fellow Italian Marco Polo (1254-1324) had spent over two decades traveling to and from Asia, including living in China for years. Polo recorded his experiences and

---

[1] Though relatively obscure, Count René is a fascinating figure of the early modern period. He had connections to Columbus, Leonardo da Vinci, the Medici family, and Joan of Arc (#27) while shrewdly angling his way into a dozen noble and regal titles. The website Ancient Origins honored him with a *Game of Thrones* comparison, dubbing him the Renaissance's "Littlefinger."

returned to publish his often exaggerated findings of China's extreme wealth. Polo's embellishments made the East's call powerfully seductive.

As these drips of goods and information leaked into the West, Europeans gradually saw east Asia as a considerably luxurious region with valuable exotic goods. Western leaders and merchants dreamed of directly securing gems, silk, and spices then selling them for colossal profit to eager Western consumers. Though these goods were rare in Europe, their assumed ubiquity in India and China would make them cheap purchases.

The hard part, of course, was acquiring these goods in Asia and returning them to Europe in an efficient, relatively cheap way in order to sell them for a meaningful profit. For most of history, Western merchants had been content to use the old pathways and the Arab world as a sort of trading hub between the two peoples.[2] It was not an ideal approach, however. Response time for demand was extremely slow. The most practical route from Paris to Beijing measures over six thousand miles, or about a two-year round trip on foot. Natural hindrances—mountains, deserts, and hot climate—were sizable challenges for traders working the route, as were robbers. A still greater deterrent was the sheer cost of a trading expedition, since an intrepid trader required assistants and pack animals, all of which must be paid and/or fed. These costs eroded a trader's profits.

Most Western merchants didn't even venture the route themselves; instead, they hired local "middlemen" who would travel a small leg of the

---

[2] The Arab world's location as Westerners' halfway point to the Far East earned it a nickname that has stuck despite a spherical world making it nonsensical—the "Middle" East. As Western and Eastern ideas and goods converged there, the Middle East, for a time, advanced beyond them both.

journey and transact the money and goods with other middlemen at points along the way. There could be a dozen or so of these middlemen, each of whom would of course require a fee. Often some goods or money would go "missing."

Worst yet, in the centuries before Columbus, the relationship between Westerners and the Arabs soured. The aggressive Seljuk Turks grabbed control of the Holy Land in the early 1000s and destroyed important Christian sites. The Crusades to defend Christianity and recapture these lands further tarnished the West's relations with the Middle East. In 1453, the Ottoman Turks conquered Constantinople, which ended the Christian Byzantine Empire and cut off the primary passage in and out of Europe through modern Istanbul. After Polo's findings had piqued the interest of the West, trade with the East became more difficult than at any point since ancient Rome.

And so, by the 1400s, we find a confluence of factors that encouraged Westerners to find a different route to Asia: an intense desire to acquire more Eastern goods, aspirations to do so efficiently, and the loss of trading options through the Middle East. Under those circumstances, one can understand why Portugal looked to sail around Africa. Ships could carry more goods than caravans, "middlemen" were unnecessary, Muslim lands could be avoided, and even the circuitous sea route would be faster and safer than traversing thousands of miles hoping to avoid deserts and mountains.

By 1488, Portugal arrived on the cusp of success when explorer Bartolomeu Dias reached Africa's southernmost point.[3] As Dias raced home to tell Portuguese leadership of his achievement, Christopher Columbus was 37 years old and an accomplished navigator and captain. He had monitored Portugal's exploration with much interest, but he was critical of the plan. It had taken Dias about seven months to sail from Portugal to the tip of southern Africa, which was further away than anyone had guessed. A mission around Africa and all the way to India would likely take ten months to a year—and twice that for a round trip. It wouldn't be that much faster than a land route.

Columbus had a better idea.

A few years earlier, in 1485, Columbus had been granted an audience with Portugal's King John II, and he came armed with a daring proposal. He claimed that navigating around Africa made the journey to Asia needlessly long. Columbus's alternative was that sailing across the "Great Western Ocean"—what we now call the Atlantic—would reach Asia in a straight shot. In other words, to reach the East, he would sail... west.

West!

Columbus vowed to cross the ocean, reach Asia, and return much quicker than a circum-African route would take.

---

[3] The region had rough seas, so Dias named it *Cabo das Tormentas*—the Cape of Storms. King John II, not wanting other Portuguese explorers to be dissuaded, commanded a new name: *Cabo da Boa Esperança*—the Cape of Good Hope.

Christopher Columbus

A round Earth was an accepted assumption by educated Europeans[4], one that made Columbus's premise conceivable, even in King John's eyes. However, it was the *size* of the planet that was still up for debate. Columbus thought this optimistically fast journey was possible due to some dubious, contemporary calculations that Asia lay only 2,400 miles to Europe's west.

King John considered Columbus's proposal, but he ultimately rejected it. Though in theoretical agreement about a western voyage eventually reaching Asia, competing estimates over the size of the earth—and, therefore, the size of the Great Western Ocean—made it a risky investment. Columbus had asked for several ships, crews to staff them, and supplies to keep them all alive—all for a mission that might never return. Portuguese progress sailing down the coast of Africa was slow, but at least it was safe. The persistent Columbus returned three years later, but John, who soon received news of Dias's accomplishment, had even less incentive to acquiesce. Portugal was on the precipice of establishing its Indian trade route without Columbus's gamble.

---

[4] Were you taught that everyone assumed the earth was flat until Columbus proved it was round? If so, you were taught wrongly. First of all, Columbus sailing to America and back proved nothing about the earth's shape. More than that, there was no flat earth assumption to disprove! A round earth had been known to Westerners dating back to, of course, the ancient Greeks. The evidence abounded: the earth casts a rounded shadow during a lunar eclipse; ships that sail over the horizon slowly descend into it; constellations can rise higher in the sky or be blocked altogether, depending on one's latitude; places on Earth get different amounts of daylight at different times; and more. Unlike, say, heliocentrism, the round-Earth premise was generally not lost by educated Europeans, even during the Middle Ages. The Church was not invested in a flat earth like they were geocentricity.

Incredibly, we have flat-earthers today, because of course we do.

Columbus, disappointed but headstrong, searched for a new patron. He returned to his home peninsula and met with leaders of two accomplished seafaring city-states: Venice and his childhood home of Genoa. Neither was interested, as the recent fall of the Byzantine Empire had allowed them to dominate trade with wealthy Arab territories in the eastern half of the Mediterranean. Columbus also sent his brother to pitch the idea to English king Henry VII, but Henry's priorities lay elsewhere, and he delayed.[5]

During this delay, just one European leader showed interest in Columbus's proposal. Soon, she and Columbus forged the most consequential partnership in history.

Isabella of Castile was born in 1451, the same year as Columbus. This coincidence perhaps made them kindred spirits, but a more meaningful compatibility was their considerable ambition. While Columbus dreamed of crossing oceans, making a fortune, and earning glory, Isabella had spent most of her life planning how to acquire and maintain political power in an arena dominated by men.

Before Spain was Spain, Castile was the Iberian Peninsula's largest kingdom. It and other Iberian crowns had for centuries retaken Muslim

---

[5] In 1485, England emerged from its romantic civil war—the War of the Roses—with the victorious Henry as the first king of the Tudor Dynasty. Stability and heir-production, not long distance trade, were his top priorities, both of which were passed on to his son, Henry VIII. The Tudor Dynasty eventually ended in 1603 with the death of Henry VII's granddaughter, Queen Elizabeth. (You know her better as the 19th most influential figure in Western history.)

lands held on the Iberian peninsula.[6] This slow but successful process—known as the *Reconquista*, or reconquering—allowed each kingdom to grow, but by Isabella's time Castile had grown more than the others.

Isabella's father, John II of Castile,[7] reigned as the most powerful person in Iberia. Each of his three children—Henry, Isabella, and Alfonso—had, at some point, designs on the Castilian throne. After her older and younger brother, Isabella was initially third in line to inherit the kingdom. That was highly improbable, as the brothers would likely have children one day, each one bumping Isabella down the line of succession.[8]

Then the drama began. King John died, promoting Isabella's older brother to King Henry IV. In 1462, Henry had a daughter, Joanna, who he named heir to the throne, further relegating Isabella. However, some prominent Castilian noblemen had started to believe they could control young Alfonso, just eight years old, who they insisted should remain next in line. There were also rumors that Joanna was the result of an affair between Henry's wife and a nobleman, meaning Joanna lacked the requisite blood.

Henry's attempt at a compromise was to agree that one day his daughter Joanna would marry his brother Alfonso,[9] and that they would

---

[6] These had been Muslim-held lands ever since their seventh and eighth century conquests across west Asia, north Africa, and southwest Europe—a spread ultimately stopped by Charles Martel (#13) and reversed by his grandson, Charlemagne (#21).

[7] Not to be confused with the aforementioned John II of Portugal. They don't make it easy on us, do they.

[8] Somewhere Princess Anne is slowly nodding her head.

[9] Gross.

inherit the crown together. However, Henry, not unreasonably bothered by the idea of his daughter marrying his brother, later backed out of the deal. An ensuing rebellion attempted to overthrow him in 1465. The war lasted three years until Alfonso died either from plague, consumption, or, if you believe the rebels who backed him, poisoning.

With Alfonso dead, the rebellion turned to Isabella as their new preferred successor, but she refused to fight her older brother and instead worked toward diplomacy. She eventually won him over and was made heir on the condition of Henry having final say on Isabelle's marriage choice.

Six years later, in 1474, Henry died, and Isabella was named Queen of Castile. Unfortunately for her, those still loyal to Joanna seized the opportunity and declared the 12-year-old queen as well. Strategically, they married her off to the 43-year-old King of Portugal,[10] a relative frustratingly also named Alfonso. Joanna backers and Portugal declared war on Isabella and her supporters, and thus began the War of Castilian Succession (1475-1479).

Isabella, however, already had her own shrewd marriage. She married Ferdinand, heir to the throne of Aragon, the second largest of the Iberian kingdoms. It was a politically successful marriage, to say the least. Together they not only won Isabelle's claim, but their marriage also formed the nucleus of modern Spain, which their heirs inherited, uniting the crowns. By their combined strength, Castile and Aragon used war and diplomacy to gradually envelope nearly all of Iberia, save their rivals in Portugal.

---

[10] Double gross.

Christopher Columbus

Now we have the context for history's most far-reaching bargain. In the late fifteenth century, Spain, a rising power, neared its completion of the *Reconquista*. Meanwhile, its last remaining rival on the peninsula—a kingdom which had just denied Isabella's very legitimacy before fighting a war against her—drew closer to Asia and its riches. A trade relationship with the East would have made Portugal the wealthiest nation in Europe, and it could leverage that wealth into dominating Isabella's fledgling nation. Europe's youngest kingdom was in danger of being strangled in its cradle.

A desperate Spanish Crown therefore heard out the proposal of a desperate Genoese navigator. Isabella in particular was drawn to Columbus. Though she initially rejected his plan in 1486, she encouraged him to stay in Spain by paying him an allowance and providing free lodging and food anywhere inside her kingdom. Though her advisers had recommended against funding his dangerous mission, she remained concerned another monarch might steal his proposal from under her.

Eventually, after Bartolomeu Dias's return to Portugal set up its long-awaited expedition to India, she was ready to roll the dice with her adventurous contemporary. She and Ferdinand promised Columbus three ships, crews to staff them, the title of Admiral of the fleet and Governor of any lands he found, and ten percent of all profits obtained for the Spanish Crown. Months of recruitment and supply procurement followed.

In August, 1492, Columbus boarded his fleet's flagship, a sizable carrack nicknamed the *Santa Maria*. Flanked by two caravels—the *Pinta* and the *Niña*—he set sail for Spain's Canary Islands, where the ships restocked, rested, and repaired.

On September 6, they cast off again, this time into the unknown. Columbus sailed south to the latitude line on which he assumed India to be, then turned due west.

After a longer-than-expected five weeks of sailing—during which he may have faced a starving mutiny that he willed away by reminding his sailors that their almost depleted supplies could never last the return voyage—an island was mercifully spotted. On October 12, 1492, Columbus and his men disembarked. They became the first Europeans to step onto what they thought was an Indian island.

But India it was not. Though Columbus had successfully crossed the Great Western Ocean, the assumption that it was Asia on the other side was flawed.

Columbus, however, had no way to know he was wrong. He had sailed down to India's latitude line, then sailed west for about 2,500 miles, eventually finding land close to where it was supposed to be. He expected to find darker skinned people that had a totally foreign culture, and, as he searched the first island and later others in the area, that's exactly what he found. These coincidences confirmed his assumptions: he was in India. Perhaps history's greatest misnomers, he called the region the "Indies" and the people that lived there "Indians."[11]

In actuality, he had encountered a subgroup of the Taíno peoples scattered across the modern Caribbean. The initial meetings with these "Indians" were positive. Even with complex verbal communication im-

---

[11] Later in history, these islands became known as the "West Indies" to differentiate them from Asia's "East Indies."

possible, the natives offered the Spanish food, water, and room to set up camp.

Columbus's top priority was finding the kind of wealth that could legitimize his mission and earn not only a return on the Spanish Crown's investment, but a return trip to the area after sailing back to Spain. He kept island hopping, including exploring Hispaniola and Cuba.

He searched and failed to find the Indian mainland. The "Indies," so far, were a bust.

Therefore, although he had forever changed world history, he generally came up empty on fulfilling his true mission. He found barely any gold, no gems, no silk, and no spices. Desperate to not let down his benefactors, he scrounged up what he could, including taking "Indians" and valuables, before making his return voyage in January with most of his men. With permission from the local tribe, 39 Spaniards stayed behind in a settlement, called La Navidad, in modern Haiti.

Columbus returned home a hero—for a while. It was assumed Columbus's claim of reaching Asia was true, a belief that persisted for a decade. Word quickly spread throughout Europe, and he became a legend across the continent.

Despite Columbus's achievement and celebrity, Ferdinand and Isabella noted he did not return with any valuable Indian spices. They were expecting black pepper, ginger, and cloves. Without sufficient gold to offset such a disappointment, Columbus exaggerated the size of the islands he found and propagated rumors of nearby "countless gold." He also described the Taínos themselves as primitive, timid, generous, naïve, and skillful. In other words, they were a bountiful, cheap labor supply.

Having no reason to doubt Columbus, a grateful Crown acknowledged his achievement of sailing to Fake Asia by giving him his own coat of arms, servants, and the command of a second expedition. Unlike his initial meager fleet, this one had 15 ships and a thousand people. In November, 1493, Columbus again sailed west into the horizon.

His armada arrived to find a key turning point in Spanish-native relations; after the colonists had purportedly tried to take gold and women, the fort at La Navidad had been destroyed and the settlers murdered. The Spanish then proceeded more skeptically with their hitherto generous hosts.

In the meantime, an increasingly frustrated Columbus continued to grope in the dark for the Asian mainland. Without spices and silks, he grew obsessed with finding a profitable trade commodity to maintain his new titles, wealth, and reputation. His appetite for gold hardly satiated by the little he found, he begged permission from the Crown to commandeer slaves from the widespread Carib tribe (after whom the Caribbean was soon named), who had been warring with the Taínos and even began picking off some Spaniards with poisoned arrows.

The practice of slavery was not new. In a 1452 papal bull, Pope Nicholas V authorized slavery of all non-Christians. In fact, only when the Portuguese began enslaving Africans did they start turning a profit on their costly expeditions down the African coast. Four decades later, Columbus, an ardent Catholic who had spent much of his life in Portugal, saw the papally-sanctioned enslavement of these new locals as a natural step, and he hoped profiting off slavery could sustain his voyages until the Asian mainland was found. Though Ferdinand and Isabella initially denied his request, Columbus soon took it upon himself to inaugurate the Atlantic slave trade anyway. In 1494, he sent nearly 600 Indian slaves to Spain, a third of whom died on the voyage.

Columbus himself remained behind and continued his hunt for gold. Supported by the guns and cannons of his more technologically advanced society, he developed a tribute system in Hispaniola where every local native over the age of 14 had to meet a gold quota. If they did not meet the quota, their hands would be severed, leading to almost certain death. With virtually no ability to meet the quota, many natives fled or committed suicide instead. He soon evolved this practice into the infamous *encomienda* system of the next century. With *encomienda*, a Spanish colonist was given natives as free labor in exchange for teaching them Spanish and Catholicism. Predictably callous treatment awaited the newly contracted slaves.

Meanwhile, every time Columbus set out to search for the mainland, he later returned to chaotic Spanish outposts. Frustrated colonists, who had left behind the comforts of Europe for this disappointing gold rush in the underdeveloped Indies, frequently behaved lawlessly. They raped native women, forcibly took wives and slaves, and killed and maimed at will. The overmatched Columbus, a better navigator than he was administrator, hastened back to Spain in 1496 to ask for more support.

Returning to the Indies in 1498, his third voyage didn't go much better. The Crown had grown weary of Columbus. His many faults—arrogance despite fruitless journeys, frequent insubordination, aimlessness in the Indies, incompetence as an administrator—began outpacing his limited return on investment. Therefore, this time on Columbus's heels was a Spanish magistrate, Francisco de Bobadilla, sent to govern in his place. While Columbus was out exploring, which included finally charting what might be a continent (we now know it was part of South

America), de Bobadilla confirmed the rumors of Columbus's disordered and brutal administration.[12] Upon the explorer's return to a Spanish settlement, the new governor had Columbus arrested, chained, and sent back to Spain, a particularly agonizing development since he thought he had finally found the Asian mainland. He remained arrested in Spain for six weeks before being granted one final audience with Ferdinand and Isabella. He defended himself and begged for one last voyage to restore their faith in him.

Two related factors worked in his request for absolution. First, while Columbus toiled on his third voyage, the Portuguese had finally circled around Africa, reached India, and sailed back. It took Vasco da Gama and his fleet 22 months to do it. Despite purchasing spices at marked-up prices and being chased away by Muslim trading rivals before filling up ships' stores, da Gama returned a three thousand percent profit on the mission. The Portuguese then ramped up their efforts in the region. The Spanish had officially lost the race to India proper.

That explains Columbus's second advantage: he was the best chance Spain had. It was still assumed that his three voyages had nibbled around

---

[12] In 2006, de Bobadilla's 48-page report was rediscovered. Containing testimonies from 23 people—enemies and supporters of Columbus included—the report accused him of punishing a man found guilty of stealing corn by having his ears and nose cut off before being sold into slavery. After Columbus was accused of lowly birth by a native woman, his brother forced her naked through the streets, then had her tongue cut off, actions Columbus applauded since they "defended the family." After an aggressive crackdown that killed many natives, he paraded their dismembered bodies through the streets in an attempt to discourage further rebellion. Consuelo Varela, a Spanish historian speaking of the document, noted, "Columbus's government was characterized by a form of tyranny. . . . Even those who loved him had to admit the atrocities that had taken place."

Asia's edges, and his third and most recent mission had finally spotted something of continental size before de Bobadilla intervened. Columbus argued he was on the verge of accomplishing the mission, and, unlike da Gama's ten-month route to Asia, Columbus's route put Asia just five or six weeks away.

The Crown gave Columbus one last chance. In May of 1502, he left Spain in his wake for the final time. He then, as usual, arrived in the "Indies" five weeks later, and then, as usual, wandered around the Caribbean. Like his third mission, he sailed west and charted more continental coastline. None of it, however, matched what Europeans knew of the Asian mainland. For two years he was there, and for two years he remained as confused as ever. There weren't even any Portuguese sailors there to shed light on the situation. He knew the Portuguese had reached Asia and were looking around the region, but there were confusingly no signs of them.

Columbus returned home from his last voyage in 1504. Sick with gout, arthritis, and ophthalmalgia for much of his adult life, he was constantly in pain and frequently bedridden. In the end, his health rapidly deteriorated. In 1506, at 55 years of age, history's most important explorer—indeed, its most influential figure—was dead.

Hindsight being what it is, we now know he was never in risk of running into Portuguese sailors in India. He thought he had reached Asia, but he literally couldn't have been further from it. He was instead on the other side of the world.

It is, without rival, history's greatest accident.[13] Though he was trying to find a route to Asia, he stumbled onto two new continents. Though he did cross the Atlantic, what he found on the other side was not the Far East, but an *entirely new West*.

Probably the first man to identify Columbus's mistake was another Italian navigator sailing under the Spanish flag, the Florentine Amerigo Vespucci. He made separate transatlantic voyages contemporary to Columbus's later voyages. During one of these trips, he sailed much further south than Columbus had, likely beyond modern Rio de Janeiro in Brazil. Realizing this continent looked nothing like what Europeans knew of Asia, he determined it must be a "*mundus novus*"—a "New World." A few years later, the German cartographer Martin Waldseemüller used Amerigo's reports to draw the first map of this New World and decided to name it after the navigator who made the determination. He called it America.[14]

In our analysis of Columbus's influence, his ignorance of his true location is but the first of several prominent counterarguments, all of which frankly hold little weight.

Without question, his estimate of 2,400 miles to cross the Atlantic and hit Asia was overly optimistic and egregiously wrong. Japan sits about 10,000 miles west of Europe; were it not for the Americas, Columbus and his men would have been dead just 30 percent into the journey.

---

[13] Sorry, penicillin.

[14] Though the map was published in 1507, the year after Columbus died, the rumors of Vespucci's theory had reached Columbus before he passed. With his typical conviction, he ignored them. Columbus died believing he had reached Asia.

Another attack against his importance includes that he never actually proved the world was round. This point is objectively true. Crossing the Atlantic is not evidence of a round Earth. It was Ferdinand Magellan's circumnavigation in 1521 that truly proved we live on a globe.[15]

Less illegitimate cases against Columbus's importance can be that he never actually "discovered America." First, not only did he never set foot on the land we now call the United States of America, he never even saw it.[16] His journeys were limited to landing on some Caribbean islands and charting some South and Central American coast.

Plus, though estimates vary, there were tens of millions of people already living in the Americas at the time. Those immigrants from the last

---

[15] Regarding Magellan, I always like to split the knowledge people have about his circumnavigation into three groups, each armed with more knowledge than the last. The first group thinks Magellan circled the globe with his famous expedition (1519-1522), becoming the first man to circumnavigate the planet. There, the second group butts in haughtily and points out that Magellan actually died in the Philippines before the remainder of his fleet continued and finished the voyage, so therefore he did not actually circumnavigate. However, the third group knows what the second group does not: Magellan may have actually been the first to circumnavigate the earth, and he even did it before his voyage's survivors finished the journey. As part of Portugal's Conquest of Malacca in 1511, he had traveled east to southeast Asian islands. He returned home in 1512. Seven years later, he departed on his famous voyage west (this time under the Spanish flag), ultimately sailing back to southeast Asia's islands for a virtual circumnavigation—just with a seven-year pit stop in Iberia. Though we're not sure if he crossed every last longitude line, he came darn close.

[16] And he certainly didn't have Thanksgiving with Native Americans at Plymouth, which took place a couple thousand miles north and OVER A HUNDRED YEARS AFTER HE DIED! (I'm sorry for yelling, but based on 15 years of teaching some surprised high schoolers, that really needed to be emphasized.)

ice age that had poured into North and South America had since propagated for 15 thousand years. Many of their descents built impressive civilizations, including wondrous empires like the Aztecs of Mexico and the Inca of South America. How could Columbus "discover" lands that were already inhabited by millions?

We can't even say Columbus was the first to successfully cross the Atlantic! Many theories of pre-Columbian contact between the Western and Eastern hemispheres exist with varying degrees of scholarly acceptance. What is almost universally accepted is that the Vikings, near the turn of the millennium, settled parts of Greenland and traveled as far as modern Newfoundland in Canada. Thus, not only did millions of people already live on the landmasses Columbus "discovered," but he wasn't even the first European to cross the Atlantic and travel there.

Each of these counterarguments is purely factual, yet they're further from the point than Columbus was from India. Columbus is a peerlessly influential historical figure, and it's not for any of the reasons debunked above.

What Columbus did was open up the Americas for European colonization, and in the process he catalyzed the age of global European empires, the genocide of millions of Native Americans, the transatlantic slave trade, and the birth of modern Western Hemispheric nations. He set the West on a trajectory to strengthen and enrich itself at the expense of nearly all other cultures. He allowed the West to extend itself not only further west, but around the globe, exporting its culture to every continent on Earth. His accomplishment deeply and irrecoverably affected Europe and the world more than any event in history.

Christopher Columbus

Let's talk about how. Once Vespucci identified the "New World" to which Columbus had sailed, the proverbial dinner bell rang, and the Americas were on the menu. Two new continents opened for European colonization. On those lands was unimaginable real and potential wealth. The real wealth was the tons of gold and silver possessed by the mainland American empires, like the Aztecs and Inca, while the potential wealth lay under fertile ground at warm latitudes, a combination that beckoned planters.

In time, New World produce was sent to Europeans. Native Americans introduced new food staples like corn, tomatoes, peanuts, beans, and potatoes. With this new diet, the European population became deliciously well fed, and its population, like its economy, began to climb at an unprecedented rate. This growth later pushed colonization as many Europeans looked to escape an overcrowding continent.

As people on each side of the Atlantic traded goods that the other side had never seen, the Columbian exchange gradually transformed the economies and societies of the old and news worlds. Of course, this development was not without its profound costs. The Columbian exchange was not limited to foods. Each side introduced new diseases to which their counterparts had never been exposed. Some diseases went from the New World to the Old. With less migration into Europe—and the diverse peoples of Afro-Eurasia having already acquired various immunities over centuries—the impacts of New World diseases were relatively limited.

Much more devastating was the impact of European diseases on the New World. In the century or so after Columbus's arrival, many estimates have up to a *90 percent* loss of Native American life, mostly from disease. Depending on the total population of pre-Columbian America, with estimates ranging from 10 to 100 million, that's up to 90 million dead in about a hundred years. Much of that is from warfare, but the diseases were deadlier, and they rapidly spread ahead of Spanish and other European conquerors. Diseases acted as a vanguard for European militaries; they significantly thinned the native population, easing the ensuing conquest.

And conquest there was. European military technology was significantly advanced compared to the natives they encountered. Cavalry, guns, and cannons (natives had neither horses nor gunpowder) overwhelmed the defenders of the continent. *Conquistadors* cut through the Americas with relative ease. Hernán Cortés, for example, arrived at Mexico's Aztec Empire about two decades after Columbus's voyage. Against a civilization of millions, he and a few thousand European soldiers, along with some native allies, emerged victorious. At their feet, a couple hundred thousand Aztecs lay dead, including their emperor, Montezuma.[17]

Across the sixteenth century, the native population of Spanish-held regions was almost totally eradicated. Those who survived diseases and warfare became slaves in the *encomienda* system, that brutal form of subjugation and forced conversion started by Columbus himself.

These three killers—disease, conquest, slavery—shattered the Native American population. On the island of Hispaniola, the first sizable island

---

[17] Lest you think this conquest can be reduced to the big bad Spanish conquering the helpless and peaceful natives, it should be noted that the Aztecs were far from innocent. Their empire included the subjugation of many surrounding tribes, which helps explain how Cortes was able to enlist some local allies. Worse, the Aztecs are notorious for their human sacrifices. Estimates, as usual, vary, but contemporary sources and archaeological evidence suggest the Aztecs averaged tens of thousands of sacrifices, including babies and children, per year. The Spanish committed their fair share of atrocities, but the Aztecs probably had even more blood on their hands than the Europeans did.

Christopher Columbus

Columbus came across, the island's population dropped from hundreds of thousands in 1495 to just a thousand in 1520. Across the region, the Taínos numbered about two million on the eve of Columbus's arrival. Within a generation, 80 to 90 percent were dead. By 1600, the tribe was on the verge of extinction. Nearby, the mighty Aztec Empire, forced to its knees by Cortés, never rose again.

After the West Indies and Mexico came the rest of Central America and much of South America. The Portuguese, all of a sudden realizing Asia wasn't the only prize, joined the conquest of the New World. They colonized the eastern half of South America and founded its Colony of Brazil.[18] Later in the 1500s, Queen Elizabeth (#19) chartered Englishmen to explore and colonize some land of its own, and for the next two centuries English colonists spread across the eastern North American coast and much of Canada. As it did so, the French, not wanting their old rivals across the channel to get the best of them, colonized Quebec, claimed the Great Lakes, sailed down the Mississippi, and founded Lou-

---

[18] In a stretch of confusion following Columbus's discovery of Fake Asia, the Spanish and Portuguese, in heated competition over trade routes and land claims in the East, were close to resuming hostilities. Pope Alexander VI, frustrated by the possibility of two Catholic empires warring with each other when there were so many new Asian pagans to convert, brought the two parties to the most influential international agreement you never heard of: 1494's Treaty of Tordesillas. As mediator, he got the two crowns to agree to a line of demarcation from pole to pole about 370 leagues off the western coast of Cape Verde. Spain would get first dibs on all land west of the line and Portugal east. Of course, just two years after Columbus's first voyage, all parties involved thought this line ran through Asia somewhere. Vespucci eventually determined otherwise. With Spain given the western portion of the continent and Portugal the eastern, this treaty begins to explain the lingual patterns of South America.

427

isiana, named after their King Louis XIV.[19] By the 1700s, these ravenous empires had almost entirely consumed the American continents.

To Europeans, America soon became synonymous with openness, growth, and opportunity. As Europeans conquered, the victories led to confidence, and confidence to more conquest. As native cultures were beaten back, Western cultures replaced them. Where hundreds of native tongues once dotted the Americas, soon the languages of Spanish, Portuguese, English, and French were spoken instead. Where natives once prayed to their local gods and spirits, the Christian God gradually displaced them.[20] Where many native societies once lived at harmony with their sacred nature, soon Western style farms, domesticated animals, terraforming, and infrastructure bulldozed the lands beyond recognition.

Of course, Native Americans weren't the only groups devastated by Columbus's discovery of the Americas. As their population dropped from disease, conquest, slavery, and maltreatment, the colonists' cheap labor supply dwindled. Fortunately for racist opportunists, the Por-

---

[19] Louisiana would later be sold to Thomas Jefferson (#24) and the United States by Napoleon (#15).

[20] Much of this Top 30 list has charted the spread of Christianity, particularly its dominant Catholic denomination. Chronologically, we start with the Christ Jesus (#7) incepting the movement, to Constantine (#23) allowing it, to Charles Martel (#13) defending it, to Charlemagne (#21) ingraining it across western Europe, and now to Columbus carrying it across the Atlantic and introducing it to the Americas. Along with Clovis and the Catholic Church, I call this alliterative group the "Seven Cs of Christianity." They help explain why Christianity became the world's largest religion and Catholicism its largest denomination.

tuguese, during their rounding of Africa, had found another option.[21] As American natives died out, the demand for African slaves rose accordingly.

Soon, the genocide of the American Indian was rivaled in horror by the Atlantic slave trade. Over the next few centuries, the process crammed about 12 million captured Africans onto thousands of transatlantic voyages. Approximately 15 percent died on the horrific Middle Passage, where disease, starvation, murder, and suicide claimed the lives of about two million Africans on the Atlantic. Many of those that arrived in the New World quickly wished they were among the dead. Auctioned off as chattel, the commodification of the African slave remains an indelible stain on Western history.

These uprooted Africans soon found themselves the unwilling fuel that fired a revitalized European economy. On their assigned plantations, slaves grew profitable cash crops to a European market that grew addicted to sugar, tobacco, and much more. Europeans, in turn, would trade their more refined goods—guns, ammunition, alcohol, and other manufactured products—to European-American colonists and to west Africans who cooperated by obtaining more slaves to send to America.

---

[21] The Portuguese also set precedents for the process of the slave trade. Many African tribes and kingdoms had long enslaved each other as prisoners of war. Capitalizing on these rivalries, the Portuguese frequently played them against each other. Portuguese sailors would trade valuable European products—like Western clothing, guns, and alcohol—to traders or leaders of one tribe for their help enslaving members of another. Similarly, with Europeans terrified of the "dark continent's" interior, the Portuguese learned to convince coastal Africans to capture central Africans and drag them to the coast before they were shackled, forced onto slave ships, and brought to their new home. Other European empires soon adopted Portugal's strategy.

This triangular trade created a symbiotic relationship between the leaders and merchants of each point.

There were long term effects on each point of the triangle, some obvious and some not. In the obvious category was the loss of life and freedom of tens of millions of Africans (who were killed or captured), and Native Americans (who steadily died off as millions of people encroached onto their land with their germs and guns). Also obvious are the aforementioned demographic and cultural transformation of America. Columbus clearly made possible the deep gashing of these many civilizations.

Less obvious is what these developments had on the long term development of Western history. As has been mentioned in earlier chapters, Europe came into the fifteenth and sixteenth centuries about as advanced, on balance, as the Arab world, India, and China. Columbus's great accident was about to shift the balance. Agricultural profits from using cheap labor on abundant land made European empires the world's greatest exporters, while the new gold and silver made them flush with capital. As new industries capitalized, economic growth had never been so easy. Farmers, shipbuilders, carpenters, sailors, soldiers, and artisans of all kinds were in high demand to fill a growing economy across the Atlantic and at ports on both sides of it.

The West shed more connections with medieval feudalism. Many with access to the influx of precious metals invested the money into new businesses to become the first modern capitalists. These businesses energized the European economy as they worked to meet insatiable worldwide demand. Europeans, colonists, African leaders, and the new Asian markets all demanded European goods, which meant Europeans went to work in mills and later factories to make them.

The triangular trade soon powered the ensuing Industrial Revolution. The invigorated economy drove technological growth and innovation. For example, profits from Caribbean sugar plantations funded the improvements made to the steam engine by James Watt (#5). Eli Whitney's cotton gin not only responded to the growing population's demand for textiles, but it also drove the growing American slave trade when the means to purify cotton made it a more realistic and lucrative export.

Much of Europe's manufactured materials relied on the raw goods and consumers in America. An industrial explosion would have been indefinitely delayed without the fuel from the New World. The population growth of the industrial period then created a demand for more raw materials from the New World and manufactured goods from the Old, which further stimulated the transatlantic economy. It was a feedback cycle that started with Columbus's discovery.

Once Western colonies gained their independence and became the dozens of Western Hemispheric nations we know today, the effects of Columbus continued. Five of these countries are in the G20. Two are in NATO. One of them is the United States, which gave us Gregory Pincus (#25), Thomas Jefferson (#24), Henry Ford (#20), Thomas Edison (#18), and George Washington (#14). The U.S. also implemented the ideology of John Locke (#4), proliferated the works of William Shakespeare (#10), sheltered Albert Einstein (#11), and worked to contain the ideology of Karl Marx (#9). The United States has surely been the West's most powerful and influential ambassador of the last century, and it twice galloped into Europe to save the Old World from itself.[22] Without European discovery of America, there is no United States.

Though one can reasonably argue that the European discovery of the Americas was inevitable, we mustn't forget that the same can be said for just about any historical accomplishment. Yet, here the timing of the accomplishment is critical. If not Columbus, who? If not in 1492, when? Would the Portuguese have found it a decade later? The English in the following century? The Chinese? The Arabs? Imagine the potential differences on the Americas. Could these have been Anglican continents that gave the world an indomitable British Empire that continues to this day? Might Americans be speaking Mandarin instead? Could the Koran be required reading across the hemisphere? All are possible, depending on who first stumbled onto the two underdeveloped continents ripe for the taking.

In an era when Columbus's reputation has had to absorb many well-deserved criticisms, we now overlook his remarkable accomplishments. It was Columbus who bravely led three ships across dangerous, uncharted waters to become history's most famous explorer. It was Columbus who convinced a nascent kingdom to fund a risky voyage, and this kingdom then became an empire that dominated the Americas—and much of the entire world—for over a century. It was Columbus who, more than anyone, altered the course of Western history. And yes, it was Columbus

---

[22] Winston Churchill, in his famous June, 1940 "We shall fight on the beaches" speech after the heroics at Dunkirk, noted that his fellow British citizens must do whatever they could to survive in the war "until, in God's good time, the New World, with all its power and might, steps forth to the rescue and the liberation of the old."

Christopher Columbus

who was a desperate, rapacious, and cruel ambassador of the West, setting painful precedents for subsequent pioneers.

It's difficult to avoid presentism (the tendency to hold historical figures to the standards of our time and place instead of their own, which is a form of cultural bias), but it's worth trying. Columbus grew up in a time where the Catholic Church sanctioned slavery and all Western kingdoms prioritized profit above all else. His job was to enrich and strengthen Spain. Since his brave voyages ultimately catalyzed a century of Spanish glory, he can be considered a success and a hero.

Regardless, even if one prefers to emphasize the negative parts of his reputation, a person's sins do not hurt their ranking on this list.[23] The Top 30 measured[24] *influence*, and no one was more influential to the development of the West, or the world, than Columbus. We couldn't even have a true "world history" until the Old World reunited with the New. The family reunion between the Western and Eastern hemispheres was 15 thousand years in the making, and it was Columbus who, albeit accidentally, made it happen. Columbus has been claimed by the Italians, the Spanish, and countries across the Americas—the latter have named many countries, districts, and cities after him—but as much as anyone in history, it's best to call him the first citizen of the world. If I took the time

---

[23] After all, on this list you'll find Adolf Hitler (#17).

[24] Is that past tense? I'm finally coming in for a landing!

to make a list of the most influential figures in all of history, he'd still rank at the top.[25]

On just this ranking of Western influence, therefore, Columbus is an even clearer number one. Unlike anyone ranked below him, Columbus is responsible for extending the West itself. Thanks to him, the Western world hopped the Atlantic and pushed all the way to the Pacific. In the process, the West not only trampled across and replaced a native culture that had populated America since the last ice age, but its own nations also strengthened beyond what was thought possible. Since the dominant theme of world history's last five centuries has been the West bringing the whole world into its sphere of influence, it's only fitting that the person most responsible for that takes the prime spot of this Top 30 ranking.

Christopher Columbus is the most influential figure in Western history.

---

[25] It's a list I've thought a lot about, and I can't think of a better final footnote to this series than to share with you the non-Western contenders for an overall Top 30 list. Here they are in a general order I think I'd rank them: Mohammed, Confucius, Buddha, Zoroaster, Alexander the Great (a Westerner who more impacted the Arab world than the West), Genghis Khan, Attila the Hun, Suleiman the Magnificent, Emperor Meiji, Cyrus the Great, Mao, Lao Tzu, and Hannibal. There are 13 names there; I'd expect the first six are slam dunk choices for a worldwide Top 30, Attila and Suleiman are likely inclusions, and Meiji is on the outside of the bubble. Look them up at your leisure. This time, I'm not doing the work for you.

About the Author

Ian Cheney has no business publishing a book, but he has friends in high places (read: his father). He founded and maintains the website *Presidential Politics for America*, which at one point had literally dozens of readers. He works as a history and government "teacher" at Waterford High School in Connecticut. His wife, Marinne, tolerates his writing hobby, and there's a 50/50 chance she will read this book. Ian and Marinne have two children, Arden and Dylan, who look forward to coloring all over any unsold copies of *Who Made the West*. The family lives happily in Gales Ferry, CT.

New London Librarium

New London Librarium is a literary publishing house that specializes in publishing books that are worth putting into print but are not likely to find the large market that profit-oriented houses require. Most of the staff are volunteers who believe in the importance of these books.

The topics of NLL books range from translations of Machado de Assis to Mother Goose rhymes illustrated by children. Special series focus on Brazil, Catholic issues, fiction, histories, art, and current events. NLL is one of the world's largest publishers of English translations of books by Brazilian writers.

The house would like to thank editors Ralph Hunter Cheney, Solange Aurora Cavalcante Cheney, and Denise Dembinski for their efforts to produce a book worthy of its words.

For more information and a catalog of titles, see NLLibrarium.com.

Index

A

Abraham: 6, 10
Adams, John: 98, 100-102, 104, 107, 235-238, 241-244, 377, 265-268, 412
Age of Exploration: 165, 321
Alexander I (Tsar of Russia): 210
Alexander the Great: 10, 32, 207, 237, 434
Alexander VI (Pope): 166, 427
Alexis I (Tsar): 75
Alighieri, Dante: 10, 40, 287
American Revolution: 95-100, 235-241, 371-374
Ananias of Damascus: 319
Anastasius of Sinai: 30
Anglo-Saxon: 15, 17, 140, 285,
Aquinas, Thomas (*Next 30*): 6, 11, 27, 32-33
Archimedes: 6, 10, 27, 262, 326
Arians (followers of Arius): 116-118, 140, 250
Aristarchus: 10, 56, 58
Aristotle (*tied at #30*): 11, 19-20, 27-35, 104, 122, 262, 269, 278, 326
astronomy, advances in: 48-58, 264-268, 280, 381-383
Attila the Hun: 2, 237, 434
Augustine of Hippo (St. Augustine) (*Next 30*): 11, 25, 27, 31, 116, 130
Augustus (Roman Emperor) (*Next 10*): 15-16

B

Babbage, Charles: 10, 57
Babylonian Captivity: 46-47
Bach, Johann Sebastian: 10
Bacon, Francis: 10, 269, 385, 388
Battle of Tours (or Poitiers): 248-259
Beethoven, Ludwig van: 10, 210
Bell, Alexander Graham: 10, 57, 180
Benedict XI (Pope): 45
Benz, Karl: 150
Bernard of Clairvaux: 31
Bismarck, Otto von (*Next 30*): 11, 184
Black Death: 62
Bohr, Neils: 57
Bolshevik Revolution: 78, 213, 300
Bonaparte, Napoleon (*#16*): 69-70, 83, 102, 148, 163, 196, 204-220, 237, 246, 292, 330, 428
Boniface VIII (Pope): 39-46
Borlaug, Norman: 10
Brexit: 163
Bruno, Giordano: 52, 54, 264,
Buddha: 2, 434
Burnett, James: 229

C

Caesar, Julius (*Next 10*): 15, 237
Calvin, John: 52-53, 340
Catherine the Great: 9, 82, 158
Catholic Reformation (Counter-Reformation): 341
Cecil, William: 167, 378
Celestine V (Pope): 39-40
Charlemagne (*#21*): 62, 121, 136-148, 196, 210, 249, 255, 257, 321, 393, 413, 428
Charles Martel (*#13*): 138, 248-259, 321, 413, 428
Chaucer, Geoffrey: 10, 287
Cheney, Glenn: xiv
Churchill, Winston (*Next 30*): 11, 432

Index

Cicero (*Next 10*): 16-17
Clement V (Pope): 45-46
Clement VII (Pope): 47, 160
Clericis laicos (papal bull): 41
Clovis (King of the Franks): 25, 62, 138, 140, 428
Columbus, Christopher (*#1*): 13, 49, 166, 218, 405-434
"Communist Manifesto": 294-295, 298, 300-301, 304, 306
Confederation of the Rhine: 148, 217
Confucius: 2, 434
Constantine "the Great" (*#23*): 25, 110-124, 257, 259, 320, 323, 341, 428
Constantinople (Byzantium) (Istanbul): 26, 32, 73-74, 82, 118-119, 122, 146, 409
Constitution (U.S.): 22, 99-102, 106-107, 239, 240-242, 244-245, 373
Continental Congress: 97-98, 104, 106, 236-238, 372
Copernicus, Nicolaus (*#28*): 48-58, 221, 227, 260-261, 264-269, 388-390, 403
Cortés, Hernan: 426-427
Council of Nicaea: 118, 121, 123, 140
Crimean War: 83, 186, 201
Crusades: 14, 32-33, 258, 324, 409
Curie, Marie (*Next 30*): 12, 57, 158
Cyrillic: 74
Cyrus the Great: 237, 434

D

da Gama, Vasco: 420
da Vinci, Leonardo: 10, 12, 49
Daguerre, Louis: 10, 402
Darwin, Charles (*#15*): 221-231
"Das Kapital": 295, 299-301, 304-305
Declaration of Independence (U.S.): 98, 100, 104, 106, 108, 202, 371-372
Declaration of the Rights of Man: 99, 374
Descartes, René: 12, 75
"Descent of Man": 221, 227
Dias, Bartolomeu: 410-411, 415
Dickens, Charles: 10
Diderot, Denis: 104, 133
Diocletian (Roman Emperor): 112-114

divine right of kings: 130, 133, 362, 366
Drake, Francis: 166, 168

E

Eastern Roman Empire (Byzantine Empire): 26, 31-32, 38, 73, 122, 141, 146, 409
Edict of Milan: 115, 120
Edison, Thomas (*#18*): 173-182, 351, 386, 403
Einstein, Albert (*#11*): 55, 266, 272-280, 330, 389
Eleanor of Aquitaine: 68, 158
Elizabeth I (Queen of England) (*#19*): 7, 158-172, 233, 284, 338, 378, 412, 427
Engels, Friedrich: 293-298, 300
Enlightenment (historical period): 12, 33, 104-105, 126, 133, 206, 217, 236, 244, 327, 343, 360-362, 372, 387, 403
Erasmus: 47, 229, 335
Eratosthenes: 10
Estates General: 3, 37, 43-44, 126, 134
Euclid (*Next 10*): 6, 16, 27, 326
European Union: 202, 216

F

Fabricius, Johannes: 270
Faraday, Michael (*Next 30*): 12, 57, 351
Ferdinand (King of Aragon): 414-415, 417-418, 420
feudalism: 39, 46, 141, 209
Fleming, Alexander (*Next 10*): 24, 67, 345, 357, 430
Ford, Henry (*#20*): 149-157, 173, 202, 356
Fracastoro, Girolamo: 311
Franklin, Benjamin: 10, 57, 98, 132, 235, 237-239, 243
Franks (Germanic tribe): 62, 137-144, 249-255, 321
Frederick (Barbarossa) (Holy Roman Emperor): 45
Frederick the Great: 129
French and Indian War: 96, 233, 235
French Revolution: 44, 69-70, 99, 106, 206, 216, 219, 241, 292-293, 374
Freud, Sigmund: 10
Fulton, Robert: 57, 351

Index

G

Galilei, Galileo (*#12*): 52, 54-55, 230, 260-271, 278, 363, 377, 381, 388-390
Gandhi, Mohandas: 2, 38
Gates, Bill: 10, 12
Gauss, Carl Friedrich: 10
German Confederation: 148, 217
Gilbert, William: 57
Glorious Revolution (1688): 367
Goethe: 48-49, 200, 221-222
Great Depression: 154, 188, 191, 194
Great Plague of 1665: 378
Great Schism (Western): 47
Gutenberg, Johannes (*#2*): 334, 391-404, 406

H

Hamilton, Alexander: 100-101, 103, 106-107, 232, 240, 242-244
Hammurabi: 6
Hannibal (Carthaginian General): 237, 434
Harriot, Thomas: 270
Harvey, William: 10, 57
Heisenberg, Werner: 57
Henry VII (King of England): 159, 163-164, 412
Henry VIII (King of England) (*Next 10*): 16-17, 159, 163-164, 340, 412
Henry the Navigator (Portuguese prince): 407
Heraclides Ponticus: 56
Hero of Alexandria: 348
Hindenburg, Paul von: 192
Hippocrates: 6, 10, 326
Hitler, Adolf (*#17*): 11, 163, 183-204, 218-220, 276-277, 343
Hobbes, Thomas (*Next 30*): 6, 12, 364-370, 372
Homer: 10, 287
Hooke, Robert: 388
Hundred Years' War: 59-68, 162
Hus, Jan: 334-335
Huygens, Christiaan: 261

I

"Index of Prohibited Books": 52, 267, 270
Industrial Revolution: 154, 216, 314, 327, 346-359, 387, 403, 431
Innocent III (Pope): 14, 38, 40, 45
Inquisition (Catholic) (Spanish): 110, 131, 219, 264, 267, 324
Isabella (Queen of Castille) (*Next 30*): 12, 61, 158, 412-415, 417-418, 420
Ivan IV "the Terrible" (Tsar): 73-74

J

James VI and I (King of Scotland and England): 169
Jefferson, Thomas (*#24*): 95-109, 133, 209, 232, 235, 237, 239, 242-243, 372
Jenner, Edward (*Next 10*): 17, 312-313
Jesus of Nazareth (*#7*): 110-111, 116-119, 123, 285, 316-329, 339-340, 428
Joan of Arc (*#27*): 60-71, 81, 127, 158
Jobs, Steve (*Next 30*): 12
John (King of England): 3
John II (King of Portugal): 410
Justinian (Roman Emperor): 146

K

Kepler, Johannes: 10, 54-55, 266, 383
Keynes, John Maynard (*Next 30*): 13
Khan, Genghis: 2, 73, 237, 434
Koch, Robert: 310

L

Lamarck, Jean-Baptiste: 224-225, 229
Lavoisier, Antoine: 10, 57
League of Nations: 194, 200, 216
Leeuwenhoek, Antonie van: 10, 57
Leibniz, Gottfried: 130-131, 379-381, 388
Lembo, Paulo: 270
Lenin, Vladimir: 9, 78, 300-301
"Leviathan": 364-366
Leo III (Pope): 40, 140, 210
Leo X (Pope): 51, 335

Index

Lincoln, Abraham (*Next 30*): xiv, 13, 222
Lippershey, Hans: 265, 269
Lister, Joseph: 57, 311, 351
Locke, John (*#4*): 75, 106-107, 128, 360-375, 387
Louis the Pious (King of the Franks): 144
Louis XIV (King of France): 3, 9, 428
Louis XVI (King of France): 3, 44, 134, 205, 214
Louisiana Purchase: 102, 107-108, 218
Luther, Martin (*#6*): 26, 47, 49, 52-53, 163, 329-345, 386-387, 397, 403

M

Machiavelli, Niccolo (*Next 30*): 13, 49
Madison, James: 99, 102-103, 240, 243
Magellan, Ferdinand: 10, 49, 423
Magna Carta: 3, 38, 46, 97, 163, 171
Malthus, Thomas: 225
Mao Zedong: 2, 301, 434
Marconi, Gugliemo: 10, 180-181, 351, 402
Marius, Simon: 270
Marx, Karl (*#9*): 291-306, 369, 403
Mary I (Queen of England): 159-164
Mary, Queen of Scots: 164
Maxwell, James Clerk: 10
medicine, advances in: 16-17, 86-94, 308-315, 353
Meiji (Emperor of Japan): 2, 434
Mendel, Gregor (*Next 30*): 13, 57
Mendeleev, Dmitri: 57
Michelangelo: 10, 49, 282, 289
Mohammed: 2, 250, 434
Montesquieu, Baron de: 133, 372
Morse, Samuel: 57
Moses: 6, 10
Mozart, Wolfgang Amadeus: 10, 284, 289
Mussolini, Benito: 9, 193-194

N

Napoleonic Code: 70, 209, 217
Nazi Party: 190-191, 276

Nero (Roman Emperor): 112
Newcomen, Thomas: 57, 348-349, 351
Newton, Isaac (*#3*): 5, 55, 75, 128, 228, 261, 264, 266, 268-269, 278-280, 377-390
Nicene Creed: 110, 116, 118
Norman Invasion: 15, 68

O

"On the Origin of Species": 226, 228
Oppenheimer, Robert: 57
Orthodox Church: 26, 80, 141, 147
Ottoman Empire: 73, 77, 82-83, 186, 409

P

Pasteur, Louis (*#8*): 307-315, 353
Paul of Tarsus (St. Paul) (*Next 10*): 11, 17, 31, 116, 319-320, 323-324
Peninsular War: 212
Pepin the Short: 137, 254
Peter (St. Peter) (Apostle): 122, 140, 331
Peter I "the Great" (Tsar) (*#26*): 72-84, 213
Petrarch (*Next 10*): 16-17, 136
Philip II "Augustus" (King of France): 38
Philip II (King of Spain): 162, 164, 338
Philip IV "the Fair" (King of France) (*#29*): 36-47, 61, 126, 147
Phoenicia: 6, 399
physics, advances in: 262-264, 275-280, 380-384
Pincus, Gregory (*#25*): 14, 85-94, 245
Plank, Max: 57
Plato (*tied at #30*): 19-28, 32-35, 80, 286-287
Pol Pot: 201, 301
Polo, Marco (*Next 30*): 13, 407
population growth: 85, 91, 185, 353-354, 358, 431
PPFA (Planned Parenthood Federation of America): 87
PPFA (Presidential Politics for America): ix, 87
"Principia" (Newton book): 384, 388
Project Apollo: 1, 263
Protestant Reformation: 26, 49, 159-160, 169, 324, 329-345, 387, 403
Ptolemy: 27, 50-51, 54, 264

Index

Puritans: 163, 168
Pythagoras: 6, 10, 27, 56

Q

Qin (Chinese Emperor): 2

R

Raphael: 10, 27, 35
Reconquista: 147, 257, 321, 413, 415
Renaissance (historical era): 11, 14, 16-17, 33-34, 144, 258, 261, 283-284, 327, 397-404
Revolutions of 1848: 217, 292, 294
Roman Catholic Church: 11, 21, 23, 25, 30, 36-47, 49-52, 110-111, 122-123, 140, 264, 266-267, 270, 321-322, 331-337, 341-344, 411, 428, 433
Röntgen, William (*Next 30*): 14
Roosevelt, Franklin Delano: 9, 108, 154, 245, 277-278
Rousseau, Jean-Jacques (*Next 30*): 14, 104, 133, 217, 372

S

Saladin: 237
Salk, Jonas: 10, 57
Sanger, Margaret (*Next 30*): 14, 87-90, 93-94, 158
Scientific Revolution: 34, 57-58, 261-270, 327, 342-434, 362, 387-388, 397-398, 403
Seleucus of Seleuica: 56
Seven Years' War: 234
Shakespeare, William (*#10*): 128, 168, 281-290, 338
Shaw, George Bernard: 70, 179, 272
Shockley, William: 57
Smith, Adam: 10
socialism: 188-189, 202, 295-306
Socrates (*Next 10*): 17, 21, 27, 32, 34, 326
Spanish Armada: 68, 167
Stalin, Josef: 9, 195-196, 197, 301

T

technology, advances in (Gutenberg): 151-155, 175-182, 261-266, 277-278, 311-313, 348-359, 383-386, 395-399
Tesla, Nikola: 10, 57, 351
Tetzel, Johann: 332
Thales: 6, 10, 269
Theodosius (Roman Emperor): 120, 321
Thirty Years' War: 341
Tolstoy, Leo: 10
Trajan (Roman Emperor): 112
Treaty of Paris (1763): 235
Treaty of Paris (1783): 99
Treaty of Tordesillas: 166, 427
Treaty of Verdun: 144, 147
Treaty of Versailles (1919): 187-190, 193-194
"Two Treatises of Government": 368, 370

U

Unam Sanctum (papal bull): 42
United Nations: 70, 200, 216
Urban II (Pope) (*Next 30*): 14

V

Valois Dynasty: 61
Vesalius, Andreas: 10, 57, 269
Vespucci, Amerigo: 422, 425, 427
Vikings (Norsemen): 144, 424
Voltaire (*#22*): 104, 107, 126-135, 217, 294, 373, 381

W

War of 1812: 103
War of the Roses: 159, 412
Washington, George (*#14*): 13, 100-101, 103-104, 107, 232-247
Watson, James and Crick, Francis: 10, 57
Watt, James (*#5*): 346-359, 387, 403, 431
Western Roman Empire: 26-27, 40, 114, 122-123, 136, 138
Whitney, Eli: 57, 152, 351, 356, 431

Index

Wilhelm II (Kaiser of Germany): 184
William I "the Conqueror" (King of England) (*Next 30*): 3, 15, 68
World War I: 185-189
World War II: 11, 154, 195-199, 277-278, 302
Wright brothers: 10, 57, 386, 402
Wycliffe, John: 334

Z

Zoroaster: 2, 434

www.ingramcontent.com/pod-product-compliance
Lightning Source LLC
Chambersburg PA
CBHW030333230426
43661CB00032B/1396/J